McCall's new book of COUNTRY NEEDLECRAFTS

McCall's new book of COUNTRY NEEDLECRAFTS

The Editors of McCall's
Needlework & Crafts Magazine

W.H. ALLEN · LONDON

COMET

Copyright © 1983 by ABC Needlework and Crafts Magazines, Inc.
First published in America by Chilton Book Company
First British edition, 1984

Printed and bound in Great Britain by
Mackays of Chatham Ltd, Kent
for the Publishers W.H. Allen & Co PLC,
44 Hill Street, London W1X 8LB

ISBN 0 491 03393 1 (W. H. Allen hardcover edition)
ISBN 0 86379 097 6 (Comet Books softcover edition)

Contents

BEDROOM MAGIC

McCall's new book of
COUNTRY
NEEDLECRAFTS

Preface

What is "country decorating"? Ask five people and you'll probably get five different answers. Words such as "traditional," "colonial," and "charm" begin to tell the story, but country decorating means much more. It's a way of combining historic decorating principles with a modern, casual ethic to achieve a comfortable, functional living space.

This book has been organized into sections. Study the photographs in each section, then select and combine for your own personal definition, because that's what country decorating is – a unique personal statement that draws together elements of past and present styles.

We begin with a history lesson of sorts – how colonial homes were furnished, from the early settlers through to the Revolutionary War. Since country decorating derives much of its style from this period, a basic knowledge of the early principles will enhance your efforts. Directions for creating and refurbishing authentic-looking details, accessories, and furniture follow the historical section, along with pictorial guides to characteristic furniture and accessories. A glossary of 18th-century decorating terms is included.

We've even provided directions for a colonial air freshener–potpourri–as well as two methods for drying flowers so you can add splashes of color to any room any time of the year!

Once you've learned the basics, you'll be ready for the remainder of the book. Color and black-and-white photographs will show you many types of projects and crafts you can do to realise your own definition of country decorating. Complete directions are given so that everyone, novice or pro, can create professional-looking items. Change colors or sizes to match your own decorating scheme, and consider this book a flexible guide to finding your own definition of country decorating.

17th-Century Early American

Where, When, and How it All Began

The overworked label "Early American" has been indiscriminately applied to everything that happened in American interior design from the 17th through the 19th Century. To be precise, it is a series of interpretations of European styles spanning roughly two hundred years and adapted from five different countries. While the more refined styles of colonial America in the 18th Century can also be considered Early American, we will first explore only the *earliest* Early American period—the "Pilgrim Century" that included the years from 1608 to 1720.

What was Happening

These were the years when the earliest settlers dared the uncertainties of a whole New World. Inspired by political and religious oppression, most of the emigrants ventured from England. Smaller groups arrived from Holland and Germany—the former to settle in the wilds of New York, the latter to colonize southeastern Pennsylvania. These intrepid souls brought with them customs, tastes, and—as best they could—tools for building a brave new world. Plymouth (Massachusetts) in the north, and Jamestown (Virginia) in the south became the centers of the loosely-grouped settlements.

Most of those who settled in the north were religious enthusiasts, the Pilgrims and the Puritans. Their towns grew up around their churches. Their farms were small and agricultural enterprise limited because it was difficult to clear the land of boulders. Thus the northern settlers turned to the small industries of fur trading, fishing and shipbuilding.

In the south, by contrast, the land was fertile, and a wealthier, agrarian economy soon began to flourish. Farms grew into plantations, and the owners started to live like lords in elaborate dwellings, surrounded by imported luxuries little known in the north. But north *or* south, the earliest settlers shared the same basic struggle . . . the struggle for survival against weather, animals and Indians.

How 17th-Century Homes were Built

The first colonists undoubtedly lived in the crudest of huts until trees could be felled to supply the logs which at first were stood on end and covered with thatched roofs. The traditional log cabin, with logs laid horizontally, was brought to America by the Swedes a few years later. These rudimentary dwellings were soon supplanted by the simple but substantial frame houses we now call Early American. Extensive pine forests had to be cleared before the land could be used, so lumber was abundant, and the homes were usually made entirely of wood. The structural beams and posts were left visible in their natural, rough-hewn state. Doors and the woodwork framing windows also went unpainted. The main beam, called the *summer beam,* ran through the center of the house and rested on the stone chimney.

The most typical houses were divided into two rooms, with a double-faced stone fireplace in the center. One side faced each room, set in a wall of unfinished horizontal or vertical pine planking. The other interior walls were plastered with a mixture of clay and animal hair. One of the two rooms was a combination kitchen, dining and living room. The other served as a bedroom for the whole family. As the family grew, wings were added to the ground floor and dormer windows to the roof

Cupboard, 1650

Slant-Top Desk

Butterfly Table, 1725

Small Table, 1650

so an attic room could also be added. Ceilings, by today's standards, were low, about seven feet from the floor.

Windows were of the casement type, with small rectangular, round, or diamond-shaped panes. The panes were made of glass, oiled paper or isinglass, separated by lead stripping.

The earliest floors were simply packed earth. These were succeeded by stone floors and finally by wide planks of pine, oak or chestnut. Occasionally, small Oriental rugs or heavy tapestries were scattered about the otherwise bare floors.

Early American Furniture

American furniture of the Pilgrim Century consisted primarily of provincial versions of English Jacobean and Restoration styles. Where the settlers were of Dutch, German or French origin, the influence of the homeland was also visible. The homes were sparsely furnished, with rarely anything but the bare essentials included. The colonists could bring very little with them from Europe, so practically all furniture had to be made by the same craftsmen who built the houses. And since most of the pieces were reproduced from memory, the copies were necessarily crude.

Living room pieces were limited to chests, cupboards, turned or wainscot chairs, stools, settles, the desk box, a trestle table, perhaps a smaller table and space-saving furniture such as the table-chair and gate-leg tables. Bedroom furniture consisted of crude four-poster and trundle beds,

Jacobean Wainscot Chair

Brewster-Type Chair, 1650

Slat-Back Chair

wooden cradles, and a few chests for storage. Nonessentials such as clocks and mirrors were rare.

Fabrics were limited to a few imported silks and some needlework and embroidery worked on basic materials which also had to be imported. Patterns, therefore, were also limited, usually to stylized florals and variations on the flame stitch.

The pieces of furniture were box-like or rectangular in design, making no concessions to the roundness of the human body. Ornamentation, although crudely executed, was often extensive, and included strapwork carving, turned legs and bannisters, applied split spindles and some painted decoration. Copying the original English pieces, oak and walnut were favored for furniture, but the more common native woods such as pine, beech, ash, cherry, maple, and cedar were frequently used.

The principal differences between 17th-Century American furniture and that of Jacobean England were in the color, the scale and the degree of refinement in decoration. American oak and walnut were lighter-grained than the English varieties, and American furniture was smaller in scale to suit the smaller rooms and low ceilings. The tools necessary for fine craftsmanship were limited in the colonies, so ornamentation was crude and moldings less elaborate.

The Most Important Individual Pieces

The most characteristic piece of furniture in the 17th-Century home was the chest. It was utilized for seating as well as for storage. The earliest chests stood flat on the floor or on squat supports. The tops were hinged for easy access, and some included a drawer at the bottom. Later, legs were added, the top fastened down for display of china and candles, and the entire storage area divided into drawers. Thus the simple chest became the popular chest of drawers.

In the meantime, two characteristic styles of chests developed—the *Connecticut chest* and the *Hadley chest,* both of which were manufactured in Connecticut. The Connecticut chest stood on short legs and had two rows of drawers below the storage area. It was made of oak and decorated with split-spindles painted black to imitate ebony. The Hadley chest had only one drawer and was decorated with crude incised ornamentation. The face of the upper portion was divided into three indented panels carved with flower and leaf patterns. Chests placed on higher legs evolved into cupboards, retaining the split spindle and panelled decoration.

Another top-opening small chest had a slanted lid and carved oak sides. It was used as storage for books, writing materials and the family Bible.

The *desk-box,* as it was called, was originally placed on top of a larger chest or a table. But eventually it, too, was placed on legs, evolving into the slant-top desk.

Most of the tables of the period had turned legs. Some were small and rectangular, with molded stretchers. Others were round, drop-leaf tables with a variety of supports for the leaf, such as swinging arms, butterfly wings or gate legs. The largest were of the trestle type, with pine tops and oak frames. They were frequently covered with tapestries or Oriental carpets.

Chairs were scarce and anything but luxurious. They were rectangular, firm, and devoid of upholstery. Occasionally, cushions were placed on the seats, but these did little to alter the austerity of the pieces. In each home there was an oak *wainscot chair* which served as the seat of honor. It had a carved panel back, curved arms and turned legs. The *Brewster chair* and its somewhat plainer relative, the *Carver chair,* had turned legs, turned stretchers and both vertical and horiziontal turned spindles. A similar type of chair, the *slat-back,* had ladder rails between the back stretchers. With the exception of the wainscot chair, these all had rush seats.

At the end of the century, the influence of the Restoration was felt when the William and Mary style was introduced. There were noticeable changes in the way wooden chairs were made. Seats and backs acquired inserts of cane. The Flemish scroll ornament came into use, and S- and C-shaped curves were seen in backs and stretchers. Walnut began to replace the formerly-favored oak. Less cumbersome side chairs with spiral turned legs and padded seats and backs covered in "Turkey work" tapestry came into fashion.

The hardware and lighting fixtures of the 17th Century were of the simplest types, because utility was the primary consideration. Latches, bolts and hinges were made of wrought iron. Candlestands and candlesticks were of iron, tin or pewter. One characteristic means of lighting was the *Betty lamp.* Similar to Egyptian and Roman lamps, it hung from the mantel of the fireplace. Old wagon wheels were often utilized for chandeliers by attaching brackets to hold candles.

18th-Century Colonial

The Decorating Style That Developed as the American Colonies Prospered

Like fashion, the furniture and decorating styles of any era reflect the economic, political and social environment of their time. This is strikingly true of the style we call 18th-Century Colonial, which came into being as the struggle for survival in the New World gradually gave way to an economic boom and significant social changes took place in the New England colonies. An aristocracy of the middle class based on financial success emerged. Boston, Newport and Philadelphia became centers of commerce, trade and wealth. New trade routes to the East inspired commerce and communication between the colonies, the Near East and the Orient. The delicate decorative arts of the East became a strong influence, introducing a refreshing change from the heavy, somber styles of the 17th Century.

The new prosperity attracted another wave of immigrants from England and Scotland, among them many expert craftsmen, carpenters and cabinetmakers. So the new aristocracy found artisans capable of satisfying their demands for more elaborate furniture and architecture copied from the current English styles. And copy they did— the customs, dress and manners of their prosperous English cousins. They wore satins and laces instead of puritanical homespun, and many had servants to serve their fine foods and wines. Coffee, tea and chocolate drinking became fashionable; parlor games grew popular. Tilt-top, pie-crust and gallery-top tables for serving tea and coffee, and card tables, gaming tables and settees to accommodate the new pastimes appeared. Chairs and settees were now stuffed, padded and upholstered. Luxurious fabrics were used freely in elaborate window treatments. The austerity of Early American bedrooms disappeared as highboys, lowboys, chests-on-chests and dressing tables came into use.

This 18th-Century Colonial period, extending approximately from 1720 to 1776, introduced Georgian architecture and the furniture styles named for Queen Anne and Chippendale to the colonies. "Georgian" refers to the reigns of the first three English kings of that name, and the period is sometimes called "American Georgian."

Georgian Colonial Interiors

The modest wood dwellings of the early settlers were replaced by more formal homes of wood, brick and stone. Dramatic entrace ways with spiral staircases appeared; larger rooms and higher ceilings made the interiors more spacious. Decorative cornices, entablatures and pilasters were applied to walls, fireplaces and windows. After 1735, the woodwork was often painted, and scenic wallpapers began to be imported about 1737. Stenciled walls and floors became popular in less-pretentious homes where expensive wood paneling was not feasible. Window treatments were elaborate, with luxurious drapery crowned by swags, jabots, cascades and valances. Floor coverings ranged from fine imported carpets to braided rag rugs produced at home.

Colonial Furniture

The names of Queen Anne and Chippendale have become synonymous with 18th-Century Colonial furniture. The most important developments of the Queen Anne style were the introduction of the curved line as an important element in furniture design, the first use of easily-carved mahogany as a cabinet wood, the adoption of Chinese motifs in furniture, and the extensive use of lacquer as a finish. The hallmark of Queen Anne furniture is the cyma, or S-shaped curve, most noticeable in the cabriole leg, which first appeared with a "club foot," followed by the claw-and-ball form.

The splat-back chair, also called the fiddle-back in America, is the most characteristic piece of furniture in the Queen Anne style. The solid back splat, echoing the graceful curves of a Chinese porcelain vase, was combined with cabriole legs and a broad seat. Solid wood or rush seats were used, but upholstered seats covered in damask, needlepoint or resist-dyed linen were more prevalent. Other chairs of the period included the easy or wing chair with its entirely upholstered frame and side wings for protection from drafts; the corner-chair or roundabout with a low, quarter-circle seat; the armchair with upholstered seat and back; and sofas or daybeds with upholstered seats. Sofas as we know them today developed a little later with the Chippendale style.

Small, round tables for serving tea and coffee had tilting tops set on tripods with cabriole legs.

The typical pie-crust edge was designed for the practical purpose of keeping dishes from sliding off. Breakfast and dining tables had drop-leaf tops combined with shell-carved cabriole legs and claw-and-ball feet.

Highboys, lowboys, dressing tables, desks and secretaries all had characteristic legs, with shell carving on the drawers as well as on the legs. Corner cabinets and high chests with split pediments were decorated in the Oriental manner by a process known as japanning, which consisted of applying gold and enamel motifs to lacquered wood.

During the Queen Anne period, framed mirrors, or "looking glasses" were first imported and widely used. Tall case clocks, or grandfather clocks, replaced small wall clocks.

The furniture of the early Georgian period flowered from the simpler Queen Anne style, and the combination of graceful curves, the extensive use of rich mahogany, and more intricate carving all contribute to the general opinion that the second quarter of the 18th Century produced some of the finest furniture ever made.

The wide acceptance of the splat-back chair continued, but now the splat was elaborately pierced and carved. The top of the chair took on the yoke-back form, with acanthus leaf and other

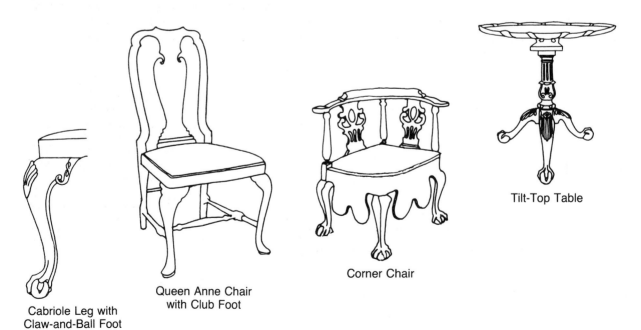

Cabriole Leg with
Claw-and-Ball Foot

Queen Anne Chair
with Club Foot

Corner Chair

Tilt-Top Table

Lowboy

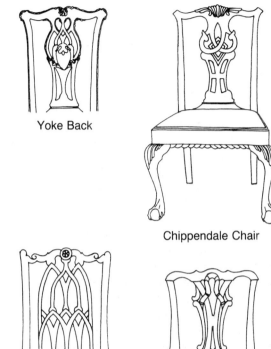

Yoke Back

Chippendale Chair

Gothic
Influence

Ribband
Back

foliage motifs substituted for the simpler shell carvings of the first quarter of the century. Wing chairs and other upholstered furniture became much more prevalent.

In 1754 the first edition of Thomas Chippendale's design book was published, and colonial cabinetmakers had access to instructions for making furniture designed by this famous London furniture maker, the foremost experimenter and innovator of his time. Although he produced furniture of every conceivable type, his artistry is most evident in the chairs he designed. The cabriole leg with carved foot and the splat back with decorative yoke top were typical of his early work. Later he combined straight legs with intricate backs copied from Gothic tracery or carved into entwining ribbons, Chinese latticework or bamboo forms. The typical Chippendale sofa is the "camel back" with upholstered frame and square legs.

His designs in the Chinese manner are classified specifically as "Chinese Chippendale." His fantastically elaborate mirror frames, combining French rococo forms with Chinese figures, are the outstanding examples of this style. This rococo influence dominated the development of the Chip-

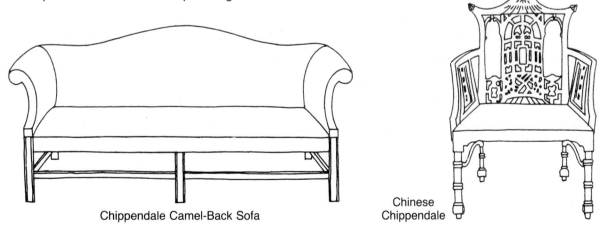

Chippendale Camel-Back Sofa

Chinese
Chippendale

pendale style in Philadelphia, with the "Philadelphia highboy" a characteristic piece, although it still displayed elements of the Queen Anne style in the legs and the shell carving.

Chippendale designs varied all the way from florid rococo to severely classic. In his latter years, the classic influence dominated, and straight lines replaced the earlier Georgian style. His work of this period, produced in conjunction with the Adams brothers during the third quarter of the 18th Century, is generally considered his best.

Other noted English cabinetmakers also published design books, and the newly style-conscious colonists avidly bought English books on architecture, interior decoration and furniture design. Those who could afford it imported English pieces; others relied on the cabinetmakers at hand to copy the designs. Many of the colonial cabinetmakers became remarkably adept at reproducing the Queen Anne, Georgian and Chippen-

American Windsor

dale styles. Some of the best, located in Philadelphia, became famous for their "Philadelphia furniture." But not all of the pieces were direct copies. A Philadelphia version of the Windsor chair was made in many variations and manufactured in surprising quantities. Found in almost every 18th-Century household, these were also used in taverns and public institutions. The rocking chair, a purely American innovation which was called a "nurse chair," developed from one form of the American Windsor, and rockers were soon applied to other types of chairs as well.

In Newport, too, noted cabinetmakers branched out to design furniture with individual characteristics. The work of three generations of Goddards and Townsends in this flourishing and cosmopolitan seaport includes some of the finest examples of American craftsmanship ever produced.

The last quarter of the 18th Century saw furniture designs by Hepplewhite and Sheraton copied by colonial cabinetmakers as Queen Anne and Chippendale styles had been copied before them. George Hepplewhite, who in turn copied French furniture of the Louis XV and Louis XVI periods, was responsible for a newly delicate sense of line and proportion in English—and therefore colonial—furniture. His most typical pieces were chairs with slender, tapered legs. The backs of the chairs, in shield, camel, oval, heart or wheel shapes, had a light and airy effect achieved by delicate design rather than by carving.

Philadelphia
Highboy

The third great English designer, Thomas Sheraton, published *his* design book in 1791, still in time to have tremendous influence on 18th-Century furniture. His chair legs were also straight, but straight lines dominated his designs even more than those of Hepplewhite. His chair backs were rectangular in shape, with curves used only to connect straight lines or rectangular divisions. He did, however, use decorative center splats in the form of gracefully curved vases. He used color and inlay more frequently than carving and was the first to use porcelain plaques for decoration. His linear forms found favor in the colonies as well as in England, and are still a strong influence on contemporary design.

18th-Century Accessories

Unlike the early settlers, whose small furnishings were limited to purely functional accessories, the 18th-Century colonists had access to many additional luxuries due to the expanding trade with Europe and the Orient. In addition to silk and damasks, there was wallpaper from China and England, decorative Oriental china, English china including Staffordshire and Wedgewood, and the blue and white Delft tiles from Holland which were often used to decorate fireplace openings. Lighting fixtures from England and France in the form of bronze and marble candelabras, gilt and crystal sconces and scroll-armed chandeliers were also imported. Painted or embroidered fire screens for protection from drafts and heat were decorative as well as functional.

Pewter continued to be used for tableware, but as the colonists became more affluent, the use of silverware increased. The designs were patterned after English pieces of the Queen Anne period, but American silversmiths tended to eliminate embellishment and concentrate on simplicity of line. Paul Revere was the most famous of the colonial silversmiths and many of his designs are still being reproduced.

Hepplewhite
Shield-Back Chair

Block-Front Desk

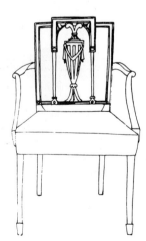

Sheraton Arm Chair

Do-It-Yourself
Early American Details

Authentic 17th-Century houses that still exist are few and far between, but enterprising manufacturers have come up with many ingenious products to help give any home the much-coveted Early American look. Here are a few that are widely available plus some interesting accesories you can make yourself. Necessity forced the industrious early settlers to make most of their own small furnishings—you can copy their ideas for fun!

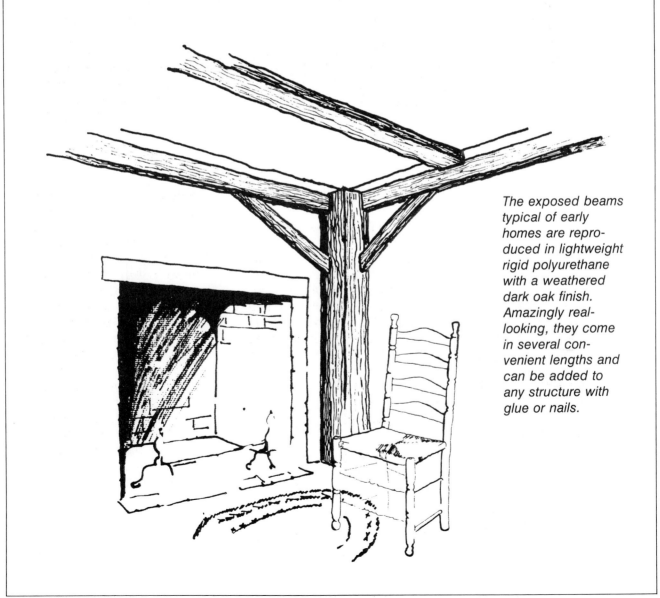

The exposed beams typical of early homes are reproduced in lightweight rigid polyurethane with a weathered dark oak finish. Amazingly real-looking, they come in several convenient lengths and can be added to any structure with glue or nails.

You can have the 17th-Century look of random plank floors with the 20th-Century durability of pure vinyl sheathing. Genuwood II resilient flooring sandwiches real hardwood veneers between a thick layer of clear vinyl on top and a layer of core vinyl on bottom. Planks come in 4", 6" and 8" widths and in 36" to 48" lengths, either pegged or plain. In six wood veneers, including walnut, English brown oak and rosewood. By PermaGrain Products from G.S. Associates, 150 E. 58th Street, New York, N.Y. 10022

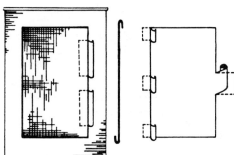

A pierced "Paul Revere" lantern can be made from two tin cans and a funnel. Remove top from a large fruit juice can and cut opening for door with tin snips, allowing for two $\frac{1}{4}''$ wide hinges to be folded back on one side. Fold other raw edges under. From second can, cut door $\frac{1}{2}''$ larger on all sides than opening, plus three hinges to fit around the two on one side of opening. Fold raw edges under on other three sides. Using a nail and wood chisel (with a log inside can to prevent buckling), hammer pattern in can, door, and a funnel that fits over can. Cut off spout of funnel and make a handle from a strip of tin. Fold sharp edges back and insert ends into top of funnel; twist to hold handle in place. Pierce funnel and top of can in six places and fasten with wire. Cut candle holder from galvanized tin and solder to bottom of can. Place door over opening; thread heavy wire through hinges.

The look of small-paned windows, so prevalent in the 17th Century, is a snap to have with snap-in vinyl grilles available at many lumber yards. They come for openings as small as three by four feet and in many other sizes as well. Or, even more do-it-yourself, buy black lead tape and lead adhesive at a nearby hobby shop and create your own small diamond-shaped "panes" for mere pin money.

A wooden candlestand, such as those whittled out by early settlers on long winter evenings, is easy to construct. Start with a half-log about 10" long and drill a ¾" hole in center of the round surface. Taper one end of a 1" × 1" hardwood post, about 25" long, and insert in hole in log. In 1" × 2" piece of hardwood, approximately 9" long, drill two holes for candles, mark a 1" × 1" square hole at center for post, and drill a ½" hole for peg next to marking for square hole. Saw 1" × 2" in half lengthwise and check out square hole. Place two sections of 1" × 2" together around post 2" from top. Screw these two parts together with a screw at each end and one at center going through post. Drive peg into hole. (Peg was originally used to wedge candle-arm in place so it could be moved up and down to adjust height.)

A Collector's Guide to Americana

FANCY CHAIRS

Lightweight wood chairs produced in volume in the early 1800's. The name most often associated with this type is Lambert Hitchcock, the only manufacturer to label his chairs. Fancy chairs were always painted and decorated with stenciled gold leaf or bronze. Hitchcock chairs, decorated with copies of the original stencils, are still being produced in the original Hitchcock factory.

DRY SINK

Classified as cottage furniture, it once served the function of our kitchen sink. The sunken top was lined with galvanized tin to hold the dishpan or washtub, making it easily convertible to its present day use as a bar or a decorative planter.

FOUR-POSTER

A large 18th-Century bed with four tall, turned posts at the corners to support draw curtains or a canopy.

GODDARD DESK

An 18th-Century desk displaying concave and convex shell carving on each of the three sections of the block front. The block front refers to a center panel, recessed for leg room.

HADLEY CHEST

An oak or pine chest from the 1600's. The front is divided into three panels and carved, intaglio-fashion, with birds, leaves and arabesques.

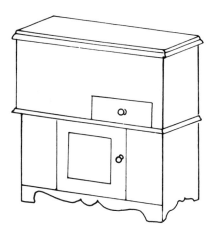

LIFT-TOP COMMODE

The best example of cottage furniture seen today, originally the counterpart of the modern bathroom. The top held a bowl and water pitcher, the drawer, soap and towels; the bottom was for other "temporary" storage.

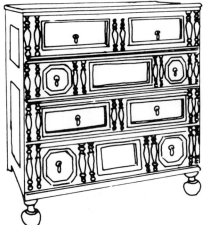

OAK CHEST

A low chest of drawers decorated with split spindles and raised molding around the drawers. The expert woodworking was typical of the New England cabinet makers of the 1600's.

PATCHWORK QUILTING

The craft of sewing pieces of fabric together by means of seams. Whether rich or poor, all women of Colonial America practiced this craft and each colony had its distinctive geometric pattern. When the piece grew to the desired size, it was hand quilted onto a backing of cotton wadding.

PENNSYLVANIA DUTCH

Descriptive term for the whimsical furniture decorations and folk art of the German and Swiss immigrants to Pennsylvania in the 17th and 18th Centuries. Common motifs were hearts, flowers and birds stenciled or painted on chests, chairs and trunks.

PEWTER

An alloy of tin and copper used in Colonial America for dinnerware. Characteristic pieces are the eight-inch plate, pitchers and teapots.

Early American Chairs

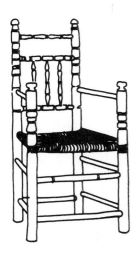

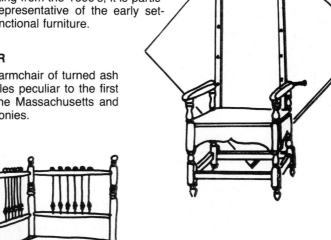

CHAIR-TABLE

Literally a chair with a large round or square hinged back that turns into a table. Dating from the 1600's, it is particularly representative of the early settlers' functional furniture.

CARVER CHAIR

A straight-back armchair of turned ash posts and spindles peculiar to the first settlements in the Massachusetts and Connecticut Colonies.

CORNER CHAIR

A chair built to fit diagonally or catty-corner into a corner. The style dates from the late 17th Century.

BOSTON ROCKER

A wood rocking chair with a high spindle back manufactured in New England in the early 18th Century. Back slat and front edge of the seat are decorated with stenciled designs.

WAGON SEAT

A Pennsylvania Dutch wooden bench with rush seat and decorated back.

WAINSCOT CHAIR

Heavily carved oak arm chair dating from the 17th Century, corresponding to the English Jacobean style.

WING CHAIR

Early 18th-Century easy chair with lateral wings, designed to shelter its user from drafts and capture the heat when placed before a fireplace.

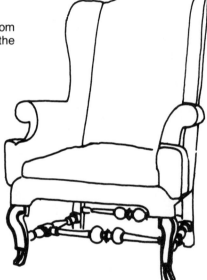

WINDSOR CHAIR

A style originated by English wheelwrights who fitted spindles into the seat as they fitted spokes into a wheel. It became so popular in America that by the time of George Washington there were nine variations.

WRITING CHAIR

Chair with large, flat right arm that served as a writing surface. Usually a Windsor style with spindle back.

How to Slipcover an Early American Wing Chair

The easiest and most accurate method of making a slipcover is to pin and fit the fabric right on the chair. Working on one section at a time, place fabric against chair right side out to make pattern matching easy. Be sure lengthwise grain of fabric is precisely vertical before pin-fitting each piece, and check again before cutting. Place fabric on each section so the pattern matches or blends well with the pattern on adjoining pieces. On a wing chair, center the design so the pattern continues from the inside back across the seat and down the front drop of the chair, and so inside wings and inside arms match and the fronts of the arms also match. If there is a cushion, the pattern on the top of the cushion should match the inside back of the chair. Outside arms and back do not have to match because they can't be seen at the same time.

When pin-fitting each section, mark seam lines along exact edge of chair (or section) with pins or chalk; when cutting, add 1″ extra on all sides of each piece for seam allowance. When placing welting on fabric, place stitching line of welting along edge of chair (or section), with seam allowance of welting to outside. The seam line on fabric and stitching line of welting will thus coincide; the slipcover will be stitched together along stitching line of welting. Baste all seams and try the slipcover on chair before final stitching so any alterations required for a smooth fit can be made at this point.

Start by placing fabric down inside back of chair and across seat, allowing 8″ for tuck-in between inside back and seat. Allow enough fabric along side edges of inside back to tuck in as far as possible between inside back and inside wings. Allow 4″ on each side of seat for tuck-in. Place welting along front edge of seat, clipping seam allowance to go around the corners. Stitch in place, following stitching line of welting. Place welting across upper edge of inside back; stitch in same manner. (See Diagram 1.)

Fit and cut fabric for inside wings, allowing extra fabric for tuck-ins where inside wings meet inside back. Fit and cut fabric for tops of arms.

Seam inside wings and tops of arms together where they meet. Place welting along lower edge of inside wing, around edge or arm, and up outside edge of wing to top of chair where inside wing meets inside back. Ease in extra fabric or make small pleats to allow for roundness of wing along the top curve. (See Diagram 2.) Repeat on other side.

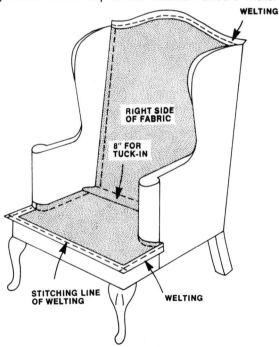

WELTING

RIGHT SIDE OF FABRIC

8″ FOR TUCK-IN

STITCHING LINE OF WELTING

WELTING

DIAGRAM 1

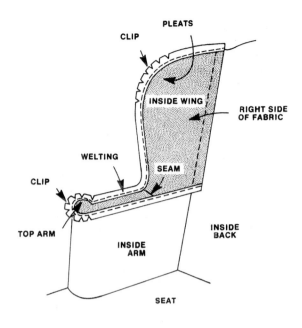

DIAGRAM 2

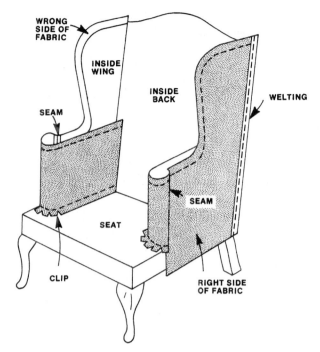

DIAGRAM 4

Fit and cut fabric to cover front and side drop of seat. Stitch in place, following stitching line of welting already attached to front edge of seat. (See Diagram 3.)

Fit and cut fabric for outside wing and arm. Cut and fit fabric for inside arm, allowing for tuck-in where inside arm meets inside back, and allowing 5″ for tuck-in along bottom edge. Clip bottom edge to go around front curve of arm. Stitch arm sections together down outside arm as shown in Diagram 4. Attach welting to back edge of outside wing and arm. (See Diagram 4.) Repeat on other arm.

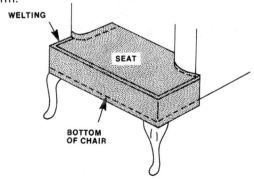

DIAGRAM 3

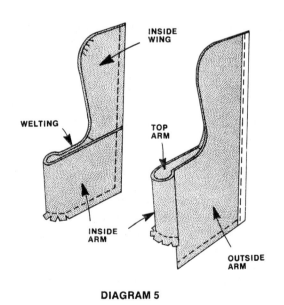

DIAGRAM 5

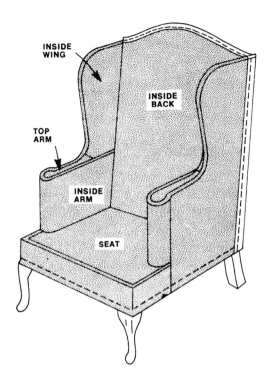

DIAGRAM 6

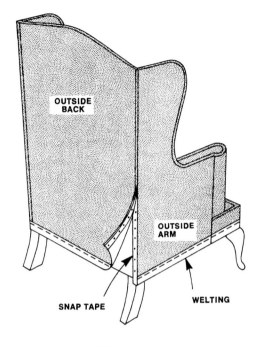

DIAGRAM 7

Stitch outside and inside wing and arm sections together, following stitching line of welting. (See Diagram 5.) Stitch lower edges of inside arms to seat. Stitch back (tuck-in) edges of inside arms to inside back. (See Diagram 6.)

Place fabric on outside back of chair and mark outline. Pin outside back to top of inside back and to outside wings. Try cover on chair, opening one side as much as necessary to place cover in position on chair. Make any necessary adjustments, then remove cover and stitch. Stitch snap tape or zipper to opening. Place welting around lower edge of chair (including back, sides and front), with stitching line of welting exactly at lower edge of chair. Stitch welting in place. (See Diagram 7.)

Cut under-seat flaps for sides 1″ longer than distance between front and back legs, and half the width of underside of chair. Make $\frac{1}{2}$″ hems on both ends and along one side of each flap. Cut three 10″ lengths of $\frac{1}{2}$″ twill tape and stitch to hemmed side of each flap for ties. Stitch flap to bottom of slipcover along each side, following stitching line of welting. (See Diagram 8.) Make

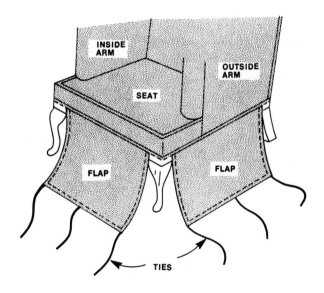

DIAGRAM 8

front and back flaps in same manner. Put cover on chair; pull side flaps under chair and tie together. Turn seam allowance of welting under at corners; tie front and back flaps together.

To cover cushion, place fabric on top, right side up, and pin welting around all edges. Clip seam allowance of welting to go around corners and curves. (See Diagram 9.) Trim fabric 1″ beyond stitching line of welting. Repeat for bottom of cushion.

Cut a boxing strip 2″ wider than depth of cushion and long enough to go around the front from the "X" mark on one side to the "X" mark on the other side, plus 2″. (See Diagram 9.) Cut two strips 2″ wider than one-half the depth of cushion and long enough to go around the back from "X" to "X", plus 2″. Fold 1″ under along one long side of each back strip. Place the two strips over the zipper with folded edges touching at center of zipper. Stitch along each side of zipper. (See Diagram 10.)

Taking 1″ seams, stitch front and back boxing strips together to form a complete circle. Place boxing strip on top section of cover, right sides together and raw edges flush. Stitch along stitching line of welting. (See Diagram 11.) Open zipper and attach other side of boxing strip to bottom section of cover in the same manner.

If your chair has a square or rectangular cushion, have zipper reach from the center of one side, around back to center of other side. Make boxing strips and attach in the same manner as above.

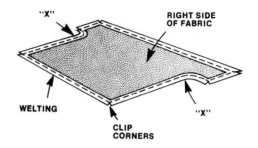

DIAGRAM 9

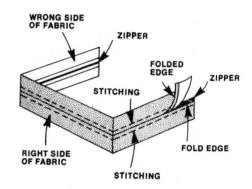

DIAGRAM 10

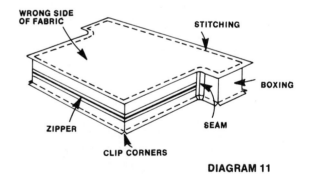

DIAGRAM 11

New Life for an Old Chair

Our 17th-century ladder-back chair, after languishing many years in a Maine attic, was still sturdy despite its dilapidated seat. We removed the worn splints, then followed the same "over two, under two" weaving pattern for the new seat. If your chair seat has another pattern (such as "over two, under three"; or "over four, under four," etc.), you can still duplicate its design by following

Early American ladder-back chair, in fine condition except for worn-out woven seat, is a good candidate for restoration.

Rewoven ash-splint seat restores usefulness of antique chair. For seat, chair must have seat rails on all four sides.

Fig. 1. Place square so angle touches back post and edge parallels back rail. Mark the front and back rails at outer edge of square, both sides.

our method. Consider the size and shape of seat openings as well as the width of your splints when choosing a pattern. The ash splints we used suit the rustic character of this chair. After weaving, the splints were finished with a wood sealer; the chair was left in its original barn red. Directions begin at right.

EQUIPMENT: String. Scissors. Deep pan about 18″ in diameter. Sponge. Cardboard 6″ × 18″. Ruler. Pencil. Clamp clothespin. Stapler. Screwdriver. Longnosed pliers.

MATERIALS: Glycerine (clear and odorless) approx. 1 pint. Ash splint, 5 coils, $\frac{5}{8}$″ or 3 coils, 1″.

GENERAL DIRECTIONS: To prepare chair for new seat, cut old seat away from chair. Remove any tacks, nails, and dust from seat rails.

To prepare splint for weaving, pull one strand of splint from hank. Bend the strand to determine right and wrong side. The right side bends smoothly while the wrong side splinters. With right side out, roll strand to fit in pan. Prepare four strands in same manner and place in pan.

To prepare soaking solution, mix glycerine and warm water in the ratio of one part glycerine to 10 parts water. Make enough to completely cover four strands and pour into pan. Let strands soak about $\frac{1}{2}$ hour. Use sponge to keep chair seat damp while working on it.

To prepare for the actual weaving of the seat, you must first wrap the warp around the seat rails from back to front of chair.

To make sure that the warp strands are straight, it is necessary to mark the front and back rails in the following manner. From cardboard cut out a carpenter's square that will fit your chair as indicated in Fig. 1. Place it so that it touches the back post and is parallel with the back rail. Mark the front rail at point where outside edge of carpenter's square crosses it. Do the same for other side of seat. On front rail, mark center between the marks. On back rail, mark center between posts.

Remove one strand from pan: wipe off excess water with sponge. Place another strand in pan each time you remove one. Tie end of strand to left side rail with right side of strand touching rail.

Fig. 2. Tie strand of splint to left rail of chair, then bring it under and over back rail, and then wrap it over and under the front rail.

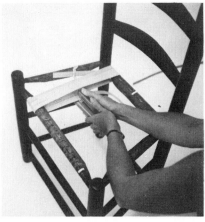

Fig. 3. Attach new strand on the underside of seat. Put new strand under old strand, overlapping 2½″; staple together in three places.

Pull strand under and over back rail. Keeping strand taut, pull to front rail; with outside edge at mark, wrap it over and under rail (Fig. 2). Pull strand to back rail and continue in this manner until you come to the end of strand. Make sure that strands are as close together as possible and are equally taut. Hold end of strand with clothespin. Always join strands on the underside.

To attach new strand, place the new under the old, allowing them to overlap about $2\frac{1}{2}''$. Staple them together in three places, 1" apart (Fig. 3); using pliers, flatten staples.

Continue to wrap strands until you reach the mark on the right side of front rail. Hold with clothespin to adjacent strip. Loosen the last strand over back rail. Remove clothespin; pull strand under and over back rail and under preceding strand. Now, bring strand under side rail, turned so that right side is down and is diagonally in front of back post (Fig. 4).

After pulling all strands tight, weave across as in Fig. 4. The pattern is over 2, under 2, but, if you have an uneven number of warp strands, start by pulling the weaving strand under one and then establishing the pattern of over 2, under 2. The pattern is worked the same on the underside.

As you can see in Fig. 5, the pattern moves one strand to the left each time. Join weaving

Fig. 4. *Bring strand under side rail diagonally in front of back post and weave across under the first strand, then over two and under one.*

strands on the underside, same as warp strands. Cover staples later.

Continue weaving until you have space to attach two more warp strands, as indicated in Fig. 5. Hook warp strand over weaving strand and fold end so that it remains between top and bottom of seat; do the same on underside and cut off excess. Continue weaving, keeping in pattern. After you have completed four rows, cut the string holding the first warp strand. It will be held in place by the weaving. Add more warp strands whenever you have space as you did before.

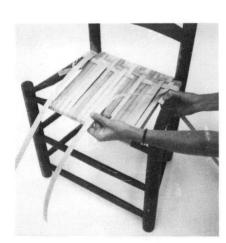

Fig. 5. *Attach more warp strands when you have space by hooking them over weaving strands at sides, then hook in weaving on the underside.*

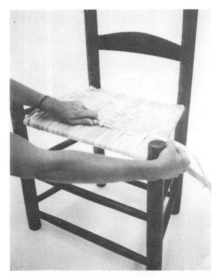

Fig. 6. *As you weave closer to front of seat, warp strands become tighter. Use screwdriver or similar tool to help push down warp threads.*

Glossary of 18th-Century Decorating Terms

Architrave: The lowest, horizontal section of the three main parts of the classical entablature, immediately above the capitals of the columns and below the frieze. The term is also used to define moldings used in a similar way as door or window trimming.

Bandy Leg: Lay term for cabriole leg with club foot. It preceded the cabriole leg with claw-and-ball foot in 18th-Century furniture.

Bolection Molding: Molding which projects sharply beyond the woodwork or wall to which it is applied (usually into the room). In the 18th Century it was frequently used as a fireplace trimming in lieu of a mantel shelf.

Cabriole Leg: A cyma-curved furniture leg designed in the form of a stylized animal's leg with knee, ankle and ornamental foot.

Case Clock: A clock with its works enclosed in a tall case. In the Queen Anne period, large case clocks replaced small wall clocks. Also called grandfather clocks in the colonies.

Claw-and-Ball Foot: A type of carved foot used with the cabriole furniture leg. It consists of a bird's claw grasping a ball. Introduced in early 18th Century England (after the club foot). Possibly of Oriental origin.

Club Foot: A foot used on the cabriole leg in early 18th-Century furniture. The foot flares into a flat, rounded form which rests on the floor. Sometimes called a pad foot.

Cornice: In classical architecture, the topmost, projecting section of the three main parts of the entablature. Often used on interior walls without the lower two sections. Now also a term for the decorative band at the top of a window that conceals drapery hardware.

Cyma Curve: A graceful, S-shaped curve which was the main hallmark of Queen Anne furniture.

Dado: Term for the lower section of a wall, when treated differently from the surface above it. Usually topped with crowning or cap molding, which was sometimes called a chair rail.

Decalcomania: A form of decoration in which printed designs on thin, specially-treated paper are transferred onto other materials. An extremely popular and fashionable hobby as well as a technique used by professionals to decorate furniture during the 18th Century.

Entablature: In classical architecture, the portion of the order supported by the column, consisting of the architrave, frieze and cornice. Also the upper section of a wall.

Fiddle-Back Chair: An American Colonial, rush-seated chair in Queen Anne style. Solid back splat approximated a fiddle-back or vase shape. Called a splat-back chair in England.

Frieze: The middle, horizontal section of the three main parts of the classical entablature. Usually a flat surface decorated with ornamental features or with carving. Often used on interior walls without the architrave or cornice.

Continued on page 41

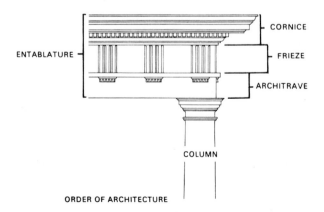

ENTABLATURE — CORNICE, FRIEZE, ARCHITRAVE

COLUMN

ORDER OF ARCHITECTURE

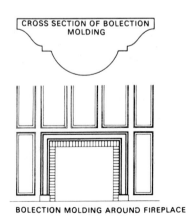

CROSS SECTION OF BOLECTION MOLDING

BOLECTION MOLDING AROUND FIREPLACE

Sampler motifs make handsome patterns for needlepoint pillows, especially in Colonial colors of blue and ecru. Alphabet and Wedding Pillows, each 14" square, work well together or alone. Directions on page 44.

Early settlers first used hand-hooking to make coverings for the bed, and later for the floor. By looping strips of fabric through monk's cloth or burlap, you can make the American primitive designs shown here, and add folk-art charm to any room. See page 46 for directions.

34

The charming tradition of stenciling floors began when early settlers, in an effort to imitate the carpeting of the Old World, began painting simple decorations on their bare floors. This simple motif, rows of baskets divided by flower repeats, was a favorite quilt design in the nineteenth century. Directions on page 48.

The delicate, Egyptian-inspired lotus repeats four times in each square. Simple green leaves form a pinwheel effect in the center of each group. Since such a striking overall pattern is created by repeating the square, we used it four times in the pillow, then added extra stripes for a border. Directions on page 51.

Delightful motifs, straight from antique quilts, are perfect patterns for stenciling and needlepoint.

Bouquet-in-a-basket is stenciled on velveteen in the manner of 19th-century theorem painting. Framed here with an old gilt frame, the picture is an almost-genuine antique! What's new are the modern acrylic paints you'll use for easy stenciling. Picture measures 14" × 18", unframed. Directions on page 53.

Striking as decorator accents, beaded flowers in attractive blues and white add garden freshness that lasts forever. Our arrangement is simple to do; all you need is lots of time. Begin your bouquet by making a flower at a time; add one beaded bloom to an arrangement of greens, then add another a week later. Directions on page 54.

Home Sweet Home pillow is patterned with simple repeating shapes and warm bands of color. Worked entirely in continental stitch; directions are on page 58. Tulip pillow, extra big at 19" square, is appliqued in four brown prints, both dainty and bold. Simple quilting follows line of applique. Directions begin on page 60.

Boudoir boxes fit one inside the other. Each box is padded inside and out to protect jewelry or other valuables. Leaves, etched on sides, top, and bottom, are machine quilted. Directions on page 60.

SCROLLED PEDIMENT ON TOP OF HIGHBOY

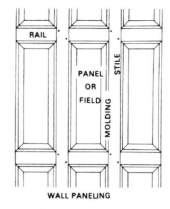

WALL PANELING

Continued from page 32

Gallery: A miniature railing, either pierced or solid, along the edge of a table top or a shelf. Specifically, a gallery-top table.

Highboy: A tall chest of drawers on a tablelike base or a lowboy. In the 18th Century, it was usually designed with either a flat molded top or a scrolled pediment top.

Japanning: A process used extensively in the 18th Century in which metalwork and furniture were completely covered with colored lacquer and the decoration raised and painted with gold and colors. Many ornamental motifs were used, including foliated scrollwork and pseudo-Chinese motifs. Amateur japanning became a fashionable hobby during this period.

Lowboy: A side table with drawers, standing approximately three feet high. It was frequently decorated with quarter-round, fluted stiles and carved with recessed shell motifs. In England, it was known as a dressing table.

Order: A style of building. In classical architecture, a type of column and entablature considered the definitive unit of a style. For example, there were three major Greek orders, or styles: Doric, Ionic and Corinthian.

Pediment: Originally, the triangular space forming the gable on each end of a Greek temple. In 18th Century furniture, an ornamental feature at the top of highboys and secretaries, generally triangular in shape but broken or segmented in decoratively carved forms.

Piecrust Edge: The upstanding edge of a small, round table carved or molded in scallops. Used especially on revolving, tilt-top tables.

Pilaster: A flat, vertical wall projection, or false column, with the general proportions and the same divisions (capital, shaft and base) as a free-standing column. Popular as a wall treatment during the late 18th Century.

Rails: In wall paneling, the horizontal strips of the frame, used to separate the panels.

Resist-Dying: A method of dying fabric in which the pattern area is covered with a chemical paste or paraffin. When the cloth is dyed, the covered parts resist the dye and retain their original color. In the 18th Century, resist-dyed linen was commonly used to cover chair seats.

Roundabout Chair: Chair designed to fit into a corner, with a low back on two adjoining sides of a square seat. Also called a corner chair.

Secretary: A tall writing desk, especially one in which the top section was used for books.

Settee: A long seat or medium-sized sofa with a high back, seating several persons.

Shell Carving: Carving in the form of a shell, a typical design motif used in the 18th Century to ornament the knees of cabriole legs, the tops of chair splats and other furniture.

Stenciling: A method of decorating or printing a design on a surface by brushing ink or dye through a cut-out pattern. Employed to decorate both walls and floors in small houses where wood paneling and rugs were not used.

Stiles: In wall paneling, the vertical strips of the frame, used to separate the panels.

Potpourris

The perfect accent for a country-flavored room would have to be a sweet-scented potpourri. Popular with the American colonists, potpourris served two purposes—they were wonderful air fresheners, and, when placed in a glass jar or bottle, they could be quite decorative. Making your own potpourri can be an enjoyable, personal, and rewarding craft. Everyone has his own preferences in fragrances and flowers—the number of perfumes on today's market attests to that fact. Therefore, the recipe we offer you below is intentionally nonspecific. Tailor your potpourri according to the flowers and herbs you can grow in your area and obtain from a florist, and to your tastes in fragrances.

Ingredients

4 cups dried petals (Suggestions: roses, geraniums, camomile, violets, lilac, honeysuckle, lily-of-the-valley, carnations, nasturtium, white jasmine)
1 Tbls. herbs or spices (Suggestions: allspice, ground cloves, cinnamon, sage, tarragon, thyme, mint, lemon verbena)
$\frac{1}{3}$ cup powdered fixative (such as orrisroot)
3 drops of essential oil (such as rose, lavender, bayberry, orange blossom, sandalwood)

Directions

Mix above ingredients together. Place in airtight jars. Stir once or twice each week. After four weeks, potpourri will be ready for use.

A well made potpourri will smell delightful for a long time. If fragrance starts to fade, you can revitalize it with a drop of brandy or cologne.

Obtaining Your Materials

Most pharmacies sell orrisroot and essential oils. Flower petals can be bought from larger hobby shops, but you will derive more pleasure from your potpourri if you grow the flowers and herbs yourself. Pick them in the early morning, after the dew has dried. Spread them on a window screen. Keep dust off them by making a canopy of cheesecloth (supported by jars to keep it from touching petals and leaves.) Place in a dry, airy place (attics are often ideal) until petals are crisp—about ten days. Turn mixture over a few times during this period.

Note: Colors of petals dried in this way will look faded. Potpourri can be concealed in an opaque sachet made from a handkerchief or other fine fabric. However, if you want to display your potpourri in a clear glass or shallow bowl, add flower petals dried by the silica gel or borax methods. These petals will provide color and texture, making your potpourri much more attractive.

Dried Flowers

Arranged in a pretty basket or bowl, dried flowers are appropriate in any country decorating scheme. Place a basketful on the fireplace mantel, on a shelf, or anywhere else you please.

EQUIPMENT: For Silica Gel Method: Silica gel. Closed container for drying.

For Borax Method: Borax. Open container for drying. Strainer. Spatula. Watercolor brush. **For Both:** Stiff paper for markers. Pencil. Sharp knife.

MATERIALS: Flowers to dry. Crystal clear spray acrylic. Plastic foam. Sphagnum or other decorative dried moss. Floral tape. Floral picks (or wooden toothpicks). Basket containers.

GENERAL DIRECTIONS: We dried carnations, roses, daisies, varieties of chrysanthemums, larkspur, and the leaves from roses and daisies. In general, thick heavy-textured flowers do not dry well by either the silica gel method or borax method.

Pick flowers in perfect condition, at their peak bloom and on a warm sunny day. If there is moisture in the flower heads, allow stemmed flowers to stand in 2″ to 3″ of warm water until the heads are completely free of moisture. Because flowers may shrink or fade in drying or break in handling, gather at least twice as many flowers as you think you may need. Discard any flowers with insects or imperfections.

To prepare, carefully strip or cut leaves from stem and cut off stem about 2″ to 3″ from flower head. Leaves and stems can be dried separately.

SILICA GEL METHOD: Silica gel is available from most hobby and craft stores. Dry flowers, following manufacturer's directions.

BORAX METHOD: Pour borax into a strainer and sift a 2″-to-3″ deep layer of borax into drying box. Place flower face down in the borax. Place flowering sprays and leaves directly on borax. Pour more borax carefully around and over flowers until completely covered. Allow some borax to lie between the petals to support them and help the flower retain its natural shape. Make and position markers for flowers with their name and date. The length of drying time depends upon the texture of the flower. Place an extra flower in box for test flower; it is dry when texture is like taffeta. Check test flower so as not to overdry the flowers.

To remove flowers, use spatula under flower head and work carefully. Remove any borax clinging to petals, using a watercolor brush.

FINISHING: To protect dried flowers and make arranging them easier, stick short stems temporarily in a long piece of plastic foam so that blooms and leaves are standing. Spray with several light coats of clear acrylic in a well-ventilated room. Allow to dry.

ARRANGING: Use various types of low baskets for containers so that the short 2″ to 3″ stems will be sufficient to arrange flowers. Wedge a chunk of plastic foam in basket or anchor with floral tape; cover with decorative dried moss. Balance colors and textures to make a pleasing arrangement. Insert short stems into foam and use floral picks or toothpicks to secure flowers and leaves where necessary. Conceal all picks with floral tape.

ALPHABET AND WEDDING PILLOWS

Shown on page 33

SIZE: 14″ square.

EQUIPMENT: Masking tape. Pencil. Ruler. Scissors. Tapestry needle. Sewing needle. Straight pins.

MATERIALS: Mono needlepoint canvas, 19″ square; for Alphabet Pillow, 10 mesh-to-the-inch; for Wedding Pillow, 12 mesh-to-the-inch. For each pillow: Persian yarn, see color key for colors and number of ounces needed (in parentheses). Navy velvet or cotton velveteen fabric for backing and welting, 45″ wide, ½ yard. Cable cord ¼″ in diam-

eter, 1¾ yards. Navy extra-strong sewing thread. Muslin for inner pillow, 36″ wide, ½ yard. Polyester Fiberfill for stuffing.

GENERAL DIRECTIONS: Read General Directions for Needlepoint on page 307. On center of canvas, mark outline of needlepoint area, leaving margin as indicated in individual directions. Mark horizontal and vertical center lines of needlepoint area on canvas.

Work design according to individual directions and color key.

COLOR KEY FOR ALPHABET PILLOW

◉ NAVY (1)

☐ ECRU (5)

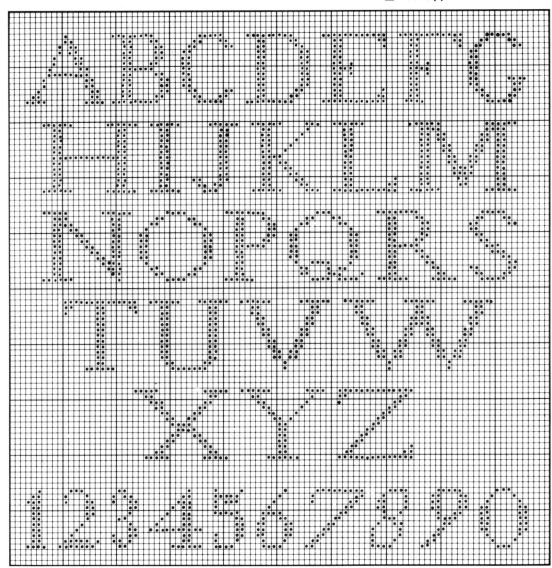

44

Finishing: Block completed needlepoint following directions on page 307. When dry, trim canvas margins to ½″. Follow directions on page 307 to assemble pillow.

ALPHABET PILLOW: Leave a 2″ margin all around design area. Following chart, work letters and numbers in navy yarn, continental stitch, then fill in background with ecru yarn, mosaic stitch. Use all three strands of yarn in needle.

WEDDING PILLOW: Leave a 1″ margin all around design area. Use two strands of yarn in needle. Following chart and color key, work man's shortcoat and lady's apron in mosaic stitch. Work rest of pillow front in continental stitch.

COLOR KEY FOR MARRIAGE PILLOW

☐ ECRU (4)
⬠ MEDIUM BLUE (⅓)
⊙ NAVY (⅔)
☒ RUST (¼)
☑ PEACH (⅓)
⊡ MEDIUM GREEN (1⅛)
⑤ DARK GREEN (⅓)
⊙ FLESH (⅛)
▲ BROWN (⅛)

HAND-HOOKED RUGS
Shown on pages 34 and 35

EQUIPMENT: Paper for patterns. Pencil. Colored pencil. Scissors. Ruler. Dressmaker's tracing (carbon) paper. Dry ballpoint pen or tracing wheel. Thumbtacks. Large sewing needle. Susan Bates 5″ straight rug hook. Masking tape. Optional: Rug frame. Fabric strip cutter. Softwood surface.

MATERIALS: Wool fabric from old garments or blankets; use solid colors, plaids, tweeds, herringbones, stripes, or paisleys (avoid hard fabrics such as gabardines or worsteds, very soft fabrics such as cashmere, or easily frayed fabrics such as diagonal weaves); see individual directions as well as illustration for colors. Foundation fabric such as monk's cloth or open-weave burlap, at least 6″ wider and longer than finished rug size. Rug binding 1½″ wide, to go around perimeter of rug. Carpet thread.

DIRECTIONS: Read General Directions for Hand-Hooked Rugs, page 293. **Patterns:** With sharp colored pencil, draw lines across patterns by connecting grid lines. Complete quarter pattern indicated by dash lines for "1724" rug; upper left corner is given. Enlarge patterns by copying on paper ruled in 2″ squares. Spread foundation fabric out on a softwood surface, if available; thumbtack edges in place, keeping threads of fabric straight in both directions. Otherwise, weight edges with heavy objects to keep fabric from shifting. Place carbon face down on fabric; lay pattern face up over carbon, centering on fabric; tape in place. Go over lines of design with dry ball-point pen to transfer.

Edging: Before attaching foundation to frame and hooking design, whipstitch one edge of rug binding to edge of marked rug design, using large sewing needle and carpet thread; binding will extend beyond rug design, flat against excess burlap, until hooking is completed.

Planned Fabric: See individual directions for specific amounts of fabric needed. As a general rule, one-half pound of wool fabric will hook approximately one square foot of rug; or, any area to be hooked requires about four times its size in wood fabric.

In planning colors for each rug, limit your choices to a very few main colors, but use a variety of shades within each color. For these primitive rugs, avoid extremely bright shades. If you will be using a very dark background, work the design with medium to light values; if your background is light, use medium to dark values in the design. For borders, repeat color(s) used in rug design.

When hooking with used wool fabrics, first wash them well to remove soil and excess dye. For these rugs, cut fabric into strips 12″ long by ¼″ wide. If a fabric is thin, cut strips ½″ wide, then fold them in half as they are hooked. Cut strips on straight of goods, removing selvage and tearing the first inch or so to establish correct cutting line.

To Hook: Attach foundation tautly to a frame if desired, following manufacturer's directions; marked design faces up. Before beginning to hook rug, practice making loops on an outside area. Following General Directions and color illustrations on pages 44-45, hook rug.

Finishing: Remove rug from frame. Trim excess foundation fabric to 1¾″ all around. Turn fabric to back of rug, turn in raw edge ½″, and slip-stitch 1¼″ hem to back of rug, mitering corners. Fold binding to back of rug, covering hem, and slip-stitch in place.

WEDDING RUG (opposite): 30″ × 44″.

Materials: Wool fabric as described under Materials, above: Khaki for main background, 1¾ lbs. (World War I army uniforms were used for rug shown.) Beige for corner squares and details, ¼ lb. Soft reds for flowers, vase, and outlining, ½ lb. brown for stems, 1 oz. soft colors for birds, ½ lb. blues for leaves and flowers, ½ lb. scraps from other areas of rug for border.

"1724" RUG (opposite): 27″ × 34½″.

Materials: Wool fabric as described in Materials above: Two shades of oyster white for main background, 1¼ lbs. Khaki for center oval background, "lamb's tongue" outer border, and details, 6 ozs. Dark blue for oval and border outlines and center flower details, 6 ozs. Light slate blue for center "tongues," 2 ozs. Variety of reds (rose, brick, rust) for flowers, hearts, and details, 11½ ozs. Brown for horses and stems, 5½ ozs. Gray-green for border "tongues" and leaves, 2 ozs.

Blue-gray for chicks, 4 ozs. Black for horses' details, 4 ozs.

NEVER NEVER RUG (below): 31″ × 66″.

Materials: Wool fabric as described in Materials above: Off-white for background, $3\frac{1}{2}$ lbs. Two or three reds for flowers and border, $1\frac{3}{4}$ lbs. Dark and medium browns for tree trunk, fish, horse, and outlining, 2 lbs. Yellow-green and blue-green for leaves, $\frac{3}{4}$ lb. Black for horse and cat, 1 lb. Two yellows for corner birds, 1 lb. Two blues for center bird, $\frac{1}{2}$ lb. White for cat details, $\frac{1}{4}$ lb. Light browns for border, $1\frac{1}{2}$ lbs.

"1724" RUG

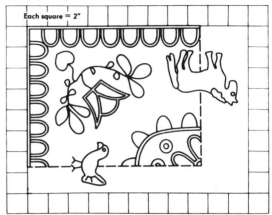

WEDDING RUG

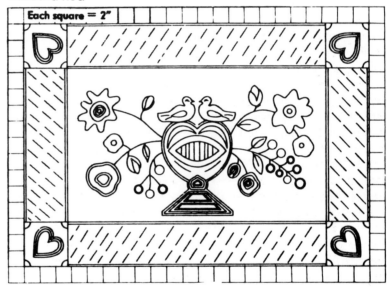

NEVER NEVER RUG

BASKET AND LOTUS STENCILED FLOORS

Shown on pages 36 and 37

EQUIPMENT: Paper for patterns. Ruler. Pencil. Jigsaw. Stencil material: Clear acetate in flat sheets, .0075 gauge; or frosted mylar, .005 gauge. Drawing pen, #2 Rapidograph, with India ink. Household utility or mat knife with fresh blades (not heavy-duty blades). Wide brush or roller for masonite. Wide brush or roller for polyurethane. Extra-large stencil brushes, 1"-diameter bristle, one for each color. Piece of glass with filed edges 10" × 12", $\frac{1}{4}$" thick. Piece of white paper 10" × 12". Saucers for mixing paint, one for each color. Palette knife. Paper towels and facial tissues. Masking tape. Frosted, translucent tape. Glass bowl for cleaning stencils. Four empty coffee cans for cleaning brushes. Mild liquid detergent. Rubber bands.

MATERIALS: Tempered masonite $\frac{1}{8}$" thick (see below for amount). Oil or water-base flat enamel paint for background. Instant-drying Japan paints for stenciling, see color keys or use desired colors. (**Note:** Actual-size stencils, stencil brushes, and Presto-Dri Japan paints, available from American Decorative Arts, Inc., Dept. MN 18, Dorset, Vermont 05251.) Spray-on and polyurethane varnish (turpentine, not plastic). Cement for floors. Turpentine or mineral spirits for thinner.

DIRECTIONS: Note: Read directions through first. Have an extra masonite square and stencil on hand as a test. Go through the entire procedure on this tile to practice before doing floor tiles.

To Prepare Masonite Squares: Determine the number of masonite squares you will need for your floor; the size of each square tile is given below. You can adjust the design by eliminating or adding borders or parts of design, making squares larger or smaller to fit your floor.

Cut masonite into square tiles with jigsaw or have them cut for you. Be sure the squares are cut with precision. With brush or roller, apply two coats of oil or water-base flat enamel to each square for background color; let paint dry between coats.

To Make Stencils: Enlarge patterns by copying on paper ruled in 1" squares. Cut a piece of stencil material 1" larger all around than masonite square.

Mark the exact dimension of the square centered on the stencil sheet with pen and ink.

Tape pattern to smooth surface. Place the stencil sheet centered over pattern; tape to secure. With pen and ink, trace the areas marked #1. Trace a second stencil in the same manner as first, for areas marked #2. Repeat for third stencil, tracing areas marked #3. Mark the stencils #1, #2, and #3. If errors occur in inking, use slightly moistened tissue to wipe away lines.

With pen and ink, trace some of the shapes from stencil #1 onto stencils #2 and #3, using broken lines rather than solid lines. These broken lines will serve as register marks for accurate placement of stencils #2 and #3 and are not to be confused with the solid cutting lines.

Place each stencil on glass and place sheet of white paper under glass to make design lines more visible. With utility or mat knife, cut out the shapes marked with solid lines from each stencil. Cut slowly and carefully, lifting the blade only after an entire area has been cut out. Always cut toward you and turn stencil as necessary with your other hand. Change blades as often as necessary.

To Prepare Japan Paint for Stenciling: Stir paint well with spoon before using. Place about $\frac{1}{2}$ teaspoon of paint in a saucer. Add two or three drops of turpentine or mineral spirits; mix thoroughly with palette knife until paint is the consistency of soft butter. To mix shades, add only small amounts at a time. You will find that you need only a small amount of paint for a large area of stenciling, as you will be using only a trace of paint on the brush.

Check the paint every few minutes to be sure it is not drying. If it is, add two or three drops of turpentine or mineral spirits with spoon; blend with palette knife. The paint should always have a look of shiny wetness.

For Brushing Technique: After dipping brush in paint, rub off paint from the brush onto paper towel until paint has a soft, even, shaded quality. To stencil, hold brush like a pencil with fingers close to bristle. Use your other hand to press the stencil down flat while working. Work brush in a broad circular motion from outer contours of open space to center until area is covered with paint. Keep a tissue moistened with turpentine or spirits handy to clean paint off fingers or stencil while working, as necessary.

To Stencil: For easier stenciling, tape four tiles together on wrong side. Work with right side up. Tape stencil #1 in place on tiles. Stencil color or colors, one at a time, as indicated by color key. Repeat with the other four tiles before going on to the next stencil. Let dry.

Tape stencil #2 in place on tiles, lining up register marks with areas already stenciled. Stencil; let dry. Repeat with stencil #3.

Let paint dry for one week. Then lightly spray on one coat of varnish to protect the stencil paint. Thin polyurethane varnish just slightly to avoid pebbly surface. With roller or brush, apply two coats of polyurethane, drying between coats. Cement tiles to floor. When cement is dry, apply a third coat of polyurethane.

To Clean Brushes: Note: Never immerse stencil brush in turpentine to clean bristles while you are stenciling. Instead, moisten paper towel with turpentine and wipe bristles as needed, while you work. To be sure brush is dry, squeeze with tissue.

When you have finished stenciling for the day, clean brushes thoroughly. Label the three empty coffee cans #1, #2, and #3, for three rinses. Pour enough thinner into each so bristles will be immersed. Swish brushes well in first rinse and squeeze out thinner on inside of can or paper towel. Repeat several times. Repeat in can #2, and then in can #3. Dry brushes well on paper towels. Then put brushes in a fourth coffee can filled with warm water and mild liquid detergent. Rinse several times until clean. Dry with paper towels. Place rubber band around bristles so brushes will dry in their proper shape.

To Clean Stencils: Never immerse acetate stencil in water. Be very gentle with stencil while cleaning, as it can break easily. Always clean immediately after you have finished stenciling for the day. The longer you wait, the harder it is to remove the paint. If properly cleaned, stencils can be as good as new.

Remove masking tape. Pour $\frac{1}{4}$ cup turpentine into bowl. Cover work surface with paper towels. Place stencils on towels and, with tissue moistened with turpentine, wipe gently on both sides while holding stencil flat on towel. Replace towels and tissue as necessary.

You can repair broken stencils with transparent tape on both sides. Trim away excess tape. Keep stencils pressed flat for storage.

To Clean Saucers: Pour some turpentine into saucer and wipe out with towel. Scrape off paint with palette knife, if necessary.

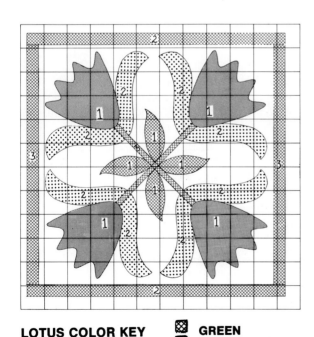

LOTUS COLOR KEY

⊠ GREEN
▦ RED
⊞ ORANGE

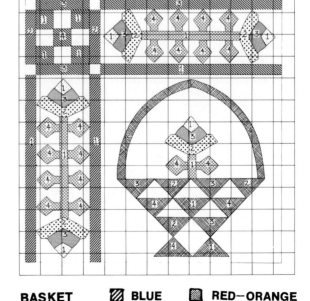

BASKET COLOR KEY

▨ BLUE
⊠ GREEN
⊡ ORANGE
▦ RED—ORANGE
⊟ YELLOW
⊠ LT. GRAY

BASKET
COLOR KEY

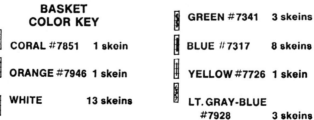

CORAL #7851	1 skein		GREEN #7341	3 skeins
ORANGE #7946	1 skein		BLUE #7317	8 skeins
WHITE	13 skeins		YELLOW #7726	1 skein
			LT. GRAY-BLUE #7928	3 skeins

BASKET AND LOTUS PILLOWS

Shown on pages 36 and 37

EQUIPMENT: Masking tape. Scissors. Waterproof marking pen. Ruler. Tapestry and sewing needles. Sewing machine with zipper foot or cording foot attachment. **For Blocking:** Rustproof thumbtacks. Soft wooden surface. Brown paper. Square.

MATERIALS: Mono needlepoint canvas, 14 mesh-to-the-inch, about 5″ larger than finished pillow size. DMC Persian 3-ply yarn: amounts and colors listed in individual color keys. Heavy fabric for backing in color to coordinate with needlepoint, 1″ larger all around than finished pillow, plus enough bias strips for piping for perimeter of pillow (see directions below). Cording $\frac{1}{4}$″ diameter, enough for circumference or perimeter of pillow, plus 1″. Sewing thread to match backing fabric. Muslin for inner pillow, 45″ wide, $\frac{1}{2}$ yard for each. Polyester fiberfill for stuffing. All-purpose glue.

GENERAL DIRECTIONS: To Work Needlepoint: Read Needlepoint How-To's on page 306. With pen and ruler, mark outline of finished pillow size in center of canvas, leaving equal margins all around.

Following individual directions, charts, and color keys for each, work in straight stitches over several threads of canvas, varying length of stitches as indicated. Grid lines on charts represent threads of canvas. Use two strands of yarn in needle for all pillows.

When needlepoint is complete, block as directed on page 307.

Finishing: To Make a Needlepoint Pillow: After needlepoint is blocked, trim canvas margins to $\frac{1}{2}$″. Cut backing fabric same size as trimmed canvas. Make and attach piping (see directions below). With right sides facing, stitch backing and needlepoint together, making $\frac{1}{2}$″ seams; leave opening at center of one side for inner pillow. Trim off corners of canvas diagonally; apply a little glue to trimmed edges. Whip canvas margins to back of needlepoint; turn right side out. Insert inner pillow (see below) through opening. Add stuffing in corners if necessary. Turn in raw edges of opening and slip-stitch closed.

To Make Inner Pillow: Cut two pieces of muslin the same shape as pillow but measuring 2″ wider and longer than finished pillow size. (If you wish pillow to look very firmly stuffed, cut muslin 3″ wider and longer than pillow size.) With right sides facing, sew edges together with $\frac{1}{2}$″ seams, leaving an opening large enough for your hand in center of one side. Clip into seams at corners. Turn to right side. Stuff inner pillow fully. Turn in raw edges of opening; slip-stitch closed.

To Make Fabric Piping: After cutting the backing for a needlepoint pillow, cut $1\frac{1}{2}$″-wide bias strips from remaining fabric. Join strips to make one strip long enough to fit perimeter or circumference of pillow with $\frac{1}{2}$″ overlap. Lay $\frac{1}{4}$″-thick cable cord along center length of strip on wrong side of fabric. Fold strip over cord and stitch, with zipper or cording foot, along length of strip close to cord.

With raw edges of piping facing out, baste piping to right side of blocked and trimmed canvas, keeping piping seam along edges of needlepoint and rounding corners slightly. Overlap piping ends $\frac{1}{2}$″ on one side; trim off any excess. To fit ends together, cut off one end of cord $\frac{1}{2}$″ inside fabric casing; turn in casing $\frac{1}{4}$″. Insert other end and slip-stitch fabric of both ends together. Stitch piping to needlepoint. Finish needlepoint pillow as directed above, stitching needlepoint and backing together with piping in between.

BASKET: $12\frac{3}{4}$″ × $13\frac{3}{4}$″.

Mark outline of pillow size in center of canvas. Mark area into quarters with horizontal and vertical lines going through exact center. Following chart, work lower right half of vertical center panel, starting in exact center of canvas, indicated on chart by star. Following color key, work flowers and leaves first, then fill in background, making stitches horizontally, vertically, or diagonally as indicated on chart. Then complete lower left half of panel, working chart in reverse. Work upper half of panel in same manner, following chart in reverse from center star. Complete the two blue and white border rows on both sides of center vertical panel. Complete the two blue and white rows going across horizontal center of pillow, as shown on chart; add another row of white on other side of blue row.

LOTUS
COLOR KEY

CORAL #7851	4 skeins
GREEN #7346	4 skeins
RED #7666	4 skeins
WHITE	10 skeins

Work basket motif in each quarter, reversing design for upper baskets. Fill in outer borders as shown on chart.

Finish pillow as instructed in General Directions.

LOTUS: About 15½″ square.

Mark outline of pillow size in center of canvas. Mark two corner-to-corner diagonal lines, dividing square into quarter sections and indicating exact center where lines cross. Count four holes to left of center, then four holes up; mark with pin. Begin working at pin (corresponding to star on chart), making inner green border around flower in lower left of pillow. Continue green border pattern, repeating to outline four equal flower areas. Within each flower area, make a second diagonal line and a horizontal and vertical line, all crossing in center. Starting at center of one flower area, work stems, leaves, and flowers, then fill in background. Work remaining flower areas, then complete outer border, following chart. Finish as in General Directions.

STENCILED BOUQUET
Shown on page 38

SIZE: 18″ × 14″, unframed.

EQUIPMENT: Read General Directions for Stenciling on page 305. Medium-size stencil brushes.

MATERIALS: Cotton velveteen, light brown (or desired color), 36″ wide, ½ yard. Acrylic tube paints in colors shown, or as desired. All-purpose glue. For Mounting: Cardboard, 18″ × 14″.

DIRECTIONS: Enlarge pattern by copying on paper ruled in 1″ squares. Trace design. Cement tracing at corners and edges onto stencil paper 18″ × 14″.

Cut stencil following General Directions on page 305. To paint, use acrylic paints full strength. Use small amounts of paints when experimenting to mix colors. Use scraps of stencil paper for palette.

On a flat working surface covered with paper, center and tape fabric in place; make sure fabric is taut. Tape stencil to fabric. To stencil, see Gen-

Stenciled Bouquet Pattern

eral Directions. Paint, following colors in illustration or as desired.

When all areas are stenciled, remove stencil carefully and let paint dry thoroughly. To clean, wash brushes in water; gently wipe stencil with a wet rag.

Mounting: Center velveteen on one surface of cardboard; turn over and tape 2″ margins to back of cardboard, making sure fabric is taut. Frame as desired.

BEADED BOUQUET
Shown on page 39

EQUIPMENT: Jewelers pliers, wire cutter.

MATERIALS: Round beads, size 11/0, in these approximate amounts: 12 bunches opaque white, 1 bunch transparent white opal, 16 bunches opaque royal blue, 12 bunches transparent light blue, 2 bunches opaque yellow, 18 bunches transparent medium green. Stem wires: Three packages 16-gauge, 12″ long (42 count); Three packages 14-gauge, 12″ long (26 count). Ten rolls green floral tape. Three spools silver-colored lacing wire. Fifteen spools silver-colored beading wire, 28-gauge (90 yards per spool). Large pedestal vase.

GENERAL DIRECTIONS: Unwind about one yard of 28-gauge wire and wrap it once around thumbtack pushed into one end of spool (to keep remaining wire wound neatly on spool). Carefully pull one strand of beads from bunch; knot thread at one end. At other end of strand; insert end of wire through five or six beads at a time and carefully pull thread out. Continue until designated number of beads have been strung on wire, unwinding more wire from spool as needed; allow at least 12″ of extra wire and rewrap wire around thumbtack. Knot or crimp wire at threading end; do not cut beaded wire from spool. Keep beading close and tight so as little wire as possible shows.

Basic techniques for shaping flowers from wire threaded with the required number of beads are given here. Refer to specific directions for amounts and colors of beads required for individual flowers shown in photograph of bouquet.

Basic Loop: The basic loop is used to form petals and leaves and can be made with rounded or pointed ends. Slide designated number of beads from spool onto wire and to within 3″ of knotted end. At end of beads opposite knot, make a bare wire loop, using about 6″ of wire; twist several times to secure loop (Diagram 1). Slide the same number of beads as in first row up to loop, adding two more if making a rounded end, or four more if making a pointed end. Curve this second row up and around one side of first row and loop wire around bare wire just above beads. For third row, slide up same number of beads as in second row, plus two or four additional beads, depending on whether end if to be rounded or pointed (Diagram 2). Curve this row down on other side of first row and twist wire around original twist. Continue making additional rows, adding two or four beads to each (depending on rounded or pointed end) and curving wire to alternate sides; finish at loop end, which will be stem of flower. Cut wire from spool 4″ from beading; cut knotted end of wire $\frac{1}{4}$″ from beads and bend end down behind beads. Cut loop open and twist ends together with end of wire cut from spool. Flatten and shape completed leaf or petal.

Single Loop: Slide designated number of beads to within 3″ of knotted end of wire; shape beaded wire into loop. Cross bare ends of wires and twist together twice (Diagram 3). For continuous single loops, continue making loops in same manner, always twisting wires together between each loop. When loop is complete, leave 4″ of bare wire and cut from spool.

Crossover Loops: Make single loop of designated number of beads but twist wires only once; then curve beaded loop into a long oval shape. Slide up same number of beads as in single loop; carry half of beads across face of loop, with wire between two top beads of single loop (Diagram 4). Bring remaining half of beads down behind single loop and twist wires twice. Flatten and shape completed petal with your fingers. Continue making crossover loops. When desired number of petals are completed, leave 4″ of bare wire and cut from spool.

For a three-row petal, string a single loop as for above but then thread on only half as many beads as for loop. Carry beads across face of loop as before, but carry bare wire rather than beads down back of loop. Flatten petal so bare wire does not show.

Straight Stamens: For one pair of stamens, thread 40 yellow beads onto 28-gauge wire. Coil the end of the wire tightly around a large needle three times; remove needle. Slide 20 beads up to coil and make a 6″ loop of bare wire below beads. Slide remaining 20 beads to loop and coil the spool end of wire around the needle three times. Cut wire at both ends close to coils. Cut bottom of loop open and twist cut ends of wire together.

Button Center: Construct same way as for basic loop. Begin with base of three beads, then second row of six, and third row of six. For larger button, add two rows at a time, one to each side of first row and each pair of rows, having three more beads than previous row. Cut from spool and twist all wires together under button several times.

Wrapping Stem with Beads: String two strands of green beads onto lacing wire. Wrap 1″ of bare wire at end without knot around the stem below flower. Slide beads up to flower and wrap beads tightly around stem by twirling flower with one hand while holding beaded wire taut with other hand. (Holding flower upside down may make it easier to wrap beads tightly.) Cover stem with beads to within several inches of bottom end and wrap wire around stem several times; cover exposed wire and stem with tape.

Leaves: To make narrow leaf, thread about 27″ of green beads onto wire. Leaf is made in Basic Loop technique, with a starting row of beads about 5″ long. Work five rows, making a pointed top and rounded bottom (at loop end). If you have trouble keeping rows flat and close together, use a bobby pin to hold them in place. When beading is complete, reinforce leaf with lacing across the center: Using a short length of lacing wire, wrap the middle of the wire once around the center row of leaf, halfway between top and bottom. Then, working outward to each side, wrap the lacing wire once around each row, keeping the rows close together; wrap wire twice around each outside row and cut wire close to beads.

To make wide leaf, thread about 77″ of green

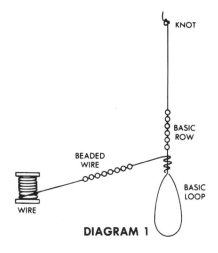

DIAGRAM 1

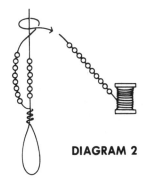

DIAGRAM 2

DIAGRAM 3

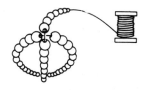

DIAGRAM 4

beads onto wire. Leaf is made in Basic Loop technique, with a starting row of beads about 6″ long. Proceed in same manner as for narrow leaf, but make this leaf eleven rows wide. When beading is complete, cut wire at knotted end to 1½″ length. Place stem wire down center of underside of leaf, even with top of leaf. Wrap top end of leaf wire around stem wire; twist bottom end of leaf wire around stem wire. Lace as for narrow leaf, but begin lacing at stem wire.

Assembly: If flower has a center, arrange petals in a circle around lower edge of stamen or button. Twist ends of all wires together several times. To make smooth stem, cut off ends of wires at slightly varying points. Cut stem wire of appropriate gauge to desired length. Hold flower wires against stem wire. Tear off about 20″ of floral tape and stretch it; then wrap it smoothly around stem wire, working diagonally downward and overlapping edges of tape so wire is completely covered. Attach leaves by wrapping them onto stem so their tips are level with bottom of flower; continue wrapping down the stem. Shape flowers and leaves, arranging them as desired.

FLOWERS

Pansy Buds: Bouquet has four blue and four white buds. For each, thread wire with 162 beads of desired color. Make a single loop of 8 beads; around the circumference of the first loop, make a second loop of 18 beads; around the second, make a third loop of 28 beads; this is one petal. Twist wires together twice before making a second petal in the same manner; then twist wires twice and make a third petal. Cut wire from spool 4″ from beading. For the calyx, thread 60 green beads on wire; make three continuous single loops of 20 beads each. To assemble, place calyx directly under flower bud and tape together as described in general directions.

Day Lily Buds: Bouquet has six light blue buds. To make each bud, thread wire with two strands of light blue beads. Use Basic Loop technique,

beginning with a row of 35 beads and working five rows. Make two petals; do not cut off top wire. Place the two petals together, with tips even; twist the top wires together and cut off wire. Twist bottom wires together. Make one leaf in same manner, using one strand of green beads. Twist top wire of leaf onto petals near top; twist bottom wire onto bottom of petals. Twist all together to make tight bud.

Daisy: Bouquet has 12 white daisies. Each daisy has three connected petals for top layer and six connected petals for bottom layer. Each petal is made of crossover loops, using 20 beads for each row, or 40 beads for each loop, so thread on 240 opaque white beads for top layer; thread on 480 white beads for bottom layer. To make one stamen for each daisy, thread 44 yellow beads on wire. Make a single loop of 8 yellow beads, twist wire once, then slide 14 beads up to twist. Make a 6″ bare wire loop. Then slide 14 beads up and make another single loop of the remaining 8 beads. Cut wires off close to both bead loops; cut large loop open. For calyx, thread 100 green beads on wire and make five continuous loops of 20 beads each. To assemble, place top layer of petals around stamen, then place bottom layer of petals underneath top layer and calyx underneath petals; twist wires together and tape as described in general directions. Make a narrow leaf and tape onto stem.

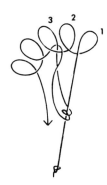

WIRE LOOPS SHOWN WITHOUT BEADING
DIAGRAM 5

Wild pansy: Bouquet has six white and eight blue pansies. Each flower is made of five petals. To begin, thread wire with about one yard of beads in desired color. Make a single loop of 8 beads. Wrap three more single loops, each one larger than the previous one, around the circumference of the original loop; fasten each row by wrapping beading wire around the wire at the base of the original loop each time you encircle it. This completes one petal of four circles. Leave $\frac{1}{4}''$ of bare wire, then form second petal as you did the first. Continue making petals until you have five in all. For stamen, thread 60 yellow beads on wire. Make five continuous single loops of 12 beads each. For calyx, thread 90 green beads onto wire; make five continuous single loops of 18 beads each. To assemble, encircle the stamen cluster with the petals; just below the petals, attach the calyx. Tape as previously directed, adding a small leaf onto each flower stem. After each flower is taped, tape pairs of flowers and one bud together until you have used all buds; tape remaining pairs of flowers together.

Bluets: Bouquet has 18 royal blue bluets, each made in three separate parts; each part requires about six strands of beads. For Part I, make 8 continuous single loops, using 1" of beads for each loop. Cut from wire, twist wires together, bend into narrow loops and give each a halftwist. For Part II, make 12 continuous single loops, using $1\frac{1}{2}''$ of beads for each loop. Cut from wire but do not twist wires together. Carefully form narrow loops and give each a half-twist. For Part III, see Diagram 5. Crimp the spool end of wire and slide 1" of beads to it. Measure 3" from the crimped end and make three continuous single loops, each formed from 1" of beads. Slide the original 1" of beads to the first loop; slide another 1" of beads from spool to third loop; bring these together and wrap bare spool wire around the end of wire at end of beads. Bring beaded spool wire up along the left side of both 1" rows, then push bare wire between third and second loops and cross the wire underneath the third loop to the left (Diagram 5). Make two more continuous single loops, each with 1" of beads; bring 1" of beaded wire along the left side of the three beaded rows; cut from

spool and twist wires together. Make six in all for each flower.

For calyx, make five continuous single loops, each formed from 1" of green beads. To assemble, wrap Part II around Part I and twist wires together. Tape to the top of a taped piece of stem wire. Wrap a piece of lacing wire just below flower to secure flower wires to stem wire. Add the six petals of Part III one at a time, wrapping tightly with lacing wire after adding each one. Wrap lacing wire down another inch, then cut; cut off excess petal wire. Add calyx at base of flower and tape as directed before. Bead the upper stem as directed; make and add a narrow leaf, placing it so its tip is even with lower edge of flower.

Tulip: The bouquet includes fifteen white tulips. Each tulip is composed of five petals. To make each petal, thread one strand of white beads onto wire. Using the Basic Loop technique, begin with a starting row of 30 beads. Make each petal of eleven rows, forming a pointed top and rounded bottom. When five petals are completed, tape together onto stem wire. Lace the petals together on inside of each tulip by wrapping lacing wire around two outer rows on each side of each petal, carrying the wire across petal from edge to edge. At beginning and end of lacing, wrap wire twice around beaded petal wire; cut lacing wire close to beading. Bead the upper stem as instructed in General Directions. Make and add two long narrow leaves, placing them so their tips are even with the lower edge of the flower.

Day Lily: Bouquet has sixteen day lilies, each with light blue petals changing to royal blue at the center. Each lily has six petals made in the Basic Loop technique with both ends pointed. In order to shade each petal from royal blue at the bottom to light blue at the top, thread beads on wire in following order: Row 7, 24 royal, 22 light blue; Row 6, 21 light blue, 22 royal; Row 5, 21 royal, 18 light blue; Row 4, 18 light blue, 19 royal; Row 3, 17 royal, 15 light blue; Row 2, 15 light blue, 14 royal; Row 1, 14 royal, 12 light blue. Make the basic loop petal, working the seven rows in exact reverse of order given, beginning with the 12 light blue beads of Row 1. Make six petals for each flower.

For stamen, make six straight stamens (three pairs), following General Directions. To make the center stamen, thread about 5″ of yellow beads onto wire. Slide 1½″ of beads up, then make three continuous single loops of 12 beads each. Slide another 1½″ of beads up to loops. Cut wire and twist ends together; give 1½″ beaded lengths several half-twists.

To assemble, place looped stamen in center of straight stamens on a short stem. Place six petals around stamen and tape together. Tape pairs of flowers together. Make three narrow leaves and add to each grouping.

Rose of Sharon: Bouquet has twenty-four roses, each consisting of three light blue petals and three variegated petals. For each light blue petal, begin with basic row of 14 beads. Use the Basic Loop technique to make petal of eleven rows with rounded top and pointed bottom. For each variegated petal, thread on beads in this order: Row 11, 13 opal, 9 royal, 21 light blue; Row 10, 22 light blue, 10 royal, 11 opal; Row 9, 11 opal, 10 royal, 17 light blue; Row 8, 18 light blue, 8 royal, 11 opal; Row 7, 9 opal, 8 royal, 14 light blue; Row 6, 15 light blue, 6 royal, 9 opal; Row 5, 25 light blue; Row 4, 22 light blue; Row 3, 19 light blue; Row 2, 17 light blue; Row 1, 14 light blue. Make variegated petals in same manner as light blue petals, working the rows in exact reverse of order given, beginning with Row 1.

For stamen, make three straight stamens of yellow beads. For looped stamen, make one single loop of 2½″ of yellow beads; give several half-twists. Arrange straight stamens around looped stamen. Arrange petals around stamen, alternating solid and variegated petals. Tape stem. Make and add a narrow leaf.

HOME SWEET HOME PILLOW
Shown on page 40

SIZE: 13″ square.
EQUIPMENT: Masking tape. Pencil. Ruler. Scissors. Tapestry needle. Sewing needle. Straight pins. Sewing machine with zipper-foot attachment.
MATERIALS: Mono needlepoint canvas, 12 mesh-to-the-inch, 18″ square. Persian yarn (3 ply): see color key for colors and number of ounces needed (in parentheses). Tan cotton velveteen for backing and welting, 45″ wide, ½ yard. Cable cord ¼″ in diameter, 1½ yards. Tan extra-strong sewing thread. Muslin fabric for inner pillow, 36″ wide, ½ yard. Polyester fiberfill for stuffing.
DIRECTIONS: Read General Directions for Needlepoint on page 306. Tape outer edges of canvas. On center of canvas, mark outline of needlepoint area, leaving margin of 1½″. Mark horizontal and vertical center lines of needlepoint area on canvas.

Dash lines along two sides of chart indicate this is a quarter of the design. Upper right corner of center design is worked, then charted design repeats in reverse for upper left corner, this time omitting stitches shown on chart to left of vertical dash line. Entire top half then repeats in reverse for bottom half, this time omitting stitches shown on chart below horizontal dash line. Pillow front is worked in continental stitch using two strands of yarn, except for areas indicated on chart by zigzagged diamond floweret A, B, or C, which are worked using three strands in straight stitches radiating outwards from a center. Diagram alongside chart shows positioning of stitches in floweret. Centermost area is worked in a variation of a straight stitch floweret; see lines on chart (at bottom left corner) indicating length of stitches; work in brown. Center mesh is covered with a French knot; see stitch detail on page 308. Working from right to left and following color key, complete top half then bottom half of center design. Remember to make all stitches face the same direction.

Following border chart, count up four meshes from the upper left corner and begin working the HOME SWEET HOME lettering. Work the houses in upper left and upper right hand corners. Turn the pillow around to work the border identically on the other side; remember to have the stitches all face the same direction. Work the same letters on the left and right side borders, omitting the houses. Fill in background of border all around with ecru stitches.

Finishing: Block completed needlepoint following directions on page 307. When dry, trim canvas margins to $\frac{1}{2}''$. Follow directions on page 307 for How to Make a Pillow.

COLOR KEY

- ⊡ **A BROWN (1)**
- ⧄ **TAN (1¼)**
- ☐ **ECRU (2)**
- ⊟ **B ORANGE (½)**
- Ⓢ **C PINK (½)**

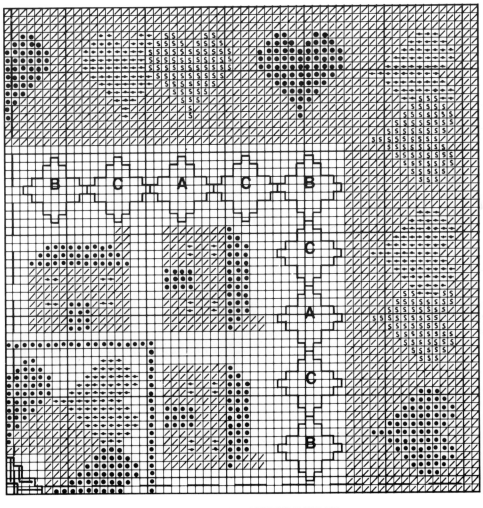

QUARTER CHART OF CENTER DESIGN

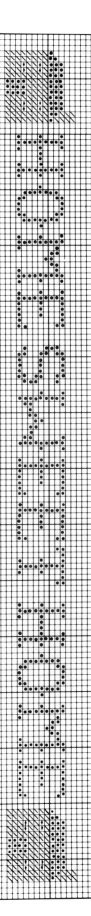

BORDER

TULIP PILLOW

Shown on page 40

SIZE: 19″ square.

EQUIPMENT: Pencil. Ruler. Scissors. Paper for pattern. Thin, stiff cardboard. Dressmaker's (carbon) tracing paper. Tracing wheel or dry ballpoint pen. Compass. Sewing and quilting needles. Tailor's chalk. Quilting frame (optional).

MATERIALS: Brown cotton fabric 45″ wide, $\frac{2}{3}$ yd. Small amounts of four cotton print fabrics in compatible colors, all including brown (in original pillow, two of the prints are small, one is medium, and one is large). Muslin, $19\frac{1}{2}$″ square. Polyester batting, $19\frac{1}{2}$″ square. Cording $\frac{1}{4}$″ wide, $2\frac{1}{4}$ yds. Loose filler for stuffing. White sewing thread.

DIRECTIONS: Read How to Appliqué on page 304. Enlarge pattern on paper ruled in 1″ squares; complete half-pattern indicated by dash lines for one-quarter of pillow design. Dotted lines are quilting lines. Make a separate cardboard pattern for each part of appliqué; use compass to draw 3″-wide circle for center piece. Marking patterns on wrong side of fabric and adding $\frac{1}{4}$″ seam allowance all around, cut one center circle and four each of remaining four pieces; cut center circle and tulip tips from medium print, tulip blossoms from large print, and two leaf pieces from two medium prints. Cut two pieces of brown fabric $19\frac{1}{2}$″ square. Set one piece aside for pillow back.

On other piece, mark horizontal and vertical center lines (fold and crease or mark with ruler and tailor's chalk). Using dressmaker's carbon and tracing wheel, transfer appliqué pattern to brown background, repeating pattern in each quarter and matching quarter-lines of circle with marked center lines of brown fabric. Following directions in How to Appliqué, pin, baste, and slip-stitch appliqués in place, starting with tulip tip and working to center, overlapping with each new piece.

Quilting: Transfer dot-line quilting pattern to appliquéd pillow front, in same manner as before. Following General Directions for Quilting on page 300, pin and baste pillow front, batting, and muslin together. Starting in center, quilt around each appliquéd piece and on marked lines, using white sewing thread double in needle.

Assembling: Cut bias strips 1″ wide from brown fabric, piecing strips for a length of about 78″. Fold long strip in half lengthwise, enclosing cording. Trim excess fabric beyond cording to $\frac{1}{4}$″. Right sides together, pin and baste pillow front, cording, and pillow back together for $\frac{1}{4}$″ seams, matching raw edges. Stitch around on three sides and the beginning and end of fourth side, rounding corners slightly. Turn to right side. Stuff pillow firmly. Slipstitch opening closed.

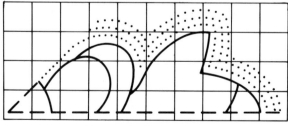

Pattern for Tulip Pillow

BOUDOIR BOXES

Shown on page 40

SIZES: 8″, 6″, and 4″ cubes.

EQUIPMENT: Pencil. Ruler. Scissors. Dressmaker's (carbon) tracing paper. Tracing wheel or dry ball-point pen. Sewing and embroidery needles. Tailor's chalk. Sewing machine.

MATERIALS: Muslin 45″ wide, $1\frac{2}{3}$ yds. for 3 boxes. Thin, stiff cardboard. Polyester batting. Loose stuffing. Green sewing and embroidery threads.

DIRECTIONS: For Each Box: Enlarge leaf patterns on paper ruled in 1″ squares. There are three patterns given for each size box. Cut six pieces of muslin, 5″ × 9″ for small box; 7″ × 13″ for medium box; and 9″ × 17″ for large box. Cut six pieces of cardboard, 4″, 6″, or 8″ square for small, medium, or large box. On each muslin piece, lightly mark a 4″, 6″, or 8″ square at one end with tailor's chalk, leaving $\frac{1}{2}$″ margin around three sides. Using dressmaker's carbon and tracing wheel,

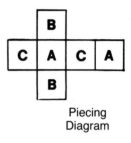

Piecing
Diagram

Patterns for Boudoir Boxes

transfer a leaf design of appropriate size within each marked square, repeating each leaf on two squares. For each muslin piece, cut a thin layer of batting and second muslin piece 4″, 6″, or 8″ square. Pin and baste batting and muslin squares behind marked area of larger piece, leaving $\frac{1}{2}″$ margin on three sides. With green sewing thread, machine-stitch on marked leaf design. Turn long side edges of piece $\frac{1}{2}″$ to underside; press. Fold piece in half crosswise, wrong sides together. Slip-stitch folded side edges together; press. Insert a cardboard square of appropriate size inside pocket made. Stuff loose filler into pocket on both sides of cardboard, concentrating filler towards center of square. Fold open edges of pocket to inside, edge of leaf side first, then edge of plain side; slip-stitch closed.

Assembling Box: When all six sides of a box have been completed, place sides together as shown in Piecing Diagram, leaf side up. Letters on diagram indicate each of the three designs for each size box. Using two strands of green floss in needle, embroider adjacent sides together with

cretan stitch (see detail on page 308). Embroider around remaining three sides of outside A piece. To form box, fold up C and B sides so they touch; the center A piece will be bottom of box. Embroider adjacent sides of C and B pieces together. Outside A piece becomes box lid.

BASKET CUSHIONS
Shown on page 63 and on the cover

SIZE: As shown, $16\frac{1}{2}″$ deep, 19″ wide at front, 17″ wide at back. (See Directions.)

EQUIPMENT: Pencil. Ruler, Scissors. Brown paper. Tracing paper. Dressmaker's tracing (carbon) paper. Tracing wheel or dry ball-point pen. Medium-size paintbrush. Small piece of glass for palette. Sewing machine. Sewing needles. Flat working surface. Masking tape. Straight pins.

MATERIALS: Closely woven black cotton fabric (see directions for figuring amount); for one cushion, we used a piece approximately 24″ × 45″. Cable cord, $\frac{1}{4}$″ diameter, enough to fit around perimeter of cushion, plus 5″. Two layers of cotton batting and one piece of muslin, size of cushion. Red and black sewing thread. Red acrylic paint.

DIRECTIONS: Enlarge basket pattern by copying on paper ruled in 1″ squares; complete half pattern indicated by dash lines. To make pattern for cushion, trace shape of chair seat on brown paper, including indentations for back posts and front legs if necessary.

On wrong side of black fabric, using brown-paper pattern as a guide, mark a top and bottom for cushion; cut out $\frac{1}{2}$″ beyond marked line. For ties, cut two strips each $1\frac{1}{2}$″ × 28″. To cover cording, cut bias strips $1\frac{1}{2}$″ wide, piecing to get length to go around perimeter of cushion, plus 5″ for rounding corners and joining ends.

Painting: On right side of cushion top, using carbon paper and ball-point pen, center and transfer basket and sawtooth border pattern. Remove pattern. Tape cushion top to flat working surface. Paint red areas following illustration. Two coats may be necessary for an opaque finish; allow to dry thoroughly between coats.

Quilting: Using cushion pattern, cut two layers

of batting and a muslin lining. Baste cushion (right side up) and lining together with batting between.

To quilt cushion top, machine-stitch through all four layers, following edges of painted shapes; start in center of basket and work out to border.

Cording: Fold fabric strip for cording in half lengthwise, enclosing cable cord in fold; machine-stitch along length close to cord. Pin covered cording to right side of cushion top, raw edges even and cording facing inward; trim ends to overlap $\frac{1}{2}$″. On one end, cut $\frac{1}{2}$″ off inner cording; turn casing in $\frac{1}{4}$″. On other end, trim away $\frac{1}{4}$″ of casing; insert inner cord into casing of first end and slip-stitch ends together.

Ties: Double-fold each strip lengthwise, right side out. Turn raw ends in; machine-stitch ends and long edge closed.

Assembling: With right sides together and cording between, machine-stitch cushion top to bottom with $\frac{1}{2}$″ seams; leave back of cushion open. Turn cushion to right side. Fold each tie in half; insert fold into a back corner of cushion. Slip-stitch cushion back closed, catching in ties.

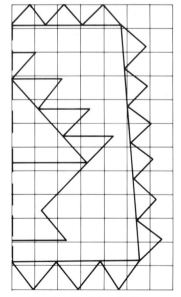

Basket Cushion Pattern

BASKET QUILT

Shown on page 63 and on the cover

SIZE: Approx. 88″ square.

EQUIPMENT: Ruler. Yardstick. Scissors. Pencil. Graph paper for patterns. Thin, stiff cardboard. All-purpose glue. Dressmaker's tracing (carbon) paper. Tracing wheel or dry ball-point pen. Tailor's chalk. Straight pins. Sewing and quilting needles. Sewing machine. Iron.

MATERIALS: Closely woven cotton fabric 45″ wide: red, $1\frac{1}{2}$ yards; black, 10 yards (includes lining). Red and black sewing thread. Cotton or polyester batting.

DIRECTIONS: Read General Directions for Quilting on pages 300 and 301. Quilt is made up of 25 pieced basket blocks, set with plain blocks and a pieced border quilted in a cable pattern.

Patterns: To make basket blocks, see Piecing Diagram. Design is made up of triangles and rec-

Continued on page 75

*Unique chair cushions take their bold design from an antique
quilt. Basket motif with border measures about 12" square.
Design is painted on fabric, then quilted for dimension.
Basket quilt is worked in old-fashioned patchwork;
directions for both begin on page 61.*

*A real Vermont village is lovingly portrayed by
one of its inhabitants. A variety of interesting
fabrics adds an authentic touch to the impression—
a bit of loop braid for a fence, sheer lace
for thin ice or a snowy peak. Winter in Waitsfield,
directions on page 76.*

*Country Christmas, our
quilted wall hanging,
is 37½" × 47" and accented
with bright embroidery
in easy stitches.
Directions on page 78.*

Man's best friend finds a resting place by the fire in Noah Webster's house. Rug, 19" × 32", is hand hooked, with wool strips looped through burlap. Pattern is from an original Edward Frost stencil. Directions begin on page 80.

*Barnyard birds are right at home in any room. Hand-hooked
rug is patterned from 1870s stencil by Edward Frost; 16" × 36".
Our directions for hooking on page 80 also give hints
for dyeing your own wool.*

67

Baby Blocks pillow uses only one diamond motif for its stepped effect. Patches must be carefully sewn together to keep the geometric crispness of design. Pattern works best when colors contrast strongly in prints and solids—here, stark black and white. Directions on page 83.

Baby Blocks, a simple but graphic patchwork
pattern, is worked in crocheted diamonds.
Three diamonds in strong colors are combined
in each block, then the blocks are sewn together
for a bold afghan. This is a perfect
take-along project—in fact, the designer
crocheted most of it on a plane, then
joined the pieces at home! Finished
afghan of Brunswick Windrush is 46" × 64".
Directions on page 85.

*Springtime flowers combine
easy embroidery stitches
with just enough beading to bloom!
Each design, $5\frac{3}{4}'' \times 4\frac{1}{2}''$.
Directions on page 92.*

*Patchwork, stenciling, quilting and woodworking are
combined to beautify any room. The tableskirt (90" diameter)
and chair cushion are of fabric strips, pieced by machine
in radiating diamond patterns. Appliques are quilted
or padded for the egg basket picture; the two-part country
cabinet, 92" × 36", of plywood and stock lumber, is as
decorative as it is practical for storage. Floor stenciling
captures the spirit of the 18th century, when colonists
painted their wooden floors with designs to imitate
the carpeting of the Old World. Our motif is derived from
one of the table skirt fabrics.
Directions for all begin on page 85.*

These Country Kids will brighten everyone's day—and they're easy to do. Actual-size patterns are simple to embroider. They're great as pictures, but could be just as cute on pillows, aprons, or other accent pieces. Country Kids directions, page 94.

Resting by the sea—three pets and their friend! All are cheerful appliques, stitched on the sewing machine with some hand-embroidered features added. Lazy Day Wall Hanging is then framed in a pretty print. Directions on page 96.

Fabric pillows are appliqued with appealing farm animals, fruit and flowers, crocheted in white, navy, and gray fingering yarn. Note the lifelike stitches—loops for woolly lamb, raised shell-stitch feathers for hen, double crochet for piggy. Pad animals, let flowers stand free for three-dimensional effect.
Directions for Farm Animal Pillows on page 98.

Continued from page 62

tangles; dimensions and shape of each patch are shown in the Piecing Diagram. Use ruler and sharp pencil to carefully draw one each of pattern pieces A, B, C, D and E on graph paper, then draw an $8\frac{3}{4}''$ square for plain block pattern. Glue paper patterns to cardboard; let dry; cut carefully along marked lines for templates. Cut several templates for each pattern piece and replace when edges begin to fray.

Patches: Use templates to mark pieces as follows: Place template on wrong side of fabric with right angles on straight of goods. Draw around template with sharp pencil held at an outward angle. Mark as many pieces as needed of each color at one time, leaving $\frac{1}{2}''$ between pieces. Cut out pieces $\frac{1}{4}''$ outside pencil lines for seam allowance; pencil lines will be stitching lines.

From red fabric cut 25 of piece A and 225 of piece B. From black fabric cut 25 of piece A, 175 of piece B, 50 of piece C, and 25 of piece D. Also cut from black fabric 16 $8\frac{3}{4}''$-square blocks, adding $\frac{1}{4}''$ all around for seam allowance; cut template in half diagonally, then cut 16 black triangles; cut template in half again, from right angle to midpoint of long side, and cut out 4 small black triangles. For border, cut 128 of piece E from both red and black fabrics.

Blocks: Assemble basket blocks, following Piecing Diagram and making $\frac{1}{4}''$ seams: Sew one red and one black piece A together along long edges. Sew one red and one black piece B together in same manner, then repeat to make 7 B/B squares. Sew B/B squares together to make a strip of four squares and a strip of three squares, keeping all black triangles at top and all red triangles at bottom of strips. Sew red edge of the 3-square strip to top black side of A/A square, then sew red edge of the 4-square strip to remaining black side of A/A square plus edge of 3-square strip. Sew one short side of each of two red B's to one end of each of two black C's. Sew each C/B strip to one side of A/B square. Sew long edge of D to long edge formed by two B triangles. Make 25 pieced blocks in this manner. Blocks should measure $8\frac{3}{4}''$ square, plus outside seam allowance.

Assembling: Main body of quilt top is assembled by placing basket blocks alternately with solid black blocks in diagonal rows, starting and ending each row with a basket block. Place all blocks in a diamond position with the baskets upright, then arrange them into rows as follows: Row 1: one block (basket); Row 2: three blocks; Row 3: five blocks; Row 4: seven blocks; Row 5: nine blocks. Pin pieces together on seam allowances with right sides facing. Stitch blocks together into rows; stitch rows together. You have now made over one-half of pieced design. Make a second section in same manner, starting with Row four and ending with Row one. Join the two sections, making a square with serrated edges. To fill out square, place large black triangles around edges between basket blocks, four on each side; place a small black triangle in each corner. Sew triangles in place. Finished piece should measure approx. 62″ square, plus outside seam allowance.

Borders: Sew one red and one black piece E

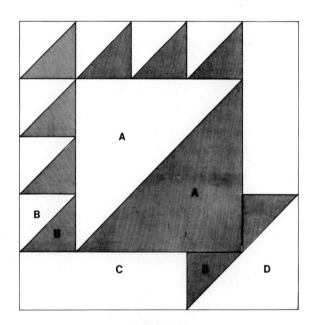

Piecing Diagram

together along long edges; repeat until there are 128 two-color squares. Sew squares together to form four strips of 32 squares each, making sure red triangles are at top of strips and black triangles are at bottom. Sew red side of each strip to each side of center quilt piece in turn so that left edge of strip is flush with left edge of center piece and right edge of strip extends one square past right edge of center piece. Stitch extended end of each strip to flush edge of adjacent strip. Piece should now meausre approx. 66″ square, plus outside seam allowance.

For black border, cut four black strips, two $11\frac{1}{4}″$ × $66\frac{1}{2}″$ and two $11\frac{1}{4}″$ × 88″. Sew shorter strips to sides of center piece, making $\frac{1}{4}″$ seams; sew longer strips to top and bottom of center piece. Quilt top should now measure approx. 88″ square.

Lining: Cut two pieces from black fabric each 45″ × 89″. Sew together on long sides with $\frac{1}{2}″$ seam, to make piece 89″ square. Press seam open. Cut batting 88″ square.

Quilting: Enlarge border quilting pattern on paper ruled in 1″ squares. Using yardstick and tailor's chalk, mark center of quilt top; draw two cor-ner-to-corner diagonal lines on center piece, crossing at center point. Working outward from the resulting X, mark parallel lines $\frac{3}{4}″$ apart to cover quilt top within border strips. Using dressmaker's carbon and tracing wheel or dry ball-point pen, transfer border pattern to top and bottom borders of quilt top; start at midpoint of borders with one cable "wave" centered, and repeat design all the way across to each side. Repeat on side borders; start at midpoint and work out to seam lines between side and end borders.

Following General Directions on pages 300 and 301, center lining, batting and quilt top together; lining will extend $\frac{1}{2}″$ beyond edges of batting and quilt top all around. Pin and baste layers together. Starting in center and working outward, quilt on all marked lines using red thread on red fabric and black thread on black fabric.

Edges: Fold excess lining to front of quilt, turn raw edges under $\frac{1}{4}″$, and slip-stitch to quilt top.

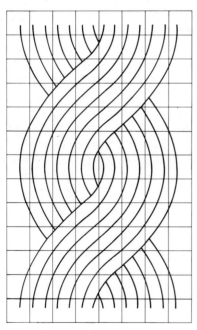

Cable Quilting Pattern

WINTER IN WAITSFIELD
Shown on page 64

SIZE: $32\frac{3}{4}″$ × $53\frac{1}{2}″$.

EQUIPMENT: Pencil. Ruler. Scissors. Paper for pattern. Dressmaker's (carbon) tracing paper. Tracing wheel or dry ball-point pen. Zigzag sewing machine.

MATERIALS: Small amounts of cotton fabrics in a variety of colors and textures, plus bits of felt, corduroy, lace, etc.; see Note below for description of original fabrics used. Three pieces of thin white fabric for backing, each $25\frac{1}{2}″$ × $46\frac{1}{2}″$. Fabric for lining 36″ wide, $1\frac{1}{2}$ yds. Matching sewing threads. Polyester or cotton batting.

DIRECTIONS: Read General Directions on pages 300-301. Enlarge pattern by copying on paper ruled in 1″ squares. Transfer entire pattern to one piece of backing, using dressmaker's carbon and tracing wheel or dry ball-point pen. Transfer outline of each appliqué to appropriate fabric.

(**Note:** In original hanging, sky and river are light blue cotton, road is blue-gray, ground is tan

Winter in Waitsfield

dotted swiss. Mountains are three prints in combinations of gray/white, blue/red, and black/yellow, plus a textured-weave dark red. Snowy peak and thin coat of ice on river are sheer white synthetic with white painted design. Covered bridge is brown and tan corduroy and black cotton. Store is tan corduroy, blue-gray cotton and heavy cutout white lace. Tree is brown cotton. Church is white felt with lace trim and green-blue corduroy door. Fence is white loop braid. Farm buildings are blue felt, red cotton print, tan and green-blue corduroy, and two shades of solid red cotton.)

Cut appliqué pieces $\frac{1}{4}''$ outside marked seam line. Cut entire river of blue, then ice coat of sheer white; ice covers river except for thin strip along right edge.

Starting at top of picture with sky and working downward through all main background pieces, pin and baste appliqués on marked backing. After each piece is basted, straight-stitch by machine along seam line. After all main pieces are stitched, add small pieces, except for lace trims, fence, and

felt church. Trim excess fabric from appliqués, $\frac{1}{8}''$ from stitching. Following General Directions, pin and baste appliquéd picture, one thin layer of batting, and second piece of backing together. Set machine on fine-stitch length and #3 stitch width. Starting in lower part of picture, satin-stitch around appliqués with matching sewing thread, covering straight stitching and raw edges; stitch ground, river and ice layer, road, buildings, and tree. Then pin lace store trim, braid fence, and felt church in place; slip-stitch around edges. Add lace trim to church. Add door to church, satin-stitching in place.

Before continuing to satin-stitch appliqués, add another layer of batting and another backing under entire piece; pin and baste as before. With the two layers of batting in place, satin-stitch around all mountain areas and around snow patch.

Remove basting. Turning back the undermost piece of backing at top, carefully snip away bottom layer of batting above top stitching line, so that sky will lie flatter than mountains. Add extra batting to white mountains at lower left, through side opening. Piece should measure $25\frac{1}{2}'' \times 46\frac{1}{2}''$, including outside seam allowance.

Borders: From pink fabric, cut four strips 2″ wide, two $25\frac{1}{2}''$ long and two $49\frac{1}{2}''$ long. Right sides together and making $\frac{1}{4}''$ seams, sew shorter strips to sides of picture, then longer strips to top and bottom.

From white-dotted navy fabric, cut three pieces 3″ wide, two $28\frac{1}{2}''$ long and one $54\frac{1}{2}''$ long. Making $\frac{1}{4}''$ seams, sew shorter strips to sides of picture and longer strip to bottom. Piece should measure $31'' \times 54\frac{1}{2}''$, including outside seam allowance.

Assembling: From lining fabric, cut piece 31″ × $54\frac{1}{2}''$. Cut a layer of batting same size. Following General Directions, pin and baste picture, batting, and lining together, but placing right side of picture against right side of lining. Straight-stitch around sides and bottom of picture, $\frac{1}{2}''$ from edge. Turn piece right side out.

Finishing: To finish top of picture and make casing for hanging rod, cut piece 6″ × 57″ from navy fabric. Stitch to top of picture, right sides together and with $\frac{1}{4}''$ seams; center top piece so that an equal amount extends at each end. After stitching, fold in excess fabric at ends and press. Fold top piece to back of quilt and turn in edge $\frac{1}{4}''$; slip-stitch to seam between casing and pink border.

Quilt around sides and bottom of picture, along seam between pink and navy borders.

COUNTRY CHRISTMAS
Shown on page 65

SIZE: $37\frac{1}{2}'' \times 47''$.

EQUIPMENT: Colored pencil. Pencil. Ruler. Scissors. Dressmaker's tracing (carbon) paper. Dry ball-point pen or tracing wheel. Sewing and embroidery needles. Iron. Quilting frame (optional). Tape.

MATERIALS: For background: Cotton fabric 36″ wide, $\frac{1}{2}$ yard light blue, 1 yard white. For appliqués: calico 44″ wide in four shades of blue (pale, light, bright*, dark), $\frac{1}{4}$ yard each; pale blue and a white

in textured weaves, light blue with white dots, $\frac{1}{8}$ yard each. For border: Bright blue calico* 44″ wide, $\frac{5}{8}$ yard. For lining: soft fabric 44″ wide, $1\frac{1}{3}$ yards. White and matching sewing thread. Six-strand embroidery floss, 1 skein each: light and bright blue, black, gray, white, yellow, gold, peach, red, light, medium and dark brown, beige, olive and bright green. Batting.

*Note: We used the same bright blue calico for borders as we did for appliqués.

DIRECTIONS: Pattern for hanging is on page 79. Using sharp colored pencil, draw lines across pattern, connecting grid lines. Enlarge pattern on paper ruled in 2″ squares. Heavy lines indicate appliqués, light lines embroidery, dotted lines quilting.

Background: Using pattern, cut sky from light blue fabric and ground from white, adding $\frac{1}{2}''$ seam allowance along inner edge (horizon) of each piece. Turn under seam allowance of white ground piece, clipping as necessary, and press flat. Place pieces together, with ground overlapping sky for $\frac{1}{2}''$. Pin, baste, slip-stitch in place, making background 36″ × $45\frac{1}{2}''$.

Appliqués: Using dressmaker's carbon and dry ball-point pen, transfer appliqué pattern to background. Following directions in How to Appliqué (page 304), cut and prepare appliqué pieces; cut trees and bushes from the four shades of blue calico (see pattern and color photograph), houses and rooftops from textured pale blue and white, smoke from dotted blue, and clouds from remnants of white background fabric. Pin, baste, and slip-stitch appliqués in place.

Embroidery: Replace pattern on background and transfer embroidery designs. Using all six strands of floss in needle, embroider as follows; see stitch details on pages 308-309 and choose colors as desired. Work large solid areas (garments, fence rail, horses) with split stitch; use a single row of split stitch for skates and to outline fence. Work smaller areas (faces, fur trim) with satin stitch. Work single lines (cross on steeple, window frames) with straight stitch. Use French knots for dots. Couch horse's rein with sewing thread.

Fingering Diagram

Areas where colors change should be "fingered"—blending strips of new and old colors as for the long and short stitch in embroidery (see diagram).

When design is complete, fill in the background in the same manner, outlining the design in background color, then filling in the areas.

To Finish: Remove rug from frame. Clip any long ends flush with loops. Cut away excess foundation just inside stay-stitching. Turn rug binding to the back of rug; slip-stitch in place, mitering corners and easing curves.

Note: Pre-dyed wool fabric may be used, but if you wish to dye your own, see the following directions.

Continuity or Dip Dyeing

This method is excellent when dyeing large areas, when dyeing to match or obtain particular colors, or when dyeing a series of shaded tones. Dip or continuity dyeing is recommended for the sky in the Rooster Rug.

EQUIPMENT: Enamel pot, 3-quart. Measuring spoon. Glass jars. Powdered fabric dyes, such as Cushing "Perfection" dye. Measuring cup. White vinegar. Tongs.

MATERIALS: Soft, firm white wool fabric, cut into 6″ × 12″ swatches.

METHOD: Wash and rinse fabric swatches; do not allow to dry. Prepare basic dye solution in glass jar, adding one cup boiling water to one tsp. dry dye. Leave a spoon in jar while pouring water to prevent the glass from cracking. Fill a pot with one quart water and add $\frac{1}{4}$ tsp. dye solution, for palest shade of desired color. Add two fabric swatches and one tbs. white vinegar. Simmer until water is clear. Rinse material under hot running water until water is clear—cold water may cause the wool to harden. Let dry. For a slightly darker shade of same color, repeat dye bath, using two new strips of material, one tbs. vinegar, and increasing the dye amount by half ($\frac{1}{2}$ tsp.). Continue process for darker shades, using following dye solution measurements for succeeding baths: 1 tsp, 2 tsp, 4 tsp, 7 tsp, 10 tsp, 14 tsp. Dye solutions may also be mixed to obtain different shades. Make certain to keep the water level at one quart for each bath. It is not necessary to change the water between baths, as long as you are using the same dye solution and are simmering fabric until the water is clear. When judging color gradations, remember that wet wool is one shade darker than dry and the blotched and unevenly dyed sections that occur add to the color interest.

Onion-Skin Dyeing

This method is good for blending odd weaves and colors. It is especially good for primitive rugs and the dyed fabrics may be used for stems, leaves, bark, feathers, scrolls, foregrounds, and backgrounds. The colors "bleed" and the onion skins add a natural dye which blends textures and values.

EQUIPMENT: Large pot or roasting pan with cover. **Optional:** Small sacks made of old nylon stockings.

MATERIALS: Dry onion skins, enough to fill pot. White vinegar, $\frac{3}{4}$ cup. Soft, firm wool fabrics in pastels, dark solids, paisleys, tweeds, textures, cut into 6″ × 12″ swatches.

METHOD: Wash and rinse fabric swatches; do not allow to dry. Place a layer of onion skins in the bottom of pot or pan, then lay several of the darkest swatches on top. (You may want to place onion skins in small bags made of old nylon stockings. This will make rinsing fabric easier once the dyeing is completed.) Sprinkle with 2 tbs. of white vinegar. Repeat this process, adding onion skins, lighter swatches, and vinegar until pot is full. Add remaining vinegar. Cover with hot water and simmer for 45 minutes. Rinse fabric thoroughly; allow to dry; cut.

SPANIEL RUG: SIZE: 32" × 19".
EQUIPMENT: See General Directions.
MATERIALS: Wool fabric in 6" × 12" swatches as follows: Black, 34; white, 16; dark brown, 5; charcoal gray, 6; beige, 12; brick, 30; dark and bright red, 4 each; forest green, 12; dark green, 4. Looseweave burlap, 40" × 25". Matching rug binding, 3 yards.

DIRECTIONS: Follow General Directions for preparing fabric strips and burlap foundation.

Hook spaniel first, starting with the facial features and following body contours. Outline eyes and muzzle in charcoal gray. Hook nose in dark brown; pupils in white. Dot white forehead with black; outline ears in gray before filling in with white and black. Hook chest and body markings in black; add gray fur details to neck. Hook fur detail lines in dark brown on legs, feet, tail. Fill in remaining body with white.

Hook inside black border; loops should face same direction. Hook upper center background forest green, lower background beige. Hook cor-

ner motifs: Work dark green leaves in concentric circles, following the veins, outline edges of flower petals in dark red, filling in with bright red; hook scrolls in solid brown with dark green highlights following the shape of scrolls with rows of loops. Hook outer brick border.

Finish, following General Directions.

ROOSTER RUG: SIZE: 36" × 16".
EQUIPMENT: See General Directions.
MATERIALS: Wool fabric in 6" × 12" swatches as follows: Black, 40; light gray, 6; dark maroon, 2; maroon, 5; dark green, 5; yellow, 5; medium brown, 8; dark brown, 2; dark beige, 4; medium beige, 32; light beige, 5; light blue, 20; peach, 2; bright red, bright green, light green, dark gray, gold, orange, one each. Loose-weave burlap, 42" × 22". Matching rug binding, 4 yards.

DIRECTIONS: Follow General Directions for preparing fabric strips and burlap foundation.

SPANIEL RUG

ROOSTER RUG

Hook chicks first, working rows in concentric circles. Hook bodies in yellow; legs and beaks in orange; eye and wing details in black. Hook hen, outlining feather markings in dark gray, then filling in body with light gray; hook comb and wattles in maroon, beak in yellow. Outline flowers in bright red then each petal with dark brown; fill in petals with deep maroon. Hook leaf veins in medium brown; fill in leaves with dark and light greens. Hook cattails in dark beige and medium brown.

Hook rooster, beginning with head: Use peach for face, bright red for side wattle and tongue, maroon and dark maroon for comb and hanging wattle, yellow for beak and black for eye and section above beak. Outline neck feathers in medium brown; add a row of light green inside tip of each feather; fill in center and top of feathers with dark green. Use "fingering" when changing colors on all feathers for blended effect. Outline feathers of center ring with dark brown; fill in tips with maroon and upper feathers with dark maroon. Complete area around feathers with medium brown. Outline tail feathers in dark brown, following contours of tail. Fill in first half of tail area with medium brown, light beige and maroon. Complete last half of tail, using only medium beige and medium brown. Hook legs and feet in gold and dark brown.

Hook ground in wavy horizontal rows of medium beige using dark beige for scratch lines. For hawk, hook outline feather markings in dark brown; fill in body in medium brown, head in dark beige, neck in light beige, beak in dark brown. Work sky in horizontal rows of shaded light blue. Outline inside border with single row of black. Hook dark beige and medium brown diamond border; hook outer black border.

Finish as directed.

BABY BLOCKS PILLOW
Shown on page 68

SIZE: 20½″ × 18″.

EQUIPMENT: Tracing paper. Pencil. Ruler. Thin, stiff cardboard. Light and dark-colored sharp, hard pencils. Scissors. Sewing needles.

MATERIALS: Closely woven cotton fabric, 36″ wide: white, ½ yard; black, 1 yard; small amounts (one piece 6″ × 7″ yields two diamonds) of five different black-and-white print fabrics, such as a small flower print, polka dots, checked gingham, a plaid, a stripe. Sewing thread in black and white. Cotton or polyester batting. Polyester fiberfill for stuffing. Unbleached muslin for lining and inner pillow, 1¾ yards. Cording, ¼″ thick, 80″.

DIRECTIONS: Cut several 1½″-wide bias strips from white fabric; set aside until later for piping. For pillow back, cut two 14″ × 19″ pieces of black. Make sure to cut pieces so that one 19″ side of each piece lies along selvedge; this avoids the necessity of hemming these edges later. Trace actual-size pattern for diamond shape. Cut several diamond patterns out of cardboard; replace patterns as edges wear from use.

Press all fabric smooth. To determine the straight of the fabric, pull a thread. Place each pattern piece on wrong side of fabric, making sure each piece is placed in correct relationship to the straight

of fabric. Diamond-shaped patches need two sides on straight of the fabric.

Using light-colored pencil on dark fabric and dark-colored pencil on light fabric, trace around each pattern. When tracing a number of pieces on one fabric, leave space between patterns for seam allowances. Patterns should be placed leaving ½″ between two—this will give you the full ¼″ seam allowance that is necessary for each. Cut 16 black diamonds, 10 white diamonds, four diamonds each from three of the print fabrics, and two diamonds each from remaining prints. Cut one cardboard diamond in half lengthwise; use one half as a pattern to cut eight long half-diamonds from white, adding ¼″ seam allowance all around. Cut another cardboard diamond in half crosswise; use one half as a pattern to cut four short half-diamonds from white fabric.

Piecing: Hold patches firmly in place, right sides facing. Using sewing thread, carefully make tiny running stitches along marked outlines to join. Begin by making a small knot; end with a few back stitches. To avoid bunching of fabric, excess thickness at seams may be trimmed as pieces are assembled. If two bias edges come together, keep thread just taut enough to prevent seams from stretching. Stitch from the wide-angled corner towards the pointed ends. It is always better to sew an edge cut on the straight of goods to one that is cut on the bias. Refer to illustration for correct placement of diamonds. Note that the long white half-diamonds are sewn along the long sides and the short white half-diamonds along the short sides. When piecing is completed, press seams in one direction.

Quilting: Read General Directions for Quilting, page 300. Pin and baste pillow top, batting, and muslin lining together. Using matching thread, quilt around edges of each patch ⅛″ in from seams.

Stitch the white bias strips together to form one 80″-long strip; press seams open. Fold strip in half lengthwise; insert cording along fold and stitch lengthwise, close to cording. With right sides facing and piping in between, pin pillow top to two black back pieces, with raw edges even and selvedge edges overlapping at center about 3″. Stitch together all around, making ½″ seams. (**Note:** Trim

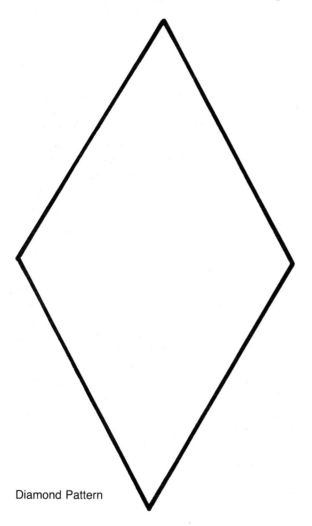

Diamond Pattern

piping ends so they overlap 1″; cut $\frac{1}{2}$″ from cording at one end and fold raw edges of piping in $\frac{1}{2}$″. Trim seam of other end of piping, and insert into other end. Continue stitching pillow top, piping, and back together.) Turn pillow right side out.

Inner Pillow: Cut two $21\frac{1}{2}$″ × 19″ pieces from muslin. Making $\frac{1}{2}$″ seams, stitch together all around, leaving opening for turning and stuffing. Turn right side out; stuff with fiberfill. Fold raw edges in $\frac{1}{2}$″; slip-stitch opening closed. Insert inner pillow in outer pillow and slip-stitch opening closed.

BABY BLOCKS AFGHAN

Shown on page 69

SIZE: 46″ × 64″.

MATERIALS: Brunswick Windrush, 5 100-gram skeins each Fisherman 90300, Dark Coffee 90293, and Burnt Orange 90611. Crochet hook size H (5 mm).

GAUGE: 4 sc = 1″; 5 rows = 1″.

AFGHAN: DIAMOND MOTIF (make 97 each of 3 colors): Ch 2. **Row 1:** 2 sc in 2nd ch from hook. Ch 1, turn.

Row 2: Sc in first sc, 2 sc in next sc. Ch 1, turn.

Row 3: Sc in each of 2 sc, 2 sc in last sc. Ch 1, turn.

Rows 4-11: Sc in each sc to last sc, 2 sc in last sc. Ch 1, turn each row—12 sc.

Rows 12-22: Sk first sc, sc in each sc across. Ch 1, turn each row—1 sc remains. End off.

FINISHING: Sew or crochet one motif of each color tog to form a six-sided figure. Make 97 blocks in this way.

First Row of Blocks: Keeping Fisherman diamonds free for bottom edge of afghan, sew or crochet 7 blocks tog, joining one edge of Dark Coffee to one edge of Burnt Orange.

2nd Row of Blocks: Repeat first row with 8 blocks. Make 7 rows of 7 blocks, 6 rows of 8 blocks. Join rows tog, alternating 7-block row with 8-block row.

PATCHWORK TABLESKIRT

Shown on page 70

SIZE: 90″ in diameter.

EQUIPMENT: Brown paper 4′ × 4′. Pencil. Yardstick. String, 4′. Scissors. Straight pins. Cardboard.

MATERIALS: Cotton fabric, 35″ or 44″ wide (all fabrics must be same weight); Fabric A, $1\frac{3}{4}$ yd.; B, $1\frac{1}{2}$ yd.; C, $\frac{3}{4}$ yd.; D, $1\frac{1}{2}$ yd.; E, 1 yd.; F, $1\frac{1}{2}$ yd.; G, $\frac{3}{4}$ yd. (**Note:** Allowance made for matching stripes and designs.) Sewing thread in colors to match fabrics. Seam binding in predominant color of fabrics.

DIRECTIONS: Use fabrics in colors desired; we used brown with white design (A), beige with black stripes (B), white with brown design (C), solid gold (D), black with gold dots (E), gold with brown design (F), gold with brown-beige-pink design (G). It is suggested you use at least one solid color. All strips are cut crosswise.

On brown paper 4′ × 4′ (if necessary, piece to make this size), make a pattern as follows:

Diagram A: Draw diagonal from corner to corner. Make a mark, point A, on this line near upper right corner (this will be center of circle). Make a compass by attaching pencil, close to point, to one end of string. Measure 45″ from pencil along string. Hold string at 45″ mark on point A; hold pencil, perpendicular to paper, in other hand with string taut. Mark a partial circle with 45″ radius. Point where diagonal meets arc is point B. Mark two points C 17$\frac{1}{2}$″ each side of point B. Draw straight lines connecting points C and A. You now have the outer dimensions of a one-eighth pattern.

Diagram B: Mark point D 7$\frac{1}{4}$″ from A and E 5″ from A; connect points D and E. Mark two points F 15″ from A; connect them. Mark point G 30″ from A. Connect points F and G. Draw 2″ wide strips as shown, parallel to lines FE, FG, and DF.

Diagram C: Connect point C to G. Draw 2″ wide strips as shown, parallel to lines FG and CG. Draw a line from G to sides, through points where 2″ strips meet. Erase guidelines through center, at top, diamond shape, and bottom triangle shape (finer lines on diagram). Dash lines indicate half of diamonds (left and right sides of diagram) and

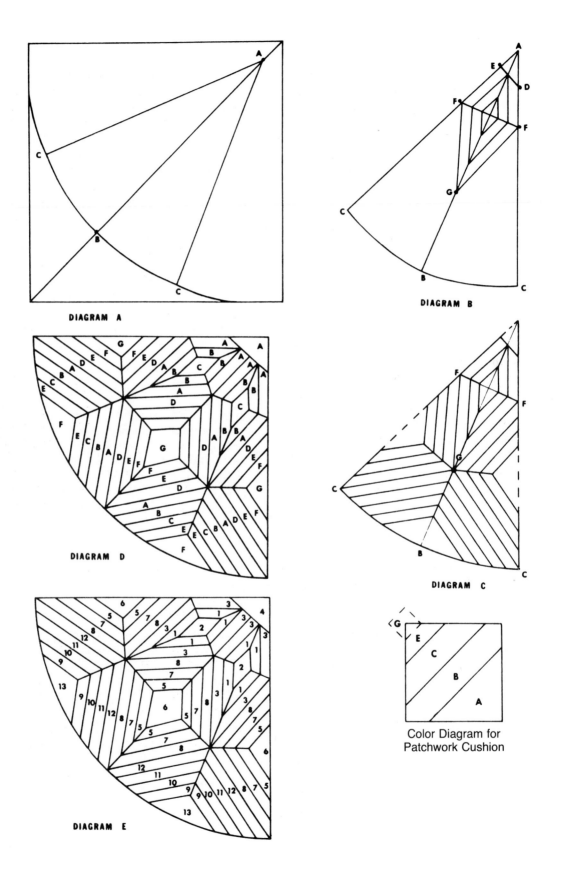

DIAGRAM A

DIAGRAM B

DIAGRAM D

DIAGRAM C

DIAGRAM E

Color Diagram for
Patchwork Cushion

one-eighth pattern for center square; complete these shapes and cut out as complete patterns.

Using paper pattern, cut a cardboard pattern for each section. Using Diagram D as a guide (letters indicate fabrics), place cardboard pattern on wrong side of fabric and mark required number of each cardboard outline with pencil or tailor's chalk. When transferring more than one pattern to same fabric, leave 1″ between pieces for seam allowance; leave 1″ allowance for hem on bottom edge of pieces that border the outside. Cut pieces $\frac{1}{2}$″ outside marked line (except border ends); use solid line as stitching line.

Assembling: All seams are $\frac{1}{2}$″; finish by overcasting edges, if desired. Press seams open as you work. Begin with diamond sections closest to center; make eight. Following Diagram E, sew the four #1 pieces in each section together in diamond shape. Sew #2 piece in place at center of #1 pieces. Then sew the four #3 pieces around the #1 pieces, and to each other. Join the eight sections by sewing the #3 pieces of adjacent sections together. Sew center square (#4) in place.

Repeat procedure for middle diamond sections: sew four inner strips of each section together, then sew center diamond in place; add surrounding strips. Sew a middle diamond section in between the center diamond sections, as shown.

For third (partial) diamond sections (at border), begin by sewing a #9 to appropriate #10 piece; then sew #11 to #10, and so on. Then, matching strips, sew these together in a V-shape. Sew piece #13 in place. Sew a completed section between middle sections, as shown.

Finishing: Trim lower edge if necessary. Stitch seam binding all around on right side. Turn under a 1″ hem.

PATCHWORK CUSHION
Shown on page 58

EQUIPMENT: Brown paper for pattern. Pencil. Ruler. Scissors. Straight pins.

MATERIALS: Small amounts of cotton fabrics in six different patterns, all of the same weight.

For cushion bottom and boxing, one fabric piece the size of chair seat, plus $\frac{1}{2}$″ all around for seam allowances and a strip for boxing $2\frac{1}{2}$″ wide and as long as the perimeter of chair seat, plus 1″ for seam allowance. Sewing thread to match fabrics. Cotton or polyester batting for stuffing.

DIRECTIONS: Use fabrics in desired colors, or see Patchwork Tableskirt directions, page 85, for our color scheme. Match letters of diagram on opposite page to those in tableskirt directions. We used F for cushion bottom and boxing.

On brown paper, make pattern exact size and shape of chair seat. Make notches in back to accommodate chair back, if desired. Cut seat shape from desired fabric, adding $\frac{1}{2}$″ all around for seam allowances. Cut boxing strip $2\frac{1}{2}$″ wide, long enough to fit around your cushion. Cut center piece G (see diagram on opposite page) $2\frac{1}{2}$″ square; set aside until later.

Mark exact center on paper pattern. With pencil and ruler, make vertical and horizontal lines to divide into four quarters. Mark point 4″ from center on one horizontal line and adjacent vertical line; draw line connecting these points. Measure 2″ out from this diagonal line and draw parallel diagonal line across quarter, marking off 2″ wide area; repeat 2″ out from this line. Repeat on other three quarter-sections. Cut these pieces out. Referring to color diagram on opposite page, pin each pattern piece crosswise on four layers of same fabric. Adding $\frac{1}{2}$″ to all edges for seam allowances, cut all four thicknesses. With right sides facing and making $\frac{1}{2}$″ seams throughout, sew four parts of one quarter together, then sew two quarters together, and then sew two halves together. At center, cut away a diamond-shaped area $1\frac{1}{2}$″ square. Pin center (piece G) in place; sew.

With right sides facing, pin and sew boxing around patchwork top; sew ends of boxing together. Pin boxing to bottom with right sides facing; leaving a 6″ opening at side, sew pieces together. Turn cushion to right side. Stuff softly. Turn edges of opening in, sew closed.

EGG BASKET PICTURE

Shown on page 70

SIZE: 15″ × 19″, without frame.

EQUIPMENT: Pencil. Ruler. Scissors. Paper for pattern. Tracing paper. Thin, stiff cardboard. Dressmaker's tracing (carbon) paper. Straight pins. Sewing needle. Tracing wheel or dry ball-point pen.

MATERIALS: Organdy 36″ wide, $\frac{5}{8}$ yd. Scraps of cotton or linen fabric in colors desired: Wall, 19″ × 23″; table, 6″ × 23″; pitcher, 7″ × 11$\frac{1}{2}$″; eggs (various shades of off-white and beige and one turquoise), about 3″ × 4″ for each; basket, 9″ × 11$\frac{1}{2}$″. Sewing thread in matching colors. Cotton batting for padding. Heavy cardboard, 15″ × 19″. Stitch Witchery® fusible web. Feather. Glue.

DIRECTIONS: Patterns: Enlarge pattern by copying on paper ruled in 1″ squares; dash lines indicate where appliqué pieces overlap; fine lines on basket indicate quilting. Trace each separate part of pattern, including wall and table of background; omit quilting lines. Glue tracings to cardboard and cut out, for two background and 14 appliqué patterns.

Background: Place wall pattern on right side of fabric and draw around. Cut out, adding 2″ margin around three outer edges and $\frac{1}{2}$″ margin on the two inner edges adjacent to table. Cut out table piece in same manner, but omitting any margin on the two inner edges adjacent to wall. Cut

piece of organdy 19″ × 23″. Following manufacturer's directions, fuse wall piece to organdy, matching pieces carefully at top and side edges. Fuse table piece to organdy, matching pieces at bottom; table will overlap wall $\frac{1}{2}$″. Using dressmaker's carbon and tracing wheel (or dry ball-point pen), transfer main outlines of appliqué design to wall-table background.

Appliqués: Read How to Appliqué (page 304). Following directions, cut appliqué pieces and stitch around. Using patterns, cut a piece of batting for pitcher and egg appliqués and baste to wrong side. Finish preparing these pieces as directed, enclosing edges of batting with seam allowance of appliqués.

For basket pieces, retrace patterns, including quilting lines. Transfer lines to basket appliqués. Cut a piece of batting and organdy for each piece. Baste top fabric and organdy together with batting between the enclosed in seam allowance. Finish preparing pieces. Quilt on marked lines, using running stitch and a single strand of brown thread.

Pin, baste, and slip-stitch appliqués in place on background, following numerical order of pattern. When stitching pitcher down, move handle in toward body of pitcher, as shown in illustration.

Finishing: When all pieces have been appliquéd, glue work to cardboard, leaving 2″ fabric margin all around. Turn margin to back of cardboard and glue down. Tuck feather in behind basket top as shown. Frame as desired.

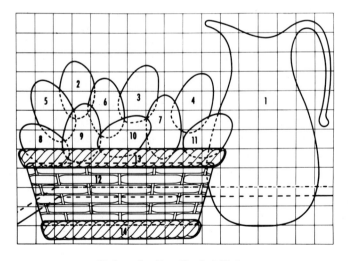

Pattern for Egg Basket Picture

TWO-PART CABINET

Shown on page 70

SIZE: Approx. $7\frac{3}{4}$ feet tall, 36″ wide.

EQUIPMENT: Metal tape measure. Pencil. Miter box. Saw. Hammer. Screwdriver. Drill with bit slightly smaller than diameter of screw shanks. Sandpaper. Large, flat paintbrush.

MATERIALS: Plywood, $\frac{1}{2}$″ thick: two $4' \times 8'$ sheets. Stock lumber: $1'' \times 1''$, 8 ft.; $1'' \times 2''$, 85 ft.; $1'' \times 4''$, 18 ft.; $1'' \times 6''$, 94 ft.; $1'' \times 12''$, 7 ft. Crown molding, 4″ wide, $7\frac{1}{2}$ ft. Panel molding, $1\frac{1}{8}$″ wide, 40 ft. Quarter-round molding, $\frac{3}{4}$″ wide, 8 ft. Screws: #10 flathead wood screws, $1\frac{1}{4}$″; $2\frac{1}{4}$″. Metal plates $1'' \times 4''$, two, and $\frac{3}{4}$″ screws (optional). Finishing nails, 1″. Eight hinges, 2″ long, and accompanying screws. Four white porcelain doorknobs, $1\frac{1}{2}$″ diameter, and accompanying screws. Wood filler. Basecoat. Satin-finish enamel, one quart. For shelves: Plywood, $\frac{1}{2}$″ thick, and lattice strips $\frac{1}{2}'' \times \frac{1}{4}''$ for facing, or clear pine shelving (amount depends on number of shelves). For shelf supports: additional amounts of $1'' \times 2''$, or stanchions and brackets. All-purpose glue.

GENERAL DIRECTIONS: Check all measurements for final fitting, and cut one piece at a time as construction progresses; the actual dimensions of stock lumber vary from source to source. Measurements for molding (the 1×4's at bottom edge of lower unit and 1×1 facing strips at top edge of lower unit) are for longest edge; miter corners before securing to cabinet or doors. Drill pilot holes to receive threads of screws, in positions indicated by dots on diagrams. Unless directed otherwise, use glue and $1\frac{1}{4}$″ screws to secure parts. Tighten screws enough so heads go $\frac{1}{16}$″ below surface; countersink nailheads. Use wood filler to smooth rough edges, to cover screws and nailheads and to fill in cracks. Let dry thoroughly; sand smooth. Following manufacturer's directions, apply two coats of sealer for basecoat, and two coats of enamel letting dry between coats.

UPPER UNIT: Top and Bottom: From plywood, cut top and bottom, each $16'' \times 36\frac{1}{2}''$, following Diagram 1. Secure a $36\frac{1}{2}''$ (1×2) piece to each long side, and a $12\frac{1}{2}''$ (1×2) piece to each short side of top and bottom (Diagram 2).

Sides: Make two sides the same. Secure three 60″ (1×6) pieces to the 1×2's on top and bottom pieces; see Diagram 3.

Back: From plywood, cut back $36\frac{1}{2}'' \times 60''$. Secure a $57\frac{1}{2}''$ (1×2) piece to each long side, long edges flush and $1\frac{1}{4}$″ from top and bottom of plywood. Using $1\frac{1}{4}$″ screws every 5″, secure back to 1×2's on top and bottom pieces, with the 1×2's of back on inside of cabinet. Secure side panels to 1×2's of back.

Front: Secure 60″ (1×2) piece to outside of front, flush with sides, top, and bottom. Secure a $34\frac{3}{4}''$ (1×4) piece across top and bottom of front. Secure a $52\frac{1}{2}''$ (1×2) piece center upright to 1×4's, using $2\frac{1}{4}$″ screws set in at an angle; or secure a metal plate at top and bottom to inside of front. Use $2\frac{1}{4}$″ screws to secure side 1×2's to top and bottom 1×4's at corners. (Diagram 4).

Molding: Nail a $19\frac{1}{2}$″ piece of crown molding to each short side, and a $42\frac{3}{8}$″ piece to the front, with the bottom edge of molding $1\frac{1}{2}$″ below top edge of cabinet.

Doors: Make two doors, left and right, constructed the same. Place three $54\frac{1}{2}''$ (1×6) pieces side-by-side with top and bottom edges even. Place three 14″ (1×2) pieces across them, one at center, and the others $2\frac{1}{2}$″ from top and bottom edge. Nail panel molding around front door edges: cut a $16\frac{3}{4}$″ piece for each top and bottom, and a $55\frac{1}{2}''$ piece for each side, then miter corners. Molding extends $\frac{1}{4}$″ beyond door edge at top, bottom, and knob side, and is flush with hinge side. Attach doorknob 34″ from top and $2\frac{1}{2}$″ in from side.

Hinges: Rout out $\frac{1}{8}$″-deep notches in edges of hinge sides of doors, 8″ from top and bottom edges. Rout matching notches in edges of front: attach hinges.

LOWER UNIT: From plywood, cut bottom $21\frac{1}{2}''$ $\times$ $36\frac{1}{2}''$, notching both rear corners to accommodate a 1×2 (Diagram 1).

Sides: For each, place four 29″ (1×6) pieces side by side, top and bottom edges even. Place two $21\frac{1}{2}''$ (1×2) pieces across them, one 25″ from top, and one 12″ from top (inside surface).

Back: From plywood, cut back $36\frac{1}{2}'' \times 29''$ (see Diagram 1). Secure a 29″ (1×2) piece to each side, with top, bottom, and sides flush with back, and two 33″ (1×2) cleats across, one 12″ from

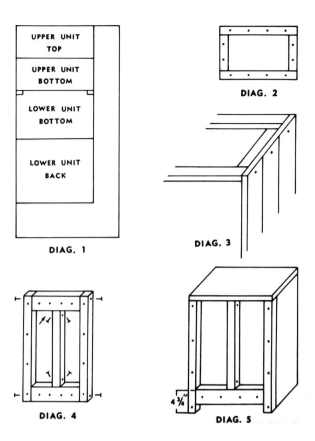

top, and one 25″ from top (inside surface). Attach back to sides, top and bottom edges flush. Add bottom, resting it on the lower 1 × 2's of sides and back; secure to all three parts, and to the 1 × 2's.

Top: Beginning flush at back, secure two 38″ (1 × 12) pieces across top edges of back and sides; this will create a slight overhang at front, after front is secured.

Front: Secure a 29″ (1 × 2) piece to front of each side, and one 34¾″ (1 × 4) piece to front edge of bottom, so top edge of 1 × 4 is 4¾″ from bottom of sides; add center upright 24½″ (1 × 2) piece in same manner as for upper unit (Diagram 5).

Secure 24″ (1 × 1) facing strips to side edges of top, and 39½″ (1 × 1) to front edge of top, mitering corners first. Secure a 23½″ (1 × 4) piece to each side, bottom edges flush with bottom edges of cabinet, and a 39¾″ (1 × 4) piece to front, mitering corners. With 1″ nails, add quarter-round molding the same dimensions as the 1 × 4's to top of the 1 × 4's.

Doors: Assemble doors in same manner as for upper unit; use three 24″ (1 × 6) pieces, and two 14″ (1 × 2) crossbars 5″ from top and bottom edges.

Add 16⅞″ panel molding to top and bottom, and 24″ molding to sides; molding is flush with top, bottom, and hinge side of doors, and extends ⅜″ beyond knob sides. Attach doorknob 2½″ in from sides at center.

Hinges: Follow directions for upper unit, placing the hinges 4″ from top and bottom.

Shelves: Cut the shelves the width and depth of cabinet, notching both rear corners to accommodate the 1 × 2's on backs of cabinet. If shelves are cut from plywood, face the front edge with lattice strips. There are two methods recommended for supporting shelves. Cleat Method: Use 1 × 2's across back and sides for supports; in lower unit, you already have these at one level—if higher or lower shelf is desired, adjust height of these pieces during construction. Add cleats to sides and back of upper or lower units during construction, making sure the height of back cleats matches height of side cleats. Stanchion Method: Secure 1 × 2's along the length of back of cabinet, next to the 1 × 2's that are there already. Secure stanchions to these, insert brackets where desired. This method allows for shelf adjustment.

STENCILED FLOOR

Shown on page 70

EQUIPMENT: Paper for patterns. Tracing paper. Ruler. Hard and soft pencils. Manila paper or envelope. Stencil paper and ready-cut stencils available at art supply stores. Use heavy stencil paper, at least 24″ long. X-acto knife. Blotter or blotting paper. Masking tape. Stencil brushes. Saucer for each color. Soft rags. Cleaning fluid. Yardstick. Brush for varnish.

MATERIALS: Water-base paints: dark blue and yellow ochre. Polyurethane varnish.

DIRECTIONS: We stenciled a floor of random planking: design can be adapted to any wooden floor. To prepare floor, remove wax, sand rough spots, and sponge clean. Enlarge pattern for floor border design on this page by copying on paper ruled in 1″ squares: complete repeat of pattern indicated by long dash line. Make tracing of complete design on tracing paper. Cut piece of stencil paper 8½″ × 24″; mark line lengthwise 4″ from one long edge; line up outer edge of border line at one side on tracing with line on stencil paper. Trace complete border design on stencil paper.

Cutting Stencils: Place stencil paper on manila paper. Cut outline with sharp knife. Hold knife at slight angle, pointing toward cut-out area to make slightly beveled edge. Cut all the way through in one stroke so edge will be clean. Turn paper so that you always cut toward you. Cut another stencil of just the flower design and one of just the dot. In stenciling large areas, such as a floor, it is necessary to cut more than one stencil for each part, as the edges will wear, creating a fuzzy print.

Preparing Paints: Carefully read instructions which come with paints. Use acrylic paints full strength. Mix colors in saucers, according to manufacturer's directions.

Painting Design: Tape stencil to floor in desired position. Dip brush in paint and rub off on piece of paper until almost dry. Since paints are very concentrated, use only a small amount on brush at a time. Paint border design on floor with a dabbing or stippling motion. To darken, go over areas with additional coats of paint. Let paint dry thoroughly. In this way, stencil border around floor, starting at center point of each wall and working to corners; line up 4″ border of stencil paper against edge of wall and paint lines and dots in blue and flowers in yellow ochre. Continue design around edge of floor, always matching up flower and dot at one end of stencil with last flower and dot painted. When dry, carefully place individual dot stencil in center of each flower and paint blue.

To make allover flower design, measure the distance from border line to border line, from one end of room to other. Divide space so that flowers are in a row with equal amount of space between

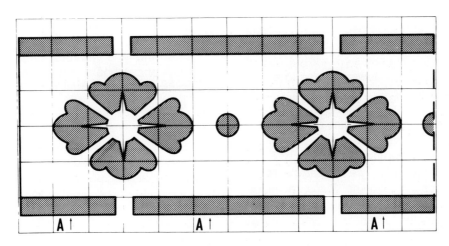

Stencil Pattern

(see illustration on page 70). Make alternate rows in which flowers are centered between flowers of the first row. We painted a row of flowers 5″ in from line of border design and opposite every other flower of border design. For alternate rows of flowers, we placed the centers 12″ from the centers of the previous row. Then we continued making rows 12″ apart on centers. When paint has dried, place individual dot stencil in center of each flower and paint blue.

Clean brushes and stencils. Wash brushes in cleaning fluid; dry well. To clean stencil, turn face down on blotter; with soft rag and a little cleaning fluid, gently wipe back clean.

When floor has dried completely, varnish twice, letting dry after each coat.

SPRINGTIME FLOWERS
Shown on page 71

DESIGN AREA: $5\frac{3}{4}″ \times 4\frac{1}{2}″$.
FRAMED SIZE: $11\frac{1}{2}″ \times 10″$.
EQUIPMENT: Tracing paper. Pencil. Dressmaker's tracing (carbon) paper. Dry ball-point pen. Ruler. Embroidery hoop. Embroidery scissors. Embroidery and sewing needles. Single-edged razor blade or X-acto knife. Sewing machine.
MATERIALS: Ecru or white linen fabric 8″ × 7″ for each. Persian yarn (3-ply), 1 yard of each color listed in Color Key. Seed beads: 170 light green, 460 each of orange and red. Fabric for frame: two coordinating prints 45″ wide, $\frac{3}{8}$ yard of one, $\frac{1}{4}$ yard of the other. Sewing thread to match beads and framing fabric. Thin but sturdy cardboard, $11\frac{1}{2}″ \times 10″$ and 7″ × 6″, for each. All-purpose glue. Masking tape. Twine or jute for piping, $\frac{1}{8}″$ diameter, $3\frac{3}{4}$ yards.
DIRECTIONS: To Transfer Each Design: Trace pattern. Mark off area $5\frac{3}{4}″ \times 4\frac{1}{2}″$ in center of linen; this is design area to be worked. Place tracing on marked area with carbon between. Go over lines of design with dry pen to transfer. Remove transfer and carbon. Tape edges of linen to prevent raveling.

To Embroider: Place linen in embroidery hoop, centering design area. Embroider, following Color and Stitch Keys; refer to Stitch Details on page 309. Use only one ply of yarn in needle. Begin by leaving an end of yarn on back and working over it to secure; run end of strand in on back to finish off. Try not to make any knots.

Wherever there is a dotted line, sew on a row of beads as follows: Thread needle with sewing thread; knot end. Bring needle up to right side of linen at start of line. Thread on a bead; take a stitch $\frac{1}{16}″$ away. Continue along line with running stitch, threading on a bead with each stitch and making each stitch $\frac{1}{16}″$ long and one or two threads apart. Make sure beads sit side by side neatly. Use light green beads for the leaves, red beads for the red flowers, and orange beads for the orange flowers.

To Frame: From $11\frac{1}{2}″ \times 10″$ cardboard, mark and cut out center area $5\frac{3}{4}″ \times 4\frac{1}{2}″$; discard center. From larger piece of print fabric, cut a piece $14\frac{1}{2}″ \times 13″$; cut out center area $4\frac{3}{4}″ \times 3\frac{1}{2}″$. Center cut-out fabric over one surface of cut-out cardboard frame. Turn excess fabric at outer edges to other surface of cardboard and tape securely. Clip into inner fabric corners down to inner cardboard corners and tape to other side. Cut smaller piece of print fabric into 3″ strips, across full width of fabric. Lay twine or jute along center length of strips on wrong side of fabric. Fold strip over twine and stitch along length of strip, close to twine. Cut and glue strips to back of fabric-covered cardboard, fitting around inner and outer edges with piping extending out.

Center and tape embroidered linen to remaining piece of cardboard, stretching fabric to make it smooth and flat; center in frame opening and glue in place.

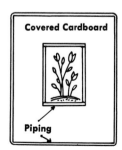

FRAME

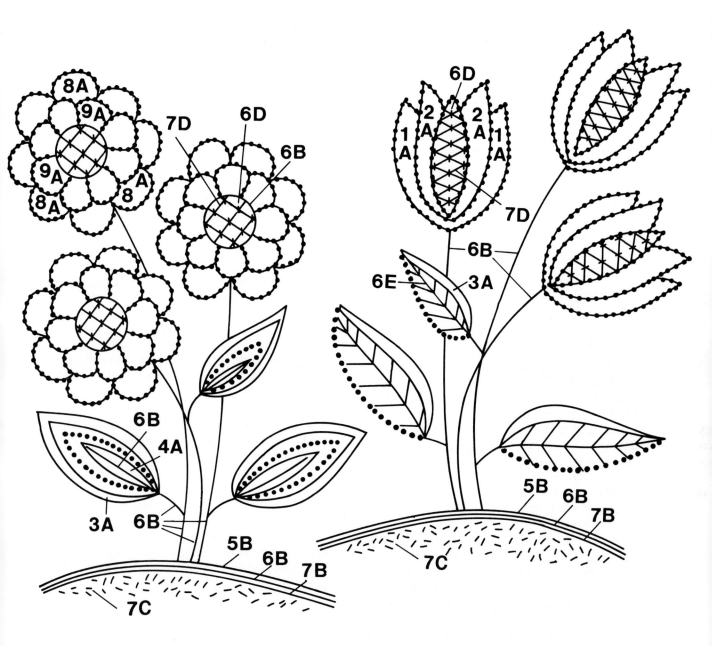

STITCH KEY

A — Satin stitch
B — Outline stitch
C — Seed stitch
D — Diagonal filling stitch
E — Fly stitch

COLOR KEY

1 — Red
2 — Coral
3 — Dk. olive green
4 — Lt. green
5 — Dk. brown
6 — Med. brown
7 — Tan
8 — Golden orange
9 — Bright yellow

COUNTRY KIDS
Shown on page 72

SIZE: Finished pictures are 7″ × 9″ each.

EQUIPMENT: Pencil. Dressmaker's tracing (carbon) paper. Tracing paper. Embroidery hoop and needle. Scissors. Ruler. Masking tape. Rust-proof tacks. Wooden surface.

MATERIALS: Yellow heavy twill-weave cotton fabric, 11″ × 18″. Six-strand embroidery floss: one skein each of light pink, light blue, green, blue, white, red, black, orange; scraps of purple, brown, gray, light brown.

DIRECTIONS: Cut fabric into two 9″ × 11″ pieces; tape edges to prevent raveling. Trace actual-size patterns for boy and girl; use dressmaker's carbon paper to transfer designs to center of each fabric piece.

To Embroider: Place one fabric piece in embroidery hoop: make sure fabric is not distorted in any way. Refer to Stitch Details on page 308. Using two strands of floss, work embroidery, following illustration on page 72, as follows:

For Boy, work blue pants, light blue cuffs, pink legs, orange hat, pink hands, and pink face in split stitch. Work brown hair, green pocket hanky, blue bundle, red mouth, and purple butterfly wings in satin stitch. Use stem stitch for red "plaid" shirt, green flower stems, blue suspenders, green neckerchief outline, and brown stick for bundle. Make French knots in orange for knee patch, green

for neckerchief, and red for suspender button. Work light blue flower petals in lazy daisy stitch. Work white and black dog in split stitch, with red satin stitch tongue.

For Girl, work green hat, white pantaloons, purple patch on apron, pink legs and pink arms in split stitch. Work black lines on bonnet and pantaloons in outline stitch. Work brown braids, purple hair bows, orange basket, gray kitten, white milk bottle, and red apples in satin stitch. Use stem stitch for red apron and bow outline, green "plaid" dress, green flower stems, and brown basket outline. Work green flower leaves and purple flower in lazy daisy stitch. Work an orange French knot for flower center.

FINISHING: To block and mount finished embroideries, read General Directions on page 308. Frame each picture as desired.

LAZY DAY WALL HANGING
Shown on page 73

SIZE: 28″ × 19″.

EQUIPMENT: Paper for patterns. Tracing paper. Pencil. Ruler. Dressmaker's tracing (carbon) paper. Dry ball-point pen. Scissors. Straight pins. Embroidery needle. Zigzag sewing machine.

MATERIALS: Medium-weight, closely-woven cotton for backing, 25″ × 16″. Calico print cotton for lining and borders, 36″-45″ wide, $\frac{3}{4}$ yard. Scraps of fabric in assorted colors, patterns, and textures (as illustrated or as desired) which are suitable for appliqué (such as light blue in plain and dotted swiss fabrics for sky, brown velour for tree, green prints for leaves and ground, blue denim for overalls, etc.) Sewing threads to match fabrics and in colors indicated below. Red six-strand embroidery floss. Two wooden dowels, each 19″ long, $\frac{3}{4}$″ in diameter.

DIRECTIONS: Enlarge pattern by copying on paper ruled in 1″ squares. Heavier pattern lines indicate cutting lines. Finer lines indicate lines and areas to be embroidered or stitched by machine.

Trace a separate pattern for each part of design. Sky pieces numbered 1-6 are seamed together. Therefore, add $\frac{1}{4}$″ seam allowance to lower edge of No. 1 and $\frac{1}{4}$″ seam allowance to upper and lower edges of the rest. Extend patterns for sky, water and grass pieces completely across the 16″ width. On hill, water and grass patterns, which are satin-stitched together, add $\frac{1}{8}$″ along lower edge where they are overlapped by next piece. Make boy's overall pattern all one piece as indicated by dash lines on pattern. Make shirt and sleeve separate pattern pieces. Make clouds one pattern piece. Continue outer sun circle pattern under cloud and add $\frac{1}{8}$″ around inner edge. Continue tree outline under leaves, boy and rabbit. All other pieces are to be cut as given on pattern.

Transfer outline of each appliqué piece to appropriate fabric, marking on right side of fabric with carbon and dry ball-point pen. Transfer fine lines for stitching onto each piece.

To Assemble: With right sides facing, sew the six sky sections together with $\frac{1}{4}$″ seams; press seams open. Pin sky to backing fabric having top edges even. Pin sea sections and sections of foreground in place. Following illustration and pattern, pin all other sections into place; baste. With a medium zigzag satin stitch and matching thread, stitch over edges of pieces. Use a narrow zigzag satin stitch for vein lines of leaves, inner body lines of larger bird and on boy's hat.

Following patterns, mark placement of flower buds on tree. Hand embroider buds with six strands of red floss in straight stitches. See Stitch Detail on page 308. With two strands of appropriate color sewing thread, embroider rabbit's features and toes, and bird's features.

Machine embroider remaining fine lines, using narrow satin stitch or straight stitching; letter A indicates straight stitching. Use color to match and contrast with fabrics being used.

To Attach Borders and Lining: From border and lining fabric, cut two pieces 25″ × 3″ and two pieces 20″ × 3″. Pin 25″ long border along each side length of finished picture, right sides facing and edges even. Stitch together with $\frac{1}{2}$″ seam on each side. Turn right sides of border out and press seams. Attach top and bottom borders in the same manner, stitching borders completely across from one side to the other. Turn right side out and press. Pin lining piece to picture front, right sides facing. Making $\frac{1}{2}$″ seam, stitch around, leaving 6″ along top unstitched for turning, and 1″ at one bottom and top corner along side to insert dowels. Turn to right side; press edges. Topstitch front and lining together around inside edges of border, $\frac{1}{4}$″ beyond picture edge. Insert dowels into openings at top and bottom. Slip-stitch all openings closed.

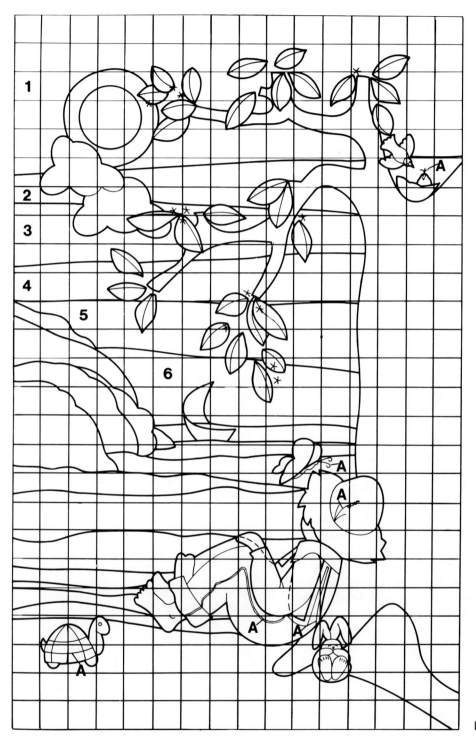

1

2

3

4

5

6

A

A

A

A

A

A

Pattern for
Lazy Day Hanging

FARM ANIMAL PILLOWS

Shown on page 74

SIZE: Each pillow, 13″ × 16½″.

MATERIALS: Fingering yarn, 3-ply, 2 1-oz. balls white (W) for each pillow or 4 balls for all three pillows, 1 ball each of gray (G) and navy (N). Steel crochet hook No. 3. Tapestry needle. Cotton for padding. Medium blue wood flannel, 54″ wide, ½ yard for one or three pillow tops. Medium blue cotton fabric, 35″ wide, ½ yard for one pillow, 1¼ yards for three pillows. Blue sewing thread. Shredded foam rubber, 2″ strip of plastic or cardboard, ½″ wide, for loop stitch (lamb).

GAUGE: 9 sc or loop sts = 1″ (lamb). 9 dc = 1″ (pig). 3 shells = 2″ (chicken).

LAMB PILLOW BODY: Front Leg Section: With W, ch 24 tightly to measure 2¾″. **Row 1:** Sc in 2nd ch from hook and in each ch across—23 sc. Ch 1, turn.

Row 2: (wrong side): Loop st in each sc across—23 loop sts. **To make loop st,** hold ½″ wide plastic or cardboard strip to back of work; insert hook in st, bring yarn back over strip and up front behind work, yo hook and through st, yo hook and through 2 lps on hook. Loops form on back of work (right side). Remove strip. Ch 1, turn.

Row 3: Sc in each loop st across. Ch 1, turn.

Row 4: Loop st in each sc across. End off; lay piece aside.

Back Leg Section: Work as for front leg section. At end of row 4, ch 1, turn.

Row 5: Sc in each of 23 sts, ch 30. From right side, sc in each of 23 sts of front leg section.

Row 6: Loop st in each sc and ch across—76 loop sts. Ch 1, turn.

Row 7: Sc in each loop st across. Ch 1, turn.

Row 8: Loop st in each sc across. Ch 1, turn. Repeat rows 7 and 8 until piece is 4¾″ from start of back leg section, end with loop st row. End off.

HEAD: With W, ch 13 tightly to measure 1¼″. **Row 1:** Sc in 2nd ch from hook and in each ch across—12 sc. Ch 1, turn each row.

Row 2 (wrong side): 2 loop sts in first sc, sc in each sc to last sc, 2 loop sts in last sc.

Row 3: Sc in each st across—14 sc.

Rows 4–11: Repeat rows 2 and 3—22 sc at end of row 11.

Row 12: 1 loop st in each of first 2 sc, sc in each of 18 sc, 1 loop st in each of last 2 sc.

Row 13: Sc in each st across—22 sc.

Rows 14–24: Repeat rows 12 and 13, end row 12.

Row 25: Sk first st, sc in next 20 sts—1 st dec at beg and end of row.

Row 26: 1 loop st in each of first 2 sc, sc in each of next 7 sc, 1 loop st in each of next 2 sc, sc in each of next 7 sc, 1 loop st in each of last 2 sc.

Row 27: Sk first sc, sc in next 18 sc—1 st dec at beg and end of row.

Row 28: 1 loop st in each of first 2 sc, sc in each of next 5 sc, 1 loop st in each of next 4 sc, sc in each of next 5 sc, 1 loop st in each of last 2 sc.

Row 29: Sk first sc, sc in next 16 sc.

Row 30: 1 loop st in each of 16 sc.

Row 31: Sk first st, sc in next 14 sts.

Row 32: 1 loop st in each of 14 sc.

Row 33: Sc in each st across.

Row 34: 1 loop st in each of 14 sc. End off.

EARS (make 2): With W, ch 3. **Row 1:** Sc in 2nd ch from hook and in next ch—2 sc. Ch 1, turn each row.

Row 2: (wrong side): 2 loop sts in each sc.

Row 3: Sc in each st across—4 sc.

Row 4: 2 loop sts in first sc, 1 loop st in each of next 2 sc, 2 loop sts in last sc.

Row 5: Sc in each st across—6 sc.

Row 6: Work in loop st, inc 1 st in first and last sc.

Row 7: Sc in each st across—8 sc.

Row 8: Repeat row 6.

Row 9: Sc in each st across—10 sc.

Row 10: 1 loop st in each sc across.

Row 11: Repeat row 9.

Row 12: Repeat row 10. End off.

TAIL: With W, ch 21. **Row 1:** Sc in 2nd ch from hook and in each ch across—20 sc. Ch 1, turn each row.

Row 2 (wrong side): 1 loop st in each sc.

Row 3: Sc in each st across.

Rows 4–12: Repeat rows 2 and 3, end with row 2. End off.

MOUTH: Beg at lower edge, with G, ch 6.

Row 1: Sc in 2nd ch from hook and in each ch across—5 sc. Ch 1, turn.

Row 2: Sc in each sc, ch 4, turn.

Row 3: Sc in 2nd ch from hook and in each of next 2 ch, sc in each of next 5 sc, ch 4, turn.

Row 4: Sc in 2nd ch from hook and in each of next 2 ch, sc in each of next 4 sc. Ch 1, turn.

Row 5: Sc in each of 3 sc. Ch 1, turn.

Row 6: Sc in each of 3 sc. End off, leave end for sewing to head. Place mouth on head, lower edge of mouth $\frac{1}{4}''$ above lower edge of head, sides of mouth equidistant from sides of head. Thread yarn in tapestry needle, sew mouth in place.

LEGS (make 4): With N, ch 4. **Row 1:** Sc in 2nd ch from hook, sc in next ch; pull up a lp in last ch, cut N. Pull G through 2 lps on hook. Ch 1, turn.

Row 2: With G, sc in each of 3 sc. Ch 1, turn. Repeat row 2 for 8 more rows. End off, leave end for sewing to body. Sew top edge of each leg to body, two legs centered on front leg section $\frac{1}{2}''$ apart, two legs on back leg section $\frac{1}{2}''$ apart, first one near front of section.

FLOWER NO. 1: Petals (make 12): With W, ch 2. **Row 1:** Sc in 2nd ch from hook. Ch 1, turn.

Row 2: 2 sc in 1 sc. Ch 1, turn each row.

Row 3: Sc in first sc, 2 sc in next sc.

Row 4: Sc in each of 3 sc.

Rows 5–8: Repeat row 4.

Row 9: Pull up a lp in each of 3 sc, yo hook and through all 4 lps on hook. Ch 1; end off (tip of petal). Run in yarn end. Place 12 petals tog in a circle, overlapping at center. Sew petals tog at center.

Center: With N, ch 4, sl st in first ch to form ring. **Rnd 1:** Ch 1, 8 sc in ring, join with sl st in first sc.

Rnd 2: Ch 1, 2 sc in each sc around. Join, end off. Sew to center of flower.

Stem: With N, ch 20. End off.

Leaves (make 2): Beg at tip, with N, ch 2. **Row 1:** Sc in 2nd ch from hook. Ch 1, turn each row. **Row 2:** 2 sc in sc.

Row 3: Sc in each sc.

Rows 4–6: Repeat row 3. End off.

FLOWER NO. 2: Petals (make 10): Work as for Flower No. 1 through row 7.

Row 8: Work as for row 9 of Flower No. 1. Place 10 petals tog in a circle, overlapping at center. Sew petals tog at center.

Center: Work as for center of Flower No. 1 through rnd 1. End off. Sew to flower.

Stem: With N, ch 18. End off.

Leaves (make 2): Work as for leaves of Flower No. 1 through row 5. End off.

FLOWER NO. 3: Petals (make 8): Work as for Flower No. 1 through row 4.

Row 5: Work as for row 9 of Flower No. 1. Place petals tog in a circle; sew tog at center.

Center: With G, work as for center of Flower No. 1 through rnd 1. End off. Sew to flower.

Stem: With G, ch 10. End off.

Leaves (make 2): With G, ch 4. Sc in 2nd ch from hook and in each of next 2 ch. End off.

FLOWER NO. 4: Petals: With W,* ch 5, sc in 2nd ch from hook and in each of next 3 ch—4 sc. Repeat from * until 8 petals have been made. End off; leave end for sewing. Make a running st around straight edge and gather petals tog in a circle. Join first and last petals tog.

Center: With W, work as for center of Flower No. 1 through rnd 1. End off. Sew to flower.

Stem: With W, ch 10. End off.

Leaves (make 2): With W, ch 4. End off. With G, make another Flower No. 4.

FINISHING: Cut one piece of flannel, 18″ × 15″. Mark off area $16\frac{1}{2}''$ × 13″, leaving margin all around for turning under. Arrange crocheted pieces on area (see illustration on page 74). With matching yarns, sew flowers in place leaving ends of petals and leaves free. Sew body and legs in place. Fold tail in half, loop side out; close tail at side and ends. Sew tail diagonally to body, loops upward. With N, make star stitch eyes on head as follows: make one straight cross-stitch, one diagonal cross-stitch over it, for each eye. Make 2 straight stitches on mouth to make an inverted T. Sew head in place, padding lightly with cotton. Sew ears to head, folding down $\frac{1}{3}$ of ear to show loops on right side at top.

TO MAKE PILLOW: Cut 2 pieces of cotton fabric, each $17\frac{1}{2}'' \times 14''$. Stitch pieces together, wrong side out, taking $\frac{1}{2}''$ seams, leaving opening for stuffing. Turn pillow right side out; press. Stuff with shredded foam rubber. Close opening. Turn under margin on pillow top, sew to pillow.

EDGING: Row 1: With W, * ch 5, 3-tr cluster in 5th ch from hook (to make 3-tr cluster, work 1 tr until there are 2 lps on hook, work another tr until there are 3 lps on hook, work another tr until there are 4 lps on hook, yo and through all 4 lps), repeat from * until edging is long enough to fit around edge of pillow, about 60″. End off, leave a length of yarn for adjustment, if necessary.

Row 2: Attach W at beg of edging, work scallop of 1 sc, 1 dc, 3 tr, 1 dc, 1 sc in each ch-5 lp across edging. End off, leave a length of yarn for adjustment. Steam-press edging. Sew in place around pillow edge through center of edging, using W and allowing scalloped edge to extend beyond edge of pillow.

PIG PILLOW: BODY: First Leg: With w, ch 9.
Row 1 (right side): Dc in 3rd ch from hook and in each of next 6 ch—7 dc. Ch 2, turn each row.

Rows 2 and 3: Dc in each dc across.

Row 4: Sk first dc, dc in each of 5 dc, 2 dc in last dc. End off. Turn leg to right side, pin to piece of paper marked Leg No. 1

Second Leg: Work as for first leg through row 3. **Row 4:** 2 dc in first dc, dc in each of 5 dc, 2 dc in last dc. End off. Turn to right side, pin to piece of paper marked Leg. No. 2.

Third Leg: Work as for first leg through row 2. **Row 3:** Dc in each of 6 dc, 2 dc in last dc.

Row 4: 2 dc in first dc, dc in each of 7 dc. End off. Turn to right side, pin to piece of paper marked Leg. No. 3.

Fourth Leg: Work as for first leg through row 3. **Row 4:** Dc in each dc across.

Row 5: Dc in each of first 6 dc, 2 dc in next dc; from right side, dc in each of 7 dc of Leg No. 3, 2 dc in each of next 2 dc, ch 21 for body, dc in each of 9 dc of Leg No. 2, 2 dc in first dc of Leg No. 1, dc in each of next 6 dc. Ch 2, turn.

Row 6: Work across in dc, make 1 dc in each dc and ch across—57 dc. Ch 2, turn each row.

Row 7: 2 dc in first dc, dc in each dc to last 2 sts, dec 1 st (**to dec,** work dc in next st until there are 2 loops on hook, work dc in last st until there are 3 loops on hook, yo and through 3 loops)—57 dc.

Row 8: Dc in each dc across, 2 dc in last st (back edge).

Row 9: 2 dc in first dc, dc in each dc across—59 dc.

Row 10: 2 dc in first dc, dc in each dc across—60 dc.

Row 11: 2 dc in first dc, dc in each dc across, 2 dc in last st—62 dc.

Row 12: Repeat row 11—64 dc.

Row 13: 2 dc in first dc, dc in each dc across, ch 6.

Row 14: 2 dc in 3rd ch from hook, dc in each of next 3 ch, dc in each dc across, 2 dc in last st—71 dc.

Row 15: Dc in each dc across, 3 dc in last st, ch 11.

Row 16: Dc in 3rd ch from hook, dc in each of next 8 ch, dc in each dc across, 2 dc in last st—83 dc.

Row 17: Dc in each dc across, 2 dc in last st—84 dc.

Row 18: Dc in each dc across.

Row 19: Sk first dc, dc in each dc across—83 dc.

Row 20: Dc in each dc, dec 1 st at end of row as before—82 dc.

Row 21: Sk first dc, dc in each dc to last 6 sts, sc in each of last 6 sts. Ch 1, turn.

Row 22: Sc in each of 6 sc, dc in each dc across, dec 1 st at end of row.

Row 23: Sk first dc, dc in each of 26 dc, sc in each of 14 dc, dc in each of 28 dc, dec 1 st in next 2 sts. Ch 2, turn.

Row 24: Sk first dc, dc in each of 28 dc, sc in each of 14 sc, dc in each of 22 dc, dec 1 st in next 2 sts. Ch 1, turn.

Row 25: Sk first 2 sts, sc in each of next 35 sts, dc in each of next 27 sts. Ch 2, turn.

Row 26: Working on head only, sk first dc, dc in each of next 22 dc, dec 1 st in next 2 sts. Ch 2, turn.

Row 27: Sk first dc, dc in each of next 19 dc, dec 1 st in next 2 sts. Ch 2, turn.

Row 28: Sk first dc, dc in each of next 16 sts, dec 1 st in next 2 sts. End off.

With N, embroider eye, make crescent-shaped eye with outline st; make several straight sts forming V in eye.

RIGHT EAR: With W, ch 10. **Row 1:** Sc in 2nd ch from hook and in each of next 8 ch—9 sc. Ch 1, turn each row.

Row 2 and 3: Sc in each sc across.

Row 4: Sk first sc, sc in each of 8 sc.

Row 5: Sk first sc, sc in each of 7 sc.

Rows 6–14: Sc in each sc.

Rows 15–20: Sk first sc, sc in each remaining sc. End off. Sew lower edge of ear to wrong side of head at top front of head.

LEFT EAR: With W, ch 13. **Row 1:** Sc in 2nd ch from hook and in each of 11 ch. Ch 1, turn each row.

Rows 2–4: Sc in each sc.

Row 5: 2 sc in first sc, sc in each of 11 sc—13 sc.

Row 6: Sc in each sc.

Row 7: 2 sc in first sc, sc in each of 12 sc—14 sc.

Row 8: Sc in each sc.

Row 9: 2 sc in first sc, sc in each of 13 sc—15 sc.

Row 10: Sc in each sc.

Rows 11–14: Sk first sc, sc in each remaining sc.

Rows 15–19: Sk 2 sc, sc in each remaining sc. End off 1 sc. Sew lower edge of ear to wrong side of head at top back of head, folding in front edge of ear for $\frac{1}{4}$".

TAIL: With N, ch 43. Sc in 2nd ch and in each remaining ch. End off.

TOES (make 4): With N, ch 6. **Row 1:** Sc in 2nd ch and in each of 4 ch. Ch 1, turn.

Row 2: Sc in each sc. End off. Sew to bottom front of legs.

SNOUT: With G, ch 4. **Rnd 1:** Sc in 2nd ch from hook and in next ch, 3 sc in last ch. Working on other side of ch, sc in next ch, 2 sc in same ch as first sc—8 sc. Join with sl st to first sc. Ch 1.

Rnds 2–4: Work around in sc, inc 2 sc at each end each rnd. Join each rnd with sl st in first sc, ch 1. End off at end of rnd 4. With N, embroider 2 lazy daisy sts on snout for nostrils.

NECK RIBBON: With N, ch 35. Sc in 2nd ch from hook and in each of 33 ch. End off. Sew in place across neck. For bow, ch 50. End off. Tie bow, sew in place on ribbon. Trim each bow end with a tassel. To make tassel, wind N 15 times around 1″ cardboard. Tie windings tog at one edge; cut through loops at other edge. Wind a piece of yarn tightly around tassel $\frac{1}{4}$″ below tied end. Knot; hide ends in tassel.

APPLE: With W, ch 13. **Row 1:** Sc in 2nd ch from hook and in each of 11 ch—12 sc. Ch 1, turn each row.

Rows 2–4: 3 sc in first sc, sc in each sc across—18 sc at end of row 4.

Rows 5–7: 2 sc in first sc, sc in each sc across—21 sc at end of row 7.

Rows 8–16: Sc in each sc.

Row 17: Sc in each of 11 sc. Ch 1, turn.

Row 18: Sk first sc, sc in each of 10 sc.

Row 19: Sk first sc, sc in each of 9 sc.

Row 20: Sk first sc, sc in each of 8 sc.

Row 21: Sk 2 sc, sc in each of 5 sc, sl st in last sc. End off. Attach yarn in 12th st of row 16.

Row 17: Sc in each of 10 sc.

Row 18: Sk first sc, sc in each of 9 sc.

Row 19: Sk 2 sc, sc in each of 7 sc.

Row 20: Sk 2 sc, sc in each of 5 sc.

Row 21: Sk 2 sc, sc in each of 3 sc. End off.

Center: With G, ch 5. **Row 1:** 2 sc in 2nd ch from hook, sc in each of 2 ch, 2 sc in last ch. Ch 1, turn each row.

Row 2: Sc in each of 6 sc.

Rows 3–5: Inc 1 sc in first and last st, work in sc across.

Row 6: Sc in each of 12 sc.

Rows 7 and 8: Sk first sc, sc in each remaining sc.

Rows 9 and 10: Sk first 2 sc, sc in each remaining sc. End off, leave end for sewing. Sew center to apple. With N, embroider 4 seeds in lazy daisy stitch.

Stem: With N, ch 7. Sc in 2nd ch from hook and in each of 5 ch. End off. Sew end to center top of apple.

Leaf: With N, ch 2. **Row 1:** 3 sc in 2nd ch from hook. Ch 1, turn each row.

Rows 2 and 3: Sc in each sc.

Row 4: Sk first sc, sc in each of 2 sc.

Row 5: Sc in each sc.

Row 6: Sk first sc, sc in last sc.

Row 7: Sc in sc. End off. Sew to side of stem.

ROSE: With W, ch 6, join with sl st in first ch to form ring, ch 1. **Rnd 1:** 12 sc in ring. Join in first sc.

Rnd 2: * Ch 3, sk 1 sc, sc in next sc, repeat from * around—6 lps.

Rnd 3: * 1 sc, 2 dc, 1 sc in next lp, repeat from * around. Join in first sc.

Rnd 4: * Ch 4, sc in back of st between next 2 petals, repeat from * around.

Rnd 5: * 1 sc, 4 dc, 1 sc in next lp, repeat from * around. Join in first sc.

Rnd 6: * Ch 5, sc in back of st between next 2 petals, repeat from * around.

Rnd 7: * 1 sc, 6 dc, 1 sc in next lp, repeat from * around. Join; end off.

Center: With N, ch 4, join with sl st to form ring. **Rnd 1:** Ch 1, 8 sc in ring. Join to first sc, ch 1.

Rnd 2: * Sc in first sc, 2 sc in next sc, repeat from * around. Join; end off.

Stem: With N, ch 19. Sc in 2nd ch from hook and in each ch. End off.

Leaves (make 2): With N, ch 2. **Row 1:** 3 sc in 2nd ch from hook. Ch 1, turn each row.

Rows 2, 3 and 5: Sc in each sc.

Row 4: Sk first sc, sc in each of 2 sc.

Row 6: Sk first sc, sc in last sc.

Row 7: Sc in sc. End off. Sew to side of stem.

FINISHING: Cut one piece of flannel, 18″ × 15″. Mark off area 16½″ × 13″, leaving margin all around for turning under. Arrange crocheted pieces on area (see illustration). With matching yarns, sew pieces in place, padding pig and apple with thin layer of cotton. Allow left ear to curl down. Fold right ear down and tack. Leave edges of petals and leaves free.

Make pillow, edging as for Lamb Pillow.

CHICKEN PILLOW: HEAD: Beg at lower edge, with W, ch 16. **Row 1:** Sc in 2nd ch from hook and in each of 14 ch—15 sc. Ch 1, turn each row.

Row 2: 2 sc in each of first 2 sc, sc across—17 sc.

Row 3: Sc in each sc.

Rows 4–9: Repeat rows 2 and 3—23 sc.

Row 10: Repeat row 2—25 sc.

Row 11: Sk first sc, sc across—24 sc.

Row 12: Repeat row 2—26 sc.

Row 13: Repeat row 11—25 sc.

Row 14: Sc in each sc.

Rows 15–17: Sk first sc, sc across.

Row 18: Sk first 2 sc, sc across.

Row 19: Sc in each sc.

Row 20: Sk first sc, sc across—19 sc.

Row 21: Sc in each sc.

Row 22: Repeat row 20—18 sc.

Row 23: 2 sc in first sc, sc across.

Row 24: Sk first sc, sc in 18 sc, ch 6 for front of head.

Row 25: Sc in 2nd ch from hook and in next 4 ch, sc across—23 sc.

Row 26: Sk first sc, sc across—22 sc.

Row 27: Sc in each sc.

Row 28: Sk first 2 sc, sc across.

Row 29: Sc in each sc.

Row 30: Repeat row 28—18 sc.

Row 31: Sc in each sc.

Row 32: Repeat row 28—16 sc.

Row 33: Sk first sc, sc across 15 sc.

Rows 34–36: Repeat row 28—9 sc. End.

BEAK: With G, ch 9. **Row 1:** Sc in 2nd ch from hook and in each of 7 ch—8 sc. Ch 1, turn each row.

Rows 2–8: Sk first sc, sc across. End off. Sew to front of head.

WATTLE: With N, ch 7. **Row 1:** Sc in 2nd ch from hook and in each of 5 ch—6 sc. Ch 1, turn each row.

Rows 2–7: Sc in each sc.

Rows 8–10: Sk first sc, sc across. End off (lower edge). Sew upper edge under head.

EYE: With N, ch 6. Join with sl st to form ring. Ch 1, make 12 sc in ring. Join in first sc. End off. Sew to head.

COMB: With N, ch 20. **Row 1:** Sc in 2nd ch from hook and in each of 18 ch. Ch 1, turn each row.

Row 2: Dc in each of first 3 sc, sc in each of 16 sc.

Row 3: Dc in first sc, tr in each of next 2 sc, dc in next sc, sc in each of 12 sc.

Rows 4 and 5: Sc in each of 12 sc.

Row 6: Dc in first sc, tr in each of next 2 sc, dc in next sc, sc in each of 8 sc.

Row 7: Sc in each of 8 sc.

Row 8: Dc in each of first 2 sc, tr in each of next 4 sc, dc in next sc, sc in last sc. End off. Sew to top of head.

BODY: Beg at top edge, with W, ch 86 to measure about 9½". **Row 1:** Sc in 2nd ch from hook, * sk 2 ch, shell of 5 dc in next ch, sk 2 ch, sc in next ch, repeat from * across—14 shells. Ch 3, turn.

Row 2 (right side): * Sc in center dc of shell, shell of 5 dc in back lp of next sc, repeat from * across, end with half shell of 3 dc in last sc. Ch 1, turn.

Rows 3 and 4: Sc in first dc, * shell in back lp of next sc, sc in center dc of next shell, repeat from * across, end with half shell in back lp of last sc. Ch 1, turn.

Row 5: Sc in first dc, * shell in back lp of next sc, sc in center dc of next shell, repeat from * across, end with sc in center dc of last shell—13 shells. Ch 3, turn.

Rows 6–9: Repeat rows 2–5—12 shells. Ch 3, turn.

Row 10: * Sc in center dc of next shell, shell in back lp of next sc, repeat from * across, end with 2 dc in back lp of last sc. Ch 1, turn.

Row 11: Sc in first dc, work in shell pat across, end with sc in center dc of last shell—11 shells. Ch. 3, turn.

Row 12: Sc in center dc of first shell, work in shell pat across, end with sc in center dc of 'last shell—10 shells. Ch 3, turn.

Row 13: Dc in first sc, sc in center dc of first shell, work in shell pat across, end with sc in last shell. Ch 3, turn.

Row 14: Sc in center dc of first shell, work in shell pat across, end with sc in top of turning ch—9 shells. Ch 3, turn.

Rows 15–19: Repeat row 12—4 shells. End off.

LEGS (make 2): With W, ch 11. **Row 1:** Sc in 2nd ch from hook and in each of 9 ch—10 sc. Ch 1, turn each row.

Row 2: Sc in each sc.

Rows 3–9: Sk first sc, sc in each remaining sc—3 sc at end of row 9. End off. Sew first 2 rows under lower edge of body, legs ½" apart.

FEET (make 2): With N, ch 9. **Row 1:** Sc in 2nd ch from hook and in next ch (first toe), * ch 5, sc in 2nd ch from hook and in each of 3 ch (2nd toe), repeat from * once (3rd toe), ch 4, sc in 2nd ch from hook and in each of 2 ch (4th toe); pull up a lp in 3rd toe, pull up a lp in 2nd toe, pull up a lp in first toe, yo hook and through all 4 lps on hook; sc in next 6 ch. End off. Sew feet to legs.

WING: First Feather: With G, ch 7.

Row 1: Sc in 2nd ch from hook and in each of 5 ch—6 sc. Ch 1, turn each row.

Row 2: Sc in each sc. Repeat row 2 until piece is 3¼" long. End off, leave end for sewing. Make 4 more pieces in this way, making one 3½" long, one 3¾" long, one 4" long and one 4½" long.

Fold each piece in half lengthwise; gather sts tog at one end (tip of feather), overcast sides tog. Place 5 feathers side by side in graduated lengths, open ends of feathers in a straight line. Sew feathers tog, leaving tips of feathers separate. Sew wing to body, gathering straight edge at front slightly and leaving wing free for 1½" at tips of feathers.

TAIL: First Feather: With W, ch 9. **Row 1:** Sc in 2nd ch from hook and in each of 7 ch—8 sc. Ch 1, turn each row.

Row 2: Sc in each sc. Repeat row 2 until piece is $5\frac{1}{2}''$ long. Shape as for wing feather.

Make two more feathers the same, $4\frac{1}{2}''$ long. With tips of feathers even, beg $1\frac{1}{2}''$ from tips, sew 2nd feather to first feather for $2\frac{1}{2}''$. Sew 3rd feather to 2nd feather for $2\frac{1}{2}''$, then to first feather at lower edge, overlapping 2nd feather.

With G, make 4th feather as for first feather, $3\frac{1}{2}''$ long. Sew to 3rd feather with tip $\frac{1}{2}''$ below tip of 3rd feather.

With W, make 5th feather as for first feather, $3\frac{1}{2}''$ long. Sew to 4th feather, $\frac{1}{2}''$ extending at tip.

With G, make 6th feather $2''$ long. Sew to 5th feather, tip $1''$ below tip of 5th feather.

With W, make 7th feather $1\frac{1}{2}''$ long. Sew to 6th feather, tip $\frac{1}{2}''$ below tip of 6th feather.

Sew tail to body, sewing top edge of body over inner edge of feathers (see picture for position of tail).

WHEAT: Stems (make 2): With N, make a ch $5''$ long. End off, leave end for sewing.

Leaves (make 6): With N, make a ch $2\frac{1}{4}''$ long. Sl st in 2nd ch from hook, sc in each remaining ch. Make 2 more leaves with ch $1\frac{3}{4}''$ long.

FINISHING: Cut one piece of flannel, $18'' \times 15''$. Mark off area $16\frac{1}{2}'' \times 13''$, leaving margin all around for turning under. Cut strands of W $2\frac{1}{2}''$ long. Knot strands along bottom and slanted back edge of head to make fringe. Trim evenly. Sew head to body.

Arrange crocheted pieces on area (see illustration). With matching yarns, sew chicken in place, padding body, head and tail with thin layer of cotton. Do not sew down tips of tail feathers, wattle or comb. Tack wattle and comb lightly to fabric. Sew wheat stems in place with backstitch through center. Tack two shorter leaves in place on upper section of left-hand stem, leaving end of leaves free. Fold leaves down; tack at fold. Sew other leaves in position in same way. With N, take several stitches near top of stems, leaving $1''$ loops. Cut through loops.

Make pillow, edging as for Lamb Pillow.

Stitch a beautiful quilt to display in any room! Mount it on a wall, fold it over the back of a sofa, or use it to cover a table, as shown. Strips of many colors are overlapped to make the Amish Pineapple Quilt; directions, page 113.

Even if you live in the city, you can create the airy feeling of a country kitchen with furnishings in natural wood tones and textures. Accessories embellished with classic motifs add to the homespun charm. Plate rack, 28" × 48", is cut from clear pine; directions on page 114. Pattern for embroidered pomegranate tablecloth adapts to any size table; page 116. Quick-point urn cushions are worked in rug yarn on five mesh-to-the-inch canvas; page 117. Plaid rug, an antique coverlet design, is woven on a four-harness loom; page 118.

107

Two-layered table cover of polished cotton is for tea time or any-time. The stenciled duo of top cloth and underskirt are made to fit a 36" round table. Berry clusters, scattered on top cloth, join in a continuous border around underskirt. Layered Skirt directions on page 119.

Choose your favorite fabric, as we've done here for the cushion and tablecloth, then "pick" the prettiest posies to stencil onto the complementary mirror frame and lampshade. Soft-sculpture frame measures 23" × 27". Directions for Stenciled Setting on page 120.

Easy crewel embroidery enhances any table. Use a cornucopia of autumn colors on natural or celery green linen; mix or match vegetables on place mats and napkin rings. Directions for Harvest Mats, page 122.

Berries-in-a-basket mat and napkin brighten a table setting; embroidery is all done on a zigzag sewing machine. Mat is 17½" × 11½"; napkin, 9 × 9¾. Strawberry Set on page 124.

Veggies to
stitch and stuff
fill a floppy burlap
basket.
Pitcher is quilted
felt.
Directions on
page 134.

Jam jars in telltale wrappings make a delightful
gift; felt fruits tell what flavor's inside. Package
in a sturdy and attractive canvas box; page 137.

*Try some appetizing appliqued
vegetable banners; muslin
is dyed to recreate
natural shades, then "mounted"
in a colorful fabric frame.
Directions on page 139.*

AMISH PINEAPPLE QUILT

Shown on page 105

SIZE: $73\frac{1}{2}'' \times 80\frac{1}{2}''$.

EQUIPMENT: Pencil. Ruler. Scissors. Thin, stiff cardboard. One or two large sheets of graph paper. Glue. Straight pins. Sewing needles.

MATERIALS: Closely woven cotton, silk, or wool fabric: black 45" wide, 4 yds.; scraps of purple, pink, beige, blue-green, dark red, royal blue, mauve. Small amount of pale blue velvet. Muslin 36" wide, $4\frac{3}{4}$ yds. Fabric for lining 45" wide, $4\frac{1}{8}$ yds. Black sewing thread.

DIRECTIONS: Read General Directions on page 300. Quilt is made up of 42 pieced blocks and a pieced border on two sides. There is no batting and no actual quilting stitch is used.

Patterns: See Piecing Diagram for one block,

$11\frac{1}{2}''$ square. To make patterns, draw same diagram on graph paper. (Use a sheet 20" square or join two smaller sheets to make that size.) Start by drawing an $11\frac{1}{2}''$ square in center of paper. Draw a 10 " square inside first square ($\frac{3}{4}$" margin all around). Draw an $8\frac{1}{2}''$ square inside the 10" square, then a 7", $5\frac{1}{2}''$, 4", and $2\frac{1}{2}''$ square, making seven concentric squares in all, with $\frac{3}{4}$" margin all around each one. Draw a $1\frac{1}{4}''$ square in center, with $\frac{5}{8}''$ margin all around.

Mark horizontal and vertical center lines over squares; extend lines out to edge of paper on all four sides. Use center lines as guides for drawing a second set of nine concentric squares, at right angles to first set; draw first square between two smallest (inner) squares of first set, as shown on diagram. For remaining eight squares, mark points every $1\frac{1}{16}''$ on all four center lines eight times,

PIECING DIAGRAM

working out from corners of square just drawn. Draw lines between center lines to connect points, making the squares.

With pencil, shade in alternate sections made by the two sets of squares, as shown by shading on diagram. Erase other working lines no longer needed (lighter lines on diagram). Glue your diagram to cardboard. Cut out cardboard pieces as indicated by darker marked lines for patterns.

Patches: Marking patterns on wrong side of fabric and adding $\frac{1}{4}''$ seam allowance all around, cut patch pieces as follows. From black fabric, cut 168 each of pieces A through G. From blue velvet, cut 42 of piece H. From remaining fabrics, cut pieces I through Q as you construct each block, cutting four sets for each block, each set in color desired. In original quilt, some blocks have a different color for each corner, but most blocks have the same color for every two opposing corners within a block. (When quilt is assembled, the colors of four adjacent blocks will combine for a pattern, rather than the colors within a block.)

Blocks: From muslin, cut 42 pieces 12″ square. Patch pieces are sewn to muslin squares for blocks. Draw two diagonal center lines on each square. Place an H piece, right side up, in exact center of square, matching corners of piece to lines drawn on square; pin in place and sew down around edges without turning under seam allowance. Place a black G piece on one side of H piece, right sides together and matching edges; sew down on marked seam line of G piece. Turn G piece to right side and press down. Join three other black G pieces around H piece in same manner. Join four colored I pieces around H-G piece, matching edges, stitching on marked lines, turning, and pressing down in same manner. Join four black F pieces, then four colored J pieces. Continue around, adding on four black pieces, then four colored pieces, until all pieces are added for one block, including the corner pieces. The raw edge of outer pieces should match raw edges of muslin base. Make 41 more blocks in same manner. Stitch around each block, $\frac{3}{16}''$ from raw edge, to hold outside pieces in place.

Assembling: Right sides facing and with $\frac{1}{4}''$ seams, join blocks into six rows of seven blocks each; arrange blocks so that adjacent colors contrast. Press seams open. Join rows together for quilt top, with $\frac{1}{4}''$ seams and again positioning colors for contrast. Press seams open. Piece should measure $69\frac{1}{2}'' \times 81''$, including outside seam allowance.

Border: Cut cardboard pattern $1'' \times 3''$. Marking pattern on wrong side of fabric and adding $\frac{1}{4}''$ seam allowance all around, cut 162 pieces from remaining fabric scraps. Join pieces on their long sides to make two border strips of 81 pieces each. Right sides together and with $\frac{1}{4}''$ seams, sew a strip to each long side of quilt top, centering strips so they extend an extra $\frac{1}{4}''$ at top and bottom; trim off excess. Piece should measure $75\frac{1}{2}'' \times 81''$.

Lining: Cut two pieces $41'' \times 73\frac{1}{2}''$. Sew together on long sides with $\frac{1}{2}''$ seams; press seam open. Lining should measure $73\frac{1}{2}'' \times 81''$.

Finishing: Place wrong sides of lining and quilt top together, matching edges at top and bottom and centering on the width so that borders extend equally on both sides; tack to hold every few inches. Turn in edges of quilt top and lining $\frac{1}{4}''$ at top and bottom and slip-stitch folded edges together. Turn in edges of borders $\frac{1}{4}''$; fold borders to back of quilt and slip-stitch to lining, making $2\frac{1}{4}''$-wide borders on front and $\frac{3}{4}''$-wide borders on back. Press all edges of quilt.

PLATE RACK
Shown on page 106

EQUIPMENT: Paper for pattern. Pencil. Ruler. Large sheet of tracing paper. Masking tape. Electric power saw. Chisel. Sandpaper. Hammer. Screwdriver. Soft cloths.

MATERIALS: Clear pine, $\frac{3}{4}''$, thick: 29″ lengths of random widths to make 4′ width for back, plus a 4′ length 5″ wide for sides. Pine 1″ × 2″, 7′. Pine shelving $\frac{3}{4}''$ thick, 7″ wide, 4′ long. Pine stripping $\frac{1}{4}''$ thick, $1\frac{1}{8}''$ wide, 8′ long. Pine stripping $\frac{1}{8}''$ thick, $\frac{3}{8}''$ wide, 8′ long. Finishing nails. Wood glue. Light brown stain. Wax, or satin-finish varnish.

DIRECTIONS: Enlarge pattern below, by copying on ruled paper in 2″ squares; complete half-pattern indicated by long dash lines. Trace pattern pieces. Go over all lines of tracing on wrong side with soft pencil.

Place the random widths of 29″ pine side by side to make an area at least 29″ × 46″. Glue pieces together along 29″ edges. Hold with two cleats of 1″ × 2″ pine, 42″ long, nailed across back, one 9″ down from top and one 8″ up from bottom. Let glue dry. Tape tracing, wrong side down, on this large piece of wood. To transfer lines to wood, go over all lines with sharp pencil. Transfer lines of side piece to 5″ wide pine twice to make two. With saw, cut out back and two side pieces. Place side pieces down flat, reversing one for opposite sides. Along this surface of each, mark and cut out two dado joints $\frac{3}{4}$″ wide, $\frac{1}{4}$″ deep where indicated by short dash lines on pattern (this surface will be inner surface of each side).

Use chisel to gouge out joint. Directly above these grooves, make small notches $\frac{1}{8}$″ × $\frac{3}{8}$″, where indicated on pattern in solid black. With straight (back) and bottom edges flush, nail side pieces to ends of back piece. Cut shelving into two $46\frac{1}{2}$″-long pieces, one $2\frac{5}{8}$″ wide, one $3\frac{5}{8}$″ wide. Insert and glue larger one into lower groove until flush with back piece. Do the same with other shelf in upper groove. Nail from sides and back to secure shelves. Cut $\frac{1}{8}$″ stripping into two $46\frac{1}{4}$″ strips. Insert into notches and glue in place along top edge of shelf. Cut the $\frac{1}{4}$″ stripping into two $47\frac{1}{2}$″-long pieces. Place across front with ends into grooves on sides; nail ends to secure. Sand smooth all round edges of the rack.

With cloth, rub stain completely over rack. Allow to penetrate for just a few minutes, then wipe away with another cloth; let dry. Finish with wax or varnish as desired.

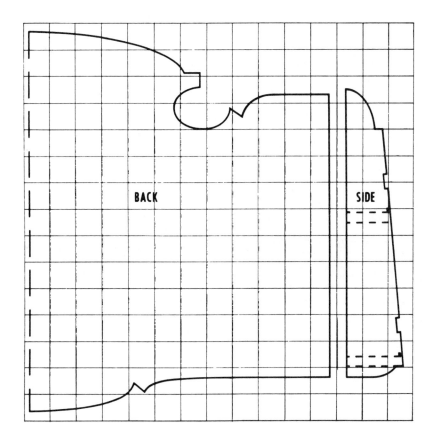

BACK SIDE

Pattern for
Plate Rack

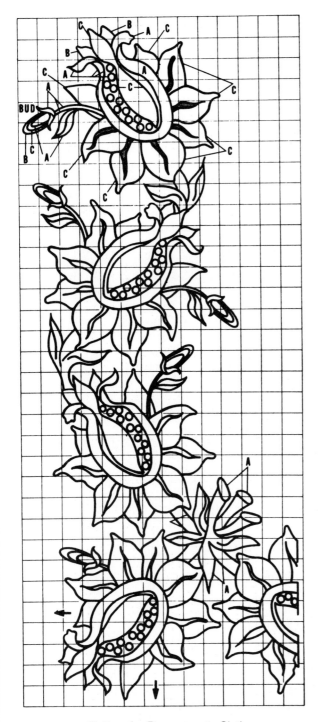

Pattern for Pomegranate Cloth

POMEGRANATE CLOTH
Shown on pages 106-107

EQUIPMENT: Tracing paper for pattern. Pencil. Ruler. Sewing machine with zigzag setting. Needle. Dressmaker's carbon paper. Embroidery hoop, 7″ diameter.

MATERIALS: Off-white linen fabric, 72″ wide, 2 yards. Off-white sewing thread (for hem). For embroidery: Belding Corticelli mercerized sewing thread, size 50 (600-yard spools): Royal Blue #1360 (A), three spools; Parakeet #1319 (B), one spool; Gala Peacock #1410 (C), three.

DIRECTIONS: Press fabric; make sure fabric is cut along straight grain, and that ends are straight. To make mitered corner: On two adjacent sides which form corner to be mitered, fold and press 1″ hem to right side of fabric. Pull point of corner up so it stands at right angles to rest of fabric; refold hem, leaving corner pulled up. Fold corner to right and left, creating a diagonal crease. Stitch together along crease. Cut off corner $\frac{1}{4}$″ from stitching. Turn mitered corner to wrong side. Repeat on all corners. Fold and press $\frac{1}{4}$″ of hem to wrong side along all edges. Refold hems to wrong side along original 1″ hem line; topstitch all around, $\frac{1}{8}$″ from inside folded edge.

Enlarge pattern by copying on paper ruled in 1″ squares. Place pattern on right side of fabric with carbon paper in between. Make sure all arrows are $2\frac{1}{2}$″ from edge of fabric which is parallel to arrow. Transfer design to fabric with a sharp pencil. Pattern as given is for lower right corner; transfer design to this area first. Then flip pattern over to wrong side, matching portion of corner motif and adjacent motif, and transfer design to right-hand side above lower right corner. Transfer design to remaining corners in same manner. Transfer entire design before beginning to embroider as the process of embroidering will pull and distort the fabric somewhat and will make exact positioning difficult.

See threads listed in Materials and pattern for color key, and refer to color illustration. Colors for all motifs are same. Set machine for close zigzag stitch to embroider all lines except shaded areas, seeds, and buds. Embroider lines

A on pattern in Royal Blue with stitch width set at #3. Embroider lines B in Parakeet, and lines C in Gala Peacock with stitch set at #4.

For remainder of design, set machine for free motion embroidery (check your book, as setting varies from machine to machine), set stitch width at #5, and remove presser foot. Place fabric in embroidery hoop with motif to be embroidered in center; work in short back-and-forth motion. Use Gala Peacock shaded to Parakeet to fill shaded areas. Work the three lines of buds in Parakeet (outer line), Gala Peacock (middle line), and Royal Blue. Work seed outlines in Royal Blue.

QUICK POINT CUSHIONS
Shown on pages 106-107

EQUIPMENT: Brown wrapping paper. Pencil. Ruler. Scissors. India ink and small, pointed brush or *waterproof* felt-tipped pen. Masking tape. Tapestry and sewing needles. **For Blocking:** Thumbtacks. Soft, wooden surface. T-square.

MATERIALS: Rug canvas, 5 mesh-to-the-inch, one piece the size of finished cushion, plus $2\frac{1}{2}''$ all around. Reynolds Tapis Pingouin 100% acrylic rug yarn (50-gram skeins): Turquoise #55, 1 skein; Bleu Franc #34, 3 skeins (one skein for

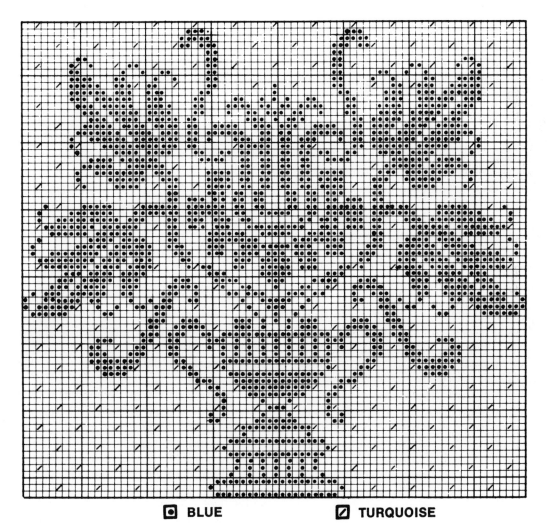

■ BLUE   ◪ TURQUOISE

Chart and Color Key for Cushions

needlepoint, plus two for twisted cord); Beige Clair #17, about 4 skeins (amount depends on size of cushion). For back: Closely woven cotton or linen fabric in off-white. For inner pillow: Muslin 36" wide, $\frac{2}{3}$ yd. For stuffing: Polyester fiberfill. Sewing thread to match Bleu Franc.

DIRECTIONS: Read directions for working a needlepoint piece, page 306. Make a paper pattern of chair seat; include indentations to accommodate back and arms, if necessary. Transfer pattern outline to canvas with ink or felt pen, leaving $2\frac{1}{2}$" canvas margin all around. Save pattern and use as a guide when blocking and making inner pillow. Mark a horizontal and vertical line at center of canvas. Determine position of design when centered on canvas. Following chart and color key, below, work design in continental stitch; use single strand yarn throughout. Work tulip design in Bleu Franc first. Then work single Turquoise stitches, working in diagonal rows, and extending the pattern to marked pattern outline. Fill in background in Beige Clair just to marked outline.

Block needlepoint, following directions on page 307. Trim canvas margins to $\frac{5}{8}$" all around. Cut back piece $\frac{5}{8}$" larger all around than paper pattern piece. With right sides facing, sew needlepoint to back, making $\frac{5}{8}$" seams; leave opening at center of back seam large enough to accommodate your hand. Trim off corners of canvas diagonally; apply a little glue to trimmed edges. Turn right side out.

Inner pillow: Cut two pieces of muslin, the same shape as paper pattern, plus 1" all around. Stitch pieces together all around, making $\frac{1}{2}$" seams; again leave opening to accommodate your hand. Clip into seams at corners; turn to right side. Stuff lightly, and slip-stitch opening closed. Insert inner pillow in needlepoint pillow; slip-stitch opening closed.

Make a twisted cord from Bleu Franc; use three strands to make cord as follows:

This method requires two people. Tie one end of yarn around a pencil. Loop yarn over center of a second pencil, back to and around first, and back to second, making as many strands between pencils as needed for thickness of cord; knot end to pencil. Length of yarn between pencils should

be three times length of cord desired. Each person holds yarn just below pencil with one hand and twists pencil with other hand, keeping yarn taut. When yarn begins to kink, catch center over doorknob or hook. Bring pencils together for one person to hold, while other grasps center of yarn, sliding hand down at intervals, letting yarn twist. Using blue thread, slip-stitch cord around edge of pillow; begin and end at center of back edge.

WOVEN PLAID RUG
Shown on pages 106 and 107

EQUIPMENT: Table or floor loom: 4-harness. Scissors. Heavy scrap yarn. Yardstick. Heavy cardboard. Tapestry needle.

MATERIALS: Scotts Woolen Mill: Bulgari 2-ply weaving wool Natural #301, 6 lbs. (for warp and plain weave weft); Craft Yarns of Rhode Island, Inc. Primitive Yarn, Persimmon #1009, 12 lbs. (for weft).

DIRECTIONS: Rug is woven in four blocks, each measuring 20" in the reed. If using a loom on which wider pieces can be woven, adjust threading accordingly. Warp loom, following manufacturer's directions, and referring to threading charts, below. Start at X's. There are nine warp threads per inch; draw them in a nine dent reed. Denting: one per dent, and one per heddle, except for selvedges where there are two warp ends in each of first and last two dents. Each warp is $4\frac{1}{2}$ yards long. Following border chart (160 ends each), thread loom for first and last blocks (border blocks); following remaining threading chart (168 ends each), thread two center blocks.

To begin weaving, leave 12" unwoven for fringe; insert several strips of cardboard in the warp threads to beat against. Weave 2" plain heading with heavy yarn of contrasting color; leave in when blocking, and remove before making fringe.

Prepare shuttles of each color; three strands of persimmon on a shuttle and four strands of natural on a shuttle. Following treading chart, weave the four blocks, repeating pattern three times; start at * on chart for second and third repeat; on third

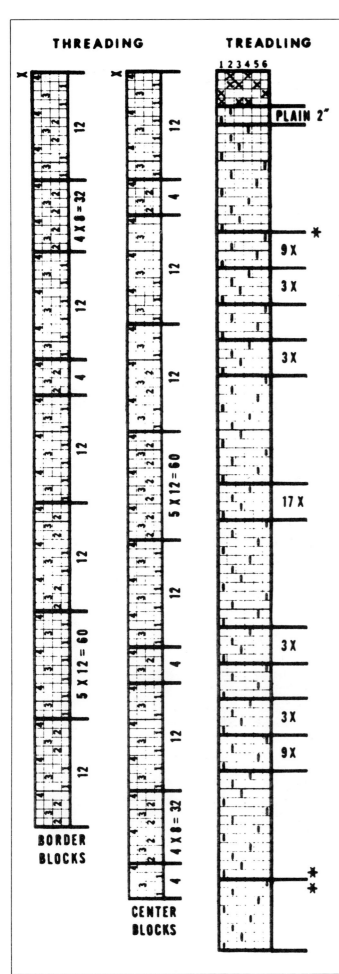

THREADING

BORDER BLOCKS

CENTER BLOCKS

TREADLING

1 2 3 4 5 6

PLAIN 2″

9 X

3 X

3 X

17 X

3 X

3 X

9 X

Threading and Treadling Chart

repeat, end at ** on chart. (**Note:** For table looms: For pedal 1 use levers 1 and 2; for pedal 2 use levers 3 and 4; for pedal 3 use levers 1 and 3; for pedal 4 use levers 1 and 4; for pedal 5 use levers 2 and 3; for pedal 6 use levers 2 and 4.) Check weft to make sure 8 picks per inch is maintained throughout. Plain weave is woven with natural; pattern is in persimmon. End each block with another 2″ plain heading. Cut weaving from loom.

To block, wash pieces separately by machine; use cold water, gentle agitation, no soap. Spread each piece out on a flat clean surface; pull into shape until each piece measures 16″ × 104″. Allow to dry partially in this position, then drape over loom or other suitable object and allow to dry completely. Whipstitch blocks together along selvedges, with natural yarn. Remove headings. For fringe, divide warp strands into groups of six; tie a large overhand knot near edge with each group; trim.

LAYERED SKIRT
Shown on page 108

SIZE: Underskirt is 94″ in diameter; top cloth is 43″ square.

EQUIPMENT: See General Directions for Stenciling on page 305. Sewing machine. Sewing needle. Tape measure. String, at least 55″ long. Yardstick. Thumbtack. Tailor's chalk. Medium-size stencil brushes.

MATERIALS: Polished cotton: blue, 45″ square; beige, 48″ wide, $5\frac{1}{3}$ yards. Iron-on seam binding tape to match underskirt, about $8\frac{1}{2}$ yards. Sewing thread to match fabrics. Acrylic paints: light green, dark green, brown, purple.

DIRECTIONS: See General Directions for Stenciling on page 305. Enlarge patterns by copying on paper ruled in 1″ squares.

Stencil as directed in General Directions. Stencil berries purple; stencil all leaves in light green first; allow to dry. Stencil tips of leaves in dark green. For branches, mix green and brown for an olive green color.

Layered Skirt Pattern

Underskirt: From beige fabric, cut two strips 48″ × 95″. With right sides facing, machine-stitch pieces together along 95″ sides with $\frac{1}{2}$″ seams. Piece should measure 95″ × 95″.

Fold fabric in half, then in quarters to find center point; mark point. Open fabric out flat again. Tack one end of string to the exact center. Tie other end of string to a pencil with exactly 47″ of string between pencil and tack. Swing pencil in an arc to mark a circle. Cut out $\frac{1}{2}$″ beyond marked circle.

Using tailor's chalk, mark a line around perimeter of circle, 5″ from raw edge. Place thick branch of larger stencil pattern along this line; repeat stencil motif approximately sixteen times around circle. Allow to dry.

To hem underskirt, turn raw edge under $\frac{1}{2}$″ all around. Finish with iron-on seam binding tape. Press skirt on wrong side of fabric.

Top Cloth: With yardstick and tailor's chalk, mark 1″ hemline all around edge of blue fabric. Mark 10 diagonal lines on fabric, to use as guidelines for stenciling as follows: Mark two corner-to-corner center lines; on each side of each center line, mark three more lines parallel to center lines and 8″ from each other.

Stencil small berry clusters where lines intersect, varying the angle of each as you go.

Turn fabric under on 1″ hemline, mitering corners. Turn raw edges under $\frac{1}{4}$″ again. Press; slipstitch along turned-under edge.

STENCILED SETTING
Shown on page 109

SIZE: Soft-sculpture mirror frame, 23″ × 27″.
EQUIPMENT: See General Directions for Stenciling on page 305. Sewing machine. Brown paper. Sewing needle. Medium-size stencil brushes.
MATERIALS: (Large-scale floral cotton or cotton-blend fabric for chair cushion and tablecloth, if you plan to design your own stencils.) Lamp-

shade with a flat paper finish; size depends upon height of lamp base. White cotton for mirror frame, 45″ wide, $1\frac{1}{3}$ yards. Green bias-binding tape, $\frac{1}{2}$″ wide, $9\frac{1}{2}$ yards. Cording, $\frac{1}{8}$″ diameter, $9\frac{1}{2}$ yards. Cotton batting. White sewing thread. Acrylic paints: blue and green. Mirror frame, 16″ × 18″. Double-faced masking tape.

DIRECTIONS: See General Directions for Stenciling on page 305. Enlarge patterns for floral designs by copying on paper ruled in 1″ squares.

Mirror Frame: From white cotton, cut four strips each 6″ wide: two $23\frac{1}{2}$″ long and two $27\frac{1}{2}$″ long. On a flat working surface, assemble four strips as follows: Two $23\frac{1}{2}$″ strips are top and bottom of frame; two $27\frac{1}{2}$″ strips are side pieces. Miter four corners to form right angles; machine-stitch along diagonal seams; cut away excess fabric $\frac{1}{4}$″ from

sewn line. Fully assembled piece should measure $23\frac{1}{2}$″ × $27\frac{1}{2}$″. Press seams flat.

We have given you modular stencil patterns. Mirror frame may be stenciled using the same flowers illustrated or others from your own fabric as desired. Before actually stenciling, draw a mirror frame on brown paper to the same dimensions as the assembled fabric piece. Plan floral design on paper, arranging leaves and flowers in a border.

With paper drawing as a guide, stencil flowers and leaves on fabric frame, following the design layout you've chosen. Allow stencils to dry thoroughly.

You will need four pieces of covered cording—two for inner edges of frame and two for outer edges. For inner edges, cut two pieces each of bias tape and cording 64″ long. Insert a piece of

Stencil for Table Setting

cording into bias tape; machine-stitch close to cording. Repeat with remaining cord and tape. For outer edges, cut two pieces each of bias tape and cording 106″ long. Assemble in same manner.

Stitch one piece of cording to inner edge of frame and another to outer edge, raw edges even and with cording facing inward; ease around corners. Overlap ends 1″. Cut $\frac{1}{2}$″ from inner cording at one end; fold raw edges of casing in $\frac{1}{2}$″. Insert other end of cording; continue stitching.

For outer boxing strip, cut a strip $2\frac{1}{2}$″ × 106″ from white fabric, piecing to get length. With raw edges even and right sides facing, machine-stitch boxing strip to frame. Overlap ends $\frac{1}{2}$″; machine-stitch together; cut away excess fabric to seam.

For inner boxing strip, cut a strip $2\frac{1}{2}$″ × 64″, piecing to get length. Stitch to inner edge of frame in same manner. Add remaining cords to outer edges of the boxing strips in the same manner as before.

For frame lining, cut a piece of white fabric $23\frac{1}{2}$″ × $27\frac{1}{2}$″. Mark and cut out center area $11\frac{1}{2}$″ × $15\frac{1}{2}$″.

With right sides facing and cording between, machine-stitch front and lining together around center opening with $\frac{1}{4}$″ seams. Turn in outer edges of lining $\frac{1}{4}$″; press. Pin to outer boxing strip, with cord facing outward. Machine-stitch outside edges together close to cord; leave one end open. Stuff frame fully; slip-stitch closed. Attach frame to mirror with double-faced masking tape.

Lampshade: Scatter stenciled flowers as desired around entire lampshade. Allow each flower to dry thoroughly before stenciling the next one.

HARVEST MATS AND NAPKIN RINGS
Shown on page 110

SIZE: Place mats, 18″ × $11\frac{1}{2}$″; napkins, 16″ square; napkin rings, 4″ × 8″.
EQUIPMENT: Colored pencil. Pencil. Ruler. Scissors. Paper for patterns. Tailor's chalk. Dressmaker's tracing (carbon) paper. Dry ball-point pen. Sewing and embroidery needles. Embroidery hoop. Iron. Padded surface. Zigzag sewing machine. Masking tape.

MATERIALS: Linen or linen-like fabric 45″ wide, 2 yards desired color (for four complete sets). Matching thread. Columbia Minerva Persian-type yarn, one 10-yard skein of each color listed in color key, unless otherwise indicated in parentheses. **For Napkin Rings:** Fusible interfacing, four 4″ × 8″ pieces, plus test scrap. Four hook-and-eye closures.
DIRECTIONS: Using sharp colored pencil, draw lines across patterns, connecting grid lines. Enlarge patterns by copying on paper ruled in $\frac{1}{2}$″ squares. Using ruler and tailor's chalk, mark four $16\frac{1}{2}$″-square napkins on fabric; cut out and set aside. In center of remaining fabric, mark four $18\frac{1}{2}$″ × 12″ place mats, and four $8\frac{1}{2}$″-square napkin rings leaving at least 2″ margins around raw edges of fabric; do not cut out pieces. Position one large motif (peas, corn, carrots, beet) over each place mat, centered between top and bottom (long edges), and 2″ from left side edge; see color photograph. Position one small motif in center of each napkin ring. Transfer designs to fabric, using carbon and dry ball-point pen.

Bind raw edges of fabric with masking tape. Place area to be worked in embroidery hoop, holding fabric smooth and taut without distortion. Embroider each design, following color photograph, individual directions, and stitch and color keys; see page 308 for embroidery stitch details. Cut 18″ lengths of yarn; separate the three strands and work with single strand throughout. Begin stitching by leaving end of yarn on back of fabric and working over it to secure. To end a strand or begin a new one, weave end of yarn through stitches on back of work; do not make knots.

For Long and Short Stitches in areas indicated by zigzag lines, blend adjacent colors, avoiding sharp demarcation lines.

Peas: Straight-Stitch all accent lines with avocado green. Outline open pods with light brown Chain Stitch.

Corn: Satin-Stitch each kernel (see supplementary key next to corn pattern; each symbol represents a color for each kernel), alternating stitches horizontally and vertically for a checkerboard effect; see arrows.

Carrots: Work carrots with horizontal Long and

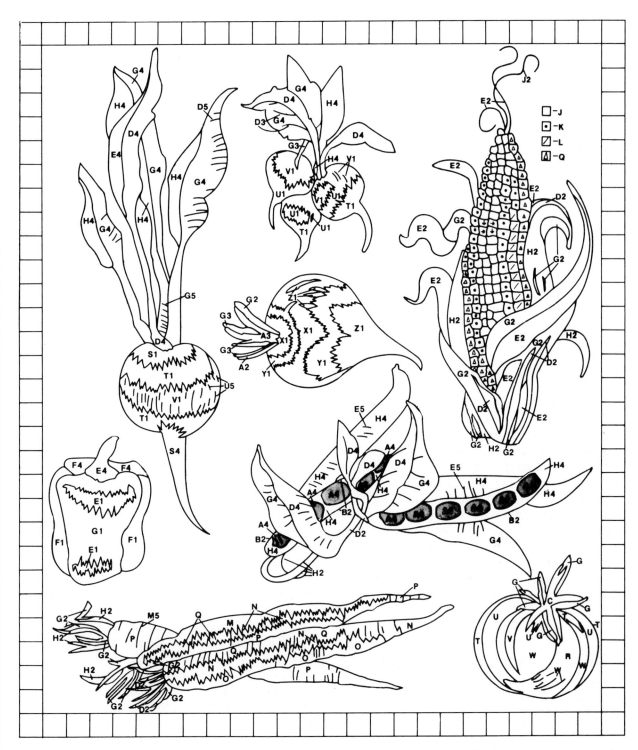

Color Key

A Spring Pea Green #575	**H** Hunter Green #520 (3)
B Light Brown #466	**J** Saffron #442
C Pea Green #540	**K** Pale Pumpkin #454
D Celery Leaf #570 (2)	**L** Pumpkin Seed #975
E Avocado #545	**M** Rust #414
F Ming Green #505	**N** Medium Orange #978
G Medium Green #510 (3)	**O** Light Orange #970
	P Burnt Orange #960
	Q Medium Gold #427 (2)

R Fireball #843
S Burgundy #236
T Cranberry #240
U True Red #R10
V Dark Red #R50
W Red #242
X Tea Rose #250
Y Neutral #020
Z Ivory #012

Short Stitch, blending adjacent colors carefully. Straight-Stitch all accent lines with rust.

Beet: Straight-Stitch accent lines on leaves with celery leaf. Work center band of beet with dark red Long and Short Stitch, accented with true red Straight Stitch.

Tomato: Work entirely in Outline Stitch.

Radishes, Turnip, Pepper: Follow stitch and color keys.

Finishing: When embroidery is complete, steam-press gently on a padded surface. Cut out pieces along marked lines.

For place mats and napkins, finish edges with maching stitching: Straight-stitch $\frac{1}{8}''$ in from raw edges all around. Press raw edges $\frac{1}{4}''$ to wrong side; baste in place. Set machine for close zigzag satin stitch and, using matching thread, satin-stitch around pressed edges, covering straight stitching. Trim away any excess fabric close to stitching.

For napkin rings, cut four $4'' \times 8''$ pieces of fusible interfacing. Test-fuse scrap of interfacing on fabric scrap to ensure compatability. Center interfacing vertically over embroidered motif on wrong side of fabric, leaving $2\frac{1}{4}''$ margins to the right and left, and $\frac{1}{4}''$ margins at top and bottom; fuse to fabric, following manufacturer's directions. Fold piece in half with right side inward and side edges together; stitch sides, making $\frac{1}{4}''$ seam; press seam open. Press top and bottom edges $\frac{1}{4}''$ to wrong side; baste. Turn fabric tube to right side; press so seam is centered in back and motif is centered in front. Slip-stitch pressed edges at top together invisibly; repeat for bottom edges; remove basting. Sew hook and eye, centered, at top and bottom edges of each napkin holder.

STRAWBERRY SET
Shown on page 110

EQUIPMENT: Paper. Pencil. Ruler. Tracing paper. Tape measure. Straight pins. Scissors. Dressmaker's tracing (carbon) paper. Sewing machine with zigzag setting. Embroidery hoop with side screw, 8″ diameter. Steam iron and two terrycloth towels for pressing.

MATERIALS: Beige medium-weight cotton fabric, 45″ wide, $\frac{1}{2}$ yd, for each place mat-napkin set (or $\frac{1}{2}$ yd. will do for two place mats). Pellon® lightweight, 36″ wide, $\frac{1}{2}$ yd. for each place mat only. Scraps of fabric for practice. White sewing thread. DMC #50 machine embroidery thread in colors listed (amounts vary, but a place mat-napkin set can be done with less than one spool each): Bright red #666, dark red #498, black #310, white (blanc) bright yellow #743, light green #703, medium green #700, pale yellow #745, and medium brown #400.

NOTE: For a better finished effect #30 Mettler machine embroidery thread (sold only at Bernina Sewing Machine Co. dealers) was used for the shading colors to add more contrast to the #50 threads.

DIRECTIONS: Enlarge patterns by copying on paper ruled in 1″ squares; complete half-pattern of place mat only; do not complete border design as this would reverse it; continue border design all around. Trace place mat pattern onto tracing paper. Draw a rectangle 9″ high × $9\frac{3}{4}''$ wide on tracing paper; trace napkin strawberry (in center of place mat pattern) onto lower left corner matching lines of pattern with ruled lines. Using dressmaker's carbon, trace both designs onto right side of fabric allowing at least $2\frac{1}{2}''$ border around each. You need not trace seed marks on strawberries nor fine lines (which indicate shading) onto fabric. Do not cut fabric around patterns. Pin Pellon® to fabric underneath tracing of place mat; machine stitch together outside the place mat edge.

To do the machine embroidery, place fabric in embroidery hoop, using the larger ring on the underside of the fabric; the smaller ring on top, on the right side (opposite the way it is used in hand embroidery). Keep fabric taut but not distorted. Practice the technique on scraps first.

Prepare sewing machine for embroidery according to individual instruction booklet. Set zigzag dial to wide (4 or 5) on stitch dial unless instructed otherwise. Remove presser foot; lower feed dogs; loosen top tension slightly. Use white sewing thread in the bobbin; thread machine according to instructions below. To do fill-in embroidery, turn the hoop so that the design section

Continued on page 133

Grandmother takes inventory of homemade jams, jellies, and pickled goods while kitty watches for mice. Piece has needlepoint background with different stitches for each fruit and vegetable. Pantry Needlepoint directions on page 141.

Perk up a dull shelf or window sill with this charming "coffee break" border. Steaming cups, pots and grid are embroidered on scalloped cloth. Directions on page 144.

Vanishing Apple needlepoint is truly irresistible. Four vignettes tell a story; unworked canvas backgrounds give a homespun look. Directions on page 153.

Set the mood—and the table—for holiday entertaining with an exciting red and white patchwork quilt.

Star blocks are joined in a square pattern, sure to make any menu shine. Tufted quilt, 73" × 85"; directions on page 154.

*Bouquets of gold underscore a table
setting rich in tradition. Each wooden mat,
$11\frac{1}{2}'' \times 18''$, is stained brown, then stenciled
in gold. Polyurethane adds protection
and shine. Directions are on page 155.*

Create a crowd of corn dolls—or one of a kind. Batik for realistic corncob look or use gingham fabric. Dolls stand about 15" tall, have delicate features and soft, muted hair color. Directions on page 158.

Stop drafts under doors and around windows with attractive Draft Stops of stenciled velveteen. Plastic lined, sand filled, stops are 39" long. Directions on page 160.

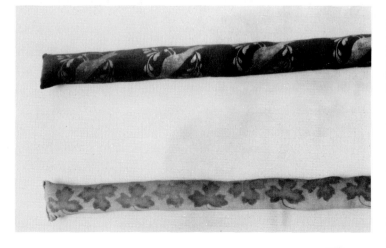

A "menu" of pot holders tells a mealtime story. Waffle, beanpot, ham, egg and fish are appliqued by hand, then embroidered or padded for extra dimension. Rickrack trims all but the beanpot. Food Pot Holders, page 161.

Cat and owl appliques adorn hot mitts—or mitts can be used as pot holders by slipping handle of pot through the side slits for a better grip. Owl, Cat Hot Mitts, page 162.

Kitchen motifs from bygone days are cut from
very modern iron-on tape, then pressed in place and machine
outlined. Quick Pot Holders, directions on page 171.

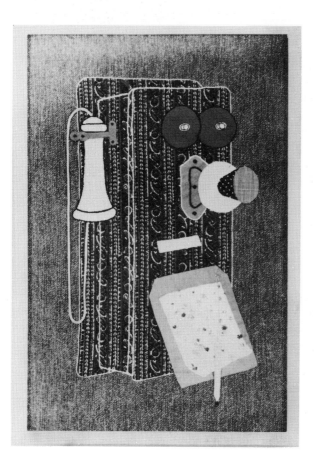

Quaint pictures in fabric applique
are made using remnants. Our
Coffee Mill is an artful
composition in green, brown, and
gold calicos. Scraps of fabric
and felt are appliqued to background and embroidered in outline
stitch and French knots. Matted
in grey and framed in gold,
picture is 16″ × 16½″. Turn-of-the-
century Wall Phone has twin bells
and separate ear and mouth pieces.
Brown paisley is slip-stitched
to background fabric for telephone box, outline stitch defines
it. Other parts are cut from
cotton fabrics and felt in
contrasting colors; French knots,
chain, and straight stitches
are also used for detailing.
Picture measures 17″ × 11¾″,
with frame. Patterns and
directions begin on page 163.

Continued from page 124

is worked on its side rather than face front. As you zigzag stitch, move hoop from side to side following the traced design shape and filling in the outlined areas. The side motion will help you to follow the outlines. To shade the embroidery, change the thread color, then zigzag over the fill-in embroidery. The fine lines indicate the general shading areas, but being exact is not crucial.

Begin embroidery by fill-in stitching strawberries using bright red threads. Shade berries with dark red. Then use black thread and the small zigzag setting to make small bartacks to resemble the seeds. You need not move the hoop at all while marking bartacks.

Next embroider the flowers: the petals are done in white then the centers in bright yellow. Stitch around the outer edges of the petals using bright yellow and a setting of "0" or fine.

Stitch strawberry caps using medium green; stitch stems with light green. For the leaves, fill in the full leaf outline using light green. Then use medium green to shade around the outer edges and the interior area where indicated by fine lines. On the leaf edges that form the border (at sides of place mat and on the napkin), use small zigzag setting to stitch over those lines.

For the basket edge border, work fill-in embroidery with pale yellow thread, but you must turn the hoop to have the stitches follow the basket outline. For the fine lines, set machine at "0" or fine and use brown thread. For the interior basket outline, use brown thread and small zigzag setting where possible; otherwise, use "0" or fine setting. For the place mat and napkin outline, use small zigzag setting and brown thread.

When all embroidery is complete, trim away

Half-Pattern for Strawberry Set

fabric close to outer stitching. To finish edges, raise feed dogs, replace presser foot, set zigzag wider and stitch around slowly while moving fabric to follow outer edges. On underside of place mat, trim away excess Pellon® in center, cutting close to embroidery. Place embroidery face down between two terry towels and steampress on underside.

FELT PITCHER

Shown on page 111

EQUIPMENT: Paper for patterns. Pencil. Ruler. Scissors. Tracing paper. Dressmaker's tracing (carbon) paper in color other than white. Tracing wheel. Straight pins. Sewing machine with zipper foot attachment. Sewing needle. Iron. Small towel. Compass. Knitting needle.

MATERIALS: Felt: White 72″ wide, $\frac{1}{2}$ yard; strip of royal blue 1″ × 20″. White sewing thread. Polyester fiberfill batting, 36″ wide, $\frac{1}{2}$ yard. Cord $\frac{1}{8}$″ thick, 20″ long.

DIRECTIONS: Enlarge patterns by copying on paper ruled in 1″ squares; complete quarter and half patterns indicated by long dash lines. Use compass to aid in drawing $4\frac{7}{8}$″ circle for pattern C.

Cut white felt into two 18″ × 36″ pieces. Pin batting smoothly to one side of one piece of felt. With pencil and ruler, mark diagonal lines 1″ apart on piece of felt with batting, first in one direction and then in the opposite direction. To quilt, machine-stitch along marked lines in each direction.

Using patterns cut each A, B, C, and D piece

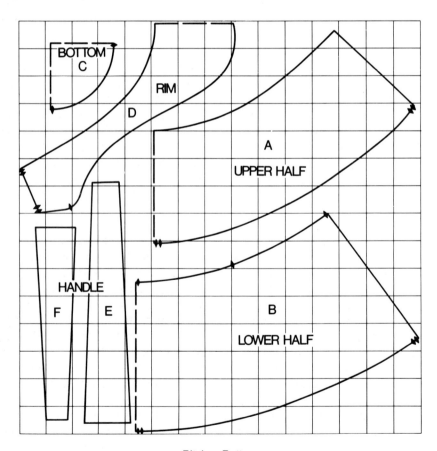

Pitcher Pattern

from plain white felt, then cut each piece again from quilted felt for lining. Cut one piece E from plain felt and one piece F from quilted felt.

For outside of pitcher, assemble plain pieces as directed below. Pin and baste pieces together, then stitch on machine, making $\frac{1}{8}''$ seams throughout. For lining, assemble quilted pieces A, B, and C separately in same manner; always pin and sew with batting facing out.

Sew pieces A and B together along wider curving edges, matching double notches. Sew ends of A-B piece together. (For lining, leave $6\frac{1}{2}''$ opening in center of end seam, so piece can be turned later.) Sew piece C to B, matching single notches.

For the handle, stitch E (top) and F together on long sides, easing the longer E sides to fit shorter F sides and thus curving handle to shape. Turn handle to right side. Machine-stitch across the top (wide) end. Stuff handle fully, using knitting needle to push in batting. Turn remaining end in $\frac{1}{4}''$; slip-stitch closed.

To make cording for pitcher rim, fold strip of blue felt in half lengthwise; insert cord into fold. With zipper foot, stitch along strip as close to cord as possible. Trim seam to $\frac{1}{4}''$.

Place the two rim pieces D together; insert cording between pieces, matching raw edges and starting and ending at single notch. Stitch along outer edges, between single notches only, with the cording between. Join ends, matching double notches. Center top end of handle into remaining opening of the rim, with the unquilted side of the handle facing the quilted side of the rim; stitch. Turn the rim to right side and sew inner edges together.

Insert inner edges of rim between the two A pieces with the unquilted piece A facing unquilted rim; match all raw edges; stitch.

Turn pitcher to right side; slip-stitch opening of lining closed and insert lining into pitcher. Slip-stitch the remaining handle end at the intersection of the four seams on the side of the pitcher.

Steam-press pitcher. To maintain shape, roll a small towel tightly into a ball shape, about the size of a fist; place it inside the pitcher at the point where you are steaming the outside; do this at all seams.

VEGGIES IN A BASKET
Shown on page 111

EQUIPMENT: Paper for patterns. Ruler. Pencil. Scissors. Straight pins. Compass. Rug, embroidery, and sewing needles. Sewing machine.

MATERIALS: For Vegetables: Unbleached muslin, 36″ wide, $\frac{3}{8}$ yard. Cotton fabric: 36″, $\frac{1}{4}$ yard each of light olive green for leeks, dark green for pepper. Orange, 8″ × 15″, for carrots. Solid purple, 9″ × 11″, and two different purple prints, each 4″ × 9″, for eggplant. Violet, 4″ × 12″, for turnip. Light green burlap, 12″ × 15,″ and yellow dotted Swiss, 4″ × 12,″ for cauliflower. (Use leftover fabrics for trims.) Rug yarn, one 70-yard skein of off-white and small amount dark green. Tan pearl cotton. Scrap of green felt. Eight pipe cleaners. Fusible web. **For Basket:** Natural-color burlap, 45″ wide, $\frac{3}{4}$ yard. Plastic foam, 1″ thick, 5″ × 10″. Tan rug yarn. **For All:** Stearns and Foster Mountain Mist Fiberloft Polyester stuffing. Matching sewing thread. All-purpose glue.

GENERAL DIRECTIONS: Enlarge patterns by copying on paper ruled in 1″ squares; complete quarter and half patterns indicated by long dash lines. Use patterns to mark pieces on wrong side of fabric; cut out $\frac{1}{4}''$ beyond marked lines for seam allowance, except where indicated. Cut other pieces without patterns as indicated; seam allowance is included in measurements. With right sides facing, pin and sew pieces together on marked lines, making $\frac{1}{4}''$ seams. Clip into seam allowances at curves. Leave each vegetable open at point indicated in individual directions; turn to right side; stuff; slip-stitch opening closed.

EGGPLANT: Following General Directions and using eggplant pattern A, cut one piece from each print fabric, reversing pattern for second piece; mark top of each piece. Using eggplant pattern B, cut three pieces from solid fabric. Sew print pieces together first along edge X-X; sew the three solid sections side by side, then sew to either side of the print sections, leaving one seam open $2\frac{1}{2}''$. Turn; stuff; sew closed.

Using leaf pattern, cut three pieces each from dark green cotton, fusible web, and light green burlap; do not add seam allowance. Following

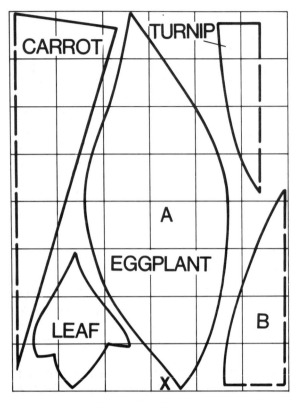

Pattern for Veggies

package directions, fuse each burlap leaf to each cotton leaf. Place one leaf, burlap side up, with two leaves, cotton sides up; wind and glue green yarn around leaf ends. Tack leaf cluster to eggplant top.

TURNIP: For lower part follow General Directions and cut six turnip sections from muslin, using pattern. Sew together, leaving one seam open. For upper part, fold 4″ × 12″ violet strip in half lengthwise, right side out. Pin long edges to right side of muslin with raw edges flush. Sew together; sew long open seam. Turn; stuff. Gather top along folded edge; leave small opening. For turnip stems, cut 12 strands, each 4″ long, from green yarn. Knot strands together at one end. Glue strands together in four groups of three strands each. Tuck knotted end into opening; tack stems to top.

PEPPER: Cut a 5½″ × 10½″ piece from both dark green cotton and muslin. Pin together, wrong sides facing. Starting at one end, mark crosswise lines on fabric with pencil: first line ¼″ in from end, then at 2″ intervals, marking five 2″ sections and leaving ¼″ at each end for seam allowance. Top-stitch the two fabrics together along pencil lines. Lightly pad each "pocket" with stuffing. Fold piece in half, green side inward; sew seam. Gather tightly around one raw edge for bottom; turn; stuff. Gather pepper top. For stems and leaves, cut 2″ × 3″ piece from light green burlap. Roll piece cross-wise into a tight stem; secure with a few stitches close to one end. To make tendrils, clip burlap at other end about halfway up stem, making six ½″ sections. Fan sections out and glue to top of pepper.

CARROT: Make three. Following General Directions, cut one piece from orange cotton, using pattern. Sew along long side; turn and stuff. Gather top, turning raw edges under and leaving a small opening. For carrot stem, cut a 2″ × 3″ piece from dark green cotton; pull threads from one long edge to fray fabric about ¼″. Roll piece crosswise into a stem; place unfrayed end into carrot top. Tack in place.

LEEK: Make three. Cut one 7½″ × 9¼″ piece each from light olive green cotton, muslin, and fusible web. Fuse wrong sides of fabrics together. Roll a piece of stuffing into a fat cigar shape, about 4″ long. Place the rolled stuffing on muslin side, having bottom of roll flush with one 7½″ side. Roll fabric snugly around the stuffing; overlap long raw edge and glue from one end to halfway up the roll. Slit the unglued end of roll into strips about 1″ wide. Make six or seven slits; starting from the outside and varying the length of the slits; make them 5″ long at the outside, 4″-4½″ long toward the inside.

Cut a piece of muslin 2¾″ × 5″; overlap long edges and glue, forming a tube. Make roots as follows (see Diagram 1): Use one strand of pearl cotton; knot end. Pass needle through outside of tube to inside, ⅜″ up from one end. Cut strand ½″

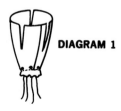

DIAGRAM 1

below fabric edge. Repeat around tube every $\frac{1}{4}''$. Using one strand of pearl cotton, gather same end of tube $\frac{1}{4}''$ up from edge, with roots hanging down. Make two slits on other end, about $\frac{3}{4}''$ apart, $1\frac{1}{4}''$ and $2''$ long. Slip piece over leek end. Bundle the three leeks together and tie with two strands of pearl cotton.

CAULIFLOWER: Cut a 12″-diameter circle from light green burlap. Gather around raw edge, leaving a $1\frac{1}{2}''$ diameter opening at the bottom. Stuff and shape into a flattened ball. With off-white rug yarn, cover the top surface (about 6″ in diameter) with flowerets made of French knots (stitch details on page 308 and color illustration on page 111). For leaves, cut 4″ × 12″ piece each from dark green cotton, yellow dotted Swiss, and fusible web. Cut pipe cleaners into eight $3\frac{1}{4}''$ lengths. Place fusible web on wrong side of green cotton. Place pipe cleaner lengths on top of web, $\frac{3}{4}''$ from one short end and $1\frac{1}{2}''$ apart. Place dotted Swiss on top of pipe cleaners. Pin along both long edges to hold pipe cleaners and fabrics in place. Fuse fabrics. Cut crosswise between pipe cleaners into eight equal strips. Glue strips to bottom of cauliflower, having ends without pipe cleaners at center and overlapping each slightly. Cut a $2\frac{1}{2}''$ circle from green felt and glue to bottom over ends of strips. Gently shape leaves to curve close to cauliflower head.

BASKET: Cut natural-colored burlap across the 45″ width into four 3″ strips. To make coil, sew the four strips together, end to end. Fold strip in half lengthwise; sew long side closed with $\frac{1}{2}''$ seams, stuffing as you sew. For basket base, cut piece of burlap 13″ × 14″. Glue around plastic foam rectangle, trimming excess at corners.

To build sides of basket, start at center of one 10″ side and glue coil to base, stitched edge facing up and folded edge flush with the bottom (see Diagram 2). Hold coil in place at bottom edge with

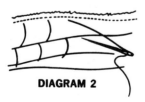

DIAGRAM 2

straight pins. When you reach the end of the round, overlap first rib and gradually begin second, so that 1″ of the first rib shows underneath. Following Diagram 2 and using tan rug yarn, sew each rib to the one before, making stitches $1\frac{1}{2}''$ apart. Continue wrapping coil around and sewing ribs together until you have four ribs. For fifth rib, turn raw edges of coil to inside of basket. Continue sewing, catching both sides of coil. End fifth rib at center of same side as beginning. Bring rib to inside and tack in place.

JAM JAR COVERS
Shown on page 111

EQUIPMENT: Paper for patterns. Ruler. Tape measure. Pencil. Scissors. Tapestry and sewing needles. Sewing machine. Compass. Pinking shears. Heavy twine, about 18′, for pulling casing over cord.

MATERIALS: For Preserves: Three 8-oz. jars of preserves. Three different soft cotton fabrics, each 15″ square. Three rubber bands. Scraps of red, yellow, and green felt. Yellow yarn, about 48″. Embroidery floss, yellow and brown. Sewing thread to match felt. Six cotton balls.

For Box: Cardboard box, 9″ × $3\frac{1}{2}''$ × $3\frac{1}{2}''$. Natural-color burlap, 36″ wide, 1 yard. Polished jute (parcel post twine), 60 yards (1 ball), for sewing burlap. Cable cord, size 300, 6 yards. Spray adhesive.

DIRECTIONS: For Preserves: Trace the three leaf and three fruit patterns given on page 138, completing half patterns indicated by dash lines. Fine lines indicate embroidery. Patterns are for 1) strawberry, 2) pear, and 3) apple. If necessary, make similar-sized simple patterns corresponding to the preserves you want to wrap. Using patterns, cut four of each from felt; pears from yellow, apples and strawberries from red, leaves from green. Cut three 16″-long pieces of yellow yarn. Using pinking shears, cut a 15″-diameter circle from each piece of fabric.

Place filled jar in the center of wrong side of fabric and gather at top with a rubber band. Referring to patterns and stitch details on page 309, embroider yellow seeds on strawberries in straight stitch and brown bud ends on pears in French knots. Place two felt fruit pieces together, wrong sides facing. Sew $\frac{1}{16}''$ in from outer edge, leaving top open. Leave needle in felt. Stuff fruit with a cotton ball; tuck end of yarn into top and continue stitching to close piece and secure yarn. Tack one leaf to each side at top. Tie decorated yarn lengths around top of jar to conceal rubber band.

For Box: Cardboard box is covered with burlap, then wrapped with a burlap-covered coil. Cut the following pieces from burlap:

A. Two pieces $4\frac{1}{2}''$ wide and 9″ long, to cover the box ends, inside and out. (Or measure the width of your box end and add 1″; for the length, use twice the height of the box end, plus 2″.)

B. One piece $9\frac{1}{2}''$ wide and 23″ long, to cover the box sides and bottom, inside and out. (Or measure your box and, for the width of this piece, use the total measurements of four times the height of the box, plus twice the width of the outside bottom of box, plus 2″.)

C. As many 3″-wide bias strips as needed to total about six yards when sewn together for coil (or eight times the perimeter of your box).

To Cover Box: Spray one side of one smaller piece of burlap (A) with adhesive; press onto one

inside end of box, over rim edge, and onto outside end, overlapping burlap on outside bottom. Repeat for other end piece.

Spray one side of the large piece of burlap (B) with adhesive and press onto box as follows: Starting at outside bottom edge of one side, press burlap onto the side, over rim edge, and onto inner side; continue pressing burlap down onto inside box bottom, on the second side, over rim edge, and onto the outer side; continue over bottom edge, and onto outside box bottom, overlapping excess fabric on the first side.

Stitch all the bias strips (C) together to make one 3″-wide strip that is about six yards long; trim seams. Cut about six yards of soft cable cord and about seven yards of strong heavy twine for pulling casing over cable cord (twine will be removed afterwards).

To Make Padded Coil: Referring to the diagram and starting at one end, work a small portion at a time as follows: Fold burlap strip in half lengthwise, right side inward; place pulling twine inside folded burlap strip; sew end of twine securely to burlap at one end; sew cable cord securely to the outside of burlap at same end. Let cable cord hang on the outside of your work. Machine-stitch long edges of burlap strip together, encasing twine; at the start, sew very close to raw edges for about 3″ to facilitate turning; continue sewing raw edges together with a $\frac{5}{8}''$ seam for the total length of the six yards. Trim the seam to $\frac{3}{8}''$, leaving strip the full width for the first 3″. Hold burlap in one hand and pull twine with the other. As burlap turns right side out, it is filled with the cable cord and the twine end becomes longer as one replaces the other. When burlap tube is turned completely right side out, cut off the first 3″ where twine and cord were attached. Taper both ends of the coil and slip-stitch closed.

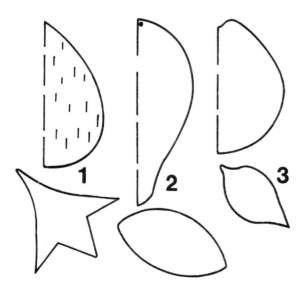

To Wrap Covered Box With Coil: Thread tapestry needle with polished jute. Starting at one bottom corner, slip-stitch coil to bottom edge of box around perimeter. Slip-stitch the next rib of coil to the one before; continue in this manner to top edge of box, ending at one corner. The coil should go around box seven or eight times. To finish box at top edge, attach the last rib of coil to the inside perimeter of box, using a blanket stitch.

VEGETABLE BANNERS

Shown on page 105

SIZE: $18\frac{1}{2}''\times 17\frac{1}{4}''$.

EQUIPMENT: Flat pan. Two spring clothespins. Wooden stick or spoon. Stove or hot plate. Iron. Newspapers. Facilities for rinsing with cold water. Measuring spoons. Paper for patterns. Thin, stiff cardboard. Tracing paper. Pencil. Ruler. Scissors. Dressmaker's tracing (carbon) paper. Tracing wheel or dry ball-point pen. Zigzag sewing machine.

MATERIALS: For each banner: one piece of small-print fabric $12\frac{1}{4}''\times 13\frac{1}{2}''$; one piece of contrasting-print fabric $16''\times 18\frac{1}{4}''$. For appliqués: unbleached muslin or white cotton fabric for dyed pieces; red-orange fabric $6''\times 8''$; small amounts of dark green and light yellow-green fabric. Small amount of polyester fiberfill. Sewing thread to match fabrics. Rit dyes, one package each of following colors: Yellow #1, Purple #13, Wine #10, Fuchsia #12, Dark Green #35.

DIRECTIONS: TO DYE FABRIC: Read directions on dye package and relate them to following procedures. Prewash unbleached muslin or white cotton fabric to be dyed. If mottled effect is needed, gather and clip wet fabric with clothespin. Place about 1" of water in flat pan and bring to boil. Add dye according to individual directions; stir well. Place wet fabric in simmering dyebath for 10 minutes. Remove fabric and unclip clothespin. Rinse in cool running water until water runs clear. Roll fabric in newspaper and squeeze out excess moisture. Hang up fabric or lay on newspaper to dry. Iron. If second color is to be added, repeat the dyeing process.

Eggplant: Add two tablespoons of purple and one tablespoon of wine dye to water. Gather wet 9" square of fabric in random folds and clip. Gathering should be haphazard so as to produce a mottled and shaded effect. Place fabric in dye pan, leaving part outside. Simmer, rinse, dry, and iron.

Asparagus: Add one tablespoon each of olive green and yellow dye to water. Dye wet $10''\times 13''$ piece of fabric; rinse. Gather four points of fabric and secure with clothespin. Prepare dyebath of two tablespoons of purple dye; submerge points of green-dyed fabric, leaving rest of piece outside pan. The result will be a mottled effect with predominantly purple shades along the edges and green shades in the center of fabric. Simmer, rinse, dry, and iron.

Radish: Dissolve two tablespoons fuchsia dye in one cup of water. Randomly gather wet 9" square of fabric and hold together with clothespin. Place fabric in dyebath so that pinched fabric remains outside. Simmer, rinse, dry, and iron.

Leaves and Stems: Dissolve one-half package yellow and one tablespoon dark green dye in pan. Place wet fabric in dye and push to one side so that part of fabric is out of water. Simmer 10 minutes. Before removing fabric from pan, spread out so that entire piece is in dye; simmer two minutes more. Rinse, dry, and iron.

TO MAKE BANNERS: Read How to Appliqué (by Machine) on page 304. Enlarge patterns by copying on paper ruled in 1" squares. Short dash lines indicate overlapped pieces; dotted lines indicate detail stitching; arrows show straight of goods. For each banner, transfer outline of complete design to center of background fabric, using dressmaker's carbon and tracing wheel (or dry ball-point pen). Trace each separate part of design, glue tracings to cardboard, and cut out for appliqué patterns. Following directions in How to Appliqué, cut each appliqué piece from fabrics indicated in individual directions; trace detail lines. Pin, straight-stitch, and zigzag appliqués in place, setting machine for wide stitch (#1). Add inner

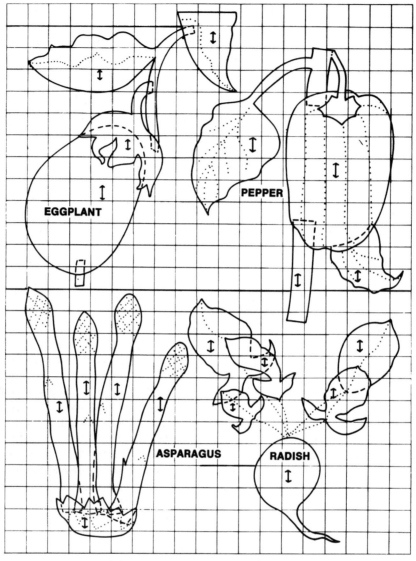

Banner Patterns

detail lines with narrow stitch (#0-1). Use machine thread for appliqués and details unless otherwise indicated.

Eggplant: Cut eggplant from a well-variegated area of dyed purple fabric; cut leaves and stems from dyed green fabric. Stitch appliqués in place. Sew on eggplant first, leaving top open; stuff lightly, then close. Pin leaves and stems in place, overlapping as indicated on pattern, then stitch.

Asparagus: Cut four stalks and one base from dyed purple-green fabric, with tips of stalks in purple area. Sew on stalks first with light green thread, overlapping as shown and stuffing lightly as you go. Then sew on base with purple thread, overlapping stalks at bottom. Stitch all detail lines with purple thread.

Radish: Cut radish from dyed fuchsia fabric, with root in lighter section. Cut two larger leaves from dark green fabric and three smaller leaves from light yellow-green. Sew on dark green leaves first, then stitch their stem lines (second and fourth on pattern) with same thread, using wide stitch. Add leaf details with narrow stitch. Sew on light green leaves, then stitch their stem lines (first, third, and fifth on pattern) with same thread, using wide stitch. Add leaf details with narrow stitch. Sew on radish with red thread, leaving bottom open; stuff lightly, then close with white thread.

Pepper: Cut pepper from red-orange fabric, leaves and steams from dyed green fabric. Sew on leaves and stems first, leaving stem that connects with pepper free. Add detail lines to leaves with dark green thread. Sew on pepper, leaving one end open; stuff lightly, then close. Add detail lines to pepper. Sew connecting stem in place.

Borders: Choose fabric for borders that contrasts with background color of appliquéd piece. Cut four strips of border fabric, each 4″ wide: two $14\frac{1}{2}$″ long and two $18\frac{1}{4}$″ long. On $14\frac{1}{2}$″ strips, turn in long edges $\frac{1}{2}$″ and press. Fold strips in half lengthwise, wrong side inward, and press. Pin and baste strips to $13\frac{1}{2}$″ sides of appliquéd piece, enclosing $\frac{1}{2}$″ edge of piece with folded edges of strip and having $\frac{1}{2}$″ extending at both ends of strip. Topstitch strips in place, $\frac{1}{4}$″ from folded edges. Sew remaining two strips to top and bottom of appliquéd piece in same manner, but turning in ends of strips $\frac{1}{2}$″ before topstitching to piece. Slip-stitch ends closed. Press. (**Note:** If you wish to hang banners with a dowel or rod, leave ends open.)

PANTRY NEEDLEPOINT
Shown on page 125

SIZE: Approximately $11\frac{1}{4}$″ × $12\frac{1}{2}$″.

EQUIPMENT: Masking tape. Scissors. Ruler. Tapestry needle. Stapler. Dressmaker's tracing (carbon) paper. Dry ball-point pen. Colored pencil. Thumbtacks. Fine-tipped waterproof felt marker.

For Blocking: Softwood surface. Brown paper.

MATERIALS: Mono needlepoint canvas 17 mesh-to-the inch, 15″ × 16″. Persian yarn, one 40-yard skein of each color listed in color key. Small amount gold metallic thread. Wooden stretcher frame, $11\frac{1}{4}$″ × $12\frac{1}{2}$″. Staples.

DIRECTIONS: Read Needlepoint How-To's on page 306. Using sharp colored pencil, draw lines across pattern by connecting grid lines. Enlarge pattern by copying on paper ruled in 1″ squares. To transfer pattern, thumbtack canvas to a softwood surface. Lay pattern on top, centered, with dressmaker's carbon between; tape pattern in place. Go over lines of design with a dry ball-point pen. Remove pattern. If necessary, strengthen lines with a fine-tipped waterproof marker. There should be four meshes between jars, one mesh between a row of jars and its shelf, and three meshes between jars at each end of shelves and side borders. In marking, it is not necessary to define each shape precisely; it will work out in stitching.

To work the design, separate the Persian yarn into three 2-ply strands. Work with either one or two of the strands in needle, as specified below for each area of design. Follow color and stitch keys on page 142. For continental stitch, see page 306. Work French knots, satin stitch, and split stitch as you would for embroidery; see details on page 309.

Begin at top of canvas with first row of jars; fill in jars with pattern stitches, then work background around them in continental stitch, starting in upper right corner. Continue working toward bottom of canvas, filling in shelves, Grandma, cat and floor as you come to them. Work border last. When working pattern stitches, complete each shape by filling in with small stitches around edges; see details. For each cross-stitch pattern, make sure to work topmost stitches always in the same direction.

Jar Tops (H19): Two strands of wool yarn with 1 strand of metallic thread in needle. Work three stitches.

Peaches (F2): Two strands. Turn canvas sideways and work four rows of long-legged herringbone from left to right (bottom to top of jar). Begin each row with a shortened version of the stitch, as shown.

Olives (C3): One strand. Work a French knot over every intersection of canvas.

Corn (H1): One strand. Lay long stitches across width of jar, then cover with continental stitch.

Plums (J4), Pickles (K5): Two strands.

COLOR KEY

A—LT. GRAY
B—WHITE
C—BLACK
D—LT. BROWN
E—DK. BROWN
F—PUMPKIN
G—LT. YELLOW
H—DK. YELLOW
I—METALLIC GOLD

J—VIOLET
K—OLIVE
L—RED
M—DK. RED
N—BLUE
O—CORAL
P—MED. GRAYS (2)
Q—LT. BLUE
R—FLESH

ADDITIONAL STITCHES

1—CONTINENTAL STITCH
3—FRENCH KNOT
9—SATIN STITCH
12—SPLIT STITCH

DE12

A1

EHI9

B1

| F2 | C3 | H1 | J4 | K5 | LM6 | N7 | J4 | O11 |

E
12

| H1 | LM6 | K5 | | O11 | C3 | H1 | F2 | N7 |

P9   P9

E
12

N7   R9   LM 6

| K5 | F2 | | | | F2 | J4 | K5 | C3 |

Q8

R9   R9

E
12

B9

| O11 | J4 | C3 | H1 | O11 | K5 | N7 | LM6 |

E
12

A1   B1   Q8

BCF
12

C1

D10

D10

P9

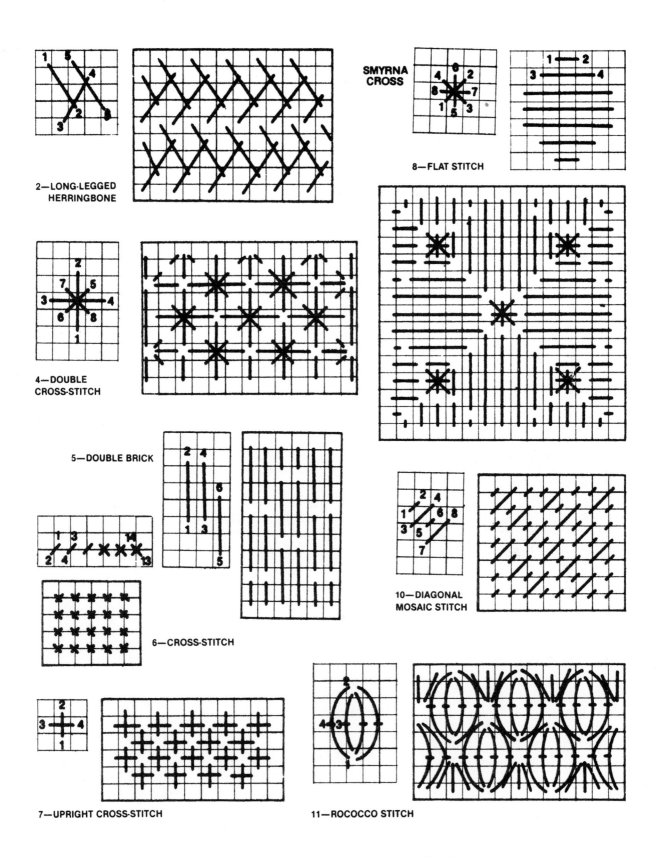

2—LONG-LEGGED HERRINGBONE

4—DOUBLE CROSS-STITCH

SMYRNA CROSS

8—FLAT STITCH

5—DOUBLE BRICK

6—CROSS-STITCH

10—DIAGONAL MOSAIC STITCH

7—UPRIGHT CROSS-STITCH

11—ROCOCCO STITCH

Cherries (LM6): One strand. Work cross-stitches at random with red, then fill in spaces with dark red.

Blueberries (N7): One strand. Complete each upright cross-stitch before going on to next.

Tomatoes (O11): One strand.

Shelves (E12): Two strands. Work one row of split stitch.

Grandma: For hair, work with two shades of medium gray in needle, one strand of each. Work

143

bun over a pencil. Work dress with two strands for flat stitch, one strand for smyrna cross-stitch. Work flesh, belt, and shoes with two strands.

Cat (BCJ12): One strand. Stagger rows of split stitch, working over two meshes for neck area, three meshes for remainder.

Floor (D10): One strand. Work diagonal mosaic stitch in one direction for right half of floor and in opposite direction for left half of floor; see pattern.

Border (DE12): Two strands (one dark brown, one light brown). Work three staggered rows of split stitch.

Finishing: When needlepoint is complete, block piece right side up, following directions on page 307. Place canvas over stretcher frame, staple to underside of frame.

"COFFEE BREAK" BORDER

Shown on page 126

SIZE: Each motif, $12\frac{1}{8}''\times16\frac{5}{8}''$, to be repeated to fit length of shelf.

EQUIPMENT: Pencil. Paper for pattern. Ruler. Scissors. Sewing and embroidery needles. Dressmaker's tracing (carbon) paper. Dry ballpoint pen. Straight pins. Embroidery hoop. Masking tape. White thread.

MATERIALS: Tightly woven white linen fabric, cut to the following measurements: depth of shelf + 13″ × length of shelf + 1″. DMC six-strand embroidery floss, bright blue or color or your choice, 3 skeins per motif.

DIRECTIONS: Using sharp pencil, draw lines across pattern, connecting grid lines, horizontally and vertically. Enlarge pattern by copying on paper ruled in 1″ squares. Place masking tape along two short sides and one long side of fabric to keep from raveling. Starting in center, plan repeated motifs along remaining long side of linen fabric, with design facing outwards. Place pattern on fabric where you have planned first repeat of motif, with scallop along raw edge. Slip carbon paper between pattern and linen and, using dry ballpoint pen, go over lines of design to transfer to fabric. Reposition pattern for second repeat, lining up placement with a straight pin. Transfer design as many times as planned. If entire motif does not fit at either end, simply continue scalloped line at bottom of design to meet outside corners of shelf. Cut along scalloped line. Using embroidery hoop and all six strands of embroidery floss, embroider scalloped edge of border in a very close buttonhole stitch, then rest of design in stem stitch (see Stitch Details on pages 302-303).

Fold, pin, press, and slip-stitch a doubled $\frac{1}{4}''$ hem on remaining three sides of fabric. Lightly press entire piece.

Pattern for Coffee Break Border

Although the Colonists' color schemes were simple, their love for bright colors is obvious. You can carry on this tradition in your decor, combining bright colors for warm—and spectacular—results. Start with the appliqued plume quilt (page 165). Finish the setting with folk-art accessories: a needlepoint sampler (page 175), rooster lamp (page 172) and tooled chest (page 169).

QUILT STENCIL BUILD STITCH

Use four techniques to recreate the charm of years gone by. The starting point for this flower-filled room is our royal blue spread with basket of flowers, quilted with white thread for definition. The dust ruffle and canopy are quick to stitch on the sewing machine. To complete the flowery setting, make comfy cushions for a chair, a simple cloth for any table. The canopy bed becomes the room's focal point—and you can construct it yourself! Counted cross-stitch is used to make a coordinating sampler. To underscore the scene, stencil a 90" floorcloth in a traditional patchwork pattern. Directions for all begin on page 175.

147

Prints, stripes and solids create our blue-on-white eight-point Winter Star quilt. Triangles and diamonds extend from octagonal center to ring of pieced squares.

We've teamed the quilt with bright crocheted
accents—a fringed afghan (54" × 69")
and soft pillow (16" × 24").
Each is worked in a geometric pattern
in popcorn crochet on afghan stitch. Make
them, as we've done, in rose-colored yarn;
they'll warm any room this winter!
Directions for all begin on page 193.

*"Milk glass" design afghan has giant monogram and
deep border of popcorns. The whole pattern is worked in
chain single crochet. And, for cold winter nights, crocheted
cases cover hot water bottles. Directions on page 198.*

Ten textured pattern
stitches borrowed
from Irish sweaters are
worked in squares,
then alternated with
plain squares to lend
variety to this handsome
afghan. Bands of garter
stitch and cable stitch
borders delineate the
patterns. Inishmore
directions on page 215.

Extra-easy knitted afghan is all in garter stitch. Four strips of black all-knit rows alternate with three made from your odds and ends of yarn. Sew strips together, cover seams with cross-stitch. Finish afghan with shell edging in crochet. Patch Panels directions on page 218.

VANISHING APPLE

Shown on page 126

EQUIPMENT: Pencil. Ruler. Scissors. Tapestry needle. Masking or adhesive tape. Single-edge razor blade or mat knife. **For Blocking:** Soft wood board. Rustproof tacks. Brown paper.

MATERIALS: Penelope double mesh needlepoint canvas, 10 mesh-to-the-inch, 36″ wide, $\frac{1}{4}$ yd. Tapestry yarn, 8-yd. skeins: 3 skeins apple red; one light red; one hot pink; one brown; one olive green; one white. Stainless steel frame with backing, 10″ × 25″ rabbet size. One sheet red paper (Color-Aid, Pantone, etc.) All-purpose glue. Mat board in color to match canvas, 6″ × 18″.

DIRECTIONS: With ruler and pencil, mark four rectangles 6″ high and 4$\frac{1}{2}$″ wide, being sure to leave 3″ margin between rectangles and 1$\frac{1}{2}$″ at top and bottom.

Read needlepoint directions on page 306. Following charts below, work needlepoint in continental stitch. Center an apple in each marked area of canvas.

Block completed piece according to directions on page 307. When dry, cut into four pieces, keeping 1$\frac{1}{2}$″ margins on all edges.

Mounting: Cut mat board into four pieces each 6″ × 4$\frac{1}{2}$″. Cover each piece with a needlepoint rectangle, folding canvas margin to back, pulling it taut, and gluing it securely; let dry. Cut red paper to fit frame; glue to frame backing. When dry, center apples on red-covered backing, being sure to leave 1″ between each picture; glue securely. Fit and secure in frame.

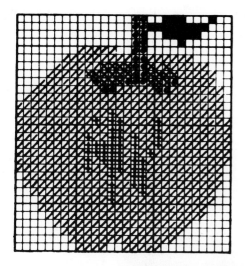
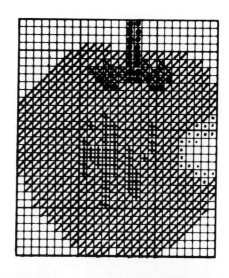

- ▨ APPLE RED
- ⊞ LT. RED
- ⊠ PINK
- ◉ BROWN
- ▩ GREEN
- ⊡ WHITE

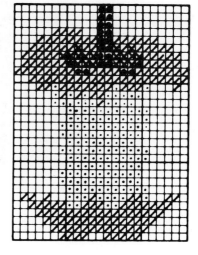

RED AND WHITE QUILT

Shown on page 127

SIZE: 73″ × 85″.

EQUIPMENT: Pencil. Ruler. Scissors. Graph paper. Thin, stiff cardboard. All-purpose glue. Sewing needle. Straight pins.

MATERIALS: Closely woven cotton fabric 45″ wide, 5 yards white, 3 yards red. White fabric for lining 45″ wide, 4¼ yards (can be same as patchwork fabric). White sewing thread. Polyester batting.

DIRECTIONS: Read General Directions for Quilting, page 300. Quilt is made up of 30 pieced blocks plus border strips. Two patterns are needed for the piecing: For pattern A, draw a 2³⁄₁₆″ square on graph paper; draw a diagonal line connecting two opposite corners. Glue paper to cardboard, let dry, and cut on marked lines for a triangle pattern. For pattern B, draw a rectangle and

mark off one corner as shown in Pattern Diagram; cut off corner and make cardboard pattern as for A. Replace patterns as edges become frayed from use.

Patch Pieces: See General Directions.

From white fabric, cut piece 25″ × 88″ and set aside for borders. From remaining white fabric, cut 360 of A and 240 of B. From red fabric, cut piece 8″ × 83″ and set aside. From remaining red, cut 480 of A.

Piecing a Block: To join pieces, hold them with right sides facing and stitch along marked seam line; if hand stitching, make small, even stitches, about 16 to the inch. Press seams to one side as you work, white fabric under red.

Make a square patch by joining a red A piece and a white A piece as shown in Fig. 1; make eight square patches. Join two patches into a row (Fig. 2); make two rows. Join the two rows for a center block (Fig. 3).

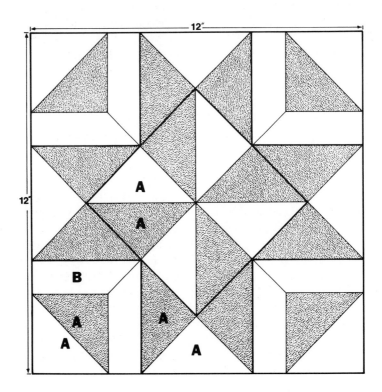

Piecing Diagram

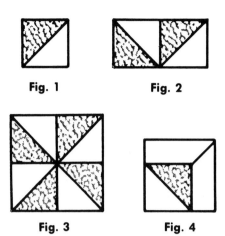

Fig. 1   Fig. 2

Fig. 3   Fig. 4

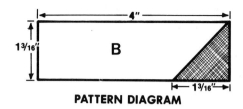

PATTERN DIAGRAM

Join two B pieces around a square patch for a corner block (Fig. 4). Make four corner blocks.

Join the four corner blocks, the center block, eight red and four white A pieces into a quilt block, as shown in Piecing Diagram. Block should measure 12″ square, plus outside seam allowance. Make 30 quilt blocks.

Assembling Quilt Top: Join the 30 quilt blocks into six horizontal rows of five blocks each. Piece should measure 60″ × 72″, plus outside seam allowance. (Before cutting border strips, measure your piece and cut longer or shorter strips if necessary.)

For first border, cut four 3″-wide strips from reserved white fabric: two 65½″ long and two 77½″ long (measurements include seam allowance). Sew strips to quilt top with ¼″ seams, leaving an equal amount at each end (2¾″); miter corners. For second border, cut four 2″-wide strips from red fabric: two 68½″ long and two 80½″ long; sew to first border in same manner. For third border, cut four 3¼″-wide strips from white fabric: two 74″ long and two 86″ long; sew to second border. Quilt top should measure 74″ × 86″.

Assembling Quilt: From lining fabric, cut two pieces 43½″ × 74″. Sew together on long edges

with ½″ seam to make lining 74″ × 86″. Cut two batting layers same size.

Place quilt top and lining together, right sides facing; place batting against lining. Pin layers together, then baste. Stitch all around perimeter of quilt with ½″ seams, leaving large opening at one end. Turn quilt right side out and slip-stitch closed.

Tufting: Place quilt flat, right side up. You will note that a square design appears wherever four blocks meet. At outer corner of each square design, insert a straight pin through to lining side; include partial squares all around edge. Turn quilt over to lining side. At each pin point, tuft quilt, using doubled sewing thread in needle: Push needle from lining to right side, leaving about 5″ of thread on lining side. Push needle back up to surface, about ⅛″ away. Tie ends in firm double knot, then clip ends to ½″.

STENCILED MATS
Shown on page 128

SIZE: 11½″ × 18″.

EQUIPMENT: Tracing paper. Ruler. Pencil. Colored pencil. Lightweight cardboard. Black felt-tipped marking pen. Rubber cement. Hard cutting surface. Waxed stencil paper, available at art supply stores. Mat knife with swivel blade. Stencil brush, #5. Transparent tape. Soft cloths. Paper towels. Newspapers. Shallow dish. Paintbrush, 1″ wide. Medium to fine sandpaper. Saber saw. Pipe clamps.

MATERIALS: For Four Place Mats: Stock size clear pine, ½″ × 12″ × 6′, or hardboard, ¼″ thick 2′ × 3′, smooth on both sides. Pine lattice for edging clear pine mats, $\frac{1}{4}'' \times \frac{1}{2}'' \times 8'$. Waterproof white glue. Walnut stain. Turpentine. Metallic gold acrylic tube paint. Clear satin-finish polyurethane.

DIRECTIONS: To Make Stencils: Use sharp colored pencil to draw lines across each stencil pattern, connecting grid lines. Enlarge patterns by copying on tracing paper ruled in 1″ squares. Go over tracings with black felt-tipped markers; mount tracings on cardboard with rubber cement.

Position and tape mounted tracings on hard cutting surface, then tape waxed stencil paper on top. Using swivel knife, cut out stencil design along black lines. If you tear or break stencil, repair with transparent tape on back of stencil and cut away excess tape. Cut a stencil for each design and several for the border design.

Preparing Wood or Hardboard: Mark and cut pine into four 18″-long pieces. To finish edges of clear pine and help prevent warping, mark and cut $\frac{1}{4}'' \times \frac{1}{2}''$ lattice to fit cut ends of each pine mat. Place glue on each cut edge and clamp on lattice strips. Remove clamps when glue is dry. If using hardboard, mark and cut four $11\frac{1}{2}'' \times 18''$ pieces.

Sand all cut edges smooth. If using pine, sand face smooth. Dust. Following manufacturer's directions, prepare stain, thinning color with turpentine as desired. Test color on scrap; adjust color as desired. Brush stain on place mats, allow to set 2 or 3 minutes, and wipe away excess stain with soft, clean cloths. Allow mats to dry overnight.

Stenciling: Position and tape stencil centered on mat. Squeeze out a small amount of metallic gold acrylic in a shallow dish. Dip stencil brush in paint and blot excess paint onto a pad of paper towels. Fill in cut-out area of stencil with paint, holding brush upright and working paint onto board with an up and down stipping motion. Carefully lift stencil and allow design to dry. For stenciled border, tape stencils in place $\frac{1}{2}$ in from outside edges. Arrange two border motifs on ends and four on long sides. Complete border; let dry. Repeat procedure described above to stencil remaining three place mat designs, using the same border motif for each.

To finish, brush two light coats of polyurethane on mats, including backs and edges; let dry.

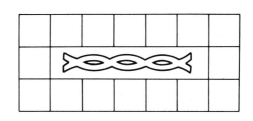

Border Design

Place mat patterns

Each square = 1″

157

CORN DOLLS

Shown on page 129

SIZE: Each doll, $14\frac{1}{2}''$ tall.

EQUIPMENT: Paper for patterns. Colored pencil. Tracing paper. Dressmaker's tracing (carbon) paper. Ruler. Scissors. Pencil or dry ball-point pen. Thumbtacks. Wooden canvas stretchers to suit. Double boiler. Sticks for stirring. Immersible thermometer. Tjanting tool, #1 or #2. Flat, stiff brush, $\frac{1}{2}''$ wide. Dye bath containers. Rubber gloves. Apron. Iron. Ironing board. Paper towels. Newspapers. Sewing needle. Sewing machine.

MATERIALS: For Five Corn Dolls: Unbleached muslin 36" wide, 2 yards (see Note below). Polyester batting. All-purpose fabric dyes in the following colors: lemon yellow, bright green, brown, purple, maroon, copper and black. Dye fixative. Table salt. Paraffin and beeswax, $\frac{1}{2}$ lb. of each. Fine-point felt-tipped marker. Matching sewing threads.

Note: If you do not want to batik the corn prints, you can substitute small-checked gingham or calico fabrics as desired. From patterns, recalculate amounts of each fabric required.

GENERAL DIRECTIONS: Using sharp colored pencil, draw lines across patterns, connecting grid lines. Enlarge patterns on paper ruled in 1" squares. Cut a 6" × 36" strip from muslin and put aside for heads. Wash remaining fabric to preshrink and remove all sizing; allow to dry. Iron. Spread fabric flat on work surface, then place patterns on right side of fabric with dressmaker's carbon between. Go over patterns with pencil or dry ball-point pen to transfer; mark $\frac{1}{4}''$ all around each shape for seam allowance. Transfer ten corncob bodies, leaves and hair pieces, grouping each set in blocks that can be cut apart. Also transfer ten head pieces (head outline only) to unwashed muslin; put aside. Cut apart blocks of bodies, leaves and hair pieces; do not cut out individual pieces.

To Prepare Wax: Prepare a mixture of half paraffin and beeswax for batik wax. With $1\frac{1}{2}''$ of water in lower part of double boiler, heat wax in top part. Stirring occasionally, heat wax to 170°F. After wax has melted, allow it to cool a little before applying to fabric. Be careful not to spill water

near pot of hot wax; the water causes wax to splatter and you can get severely burned. If fire occurs, extinguish with salt or baking soda, **not** water. Cover work surface and floor underneath it with newspapers.

To Paint with Wax: Because the lines are delicate you will work mostly with the tjanting tool. Dip tjanting in hot wax, and, being very careful not to drip wax, guide spout along marked guidelines. For larger areas, use $\frac{1}{2}''$ brush. Dip brush in wax and press out any air or moisture against side of pan. Before starting to wax fabric, test on fabric scraps first: if wax spot is dark, wax is ready; if not, allow wax to heat through.

With even strokes, apply wax to fabric areas not to be dyed by first color. Work carefully within the design area, because the hot wax has a tendency to run. Be careful not to drip wax on fabric.

To Prepare Dye Bath: Following manufacturer's directions, prepare hot dye bath, starting with lightest color. Allow dye bath to cool. Gently immerse waxed fabric into dye bath, and add dye fixative and salt as indicated. Remove fabric from dye bath and rinse in clear, cold water; blot up excess water with paper towels. Hang up straight and smooth to dry. If color is too pale, dye again.

To Remove Wax: To protect ironing board, cover it with newspapers. Place fabric on ironing board between layers of paper towels. Set iron for cotton and check frequently that iron does not become too hot. As the heat of the iron is applied, the wax will melt and be absorbed by the paper. As the paper becomes saturated, replace it with fresh paper towels. Repeat until all wax is absorbed and no wax shows on papers. Since the heat is a color-fastening agent, iron entire fabric well. Have fabric dry-cleaned to remove all traces of wax and to clean fabric thoroughly.

CORN DOLLS: Prepare yellow dye and dye corncob body fabric. Remove and dry fabric; iron. Stretch and tack body and leaf fabrics on canvas stretchers in turn, pull taut and hold in place with thumbtacks. Heat wax and brush it on corn kernels of bodies and on veins of leaves. Prepare green dye bath and dip both body and leaves in bath. Remove body fabric after a few minutes, rinse and hang up to dry. Repeat for leaves after fabric is bright green. Iron bodies to remove wax and stretch over frame again, then reapply wax to top portion of each design for about 2″ or 3″ down. Prepare brown dye and soak body fabric for a few minutes. Remove, rinse and dry.

Referring to the General Directions, iron out all wax in both leaf and body fabrics. Dry-clean if desired.

Cut apart pairs of hair pieces and dye one pair each brown, maroon, copper, purple and black. Rinse and let dry. Also, from remaining washed muslin, cut a 1½″ × 28″ strip; dye purple. Rinse and dry. Iron all dyed pieces.

To assemble dolls, cut out heads. With right sides facing, stitch pairs of heads together, leaving neck end open. Clip curves; turn heads. Stuff heads fully with pull-apart batting. With felt-tipped marker, draw in facial features. Cut out hair pieces. With right sides facing, stitch matching pairs together, leaving opening to turn. Clip curves and turn. Fold in raw edges and slip-stitch opening closed. Gather hair at center as indicated on pattern by dash lines, using needle and thread to create top knot. Shape hair, top knot out, around heads; blindstitch in place.

Cut out all bodies and leaves. With right sides facing, stitch body pieces together in pairs, leaving both ends open. Turn body; insert and pull head through neck end. Fold in raw edges around neck; blindstitch. Stuff body fully, tuck in raw edges at bottom end; hem. Insert a small scrap of muslin at bottom end, to create a base. Cut batting to shape for each leaf pair. With right sides facing and batting piece on top, stitch leaves together, leaving wide end open. Turn. Fold in raw edges at end; sew. Referring to illustration, page 129, fold leaf around bottom end of body and blindstitch leaf in place at bottom and about three-quarters up body. Make five dolls. Fold purple strip, long edges to center and then in half again lengthwise. Press. Slip-stitch strip along ends and long edge. Bind dolls together as in illustration.

Each square = 1″

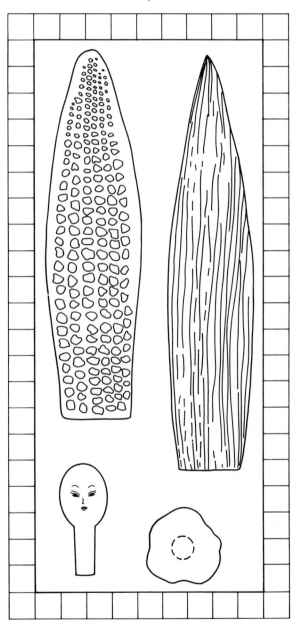

Pattern for Corn Dolls

STENCILED DRAFT STOPS

Shown on page 129

SIZE: Each about 39″ long.

EQUIPMENT: Tracing paper. Pencil. Ruler. Colored pencil. Lightweight cardboard. Black felt-tipped marking pen. Rubber cement. Hard cutting surface. Waxed stencil paper, available at most art-supply stores. Mat knife with swivel blade. Stencil brushes, #5. Small shallow dish. Transparent tape. Paper towels. Newspaper. Large funnel. Sewing machine.

MATERIALS: Cotton velveteen 45″ wide, $\frac{1}{4}$ yard each orange-red or tan. Matching sewing thread. Clear plastic drop cloth (available at most hardware stores). Transparent thread. Acrylic tube paints: metallic gold, brown, and ochre. Sand.

DIRECTIONS: Read How to Stencil on Fabric, page 305. **To Make Stencil:** Using sharp colored pencil, draw connecting grid lines across each stencil pattern. Enlarge pattern by copying design on tracing paper ruled in $\frac{1}{2}$″ squares. Go over tracings with black felt-tipped marking pen. Mount tracings and cut out stencils as directed on page 305.

Stenciling: Cut a 7″ × 40″ piece from velveteen. Cover work surface with newspapers, then tape velveteen, right side facing up, to work surface, keeping fabric taut. Tape a stencil to velveteen, centered on width of fabric as directed below for each Stop. Squeeze a small amount of acrylic paint into dish. Dip stencil brush into paint, then blot on a pad of paper toweling until brush is almost dry. Holding brush upright, work paint onto fabric with an up and down stippling motion, filling in cut-out design of stencil. Carefully lift stencil; set aside. For additional motifs, tape a dry stencil to velveteen and stencil in same manner as first motif. Allow stenciling to dry.

Golden Birds: Stencil six birds on orange-red velveteen with metallic gold paint; place bird motifs 2″ apart, with first and last motifs 3″ from end.

Autumn Leaves: Stencil 15 leaves on tan velveteen, placing first leaf 1″ from one end. Stencil outer edges of leaf brown; let dry. Fill center of leaf with ochre. Position second leaf $\frac{1}{2}$″ from first, reversing stencil and placing stem in opposite di-

rection. Continue spacing leaves $\frac{1}{2}$″ apart and alternating direction, with last leaf 1″ from end.

Assembly: From plastic, cut 7″ × 40″ piece for lining each Stop. Fold plastic in half lengthwise and stitch $\frac{1}{2}$″ seam along one short end and down long side, using transparent thread and 15-stitches-per-inch gauge. Turn plastic. Fill solidly with sand, using funnel. Turn in raw edges of open end and topstitch closed. With right side inward, fold each velveteen cover in half lengthwise; stitch as for plastic liner. Trim seams to $\frac{1}{4}$″ and turn. Insert sand-filled plastic liner; turn in raw edges of open end and topstitch.

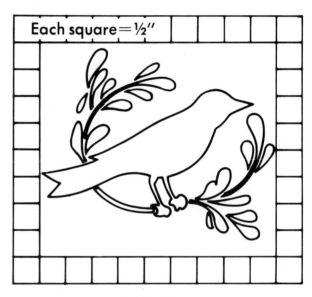

Golden Birds

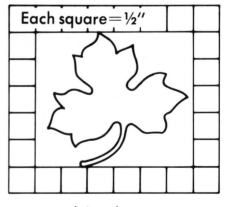

Autumn Leaves

FOOD POT HOLDERS

Shown on page 130

EQUIPMENT: Paper for patterns. Pencil. Ruler. Scissors. Sewing needle. Large-eyed embroidery needle.

MATERIALS: Tightly woven cotton fabric: two pieces approximately $6\frac{1}{2}'' \times 8\frac{1}{2}''$ for each; scraps of desired colors for food appliqués. Baby, regular, and large rickrack for edging as desired, about $\frac{3}{4}$ yard each. Sewing thread to match fabric and rickrack. Six-strand embroidery floss (see individual directions for colors). Piece of flannel or batting approximately $6'' \times 8''$ for each. Metal rings $\frac{3}{4}''$ diameter for hanging loops. Button for fish eye.

GENERAL DIRECTIONS: First read "How to Appliqué" on page 304.

Enlarge patterns by copying on paper ruled in $1''$ squares. The heavy lines indicate cutting lines; the finer lines indicate lines to be embroidered. For each, except for bean pot, cut two basic oval pieces for front and back from the same fabric, adding $\frac{1}{4}''$ for seam allowance. For bean pot, cut only one basic piece (complete outline) for back; the front is made up of four pieces sewn together. Cut the individual appliqués from fabric in colors shown, adding $\frac{1}{4}''$ all around for turning under. Following patterns, and directions on page 304, appliqué piece to right side on one basic piece.

Work embroidery following individual direc-

Patterns for Pot Holders

tions, and Stitch Details on page 308. Cut batting same size as basic piece; baste to wrong side of front, $\frac{1}{4}''$ from edge. With right sides facing, sew front and back pieces together, making $\frac{1}{4}''$ seam and leaving small opening for turning. Trim batting close to seam. Turn to right side; slip-stitch closed. Sew rickrack to outer edge on back or front. Sew ring to back at top edge.

HAM: Cut out a small circle from pink to indicate bone; clip around and turn under. First appliqué white fabric in place, then pink, then brown. Embroider lines in outline stitch with three strands of gold floss; embroider small circles in satin stitch with four strands of red floss; embroider crosses with three strands of black floss.

FISH: After appliquéing, sew on button for eye. Embroider lines on fish in outline stitch with two strands of blue floss; make the three lines on lemon in straight stitch with six strands of green floss. Make crosses and turkey work loops above and below fish with six strands of green floss.

FRIED EGG: Add thin layer of batting under egg white before appliquéing, for dimension.

WAFFLE: After appliquéing waffle and butter fabric in place, work backstitch along lines with one strand of tan floss, then make running stitch along short dash lines with three strands of brown floss.

BEAN POT: Cut the four front pieces as indicated, adding $\frac{1}{4}''$ extra all around each for seam allowance. Sew the four front pieces together; clip seams and press. Embroider letters in outline stitch with six strands of gold floss; embroider pot rim and beans with six strands of dark brown floss, as shown in illustration.

OWL AND CAT HOT MITTS

Shown on page 130

EQUIPMENT: Paper. Pencil. Ruler. Scissors. Straight pins. Zigzag sewing machine. Needle.

MATERIALS: Cotton fabric: **For Cat:** olive green and tan, each $6\frac{1}{2}'' \times 10\frac{1}{2}''$; red print, $6\frac{1}{2}''$ square; scraps of bright green, black, red. **For Owl:** olive green, $13''$ square; red print, $6\frac{1}{2}''$ square; scraps of white, black, orange. Cotton batting for pad-

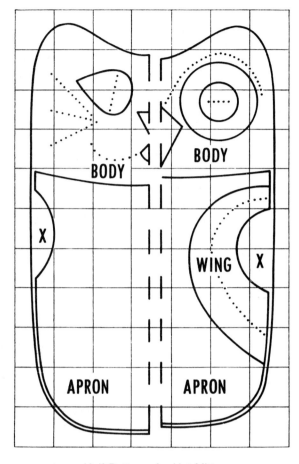

Half-Patterns for Hot Mitts

ding, $6'' \times 10''$ for each. Bias binding tape, olive green. Thread: olive green, yellow, black, bright green and red for cat: white for owl.

DIRECTIONS: Enlarge patterns by copying on paper ruled in $1''$ squares. Complete half-patterns indicated by long dash lines. Solid lines are cutting lines; dotted lines are embroidery lines.

Using patterns, cut complete outline for back of each of olive green fabric; cut another piece the same for front, using tan fabric for cat, olive green for owl. Cut padding for each the same size. Stitch padding to wrong side of back piece with zigzag stitch and olive green thread, about $\frac{1}{4}''$ inside edges. Cut away $\frac{1}{4}''$ of padding all around outside.

Cut features, for cat: green eyes, black nose, red tongue; for owl: white outer eyes, black pupils, orange beak. Baste features in place on front piece.

Using matching thread, work satin stitch on machine around each appliqué piece. For cat, make vertical irises in black satin stitch, widening slightly at center; make mouth in black satin stitch and whiskers in very narrow black satin stitch. For owl, make horizontal irises in yellow satin stitch, widening slightly at center; make eyebrows and cross at top of beak in black satin stitch. For Stitch Details, see page 308.

Cut each apron of red print fabric; cut out X area at sides. For cat, bind curved cutouts at sides with green bias tape; stitch with yellow thread in featherstitch. For owl, cut two wings of olive green; baste at each side of apron. Satin stitch wings to apron around larger curved edge with yellow thread; around smaller curved edge with featherstitch. Make center line in featherstitch with yellow thread. Bind top edge of each apron with green bias tape, using yellow featherstitch.

Place front piece over padding; pin apron in place and baste. Bind all together around outside with green bias tape, using yellow featherstitch.

For hanging loop for each, cut a piece of green bias tape $5\frac{1}{2}''$ long. Stitch long open edges together with yellow featherstitch. Fold tape in half crosswise; turn over ends $\frac{1}{4}''$. Place ends at center back of hot mitt at top and stitch in place.

FABRIC APPLIQUÉ PICTURES
Shown on page 132

EQUIPMENT: Scissors. Tracing paper. Pencil. Ruler. Single-edge razor blade. Square. Embroidery and fine needles. Back saw. Miter box. Hammer. Nail set. Sandpaper. Paintbrush.

MATERIALS: Cardboard: two pieces $15\frac{1}{4}'' \times 15\frac{3}{4}''$ for Coffee Mill; one piece $11'' \times 16\frac{1}{4}''$ for Telephone. Tightly woven lightweight cotton fabric: for backgrounds, gold and gray each $15\frac{1}{4}'' \times 15\frac{3}{4}''$ for Coffee Mill, and blue $11'' \times 16\frac{1}{4}''$ for Telephone; large and small scraps of fabric in solid colors and small designs such as paisley, calico, gingham checks, polka dots, and stripes (see illustrations on page 132 and follow individual directions for colors and patterns used). Scraps of felt: blue, yellow for Telephone; pale and olive green, tan, rust, and dark brown for Coffee Mill. Six-strand embroidery floss: black, green, tan, white. White sewing thread. For Telephone: gold metallic thread; gold cord 17″ long. All-purpose glue. **For frames:** Picture molding with $\frac{3}{16}''$ rabbet: $5\frac{1}{2}'$ for Coffee Mill; 5′ for Telephone. Wood filler. White and gold paint. Small brads.

GENERAL DIRECTIONS: Patterns are given at 50% of original; draw a $\frac{1}{2}''$ grid over patterns; enlarge patterns by copying on paper ruled in 1″ squares. Short dash lines on patterns indicate where pieces are overlapped. Following individual directions and using patterns, cut each piece of fabric, adding $\frac{1}{4}''$ seam allowance on all fabric edges. Clip curved edges; turn all seam allowances under and press flat. Cut pieces of felt as indicated in individual directions, with no seam allowances.

Pin appliqué pieces to background, placing pieces that are underneath down first. Slip-stitch in place with tiny stitches. See details for How to Appliqué on page 304.

For embroidery, use three strands of floss in needle. Stitch Details are on page 308. Make outline stitches along all long dash lines; outline those pieces indicated in individual directions in outline stitch. Solid black dots indicate French knots. Shaded areas indicate satin stitches. Tiny dash lines indicate backstitches. Dot-dash lines indicate chain stitches. Embroider some felt pieces before appliquéing, as indicated in individual directions.

Steam-press picture on back with moist cloth. Spread glue all along edges of cardboard and secure picture smoothly to appropriate-sized cardboard. Make mat for Coffee Mill as indicated in individual directions.

COFFEE MILL: Cut A and B of green calico. Cut C and D of pale green stripe. Cut E and F of rust. Cut G of white with tan check. Cut H and I of brown paisley. Cut J and M of tan felt. Cut K of dark brown felt. Cut L of olive green felt. Cut N of gold felt. Cut O of pale green felt. Cut coffee beans of dark brown and tan felt. Embroider and outline J and M with white floss before appliquéing. Appliqué all pieces except coffee beans, as indicated in General Directions. Embroider lines on A and B, D, E, and G with white floss. Outline bottom of D; outline E, F, G, and K with white

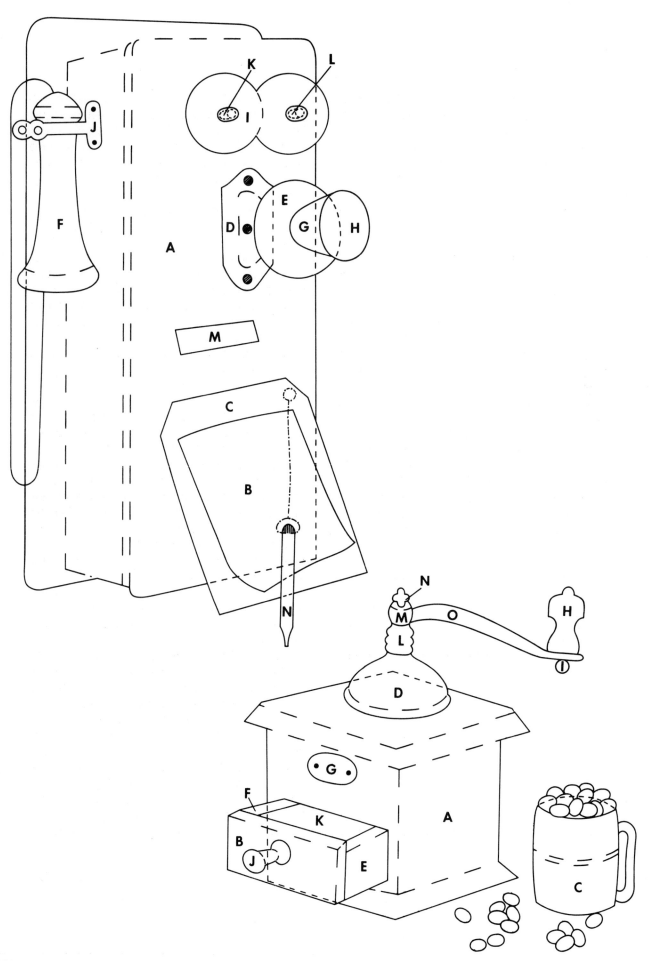

floss. Embroider lines on and outline C with medium green floss. Make French knots on G with tan floss. Tack coffee beans in place as shown, overlapping edges of some.

To make mat, measure $1\frac{1}{2}''$ from edges on all sides of second $15\frac{1}{4}'' \times 15\frac{3}{4}''$ piece of cardboard and mark, using square. Cut out center with razor blade and discard; remaining piece of cardboard is mat. Cut out piece of gray fabric the same shape as mat, with $\frac{1}{2}''$ on all sides for turning. Center mat over gray fabric. Clip fabric diagonally at inner corners. Turn excess fabric on all edges to back of mat and glue smoothly. Glue mat to picture front.

TELEPHONE: Cut A of brown striped paisley. Cut B of white with gray flower pattern. Cut C and D of solid gray. Cut E and F of yellow and white tiny gingham check. Cut G of black with white polka dots. Cut H of tiny black and white check. Cut I of rust. Cut J of blue felt. Cut K, L, M, and N of yellow felt. Work backstitch with black floss on K and L as indicated. Appliqué as indicated in General Directions, tacking on gold cord for telephone wire as shown. Embroider A with white floss. Then outline A and D with white floss. Embroider line and dots on D, and embroider lines on F with black floss. Outline F and I with black floss. With gold thread, make pencil chain and satin stitches on N for pencil eraser. Blacken tip of N in pencil or ink.

To Frame: Using miter box and back saw, cut picture molding to fit sides of picture; sand smooth. Glue and nail frame pieces together. Countersink nails and fill holes with wood filler. Paint frame with two coats of white paint; let dry. Paint front edges gold. Put picture inside frame; secure picture in place with brads.

PLUME QUILT
Shown on page 145

SIZE: 87″ square.
EQUIPMENT: Pencil. Scissors. Ruler. Thin, stiff cardboard. Tailor's chalk. Sewing and quilting needles. Quilting frame (optional). Glue.

MATERIALS: Closely woven cotton fabric 44″-45″ wide: navy, $6\frac{1}{4}$ yds. (less if you wish to piece border strips); red, 3 yds.; light orange, $2\frac{1}{2}$ yds. Fabric for lining 44″-45″ wide, 5 yds. Matching sewing thread. Navy bias binding tape, $\frac{1}{4}''$ wide double-folded, 10 yds. Polyester batting.

DIRECTIONS: Read General Directions for Quilting and How to Appliqué (pages 300 and 304). Quilt is constructed with four appliquéd blocks plus an appliquéd border.

Appliqués: Trace actual-size patterns for appliqués on next three pages; complete quarter and half-patterns indicated by dash lines; trace only one of the diamond-shaped petals for border flower. Glue tracings to cardboard and cut out, for appliqué patterns.

Following directions in How to Appliqué, cut and prepare appliqué pieces: From red fabric, cut four stars, 16 plumes, one center flower (outer section), 10 scallops, 40 diamond petals for border flower, and 16 stems. From light orange fabric, cut 16 plumes, one center flower (inner section), 10 scallops, and 32 diamond petals.

Blocks: From navy fabric, cut four blocks $34\frac{1}{2}''$ square (measurements include $\frac{1}{4}''$ seam allowance all around). Find center point of each and pin a star in place. Around each star, pin four red and four orange plumes, alternating colors and placing base of each plume in an indentation of star. Baste and slip-stitch appliqués in place, using matching thread.

Join blocks, first in pairs to make two strips, then join strips to make piece $68\frac{1}{2}''$ square. Appliqué center flower to center of piece, where all blocks meet.

Borders: From navy fabric, cut four strips $9\frac{3}{4}''$ × 87″ (measurements include $\frac{1}{4}''$ seam allowance). Find lengthwise center of each strip and pin a scallop in place along one center edge, as shown; pin an orange scallop on two strips and a red scallop on remaining strips. Place four more scallops on each strip as shown, alternating colors. Pin flower stems in place, with scallops overlapping ends, then flowers (join four diamond petals first to make complete flower); see illustration. Baste and slip-stitch appliqués in place.

Sew borders to quilt top, alternating colors and centering so an equal amount extends at each

Continued on page 169

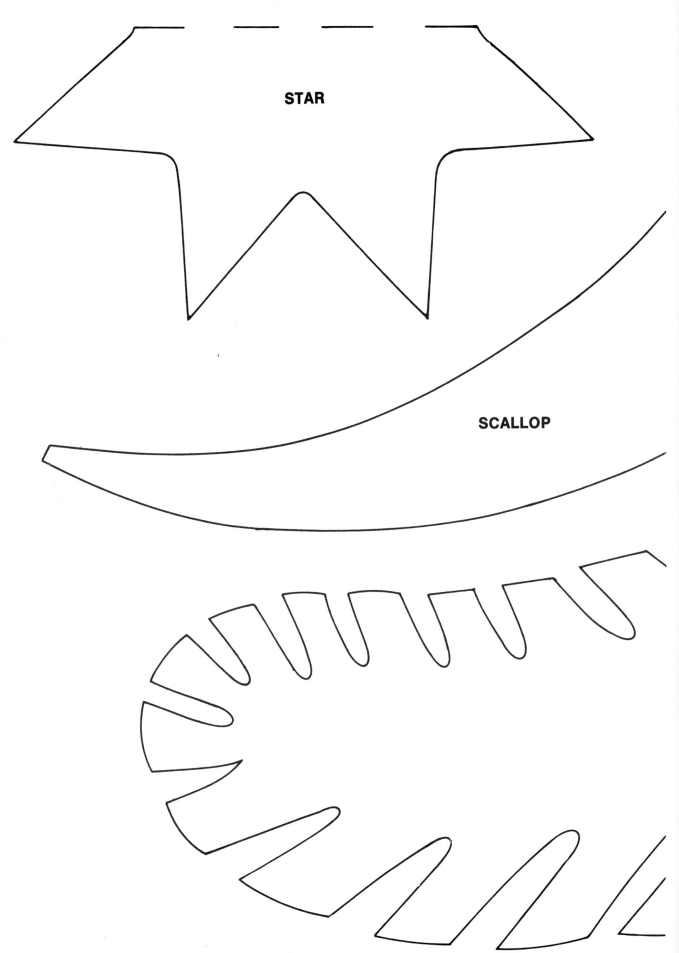

STAR

SCALLOP

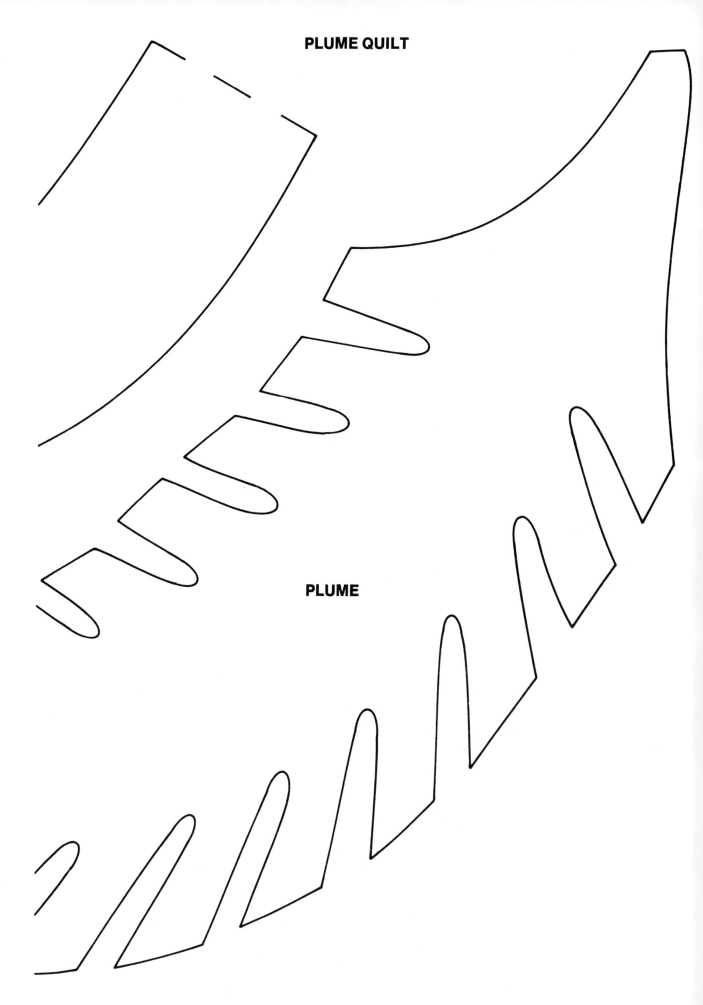

PLUME

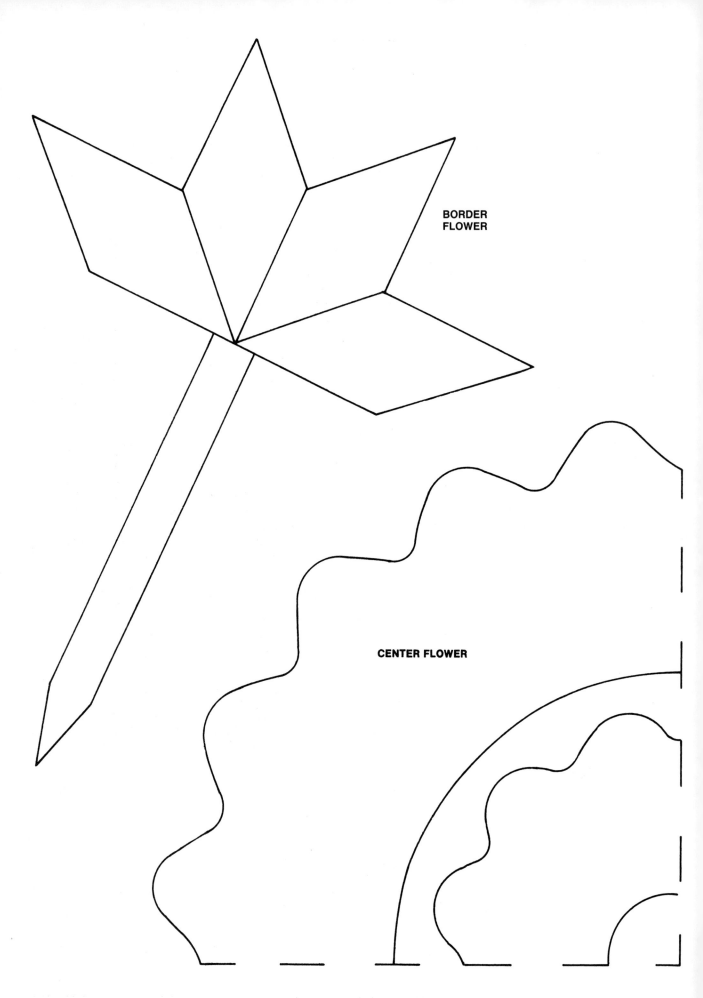

BORDER
FLOWER

CENTER FLOWER

Continued from page 165

end. Miter corners, following General Directions. Appliqué two diamond petals to inner corners of border as shown. Quilt top should measure 87″ square.

Lining: Cut two pieces 44″ × 87″. Sew together on long edges with $\frac{1}{2}$″ seams to make lining 87″ square. Cut batting same size.

Quilting: Following General Directions, pin and baste lining, batting, and quilt top together. Starting in center and working around and outward, quilt as follows: On each appliqué, quilt $\frac{1}{4}$″ in from seam; make additional quilting lines $\frac{1}{2}$″ apart on center flower, plumes, and scallops, following shape of pieces; on each star, draw lines with tailor's chalk between opposite indentations for eight diamond-shaped segments and quilt on lines. On navy background, quilt around each plume $\frac{1}{2}$″ from seam; continue quilting outward around plumes with lines $\frac{1}{2}$″ apart, following contour of plumes and covering background up to border; on border, follow contours of scallops in same manner. (If desired, mark pattern first with tailor's chalk.)

Edges: Enclose edges of quilt within bias tape; slip-stitch folded edges to front and back of quilt.

BLANKET CHEST
Shown on page 145

EQUIPMENT: Scissors. Pencil. Ruler. Paper for patterns. Tracing paper. Paintbrushes for shel-

lac and paint. Stiff, lightweight cardboard. Newspapers. Wooden modeling tool, or orangewood stick. Fine sandpaper. Very fine steel wool. Masking tape. Awl. Tack hammer.

MATERIALS: Unpainted storage chest, 38″ × 18″ × 18″ high. Clear shellac. Martin-Semour Provincial Antiquing Kit, colored desired. Maid-O'-Metal brass tooling foil, 36-gauge. Upholstery nails with antique bronze finish, $\frac{7}{16}$″ long. Contact cement.

DIRECTIONS: Enlarge half-patterns for top, front, and end designs, by copying on paper ruled in 1″ squares; half-patterns are indicated by dash lines. Copy designs on tracing paper. Cut a separate pattern out of cardboard for each brass motif.

Sand chest smooth. Give chest a coat of clear shellac; let dry. Go over chest with steel wool. Antique chest following directions on label.

Tape tracings of half-designs, pencil side down, on chest top, front, and end, with half-pattern lines at center. Go over lines to transfer designs to chest. Turn tracings over and retrace designs to complete other half. Black dots on patterns indicate placement of nails; mark dots in chest with awl, through the tracing.

Place cardboard patterns on foil; trace outlines on foil with pointed end of modeling tool or orangewood stick; cut motifs out of foil. Place motif on a padding of newspapers; with pattern tracing of motif on top of foil, go over inner design lines on each foil piece; add center vertical line to large leaves at half-pattern line. Turn foil motif over to right side, and place on a hard, flat surface.

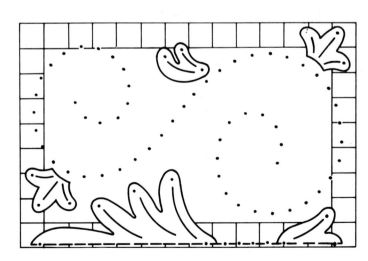

Front

Blanket Chest

Top

End

Using flat end of modeling tool, press and smooth foil all around marked lines, pushing toward lines to raise them. Continue smoothing and pressing outward to make foil flat. With right side up, make a hole at each dot on patterns, using awl. Glue foil motifs in place on chest. Hammer a nail in place at each dot of chest design and on foil pieces.

QUICK-WAY POT HOLDERS
Shown on page 131

EQUIPMENT: Scissors. Ruler. Paper for pattern. Dressmaker's carbon paper. Needle. Sewing machine.

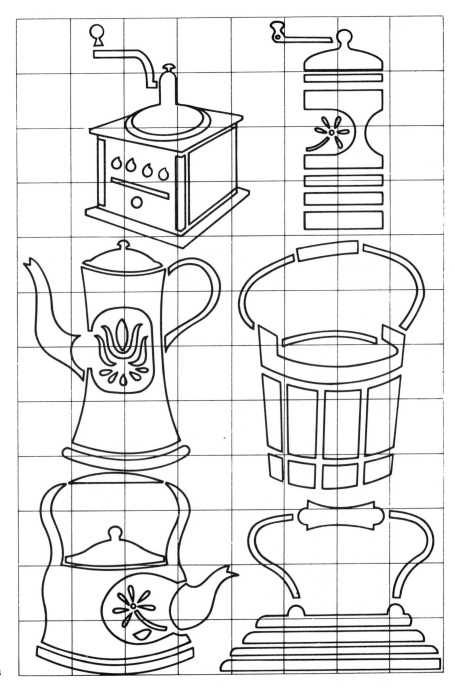

Patterns for Pot Holders

MATERIALS: Heavy cotton fabric, 7″ × 14″ for each pot holder. Bondex Iron-On Tape to contrast. Double-fold bias tape to contrast, 1 yard for each. Polyester fiberfill batting (three 7″ squares for each). Sewing thread to match fabric and tape. Six-strand embroidery floss to contrast.

DIRECTIONS: Enlarge patterns by copying on paper ruled in 1″ squares. For each pot holder, cut two 7″ squares of fabric in color desired. Cut three 7″ squares of polyester fiberfill. Referring to illustration on page 131, center one pattern diagonally on one 7″ piece of fabric; transfer with dressmaker's carbon paper, making light lines slightly inside pattern lines so that carbon will not show. With carbon paper, transfer each part of design to iron-on tape in desired color. Cut out each piece carefully. Place parts on fabric to cover carbon outlines. Set iron according to tape manufacturer's instructions; press to adhere securely.

On open flowered areas, embroider designs, using three strands of floss in needle (Stitch Details, page 308). On pepper grinder and kettle, embroider petals in lazy daisy stitch, stems in outline stitch, and flower centers in stain stitch; embroider leaf on kettle in outline stitch. On coffeepot, embroider flower in outline stitch, leaves below in lazy daisy stitch.

Place three layers of fiberfill between two pieces of fabric. Pin and baste all around edges and close to design. With small machine stitches and thread to match fabric, stitch closely around outside of each iron-on design.

Trim away $\frac{1}{4}$″ of fiberfill all around. Starting at top corner, bind edges of pot holder with contrasting bias tape; ease around corners and stitch tape in place through all thicknesses. Continue stitching edges of tape together for 3″ more at end of binding. Fold extension in half to form loop and stitch end to back of pot holder to complete.

ROOSTER LAMP
Shown on page 145

SIZE: 21″ tall (from base to comb).
EQUIPMENT: Jigsaw or coping saw and vise.

Pencil. Tracing paper. Carbon paper. T-square. Ruler. Handsaw. Medium and fine sandpaper. Pointed and small flat paintbrushes for staining. Clean rag. Drill with $\frac{5}{8}$″ and $\frac{7}{16}$″ bits. Hole saw, 2″ diameter. C-clamps. Carving knife. Ice pick or awl.

MATERIALS: Clear poplar (white wood), about: $\frac{1}{2}$″ thick, 12″ wide, $3\frac{1}{2}$ feet long; 1″ thick, 12″ × 17″. Block of 2″ × 4″ wood, 7″ long. Liquid wood glue. Flo-Stain (pigment-penetrating stain), Walnut and Scotch Pine (green) for bronze weathered effect. Brass tubing, $\frac{5}{8}$″ diameter, one piece 12″ long, one 7″ long. Running thread pipe, 24″ long, $\frac{3}{8}$″. Brass lamp socket with cord, harp, and finial. Brass seating ring. Lock nut to fit pipe.

DIRECTIONS: Enlarge bird patterns by copying on paper ruled in 1″ squares. With carbon paper, transfer bird pattern, including shaded areas, onto 1″ wood, placing pattern so that shading lines match grain of wood. Trace bird, minus shaded areas, and transfer twice onto $\frac{1}{2}$″ thick wood. Trace wing pattern and transfer twice on $\frac{1}{2}$″ wood. Cut pieces, using jigsaw or coping saw and vise. Sand pieces smooth.

Carve lines on opposite sides of matching pieces the same, leaving edges smooth. With carving knife, cut out lines as indicated on patterns, about $\frac{1}{8}$″ deep; cut tail lines a little wider than body and wing lines. On inner area of comb and head, make short thin cuts at random. On upper area of comb and wattle, jab small holes with an ice pick or awl. To assemble, use 1″ thick piece as center; glue the two $\frac{1}{2}$″ thick body pieces to each side of 1″ piece; glue a wing to each side of body where indicated on pattern. Hold pieces together with clamps until glue dries. Drill $\frac{5}{8}$″ holes in 1″ piece, into top and bottom 1″ deep as shown on pattern; drill $\frac{7}{16}$″ hole through. Sand entire form again, rounding edges softly.

Cut 2″ × 4″ wood 7″ long. Drill hole into 2″ thickness of block at center, from top, $\frac{3}{4}$″ deep. Cut a 2″ hole with hole cutter at center, from bottom, $\frac{3}{4}$″ deep. Drill $\frac{7}{16}$″ hole through center (see diagram). From 7″ side drill $\frac{7}{16}$″ hole into bottom cut-out area as shown on diagram. Sand block smooth, rounding edges.

Stain rooster and block with walnut stain, wiping off excess. When dry, paint the incised lines with

Scotch Pine stain, using fine-pointed brush; paint eye area around pupil and upper comb area with Scotch Pine; let dry. Go over lines again to give weathered bronze appearance.

TO ASSEMBLE LAMP: Run cord through threaded pipe and attach socket with harp in place below socket. Push seating ring and 12″ brass tube up threaded pipe. Insert cord and pipe through rooster and push brass tube in so it rests on ledge above small hole. Tighten socket on pipe. Run cord through 6″ brass tube and push tube up over pipe and into bottom of rooster. Run cord through 7″ block; push pipe through and insert brass tube in block so it rests on ledge. Push lock nut over cord and tighten it on pipe. Run cord out through side hole of block.

Pattern for Rooster Lamp

Block Diagram

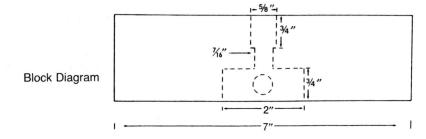

COLOR KEY

▬ FUCHSIA	☒ ORANGE	⊞ GOLD
☑ WATERMELON	▨ GREEN	☐ BLUE	⊡ YELLOW

ALPHABET SAMPLER

Shown on page 145

SIZE: 17″ × 19″.

EQUIPMENT: Masking tape. Ruler. Pencil. Scissors. Tapestry needle.

For Blocking: Soft wooden surface. Brown wrapping paper. T- or carpenter's square.

MATERIALS: Needlepoint canvas 10 mesh-to-the-inch, 22″ × 24″. DMC Laine Tapisserie (tapestry wool): gray-blue #7294, 35 skeins; bright green #7342, 4 skeins; orange #7437, 4 skeins; watermelon #7106, 2 skeins; fuchsia #7155, 2 skeins; light yellow #7433, 1 skein; gold #7473, 1 skein. Plywood, $\frac{1}{4}$″ thick, 17″ × 19″.

DIRECTIONS: Read General Directions for Needlepoint on page 306. Mark outline of sampler 17″ × 19″ on canvas with pencil, allowing $2\frac{1}{2}$″ margin all around. Use continental stitch with one strand of tapestry yarn in needle. Following chart, work design; fill in background as you go.

Block and mount according to General Directions. Frame as desired.

BED AND CANOPY

Shown on page 147

SIZE: $58\frac{3}{4}$″ × $79\frac{3}{4}$″ × 78″ tall, to fit around 54″ × 75″ standard double bed.

EQUIPMENT: Pencil. Cork-backed steel ruler. Carpenter's square. Hand saw. Backsaw. Drill with bit and countersink to fit screw sizes. Miter box. Screw driver. Mortise chisel, $\frac{1}{8}$″. Medium and fine sandpaper. **For Canopy:** Scissors. Yardstick. Sewing machine. Sewing needle. Iron.

MATERIALS: Poplar, 52 feet of 3 × 3 (actual size $2\frac{1}{2}$″ × $2\frac{1}{2}$″) in the following pieces: Four pieces 78″ for posts; one piece $56\frac{1}{4}$″ for canopy head; two pieces $79\frac{3}{4}$″ for canopy sides; one piece $58\frac{3}{4}$″ for canopy foot. White pine, 19 feet of 1 × 6 board lumber (actual size $\frac{3}{4}$″ × $5\frac{1}{2}$″) in the following pieces: Two pieces $74\frac{3}{4}$″ for side rails; one piece $53\frac{3}{4}$″ for foot. Plywood $\frac{3}{4}$″ thick, Grade A on one side, 26″ × $53\frac{3}{4}$″, for headboard. One-inch square pine strips, 6 feet as follows: Two 26″-long support strips and two $5\frac{1}{2}$″-long support strips. Wood glue. Four sets of metal side rail connectors (hook and slot type), $\frac{5}{8}$″ wide and $4\frac{1}{2}$″ long with screws. Flathead 2″ wood screws, twenty. Four flat corner braces with screws.

For Canopy: Decorator fabric with large stencil-like design as shown in photograph, 54″ wide, $5\frac{1}{8}$ yards. Matching thread.

Note: The base to support canopy is a free-standing framework that surrounds the mattress on box spring and Harvard-type frame; it does not support the bed.

DIRECTIONS: Cut notches in poplar stock as follows: Mark the exact shape of the cutout on all faces and edge of wood. Cut out the waste gradually from each side with a backsaw and chisel until face of cutout is level. Following Fig. 1, cut notch in both ends of canopy head piece. Following Fig. 2, cut notch in both ends of each canopy side and canopy foot piece. Following Fig. 3, cut notch in top of each 78″ post.

Following Fig. 4 (not to scale), lay out canopy pieces; miter foot ends of sides and both ends of foot piece and test-fit as shown; set pieces aside.

Following Assembly Diagram, glue long support strip to each side of headboard back so 26″ edges are flush. Glue $5\frac{1}{2}$″ strips to foot board in same manner. Position head and foot boards between appropriate posts, so that faces are flush as shown; assemble by screwing support strips to posts (three screws in each). Countersink all screws.

For Side Rail Connectors: Position side rails as shown, and draw outline of rail ends on posts. Center connector plate with slots on rail end; with pencil, mark plate outline for mortise. Score plate outline with chisel inside pencil mark. Cut out area to plate depth. Refit plate, making sure that clearance given for hooks is between screws and top ends of slots. Mark slots and screw holes; remove plate. Cut out slots to depth of hooks on matching plate, extending slots above marked top end of slot to accommodate hook. Screw plate in place. Center connector plate with hooks within drawn outline on post so that hooks face up. Mark outline and cut mortise as before; screw plate in place.

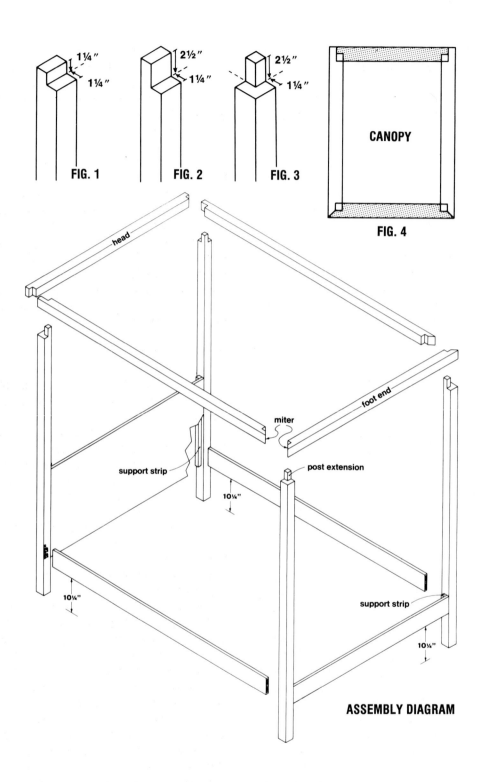

1¼″
1¼″
FIG. 1

2½″
1¼″
FIG. 2

2½″
1¼″
FIG. 3

CANOPY

FIG. 4

head

foot end

miter

support strip

post extension

10¼″

10¼″

support strip

10¼″

ASSEMBLY DIAGRAM

Assemble bed frame. Position sides of canopy on posts; screw together through post extension (formed by notching) into side piece, counter-sinking all screws. Position canopy front and back; glue in place and reinforce on top with corner braces.

Sand entire structure first with medium and then fine sandpaper. Finish as desired.

CANOPY: Cut $126\frac{1}{4}'' \times 54''$ piece from fabric for top/backdrop. Hem one 54" edge (backdrop) by turning under $\frac{1}{2}''$ twice; slip-stitch in place. Cut front panel 56" × 9", with border design running the length of the fabric. Hem short side edges and one 54" edge as for backdrop. Stitch front to top with raw edges even and with right side of front facing wrong side of top. Center canopy over frame as shown in photograph. Thumbtack to top of frame so seam is at front edge of canopy frame; thumbtack backdrop behind headboard.

BLUE QUILT

Shown on pages 146-147

SIZE: 78" × 96".

EQUIPMENT: Colored pencil. Pencil. Ruler. Paper for patterns. Dressmaker's tracing (carbon) paper. Tailor's chalk. Tracing wheel (or dry ball-point pen). Straight pins. Large safety pins. Sewing and quilting needles. Quilting frame or hoop (optional).

MATERIALS: Closely woven, lightweight polished cotton fabric 54" wide, $10\frac{3}{4}$ yards. Matching sewing thread. White quilting thread. Mountain Mist® polyester batting.

DIRECTIONS: From cotton fabric, cut two pieces 49" × 96" and four pieces $15\frac{1}{2}'' \times 96''$. Right sides facing and making $\frac{1}{2}''$ seams, sew a narrow piece to each long side of a wide piece, to make two quilt pieces 78" × 96". Press seams to one side. Cut two layers of batting same size or a little larger.

Quilting Patterns: Mark lines for quilting on right side of one quilt piece: Using ruler and tailor's chalk, mark a line 7" in from edge on two long and one short sides of piece; mark line 1" in from edge on remaining short side (top); see Quilting Diagram. Starting at one marked corner, mark points 8" apart all along the four lines. Mark grid pattern as shown in diagram, connecting marked points with diagonal lines; leave open area as shown. Around edge of grid, mark two lines in each triangle $\frac{1}{2}''$ and $1\frac{1}{4}''$ in from outer lines.

Using sharp colored pencil, draw lines across flowers-in-bowl center pattern and border pattern, connecting grid lines. Enlarge center pattern on paper ruled in 2" squares; enlarge border pattern on 1" squares. Using dressmaker's carbon and tracing wheel, transfer center design to open area of quilt piece, placing base of bowl 16" from bottom raw edge of fabric; parts of design will overlap grid area. Transfer border design to sides and bottom of quilt piece: Beginning at bottom, place pattern with arrow at left corner; repeat motif across to right corner for 32 complete motifs, plus a half motif extending from each corner. Repeat border motif along each side for 44 complete motfis, plus a half motif at bottom corner. To complete each bottom corner, extend line of both half motifs to form design shown.

Quilting: Lay unmarked quilt piece on large, flat surface, wrong side up. Lay the two layers of batting on top, smoothing out any bumps or wrinkles. Anchor batting to center of fabric by taking two long stitches in a cross. Place marked quilt piece on batting, right side up. Pin all layers together to hold temporarily, using large safety pins. Baste generously through all thicknesses: First, baste on the lengthwise and crosswise grain of fabric, then diagonally in both directions, and around sides, top and bottom.

If desired, attach quilt to a frame or insert in a quilting hoop. If using neither hoop nor frame, you can quilt in your lap, working over a small area at a time. Using a short, strong needle and strong cotton thread (or quilting thread), begin quilting along marked lines with running stitch in two separate motions: Push needle straight down through all layers with one hand, take needle with other hand, pull thread through and push up close to first stitch; see detail. Make stitches as small and close as possible; space stitches evenly so they are same size on both sides of quilt. Start in mid-

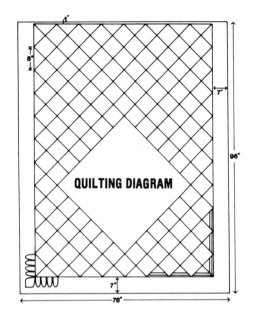

QUILTING DIAGRAM

QUILTING STITCH

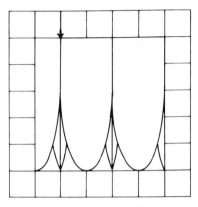

BORDER PATTERN

CENTER PATTERN

dle of quilt with flowers; stitch toward you, shifting your position as you work so that the quilting progresses evenly on all sides. When flowers and bowl are completed, stitch grid pattern, working from center out; carry lines of grid to edges of flowers and bowl, or leave as diagramed. Stitch border design.

Finishing: To bind edges, cut $1\frac{1}{2}''$-wide bias strip $9\frac{3}{4}$ yards long from remaining quilt fabric, piecing for length. Turn under one long edge and one end of strip $\frac{3}{8}''$; press carefully without stretching. Beginning at center top edge of quilt, pin bias strip to quilt with right sides facing and matching unpressed raw edge of strip with raw edge of quilt. At end of strip, pin raw end over pressed end. Machine-stitch $\frac{3}{8}''$ from raw edges all around, lifting foot and turning fabric at corners. Fold strip to reverse side of quilt; slip-stitch pressed edge in place.

BLUE PILLOW SHAMS
Shown on page 147

SIZE: $23'' \times 29''$.

EQUIPMENT: See Quilt.

MATERIALS: See Quilt. Additional fabric for two shams, $3\frac{1}{2}$ yards.

DIRECTIONS (for one): From cotton fabric, cut two pieces $23'' \times 29''$ and two pieces $23'' \times 32''$. Mark lines for quilting on right side of one $23'' \times 29''$ piece: Using ruler and tailor's chalk, mark a line $5\frac{1}{2}''$ in from edge all around. Mark second and third lines $\frac{1}{2}''$ and $1\frac{3}{4}''$ inside first line. Using dressmaker's carbon and tracing wheel, transfer border design as for quilt, making nine motifs on long borders and six on short borders; there should be $\frac{1}{2}''$ between tip of motifs and raw edge of fabric.

Quilting: Lay unmarked $23'' \times 29''$ piece on flat surface, wrong side up. Lay single layer of batting on top, then lay marked piece on batting. Baste pieces together and quilt on marked lines as for the quilt, completing front of sham.

Assembling: Fold each $23'' \times 32''$ piece in half crosswise, wrong side inward, for two pieces $23''$

$\times 16''$; press. Place quilted piece flat, wrong side up. Place folded pieces on top, matching $23''$ raw edges of each with a $23''$ edge of quilted piece; folded edges will overlap in center. Pin and baste, then stitch all around $\frac{1}{2}''$ from raw edges.

Finishing: (**Note:** It is advisable to cut pieces for second sham before cutting binding strips.) To bind edges, cut $2''$-wide bias strips $3\frac{1}{2}$ yards long, piecing for length. Bind edges of sham in same manner as for quilt, but making $\frac{1}{2}''$ seams for $\frac{1}{2}''$-wide binding, which will just meet tip of quilted border motifs.

STENCILED FLOORCLOTH
Shown on pages 146 and 147

SIZE: Bear Paw, $96''$ square.

EQUIPMENT: Colored pencil. Pencil. Ruler. T- or carpenter's square. Scissors. Paper for patterns. Large sheets of stencil paper. Felt-tipped black marking pen. X-acto knife with fresh blades. Glass $8''$ square, with filed edges. White paper $8''$ square. Two saucers for mixing paint. Paper towels. Newspaper. Masking tape $1''$ and $2''$ wide. Stencil brush. Large paintbrush. Large flat working surface. Sewing machine. Cleaning solvent. Iron.

MATERIALS: Primed cotton duck fabric $52''$-$54''$ wide: $5\frac{1}{2}$ yards for Bear Paw. Acrylic paints: royal blue, black. Heavy sewing thread. Chalk. Polyurethane.

GENERAL DIRECTIONS: Using sharp colored pencil, draw lines across patterns, connecting grid lines. Enlarge patterns by copying on paper ruled in $1''$ squares. Strengthen lines of patterns with felt-tipped marking pen.

To make stencils, place stencil paper over each enlarged pattern, taping sheets together if necessary; trace design in center of paper. Position paper on glass, centering area to be cut; place sheet of white paper under glass to make design lines visible. With X-acto knife, carefully cut out shaded areas. Cut toward you, lifting the blade only after an entire area has been cut out; change blades often.

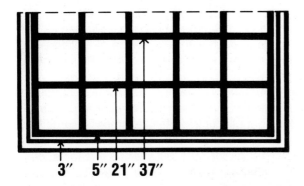

3″ 5″ 21″ 37″

Stencil Pattern

Stir paint with spoon and place about two teaspoons in a saucer. Blend in two or three drops of water; if paint appears to be drying, blend in a few more drops of water, keeping paint the consistency of soft butter throughout.

To stencil, dip brush in paint; tap flat end of bristles on saucer to remove excess. Hold brush, like a pencil, with fingers close to bristles; use other hand to press stencil down flat while working. With quick, up-and-down motions, dab paint onto fabric through stencil; do not move stencil while working or paint will smear. When finished, carefully lift stencil from fabric. If stencils begin to curl or accumulate excess paint, trace and cut out new ones.

BEAR PAW FLOORCLOTH: Cut the following panels from primed cotton duck: one 52″ × 95″ center; two 22½″ × 95″ sides. Stitch sides to center along 95″ edges, making ½″ seams. Press seams toward center; topstitch in place. Press 1½″ hem to wrong side along each edge; stitch in place. Paint entire cloth blue.

To prepare floorcloth for stenciling, lay out on flat surface, right side up. Study floorcloth diagram before beginning (dash line indicates horizontal center of floorcloth). Using chalk, yardstick and T- or carpenter's square, mark horizontal lines the following distances from, and parallel to, bottom edge of cloth: 1″, 3″, 4″, 5″, 7″, 21″, 23″, 37″, 39″; note that measurements on diagram indicate bottom edge of horizontal stripes. Give floorcloth a quarter turn and draw lines again; lines will intersect at corner. Repeat along remaining two edges, forming 25 14″-square internal blocks and two border stripes; erase intersecting lines at corners and edges for continuous borders. Following diagram, mask all unshaded areas, using 1″ and 2″-wide masking tape as necessary. Using black paint, stencil all shaded areas, following diagram and General Directions. Remove tape when paint is dry.

Following General Directions, enlarge and cut Bear Paw stencil; position stencil in center of each 14″ block and stencil with black paint. When paint is dry, coat entire surface with polyurethane.

ALPHABET SAMPLER
Shown on page 146

FINISHED SIZE: 11¾″ × 17¾″.

EQUIPMENT: Ruler. Pencil. Scissors. Embroidery hoop and needle. Straight pins. Steam iron. Sewing machine (optional). Zweigart "Florina" (ecru-colored, even-weave fabric, 14 threads-to-the-inch) 14″ × 20½″. Paternayan Persian yarn in 8-yard skeins: Medium Blue #330, two skeins; Navy Blue #305, three skeins. Illustration board 11½″ × 17½″. Masking tape.

Chart for Alphabet Sampler

Directions: Read How to Cross-Stitch on page 309. Whipstitch fabric edges to prevent raveling. Each square on chart represents two horizontal and two vertical threads on fabric; each symbol represents one cross-stitch. Separate yarn and work with single strand in needle throughout. Work all letters (dots) in Navy Blue and entire flower motif (Xs) in Medium Blue. Work all stitches over two threads in each direction.

To Stitch: With short fabric edges at top and bottom, measure 2″ down and in from upper left corner to correspond with upper left corner of chart; mark with a pin. Following chart, begin top of letter A by counting two threads down and four threads to the right, for first stitch. Work first row of alphabet. Work second row of alphabet, including top of central flower. Continue working letters and flower motif to end of chart. Work one or two of your own initials in the center of blank space at lower right corner. (It is best to plot out initial(s) in pencil on chart before embroidering.) Press embroidery, following General Directions.

To Finish: Center illustration board on wrong side of stitched fabric; fold raw edges over board and tape in place. Frame as desired.

DUST RUFFLE, CUSHIONS, TABLECLOTH
Shown on pages 146 and 147

EQUIPMENT: Pencil. Yardstick. Tape measure. Scissors. Paper for patterns. Straight pins. Sewing needle. Sewing machine. Iron. String. Thumbtack. Large softwood work surface.

MATERIALS: Decorator fabric with large stencil-like design as shown in photograph*, 54″ wide: dust ruffle, about $5\frac{1}{4}$ yards (will fit double bed; adjust yardage if necessary); chair cushions, about $\frac{2}{3}$ yard; tablecloth, measure for yardage as directed. Thread to match fabrics. Muslin for dust ruffle, see directions for amount. **For Cushions:** Coordinating fabric for backing 45″ wide, $\frac{2}{3}$ yard. Coordinating piping, about 5 yards. Fiberfill.

*Note: Major motif (flower basket including corner starts) should be about 18″ square.

GENERAL DIRECTIONS: Trim selvages from all fabrics. Measure accurately as directed; use yardstick and pencil to mark wrong side of fabric. Cut out pieces on straight grain of fabric, working around the large stencil motifs and integrating them into the design of each item, as directed. When joining pieces together to achieve width, match design carefully, allowing for seams. Stitch pieces together with right sides facing and raw edges even, making $\frac{1}{2}$″ seams.

DUST RUFFLE: Measure length and width of top of box spring. For underlay, cut muslin 1″ larger than each measurement; piece if necessary. To make hem for head of bed, turn under one short edge of muslin $\frac{1}{4}$″ twice, enclosing raw edge; press; stitch. To make pleated panels for drops, determine height of strip by measuring from top of box spring to floor and adding 4″; when cutting, position bottom edges of motifs 4″ above lower edge so as not to lose the design in hemming. Length of strip and size of pleats is determined by size of motifs and distance between them. For fabric such as ours with 18″ motifs, cut and piece strip three motifs wide for panel at foot of bed, adding 4″ of fabric beyond each end motif for corner hems and pleats. Turn raw edges at ends of strip $\frac{1}{2}$″ to wrong side twice; press; stitch. Turn bottom of strip $\frac{1}{2}$″ to wrong side; press, then turn 3″ to wrong side, enclosing raw edges; stitch. Fold each end $1\frac{1}{2}$″ to right side; press. Fold again so doubled fabric is on wrong side of strip; baste pleat across top. Divide short edge of muslin underlay in half; mark center point, then divide each half again and mark, for three points. With right sides facing, pin panel to underlay, starting $\frac{1}{2}$″ away from each side edge of underlay and pinning center of each motif to marked point on underlay. Smooth each motif to right and left of center point and pin to underlay; make a box pleat between motifs with excess fabric. Stitch in place.

For side panels, piece strip, $4\frac{1}{2}$ motifs wide, adding 4″ beyond each end for pleats. Hem side and bottom edges and make side pleats as for panel at foot of bed. With right sides facing, pin panel to underlay at each end. Pin centers of motifs, evenly spaced, along edges; make pleats with excess fabric as for first panel. Stitch side panels in place.

Continued on page 193

Cold New England nights were made warmer with this wool coverlet, woven in a square pattern and decorated in crewel embroidery designs. To recreate this 1800s coverlet, square off a plain, lightweight blanket with fabric, ribbon or embroidery; then work the blue and rust motifs in chain and satin stitch. *Directions on page 218.*

*For a room as fresh as spring itself, duplicate our
accessories. Begin by uncovering the decorating
potential of bedsheets, using a pretty
print such as the flowered trellis design we've chosen.
Sew a dust ruffle, pillow shams and a tufted
bedsheet quilt; matching curtains also
stitch up quickly. The trellis pattern with flowers
is repeated in the latch-hook rug (49" × 29"),
then a simpler trellis design is painted
on a favorite chest of drawers.
A crocheted net canopy finished with tassels adds
the perfect touch.
Directions for all begin on page 220.*

Red Pineapples (or Wild Goose Chase, whichever you see first) pattern a square quilt made of 49 identical blocks. No border is needed. Each block is pieced with triangles, strips, and a square. Quilting follows the patchwork pattern. Directions for Pineapple Quilt, page 241.

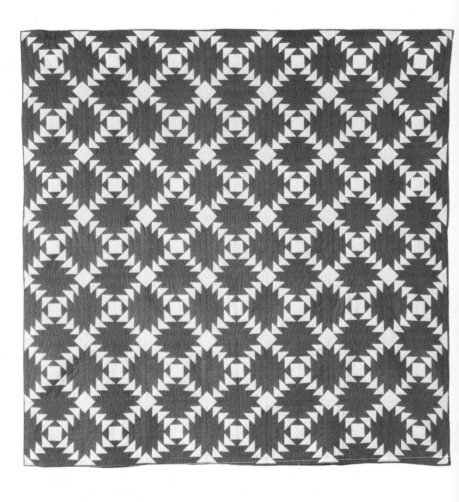

A bold red star features five little stars within and a feathered edge. Patch pieces are relatively few; star points are joined to the nine-patch center block. Coverlet is splendidly quilted with wreaths and a serpentine border. Made in Ohio, about 1870. Feathered Star Quilt, page 22?

*Little stars against jagged peaks: this rugged design,
called Delectable Mountains, is one of the few that can be traced back
to colonial days. Set with Flying Geese borders, quilt is pieced
entirely with squares and triangles. Ca. 1910. See page 227.*

The lovely orange peel pattern is not for the novice quilter;
it takes careful cutting and stitching to fit the curved patches
together. This quilt won a prize at the Indiana State Fair, around 1930.
Directions for Orange Peel Quilt are on page 242.

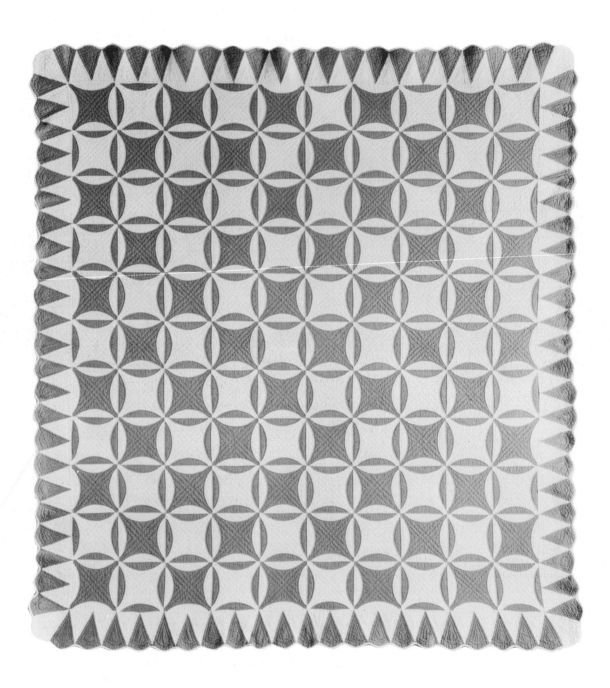

Two tiny cherubs bid "Sweet Dreams" on an open-mesh needlepoint inspired
by 19th-century perforated cardboard embroideries. Design, 10" × 23⅞",
is on 10 mesh-to-the-inch canvas with tapestry yarns. Background
is unworked for the "perforated" paper look. Leaves trim our replica
of an antique frame. Flamboyant red ruffles edge muslin pillow shams
and stylized tulips in a sprightly calico print are appliqued on an
unbleached muslin quilt; 80" × 92". Decorate with
silhouettes; directions for all begin on page 245.

Harvest Sun's eight-point star is known by many names—
Ship's Wheel, Star of Bethlehem, and Rising Sun, to name a few.
Various fabrics were used in piecing the quilt's
nine stars, each radiating from a light-colored center
in alternating lights and darks. The quilt
measures about 89" square. Directions on page 248.

Two little sunbonnet girls and two little fishermen
make a delightful quartet for a child's quilt. Add a pillow
and make it a set! Easy-pattern appliques, with
easy machine quilting; directions on page 250.

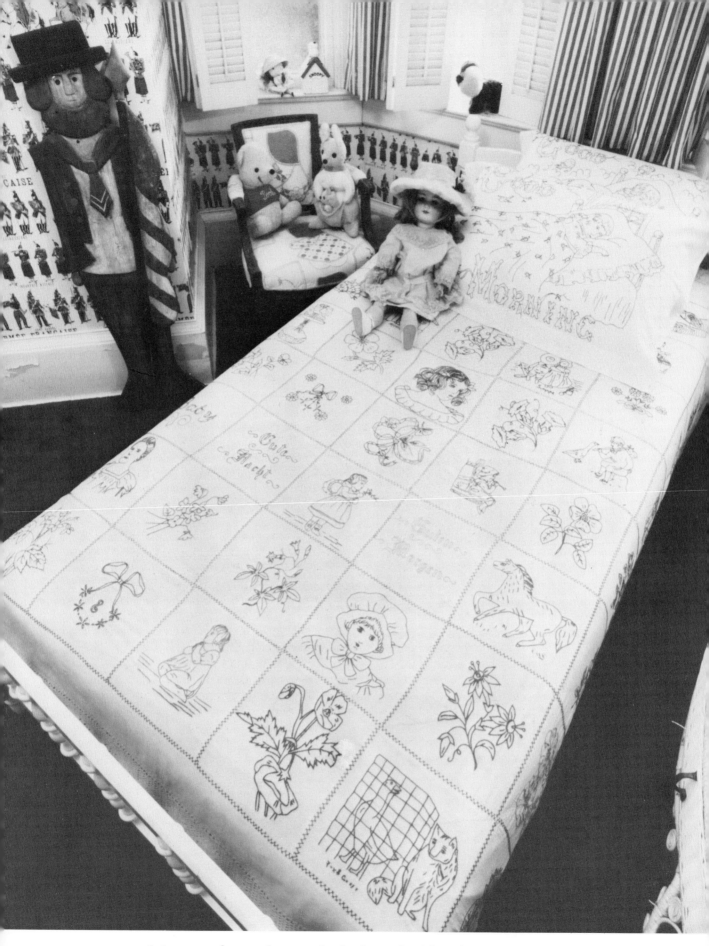

A treasured coverlet was lovingly embroidered over 100 years ago to celebrate the birth year of a little girl. We provide sixteen motifs to start you on your heirloom-to-be, as well as patterns for coordinating pillow shams; see page 253.

Continued from page 182

CUSHIONS: Make seat and backrest as follows: Use scrap muslin or brown wrapping paper to make pattern. Drape muslin or paper over area to be traced; tape or pin in place. Fit and mark shape of seat or backrest; remove and cut out pattern. Test-fit in chair; adjust so that shaped sides are symmetrical. Position and pin pattern on fabric, centering pattern over one motif; mark outline of pattern. Cut out fabric $\frac{1}{2}''$ beyond marked line for seam allowance. Cut out backing fabric in same manner.

Measure circumference of each pattern and add 1"; cut piping for each cushion to this length. With seam of piping over marked seamline of cushion, stitch piping to right side of each printed fabric piece, using zipper foot. To end piping, clip off about $\frac{1}{2}''$ of the inner core; insert other end of piping into the empty tube. Slip-stitch ends together.

To make ties for backrest, cut four strips from backing fabric, each $19'' \times 1\frac{1}{2}''$. Fold each in half lengthwise; stitch together along one short and one long edge. Turn to right side; press. Mark points on backrest fabric $1\frac{1}{2}''$ away from each top corner across top edges and down each side edge for four marks. With raw edges even pin one strip to right side of fabric at each mark; stitch in place.

Pin cushion front to backing with right sides facing and piping (and ties on backrest) in between. Stitch together, leaving opening for turning. Turn to right side and stuff with fiberfill until plump; fold raw edges $\frac{1}{2}''$ to inside and slip-stitch opening closed.

ROUND TABLECLOTH: Find exact center of tabletop; measure from center to edge of table, then down to floor. Add $1\frac{1}{2}''$ to measurement for length A. Multiply A by four to determine length of fabric needed (in inches); convert inches to yards.

Tie one end of string around pencil near pencil point; knot other end so distance between point and knot is length A. Spread fabric out on large softwood surface, wrong side up. Place pencil point at one corner of fabric. Stretch string taut along long edge, and tack knot to edge. Holding pencil perpendicular to fabric, swing pencil around to mark a semi-circle; cut out along marked line. Make second semi-circle from remaining fabric in

same manner. Pin semi-circles together at straight edges, with right sides facing. Machine-stitch together $\frac{1}{2}''$ from edges; press seam open. Turn hem under $\frac{1}{2}''$ twice, steam-pressing to ease curve. Slip-stitch in place. To finish, make small square overcloth as shown.

WHITE/BLUE STAR QUILT
Shown on pages 148-149

SIZE: $86\frac{1}{2}'' \times 110\frac{1}{2}''$.

EQUIPMENT: Pencil. Steel-edged ruler. Tracing paper. Graph paper. Thin, stiff cardboard. Scissors. Glue. Sewing and quilting needles. Tailor's chalk. Quilting frame (optional).

MATERIALS: Closely woven cotton fabric 45" wide: $5\frac{1}{2}$ yards white, 3 yards navy, $2\frac{1}{2}$ yards white-on-blue print, $1\frac{1}{2}$ yards white-on-blue striped. White lining fabric 45" wide, $6\frac{1}{4}$ yards. Polyester batting. White sewing and quilting threads. Navy double-fold bias binding tape $\frac{1}{4}''$ wide, 11 yards.

DIRECTIONS: Read General Directions for Quilting, page 300. Quilt top is entirely pieced. Make a cardboard pattern for each patch piece as follows. Label each pattern. (Dotted lines on some patterns indicate quilting designs.)

Patterns: Trace pattern A, which is shown actual size; use ruler and sharp pencil. Complete quarter-pattern indicated by dash lines for an octagon. Glue tracing to cardboard and let dry. Carefully cut out along marked lines.

For patterns B, C, E, G, H and Border Piece, mark outlines on graph paper as indicated in diagrams. Glue paper to cardboard, let dry, and cut out patterns, discarding shaded portions.

For patterns D and F, mark $1\frac{1}{4}''$ and 4" squares respectively on graph paper; glue to cardboard.

Before cutting fabric patches, test accuracy of patterns A, B and C by drawing around them on a piece of paper to recreate center star design of Main Block; see Piecing Diagram. If patterns do not fit well together, make new ones.

Patch Pieces: For each piece, place cardboard pattern on wrong side of designated fabric, with

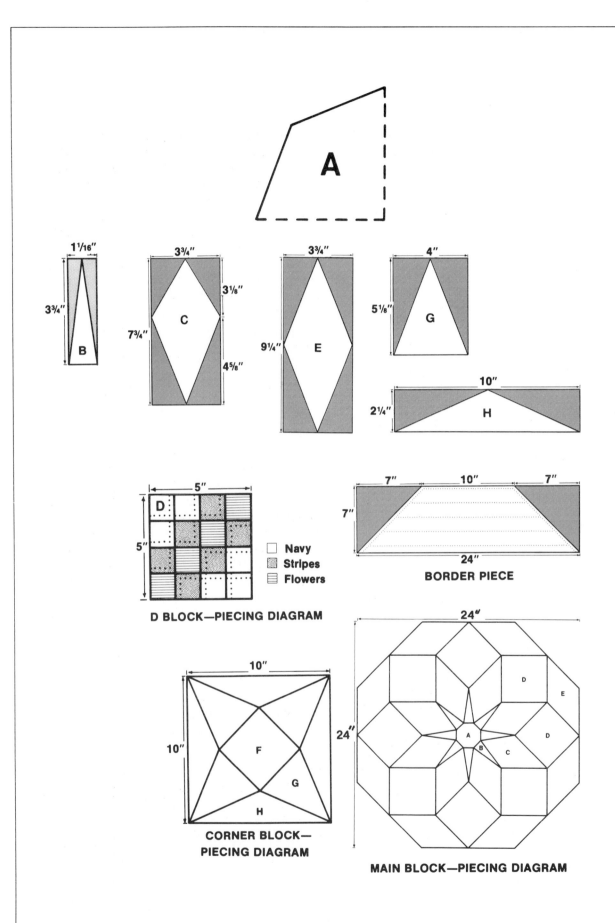

A

1¹⁄₁₆″

3¾″

B

3¾″

3⅛″

7¾″

C

4⅝″

3¾″

9¼″

E

4″

5⅛″

G

10″

2¼″

H

5″

5″

D

☐ Navy
▨ Stripes
▤ Flowers

D BLOCK—PIECING DIAGRAM

7″   10″   7″

7″

24″

BORDER PIECE

10″

10″

F

G

H

**CORNER BLOCK—
PIECING DIAGRAM**

24″

24″

A

B

C

D

E

D

MAIN BLOCK—PIECING DIAGRAM

perpendicular and parallel edges on straight of goods. Mark around pattern, holding pencil at an outward angle so point is firmly against cardboard. Mark all patterns for each fabric at one time, leaving $\frac{1}{2}''$ space between. As edges of patterns become frayed from use, replace with new ones. When all pattern have been marked, cut out patches $\frac{1}{4}''$ beyond pencil outline, which will be stitching line.

From white fabric, cut 14 Border Pieces, 80 of piece H, 96 of piece E and 576 of piece D. From navy fabric, cut 96 of piece C. From striped fabric, cut 20 of piece F, 12 of piece A and 576 of piece D. From flowered fabric, cut 80 of piece G, 96 of piece B. and 384 of piece D.

Sew patch pieces together into blocks as directed, referring to Piecing Diagrams. Holding pieces with right sides facing, stitch along marked seam line; if hand-stitching, use small, even stitches, about 16 to the inch. Press seams to one side as you work, light fabric under dark.

D Block: For one block, sew 16 of piece D together as shown in Piecing Diagram. First, sew four rows of four pieces each, then sew rows together, matching corners carefully. Block will measure 5″ square, plus outside seam allowance. Make 96 of D block, 48 with stripes of center diagonal row placed horizontally as shown, and 48 with stripes placed vertically.

Main Block: Begin sewing in center of block and work outward. Sew eight of piece B to an A piece, then sew eight of piece C between B pieces. Sew eight of block D to sides of C pieces with striped rows of each block touching; alternate horizontal and vertical stripes. Sew eight E pieces between D blocks. Block will measure 24″ each way, plus outside seam allowance. Make 12 Main Blocks.

Corner Block: Sew four of piece G to an F piece, then four of piece H between G pieces. Block will be 10″ square, plus outside seam allowance.

Assembling Quilt Top: Place main blocks together in four horizontal rows of three blocks each. In each row, join the blocks along the vertical edges of the adjacent E pieces, stitching on the marked seam lines. Then join the rows along the

horizontal edges of the adjacent E pieces. In the square spaces created between rows, sew a Corner Block, joining H pieces to the diagonal edges of E pieces. (Or you may prefer to sew in the Corner Blocks as you join rows.) Sew the remaining Corner Blocks around edge of quilt top in the triangular spaces and across each corner. Sew Border Pieces around edge between Corner Blocks, three at top and bottom, four along each side. Quilt top should measure $86\frac{1}{2}''$ × $110\frac{1}{2}''$, including outside seam allowance.

Lining: From lining fabric, cut two pieces 44″ × 111″. Stitch together on long edges with $\frac{1}{2}''$ seam, to make lining 87″ × 111″, slightly larger than quilt top. Cut batting same size as lining.

Quilting: Place lining out flat, wrong side up. Place batting on top, smoothing out wrinkles. Take two long stitches in a cross, to anchor batting to lining. Place quilt top over batting, right side up; pin layers together. Baste vertically, horizontally, diagonally, and around perimeter.

Begin quilting in center and work around and outward to edge: Using white thread, quilt all around each patch piece (except B) $\frac{1}{4}''$ in from seam; on D blocks and Border Pieces, quilt as shown by dotted lines in diagrams, marking patterns with tailor's chalk.

Finishing: Trim edge of batting and lining to match top. Enclose outside seam allowance of quilt with double-fold tape, placing wider side of tape against lining; slip-stitch one folded edge of tape to quilt top, the other to lining.

AFGHAN AND PILLOW
Shown on pages 148-149

SIZE: Afghan, 54″ × 69″, plus fringe. Pillow, 16″ × 24″.

MATERIALS: Bernat Berella "4", 16 4-oz. balls of Rose Heather #8937 for afghan, 2 balls for pillow. Afghan hook size G. Plastic crochet hook size G (for afghan). Afghan hook size F (for pillow). Pillow form, 16″ × 24″. Fabric for pillow back.

GAUGE: 7 sts = 2″; 3 rows = 1″ (afghan st panels). 4 sts = 1″; 4 rows = 1″ (pillow, size F hook).

AFGHAN: PICOT PANEL (make 4): With afghan hook size G, ch 36. **Row 1:** Keeping all lps on hook, pull up a lp in 2nd ch from hook and in each ch across.

To Work Lps Off: Yo hook, pull through first lp, * yo hook, pull through next 2 lps, repeat from * across. Lp that remains on hook always counts as first st of next row.

Row 2: Keeping all lps on hook, sk first vertical bar (lp on hook is first st), pull up a lp under next vertical bar and under each vertical bar across.

Note: The first half of every row is worked this way.

2nd Half: Work off 8 lps, ch 4 for picot, work off 4 lps, picot, (work off 6 lps, picot) twice, work off 4 lps, picot, work remaining 8 lps.

Row 3: 2nd Half: Work off 9 lps, picot, (work off 2 lps, picot, work off 6 lps, picot) twice, work off 2 lps, picot, work off remaining 9 lps.

Row 4: 2nd Half: Work off 10 lps, picot, work off 6 lps, picot, work off 4 lps, picot, work off 6 lps, picot, work off remaining 10 lps.

Row 5: 2nd Half: Work off 5 lps, picot, work off 4 lps, picot, (work off 6 lps, picot) 3 times, work off 4 lps, picot, work off remaining 5 lps. Following

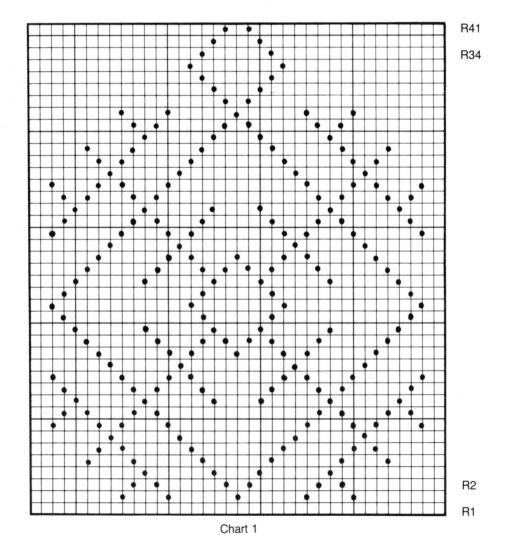

R41

R34

R2

R1

Chart 1

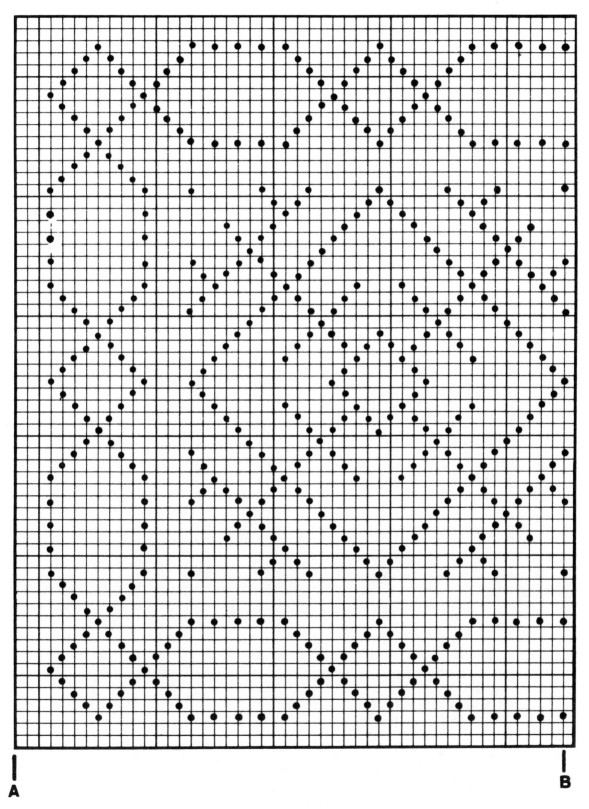

A

B

Chart 2

chart 1 for placement of picots, work to row 41. Repeat rows 2–41, 3 times, then repeat rows 2–34. Work last row, row 195, in plain afghan stitch. Bind off by marking a sl st in each vertical bar across. Mark bottom edge of each panel.

BORDER: With crochet hook, join yarn in first st of row 1 (bottom edge). **Row 1:** Sc in first st of each row to top of panel, sk 1 row at center to make 194 sc. Ch 3, turn.

Row 2: * Sk next st, dc in next st, dc in skipped st, repeat from * across, end dc in last st. Ch 3, turn.

Row 3: Repeat row 2. End off. Repeat border on other edge of panel, beg at top of panel.

FINISHING: Place 2 panels wrong sides tog, bottom edges tog. Using crochet hook, beg at bottom edge, sc panels tog from right side, working sc in each dc across. After all panels have been joined, work 3 rows of border across top and bottom edges of afghan.

FRINGE: Cut 14″ strands of yarn. Knot 3 strands tog in each sp between cross stitches across each end of afghan. Trim evenly.

PILLOW: With afghan hook size F, ch 94. Work even in afghan st for 2 rows.

Row 3: Work first half of row—94 lps on hook. **Note:** The first half of every row is worked this way.

2nd Half: Work off 7 lps, ch 4 for picot, work off 8 lps, picot, (work off 2 lps, picot) 4 times, (work off 8 lps, picot) twice, (work off 2 lps, picot) 8 times, (work off 8 lps, picot) twice, (work off 2 lps, picot) 4 times, work off 8 lps, picot, work off remaining 7 lps.

Row 4: Work first half of row—94 lps on hook.

2nd Half: * Work off 6 lps, picot, work off 2 lps, picot, work off 6 lps, picot, work off 10 lps, picot, work off 6 lps, picot, work off 2 lps, picot, work off 6 lps, * picot, work off 18 lps, picot, repeat from first * to 2nd *. Following chart 2 for placement of picots, work from A to B (center), then work back to A, omitting center picots already made. Work to top of chart, ending with 2 plain afghan st rows. Sl st in each vertical bar across last row. End off.

FINISHING: Cut pillow back same size as pillow top. Stitch pieces right sides tog, on 3 sides. Turn to right side. Insert pillow form. Close opening.

INITIAL AFGHAN
Shown on page 150

SIZE: 48″ × 66″.

MATERIALS: White yarn of knitting worsted weight, 13 4-oz. skeins. Crochet hook size J.

GAUGE: 8 sts = 3″; 8 rows = 3″.

AFGHAN: Beg at lower edge, ch 132.

Row 1: Ch-sc in 2nd ch from hook and in each ch across (to make ch-sc, pull up a lp in st, ch 1, yo hook and through 2 lps on hook)—131 ch-sc. Ch 2, turn each row.

Row 2 (right side): Sk first st (ch 2 always counts as first st), ch-sc in each of next 4 sts, popcorn in next st (to make a popcorn, work 4 ch-sc in st, drop lp off hook, insert hook in sp before first ch-sc of group, pick up dropped lp and pull it through sp); (ch-sc in next st, popcorn in next st) 3 times, (ch-sc in each of next 7 sts, popcorn in next st, ch-sc in next st, popcorn in next st) 10 times, ch-sc in each of next 7 sts, popcorn in next st, (ch-sc in next st, popcorn in next st) 3 times, ch-sc in each of last 5 sts—131 sts.

Row 3 and All Odd Rows: Sk first st (ch 2 is first st), ch-sc in each st across, ch-sc in top of turning ch 2.

Row 4: Working from chart, sk first st, work 2 ch-sc, (popcorn, ch-sc) 5 times, popcorn, 3 ch-sc, * (popcorn, ch-sc) 3 times, popcorn, 3 ch-sc, repeat from * across to last 14 sts, (popcorn, ch-sc) 5 times, popcorn, 3 ch-sc. On chart, each plain square is 1 ch-sc, each X is 1 popcorn. One-quarter chart is given. Follow chart across to center st, marked with arrow, work center st only once, follow chart back to side edge. Continue to work from chart.

Before reaching frame for initial, find center st of first row of desired initial. This center st is represented by solid square on chart. Fill in as much as possible of first row of initial on chart so that you can start your initial in the right place. Work from initial chart thereafter for the center section of afghan. When half of afghan has been completed, read chart from top down to row 1.

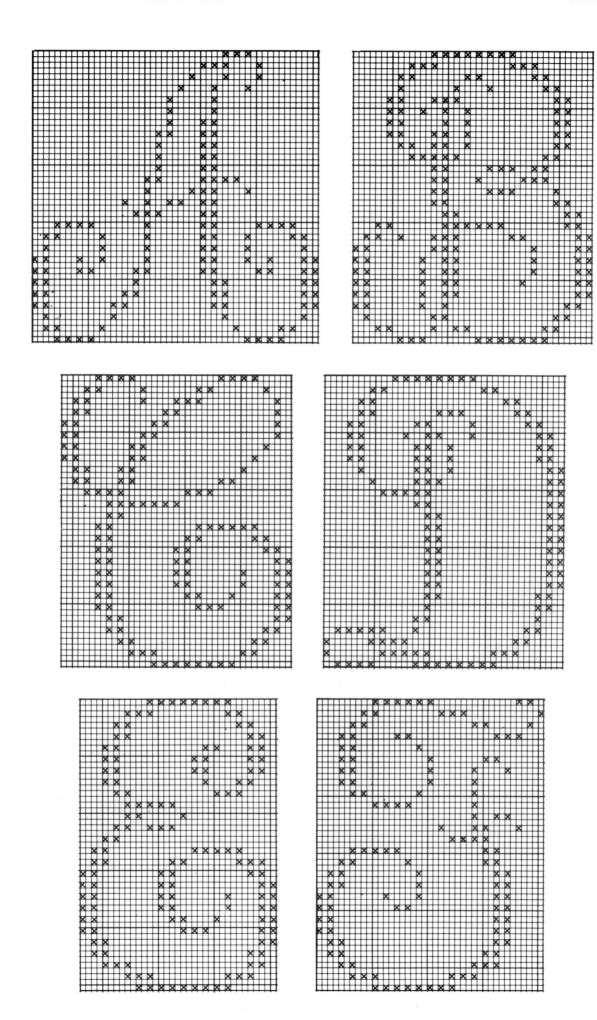

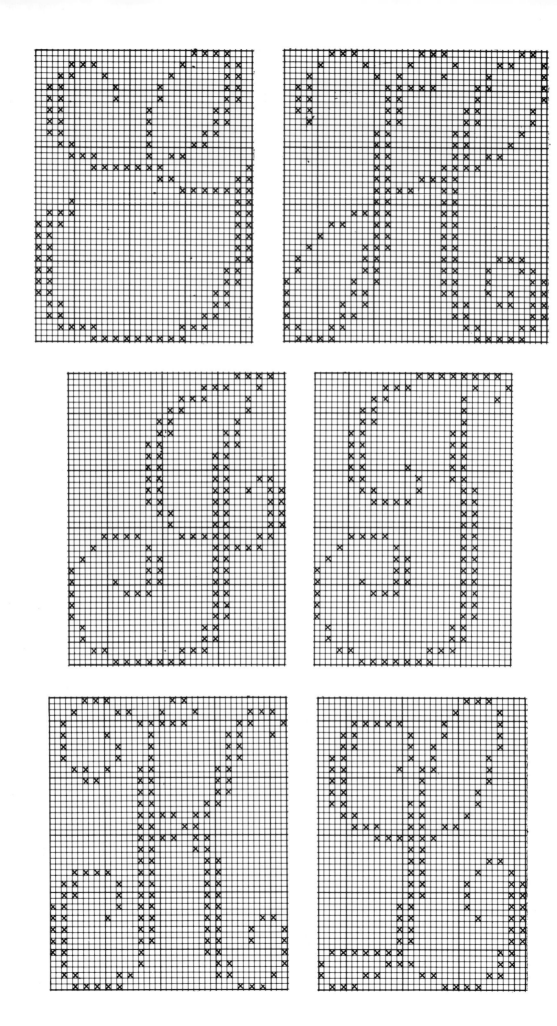

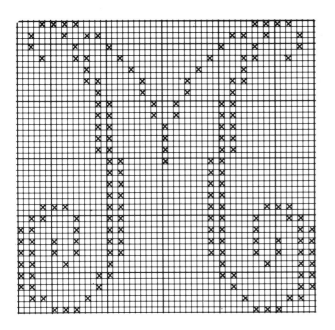

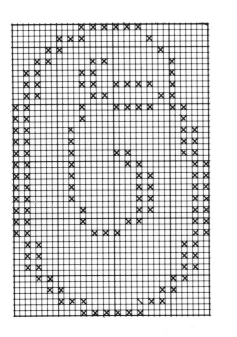

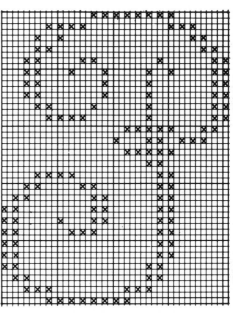

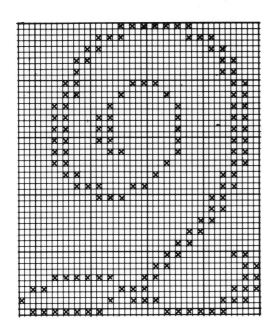

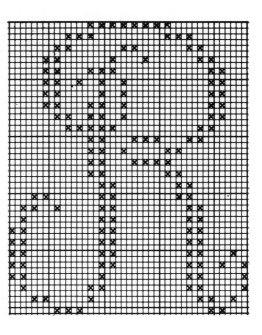

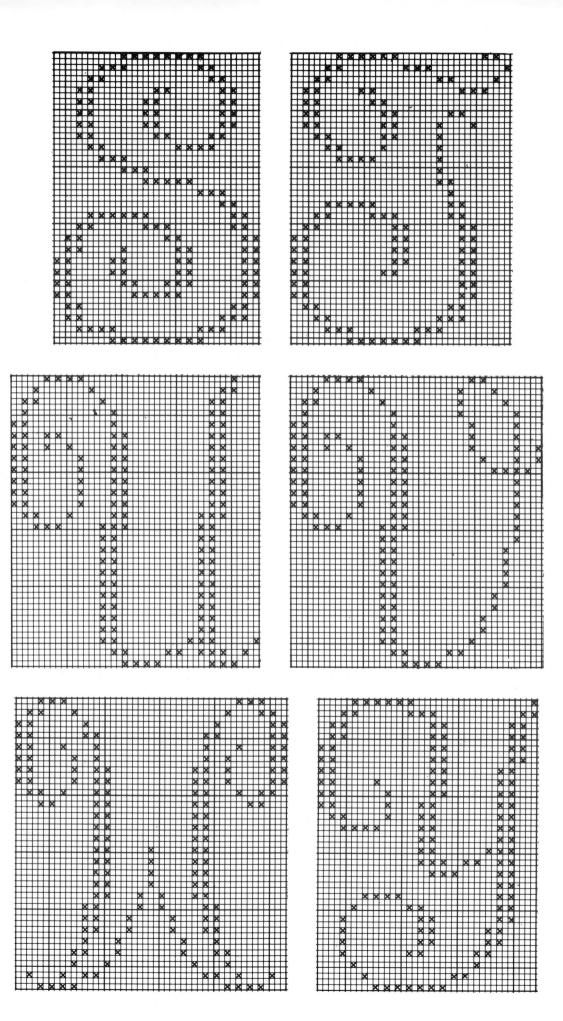

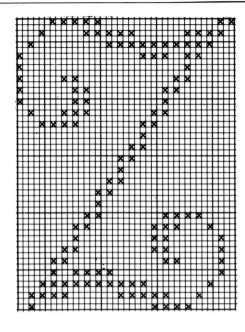

ROSEBUD COVER
Shown on page 150

SIZE: Fits standard hot water bottle.

MATERIALS: Yarn of knitting worsted weight, 2 ozs. each of white (W) and pink (P), 1 oz. light olive green (G). Crochet hook size G

GAUGE: 4 dc = 1″; 2 rows = 1″.

COVER: First Side: With W, ch 33. **Row 1:** Dc in 4th ch from hook, dc in each of next 29 ch. Ch 3, turn each row.

Row 2: Sk first dc, dc in each dc across, dc in top of ch 3—31 dc, counting ch 3 as 1 dc.

Row 3 (right side): Lay strand of G across top of work and work over it until needed. With W, sk first dc, dc in next 2 dc, changing to G in last dc. (To change colors, work dc until last 2 lps on hook, drop color to wrong side, finish dc with new color.) * Working over W, work G dc in next dc, finish dc with W. With W, working over G, dc in next 5 dc, change to G. Repeat from * 3 times, work G dc in next dc, work W dc in last 2 dc and in top of ch 3. Cut G.

Row 4 (wrong side): Lay strand of P across top of work. With W, sk first dc, dc in next 2 dc, change to P in last dc. * Working over W, work P 3-dc cluster in next dc, changing to W. (To make 3-dc cluster, hold back last lp of each dc on hook, work 3 dc in same st, drop P to front, pick up W and

pull through all lps on hook.) With W, working over P, dc in next 5 dc, change to P, repeat from * across, end dc in 2 dc, dc in top of ch 3. Cut P.

Rows 5 and 6: Repeat row 2.

Row 7: Lay strand of G across top of work. With W, sk first dc, dc in next 5 dc, * change to G. With G, dc in next dc, change to W. With W, working over G, dc in next 5 dc, repeat from * 3 times, dc in top of ch 3. Cut G.

Row 8: Lay strand of P across top of work. With W, sk first dc, dc in next 5 dc, * change to P. With P, 3-dc cluster in G dc, change to W; with W, working over P, dc in next 5 dc, repeat from * 3 times, dc in top of ch 3. Cut P.

Rows 9 and 10: Repeat row 2.

Rows 11–20: Repeat rows 3–10, then repeat rows 3 and 4.

Row 21: Sk first dc, (yo hook, pull up a lp in next dc, yo and through 2 lps) twice, yo and through 3 lps on hook (1 dec), dc in each st across to last 2 sts, dec over last 2 sts, do not work in ch 3 (2 dec).

Row 22: Sk first dc, dec over next 2 sts, dc in each st across to last 2 sts, dec over last 2 sts, do not work in ch 3.

Row 23: Dec 1 st as before, G dc in next dc, work in pat across, dec 2 sts as before.

Row 24: Work in pat across, dc in last st.

Row 25: Work even in dc across.

Row 26: Repeat row 22.

Row 27: Dc in next dc, G dc in next dc, work in pat across, dec 1 dc in last 2 sts, dc in top of ch 3.

Row 28: Dc in first st (1 inc), work in pat across, 2 dc in top of ch 3 (1 inc).

Row 29: Inc in first and last st—21 dc.

Row 30: Work even. At end of row 30, ch 1, turn.

Edging: Sc in each st across top, 2 sc over ch 3, 2 sc in end st of each row to lower edge, sc in each ch across lower edge, 2 sc in end st of each row to top. Sl st in first sc. End off.

SECOND SIDE: Work as for first side substituting P for W and W for P.

FINISHING: Embroider 2 G lazy daisy sts on row below each rosebud for leaves (see Stitch Details on page 308). With P, sc 2 sides tog, working through back lps only, from beg of row 20, down around bottom to end of rwo 20. Continue to work sc in back lp of each sc of first side only to beg of rnd. End off. With G, sl st in back lp of each P sc around. For tie, make a G ch 20″ long. Sl st in each ch across.

ROSE COVER

Shown on page 150

SIZE: Fits standard hot water bottle.

MATERIALS: Yarn of knitting worsted weight, 1 4-oz. skein white, 1 oz. light olive, small amounts of pink, dark pink and dark olive. Afghan hook size H. Crochet hook size H. Tapestry needle.

GAUGE: 4 sts = 1″; 4 rows = 1″.

COVER (make 2 pieces): With white, ch 30.

Row 1: Keeping all lps on hook, pull up a lp in 2nd ch from hook and in each ch across.

To Work Lps Off: Yo hook, pull through first lp, * yo hook, pull through next 2 lps, repeat from * across. Lp that remains on hook always counts as first st of next row.

Row 2: Pull up a lp in sp between first and 2nd sts (an inc), pull up a lp under each vertical bar across to last sp, pull up a lp in sp (an inc), pull up a lp under last vertical bar—32 lps on hook. Work lps off as before.

Row 3: Repeat row 2—34 sts. Work even in afghan st until piece is 9½″ from start.

Dec 1 st each side each row 8 times. To dec, pull up a lp under 2nd and 3rd vertical bars tog at beg of row, under 3rd and 2nd vertical bars from end of row. Work even on 18 sts for 4 rows. Inc 1 st each side every other row twice. Work even for 2 rows.

Change to crochet hook, sl st in each st across top. Cut white. With light olive, 2 sc in end st, sc in each end st to lower edge, 2 sc in corner, sc in each ch across lower edge, 2 sc in corner, sc in each end st to top, 2 sc in corner, sc in each sl st across top. Join; end off.

Embroidery: Following chart, embroider rose in cross-stitch on front piece (see page 309).

FINISHING: Steam-press pieces. With light olive, sl st pieces tog along wide section of cover (below top decreases) and across bottom, picking up back lps of sc only.

Tie: With light olive, ch 75. Sl st in each ch across. Sew mid-point of tie to one edge of cover at narrow section.

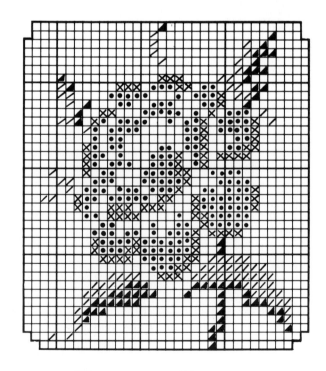

◪ LT. OLIVE		⊙ PINK
◢ DK. OLIVE		☒ DK. PINK

Traditional Irish patterns are a challenge to the knitter, but nothing makes a more luxurious coverlet than the rich textures of Aran. Seven panels of embossed stitches make up this Nosegay Aran Afghan; directions on page 256.

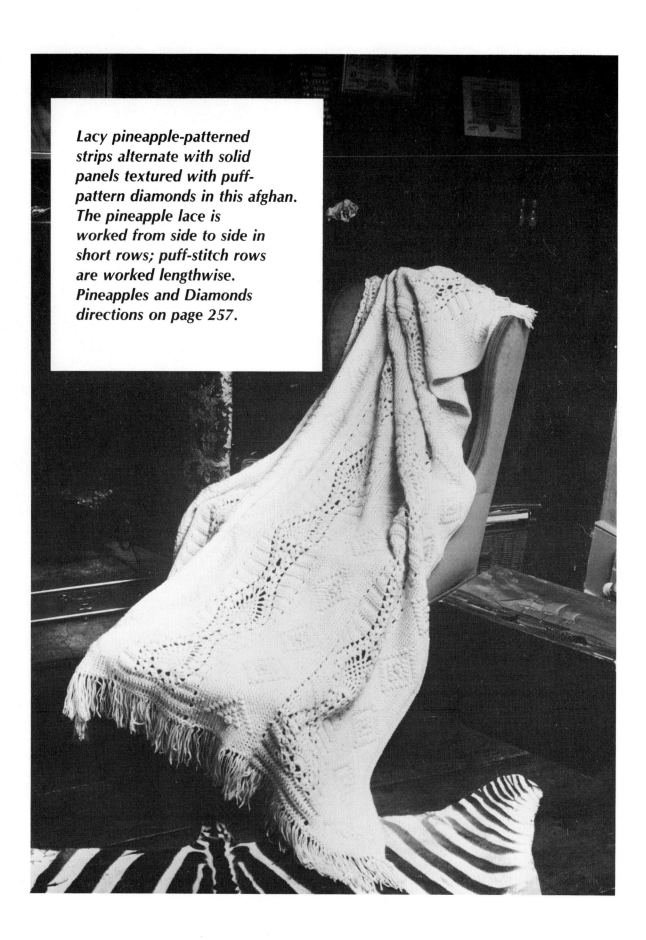

Lacy pineapple-patterned strips alternate with solid panels textured with puff-pattern diamonds in this afghan. The pineapple lace is worked from side to side in short rows; puff-stitch rows are worked lengthwise. Pineapples and Diamonds directions on page 257.

Two heirloom afghans, one to knit, one to crochet, add to the charm of country decor. Irish Fisherman Afghan, left, is knit in one piece with double strand of yarn; directions on page 259. Popcorn Square, crocheted, can be used as afghan or bedspread; directions on page 255.

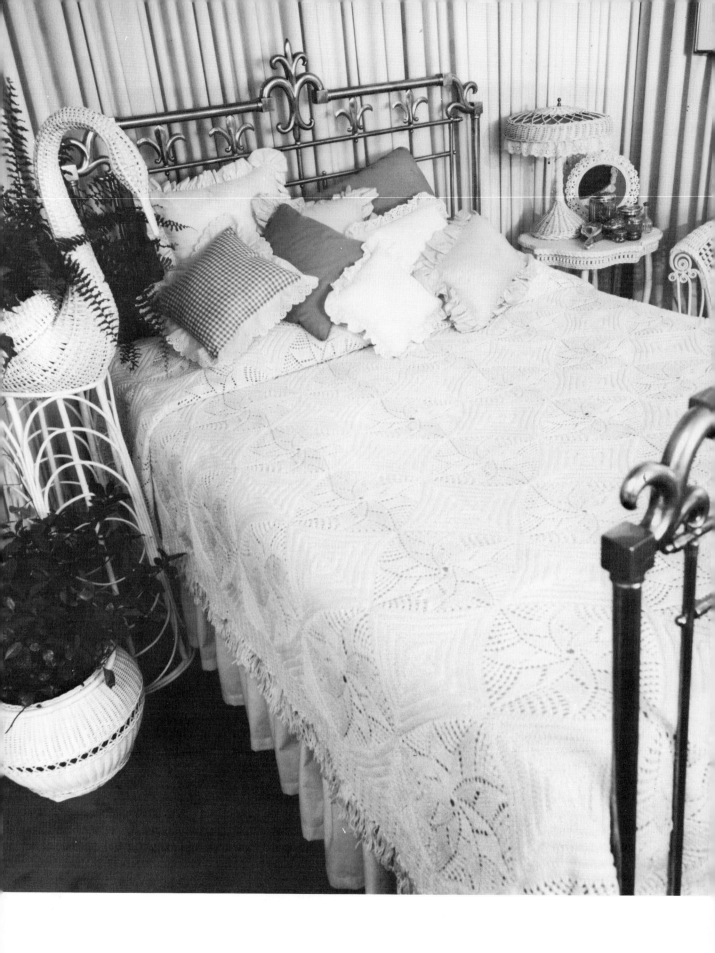

Swirling stars adorn a knitted bedspread, made in squares for a project that can travel with you (below). Stars are knitted from the center out, using double-pointed needles; the striped corners are Quaker-stitched. Shown here in double-bed size, you can easily adapt it to any size by adding or subtracting squares. Star Bedspread directions on page 260.

*Charming water lilies float on a background of
flat stitches, open mesh, and nubby popcorns.
Hexagon motifs are worked separately, then
sewn together for the size you want and fringed
on three sides with the bedspread cotton.
Water Lily Bedspread, directions on page 261.*

Bridal Rose Afghan features
three-dimensional roses on a field of white.
Three rings of raised petals form
each rose on a flat background of double crochet
and chain loop patterns. Directions on page 264.

This Colonial Bedspread is timeless in its
appeal, as lovely on a four-poster
as it is with contemporary furnishings.
Square motifs are centered with rosettes
in relief, have rows of raised popcorns
and openwork filet crochet. Knotted fringe
finishes sides and lower edge.
Directions on page 265.

213

Nautical Stars and Bars afghan in red, white and blue is made of four identical strips knitted in a repeat pattern. The stars within stars are worked with bobbins so colors do not have to be carried across the white background; directions on page 267.

INISHMORE
Shown on page 151

SIZE: About 52″ × 60″, without fringe.

MATERIALS: Unger's Roly Poly, 3½-oz. ball, 10 balls Off White. Knitting needles No. 8. One dp needle. Aluminum crochet hook size H.

GAUGE: 9 sts = 2″.

PATTERN 1 (Bobble Pat—17 sts): **Row 1** (right side): * K 1, p 1, repeat from *, end k 1.

Row 2: Purl.

Row 3: * Bobble st (k 4sts in 1 st, alternating from front to back. Turn, p these 4 sts. Turn, sl 1, k 3 tog, pass sl st over last st), p 1, k 1, p 1, repeat from *, end bobble st—5 bobbles.

Row 4: Repeat row 2.

Row 5: Repeat row 1.

Row 6: Repeat row 2.

Row 7: * K 1, p 1, bobble st, p 1, repeat from *, end p 1, k 1—4 bobbles.

Row 8: Repeat row 2. Repeat these 8 rows for pat 1.

PATTERN 2 (Diagonal Left—17 sts): **Row 1** (right side): P 1, (k 3, p 3) twice, k 3, p 1.

Row 2: (P 3, k 3) twice, p 3, k 2.

Row 3: Repeat row 2.

Row 4: Repeat row 1.

Row 5: K 2, (p 3, k 3) twice, p 3.

Row 6: Repeat row 5. Repeat these 6 rows for pat 2.

PATTERN 3 (Diagonal Right—17 sts):

Row 1 (right side): P 1, (k 3, p 3) twice, k 3, p 1.

Row 2: K 2, (p 3, k 3) twice, p 3.

Row 3: Repeat row 2.

Row 4: Repeat row 1.

Row 5: (P 3, k 3) twice, p 3, k 2.

Row 6: Repeat row 5. Repeat these 6 rows for pat 3.

PATTERN 4 (Box St—17 sts): **Row 1** (right side): K 1, (p 3, k 3) twice, p 3, k 1.

Row 2: P 1, (k 3, p 3) twice, k 3, p 1.

Rows 3 and 4: Repeat row 1.

Row 5: Repeat row 2.

Row 6 : Repeat row 1. Repeat these 6 rows for pat 4.

Box A

STOCK ST	PATTERN 1	STOCK ST
PATTERN 2	STOCK ST	PATTERN 3
STOCK ST	PATTERN 1	STOCK ST

Each box within box is 17 sts and 20 rows

Box B

STOCK ST	PATTERN 9	STOCK ST
PATTERN 10	STOCK ST	PATTERN 10
STOCK ST	PATTERN 7	STOCK ST

Each box within box is 17 sts and 20 rows

Box C

STOCK ST	PATTERN 7	STOCK ST
PATTERN 6	STOCK ST	PATTERN 6
STOCK ST	PATTERN 8	STOCK ST

Each box within box is 17 sts and 20 rows

Box D

STOCK ST	PATTERN 4	STOCK ST
PATTERN 5	STOCK ST	PATTERN 5
STOCK ST	PATTERN 4	STOCK ST

Each box within box is 17 sts and 20 rows

16 rows garter st

Box C

16 rows garter st

Box B

16 rows garter st

Box A

16 rows garter st

Box D

16 rows garter st

Box C

16 rows garter st

12 sts—Right Cable

12 sts—Left Cable

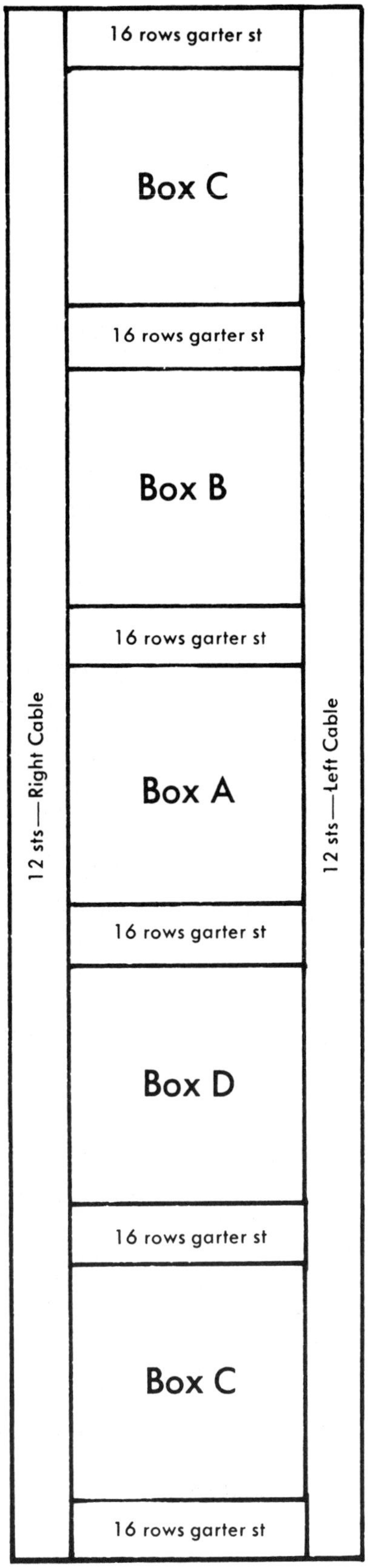

PATTERN 5 (Seed and Cable—17 sts):
Row 1 (right side): P 1, (k 3, p 1, k 1, p 1) twice, k 3, p 1.

Row 2: (P 5, k 1) twice, p 5.

Row 3: P 1, (sk 2 sts, k next st, k the 2 skipped sts, sl knitted st already worked off needle, p 1, k 1, p 1) twice, sk 2 sts, k next st, k the 2 skipped sts, sl knitted st already worked off needle (cable twist—CT), p 1.

Row 4: Repeat row 2.

Row 5: Repeat row 1.

Row 6: Repeat row 2. Repeat rows 3–6 for pat 5.

PATTERN 6 (Seed St—17 sts): **Row 1:** K 1, p 1) 8 times, k 1.

Row 2: (P 1, k 1) 8 times, p 1.

Row 3: Repeat row 2.

Row 4: Repeat row 1. Repeat these 4 rows for pat 6.

PATTERN 7 (Raised Diagonal Right—17 sts):
Row 1: * K 2, sk 1 st, insert needle as to p in next st, turn and k the skipped st, take the 2 sts off left-hand needle (2 twist right or 2 TR), repeat from *, end k 1.

Row 2 and All Even Rows: Purl.

Row 3: K 1, (2 TR, k 2) 4 times.

Row 5: (2 TR, k 2) 4 times, end last repeat, k 3.

Row 7: K 3, (2 TR, k 2) 3 times, 2 TR.

Row 8: Purl. Repeat these 8 rows for pat 7.

PATTERN 8 (Raised Diagonal Left—17 sts):
Row 1: K 1, * sk 1 st, k next st from back, insert needle in skipped st as to p and sl both sts off left-hand needle (2 twist left or 2 TL), k 2, repeat from *.

Row 2 and All Even Rows: Purl.

Row 3: (K 2, 2 TL) 4 times, k 1.

Row 5: K 3, (2 TL, k 2) 3 times, 2 TL.

Row 7: (2 TL, k 2) 4 times, end last repeat k 3.

Row 8: Purl. Repeat these 8 rows for pat 8.

PATTERN 9 (Raised Box St—17 sts): **Row 1:** (P 2, k 1) 5 times, p 2.

Row 2: (K 2, p 1) 5 times, k 2.

Row 3: Knit.

Row 4: Purl. Repeat these 4 rows for pat 9.

PATTERN 10 (Snake St—17 sts): **Row 1:** (right side): (P 2, k 3) 3 times, p 2.

Row 2 and All Even Rows: (K 2, p 3) 3 times, k 2.

Row 3: (P 2, sk 2 sts, k next st, k 2 skipped sts, sl knitted st already worked off left-hand needle) 3 times, p 2.

Row 5: (P 2, sl 1 st to dp needle, hold in front, k 2, k st from dp needle) 3 times, p 2.

Row 6: Repeat row 2. Repeat rows 3–6 for pat 10.

RIGHT CABLE (RC—12 sts): **Rows 1 and 3:** K 12.

Row 2 and All Even Rows: K 2, p 8, k 2.

Row 5: K 2, sl 4 sts to dp needle, hold in back of work, k 4, k 4 from dp needle, k 2.

Rows 7, 9 and 11: Repeat row 1.

Row 12: Repeat row 2. Repeat these 12 rows for RC.

LEFT CABLE (LC—12 sts): Work as for RC, but on cable twist, sl 4 to dp needle, hold in front of work, k 4, k 4 from dp needle.

STRIP 1: Cast on 77 sts. **Row 1:** Work 12 sts RC (see Right Cable), k 53, work last 12 sts RC. Repeat row 1 for 15 times more (garter st border, RC each side). The 12-st RC will be worked each end for entire strip.

BOX A: Row 1: Work RC, k 17, sl 1 with yarn in back, 17 sts pat 1, sl 1 with yarn in back, k 17, work RC.

Row 2: RC, p 17, p the sl st, 17 sts pat 1, p the sl st, p 17, RC. Repeat rows 1 and 2 until there are 20 rows.

Row 21: RC, 17 sts pat 3, sl 1 with yarn in back, k 17, sl 1, 17 sts pat 2, RC.

Row 22: RC, 17 sts pat 2, p the sl st, p 17, p the sl st, 17 sts pat 3, RC. Repeat rows 21 and 22 until there are 20 rows in this group of boxes.

Rows 41–60: Repeat rows 1 and 2. See diagram, Box A.

BOX B: K 16 rows garter st (k each row) with RC at each end as established.

Row 1: RC, k 17, sl 1, 17 sts pat 9, sl 1, k 17, RC.

Row 2: RC, p 17, p the sl st, 17 sts pat 9, p the sl st, p 17, RC. Repeat rows 1 and 2 until there are 20 rows.

Row 21: RC, 17 sts pat 10, sl 1, k 17, sl 1, 17 sts pat 10, RC.

Row 22: RC, 17 sts pat 10, p the sl st, p 17, p

the sl st, 17 sts pat 10, RC. Repeat rows 21 and 22 until there are 20 rows in this group of boxes.

Rows 41–60: Repeat rows 1 and 2. See diagram, Box B.

BOX C: K 16 rows garter st with RC at each end.

Row 1: RC, k 17, sl 1, 17 sts pat 8, sl 1, k 17, RC.

Row 2: RC, p 17, p the sl st, 17 sts pat 8, p the sl st, p 17, RC. Repeat rows 1 and 2 until there are 20 rows.

Row 21: RC, 17 sts pat 6, sl 1, k 17, sl 1, 17 sts pat 6, RC.

Row 22: RC, 17 sts pat 6, p the sl st, p 17, p the sl st, 17 sts pat 6, RC. Repeat rows 21 and 22 until there are 20 rows in this group of boxes.

Rows 41–60: Repeat rows 1 and 2, working pat 7 instead of 8 so diagonal goes in opposite direction. See diagram, Box C.

BOX D: K 16 rows garter st with RC at each end.

Row 1: RC, k 17, sl 1, 17 sts pat 4, sl 1, k 17, RC.

Row 2: RC, p 17, p sl st, 17 sts pat 4, p sl st, p 17, RC. Repeat rows 1 and 2 until there are 20 rows.

Row 21: RC, 17 sts pat 5, sl 1, k 17, sl 1, 17 sts pat 5, RC.

Row 22: RC, 17 sts pat 5, p sl st, p 17, p sl st, 17 sts pat 5, RC. Repeat rows 21 and 22 until there are 20 rows in this group of boxes.

Rows 41–60: Repeat rows 1 and 2. See diagram, Box D.

BOX E: K 16 rows garter st with RC at each end as established. Work as for Box A. K 16 rows garter st with RC at each end. Bind off.

STRIP 2: See diagram.

STRIP 3: Work same as for Strip 1, working 12 Left Cable sts each side of strip, instead of Right Cable each side.

FINISHING: Wet block each strip if necessary. Wet with cold water, lay on a towel to measurements. Dry away from heat and sun. Weave Strip 2 to one side of Strips 1 and 3. From right side, sl st along each side edge, making sure work lies flat. For fringe, cut 12″ strands. Knot 4 strands tog in end st at bottom edge and in every 3rd st across. Repeat fringe on top edge.

PATCH PANELS
Shown on page 152

SIZE: 56″ (across 7 strips) × 50″ (length of strips).

MATERIAL: Yarn of knitting worsted weight, 7 4-oz. skeins black, about 22 ozs. of assorted colors. Knitting needles No. 6. Crochet hook size F.

GAUGE: 5 sts = 1″.

STRIPS: With black, cast on 40 sts. Work in garter st (k every row) until strip is 50″ long or desired length. Bind off. Make 3 more black strips. Work 3 colored strips the same, changing colors as desired.

FINISHING: With black, alternating black and colored strips, weave edges of strips tog. With one color, embroider a row of cross-stitch over each seam (see page 309), working half of each cross from bottom to top, then coming back to finish each cross.

Edging: Row 1: With hook, from wrong side, attach black to corner of afghan. Working across bound-off edge of 7 strips, sc in first st, * ch 3, sk 2 sts, sc in next st, repeat from * across. Ch 1, turn.

Row 2: 5 dc in first ch-3, sp, * sc in next sp, 5 dc in next sp, repeat from * across. End off.

Work same edging at opposite edge.

EMBROIDERED COVERLET
Shown on page 183

SIZE: 66″ × 82½″.

EQUIPMENT: Colored pencil. Pencil. Ruler. Yardstick. Tailor's chalk. Scissors. Paper for patterns. Dressmaker's tracing (carbon) paper. Dry ball-point pen or tracing wheel. Straight pins. Sewing and embroidery needles. Embroidery hoop or adjustable wooden stretcher frame. Steam iron. Padded surface.

MATERIALS: Twin-sized (66″ × 90″) lightweight blanket (wool, cotton, or polyester) with whipstitched edges, ivory or white (see Blanket Note). Paternayan Paterna Persian Yarn, 40-yard skeins: navy #321, 9; rust #242, 7. **For Border/Box Design:** Woven borders of original coverlet can be imitated with embroidery or appliqués. **For

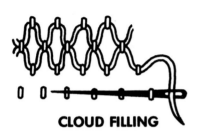

CLOUD FILLING

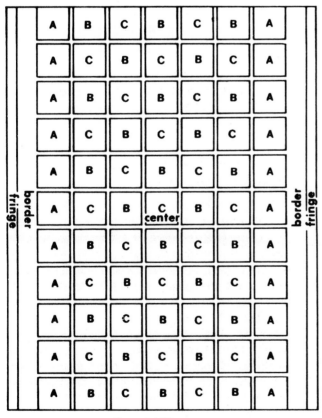

A	B	C	B	C	B	A
A	C	B	C	B	C	A
A	B	C	B	C	B	A
A	C	B	C	B	C	A
A	B	C	B	C	B	A
A	C	B	C center	B	C	A
A	B	C	B	C	B	A
A	C	B	C	B	C	A
A	B	C	B	C	B	A
A	C	B	C	B	C	A
A	B	C	B	C	B	A

border fringe

border fringe

Coverlet Diagram

A

B

C

Crewel Motifs

Appliqués: Lightweight wool or muslin fabric 36″ wide, in color to coordinate with embroidery, $2\frac{1}{4}$ yards. (Or use blanket binding and $\frac{1}{2}$″-wide ribbon.) Matching thread. **For Embroidery:** Paternayan Persian Yarn, blue #350, eight 40-yard skeins.

BLANKET NOTE: The coverlet shown on page 183 was woven to 66″ × $82\frac{1}{2}$″; trim the purchased blanket to length and whipstitch upper and lower edges, **OR** you can make your own blanket from wool, monk's cloth, or any medium- to heavyweight fabric; cut fabric to 66″ × $82\frac{1}{2}$″.

DIRECTIONS: Find center of blanket by basting a straight line from center of one edge to center of opposite edge; then baste another line from center of third edge to center of fourth edge. Basting threads will cross at center of blanket. For vertical lines of box design, measure and mark several points along length of blanket $3\frac{3}{4}$″ to the left and right of vertical basting line; lightly draw two $82\frac{1}{2}$″ lines through these marks with tailor's chalk. Draw three lines to the left and three lines to the right of these lines $7\frac{1}{2}$″ apart, for eight vertical lines. Measure $4\frac{1}{4}$″ to the left and right of outer vertical lines and draw two more lines for border (these are outer border edges). For horizontal lines, measure and mark points $3\frac{3}{4}$″ above and below widthwise basting line; lightly draw two lines through these marks with tailor's chalk, beginning and ending lines at inner edges of borders. Draw four lines above and four lines below these lines, all $7\frac{1}{2}$″ apart for 10 horizontal lines; you should have 77 squares.

To appliqué the border/box design, cut the following pieces from wool or muslin fabric: two borders, $4\frac{3}{4}$″ × 83″; six verticals, 1″ × 83″, piecing for length if necessary; ten horizontals, 1″ × 62″. Turn ends of horizontals under $\frac{1}{2}$″; turn ends of all other pieces and all side edges under $\frac{1}{4}$″; press in place. Pin borders in marked positions; slipstitch in place, along ends and inner edges only. Pin six verticals centered over marked lines; slipstitch in place. Pin ten horizontals centered over marked lines and overlapping verticals and borders; slip turned-in ends under outer edge of each border; slip-stitch.

To embroider the border/box design, draw lines $\frac{1}{4}$″ above and below marked grid lines to make $\frac{1}{2}$″-wide bands across the coverlet; see Coverlet Diagram. Separate Persian yarn into three strands. Use one strand in needle to fill in bands and border with cloud filling stitch (or any desired); see embroidery stitch details on page 309. To keep cloud-filling stitches straight, use ruler and tailor's chalk to mark rows of dotted lines about $\frac{1}{4}$″ apart for length of border; embroider straight stitches on these lines.

To embroider **crewel motifs,** use sharp colored pencil to draw lines across pattern, connecting grid lines. Enlarge A, B, and C patterns by copying on paper ruled in 1″ squares. Using dressmaker's carbon and dry ball-point pen, transfer one motif to center of each box, following Coverlet Diagram and color illustration for placement. Separate the three strands of Persian yarn and use one strand in needle: Embroider tiny ovals in satin stitch; embroider all other areas in chain stitch. Embroider A and inner lines of C with rust; embroider B and outer lines of C with navy.

If desired and if fabric is suitable, fringe side edges as shown in illustration; zigzag-stitch by machine close to fringe to secure.

To Block: Place finished embroidery face down on padded surface. Steam-press gently.

TRELLIS RUG
Shown on page 184

SIZE: 29″ × 49″.

EQUIPMENT: Latch hook. Scissors. Tapestry needle.

MATERIALS: Brunswick Orlon Acrylic Rug Yarn (320 pieces per package): see key for color numbers and number of packages needed (in parentheses). Brunswick rug canvas, 3.3 mesh-to-the inch, 36″ wide, $1\frac{1}{2}$ yards. Carpet thread. Rug binding, $4\frac{1}{2}$ yards (optional).

DIRECTIONS: Read directions (opposite page) for How to Latch Hook. Place canvas on table with selvage edges at sides and about 3″ of canvas extending off table toward you; roll up op-

Continued on page 222

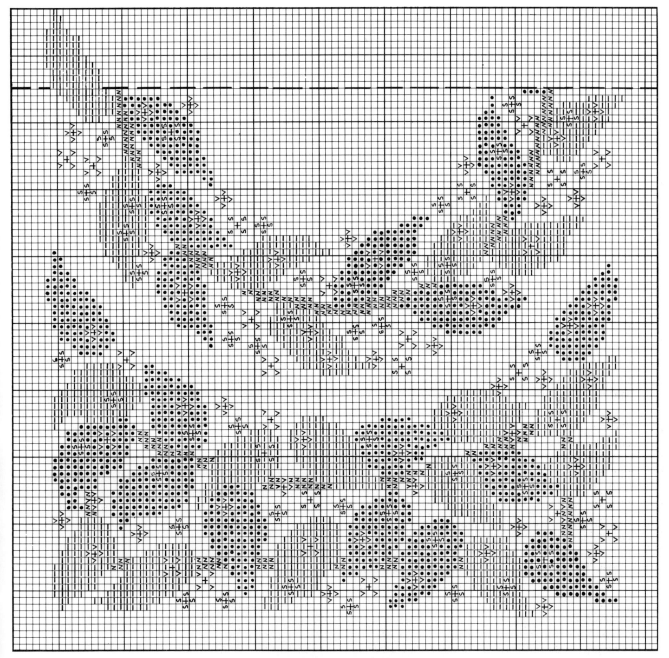

Half-Chart for Trellis Rug

How To Latch Hook: Fold yarn over shank of hook, **Fig. 1;** hold ends with left hand. With hook in right hand and latch down, push hook down through mesh under double horizontal threads and up, **Fig. 2;** draw hook toward you, placing yarn ends inside hook, **Fig. 3.** Be sure the yarn is completely inside hook when the latch closes. Pull hook back through canvas, drawing yarn through loop. Tighten knot by pulling yarn ends, **Fig. 4.**

☐ White #149 (29)
⊡ Apple #145 (9)
⦿ Shamrock #141 (9)
⊠ Nutmeg #105 (2)

ⓢ Orchid #163 (2)
⊵ Sky Blue #171 (2)
⊞ Medium Yellow #116 (1)

FIGURE 1

FIGURE 2

FIGURE 3

FIGURE 4

posite end. Turn five rows of extended canvas to front; work first five rows through this doubled canvas for a finished end. Measuring 3½″ in from right selvage, work first row across from right to left, following bottom row of chart and color key; each square on chart represents one knot. (Or work from left to right, if you find it easier.) Continue to work across in rows to dash line at top of chart, for half of rug; complete leaf beyond dash line.

To work second half of rug, follow chart in reverse, not repeating leaf at upper left. When five rows from end of chart, cut off excess canvas beyond ten rows. Turn five rows to front and work last five rows of rug through doubled canvas.

Turn long edges to back of rug, leaving on selvages or trimming canvas to 2″. Slip-stitch edges in place with carpet thread, trimming corners. If desired, add rug binding over canvas edges and across ends, slip-stitching both edges of binding and mitering corners.

CROCHETED NET CANOPY
Shown on page 185

SIZE: Directions for twin sized bed, 81″ × 40″. Changes for double size, 81″ × 56″, are in parentheses.

MATERIALS: American Thread Giant Mercerized Crochet Cotton, 14 (18) 550-yd. balls. Steel crochet hook No. 4.

GAUGE: 4 meshes = 3″; 5 rows = 2″ (2 strands of cotton).

Note: Use thread double throughout.

CANOPY: TOP: With 2 strands, make a chain a few inches longer than width of bed frame.

Row 1: Sc in 10th ch from hook, * ch 7, sk 4 ch, sc in next ch, repeat from * across until piece is width of bed frame. (Extra ch can be cut off or unraveled.) Ch 7, turn.

Row 2: Sc in first lp, * ch 7, sc in next lp, repeat from * across. Ch 7, turn. Repeat row 2 until piece is 81″ long or long enough to fit top of bed. Ch 7, turn.

Last Row: Sc in first lp, * ch 4, sc in next lp, repeat from * across. End off.

DROP EDGING: FIRST POINT: With 2 strands, ch 7. Join with a sl st to form ring. (Tassels are attached later to rings.)

Row 1: Ch 7, 3 tr in same ch with sl st, ch 2, tr in same ch. Ch 7, turn.

Row 2: 3 tr in 7th ch from hook, ch 2, sc in middle tr of 3 tr, ch 2, 3 tr in 3rd ch of turning ch, ch 2, tr in same ch as 3 tr. Ch 7, turn.

Row 3: 3 tr in 7th ch from hook, ch 2, sc in middle tr of 3 tr, ch 2, 3 tr in sc, ch 2, sc in middle tr of 3 tr, ch 2, 3 tr in 3rd ch of turning ch, ch 2, tr in same ch. Ch 7, turn.

Row 4: 3 tr in 7th ch from hook, (ch 2, sc in middle tr of 3 tr, ch 2, 3 tr in sc) twice, ch 2, sc in middle tr of 3 tr, ch 2, 3 tr in 3rd ch of turning ch, ch 2, tr in same ch. Ch 7, turn.

Row 5: 3 tr in 7th ch from hook, ch 2, sc in middle tr of 3 tr, ch 2, 3 tr in sc, ch 2, sc in middle tr of 3 tr, ch 7, sc in middle tr of next 3 tr, ch 2, 3 tr in sc, ch 2, sc in middle tr of next 3 tr, ch 2, 3 tr in 3rd ch of turning ch, ch 2, tr in same ch. Ch 7, turn.

Row 6: * 3 tr in 7th ch from hook, ch 2, sc in middle tr of 3 tr, ch 2, 3 tr in sc, ch 2, sc in middle tr of 3 tr, ch 7, sc in next lp *, ch 7, ** sc in middle tr of 3 tr, ch 2, 3 tr in sc, ch 2, sc in middle tr of next 3 tr, ch 2, 3 tr in 3rd ch of turning ch, ch 2, tr in same ch. Ch 7, turn.**

Row 7: Work from first * to 2nd * of row 6, ch 2, 3 tr in next sc, ch 2, sc in next lp, ch 7, work from first ** to 2nd ** of row 6.

Row 8: Work from first * to 2nd * of row 6, ch 2, 3 tr in next sc, ch 2, sc in middle tr of 3 tr, ch 2, 3 tr in next sc, ch 2, sc in next lp, ch 7, work from first ** to 2nd ** of row 6.

Row 9: Work from first * to 2nd * of row 6, (ch 2, 3 tr in next sc, ch 2, sc in middle tr of 3 tr) twice, ch 2, 3 tr in next sc, ch 2, sc in next lp, ch 7, work from first ** to 2nd ** of row 6.

Row 10: Work from first * to 2nd * of row 6, (ch 2, 3 tr in next sc, ch 2, sc in middle tr of 3 tr) 3 times, ch 2, 3 tr in next sc, ch 2, sc in next lp, ch 7, work from first ** to 2nd ** of row 6.

Row 11: Work from first * to 2nd * of row 6, (ch 2, 3 tr in next sc, ch 2, sc in middle tr of 3 tr) twice, ch 7, sc in middle tr of next 3 tr, ch 2, 3 tr in next sc, ch 2, sc in middle tr of 3 tr, ch 2, 3 tr in next sc, ch 2, sc in next lp, ch 7, work from first ** to 2nd ** of row 6. At end of row 11, do not ch 7. End off.

SECOND POINT: Work as for first point through row 11. Before ending off, sl st in 5th ch of ch 7 at beg of row 11 of first point. End off. Work as many points as needed to fit around all four sides of canopy, joining each point to previous point as second point was joined to first point. Plan points to start and end at corners of canopy. For instance, if point is 10″ wide, plan 4 (6) points across front and back of canopy, 8 for each side. If point is 9″ wide, plan 5 (6) points across front and back of canopy, 9 for each side. When all points are made and joined, open up the sl st at end of row 11 of first point and join to last point made.

Row 12: With 2 strands, make lp on hook; sc in middle tr of first shell (a shell is 3 tr) of any point. * Ch 2, shell in next sc, ch 2, sc in middle tr of next shell, ch 2, shell in next sc, ch 2, sc in next lp, ch 7, (sc in middle tr of next shell, ch 2, shell in next sc, ch 2) twice, sc in next lp, (ch 2, shell in next sc, ch 2, sc in middle tr of next shell) twice, ch 7, sc in next lp, (ch 2, shell in next sc, ch 2, sc in middle tr of next shell), ch 2, shell in joining between points, ch 2, sc in middle tr of first shell of next point, repeat from * around, end ch 2, sl st in first sc.

Row 13: Sl st in each of 2 ch, sl st in next tr, sc in middle tr of shell, * ch 2, shell in next sc, ch 2, sc in middle tr of next shell, ch 2, shell in next sc, ch 2, sc in next lp, ch 7, sc in middle tr of next shell, (ch 2, shell in next sc, ch 2, sc in middle tr of next shell) 3 times, ch 7, sc in next lp, (ch 2, shell in next sc, ch 2, sc in middle tr of next shell) twice, (ch 7, sc in middle tr of next shell) twice, repeat from * around, end ch 7, sl st in first sc.

Row 14: Sl st to middle tr of next shell, sc in same tr, * ch 2, shell in next sc, ch 2, sc in middle tr of next shell, ch 2, shell in next sc, ch 2, sc in next lp, ch 7, sc in middle tr of next shell, (ch 2, shell in next sc, ch 2, sc in middle tr of next shell) twice, ch 7, sc in next lp, (ch 2, shell in next sc, ch 2, sc in middle tr of next shell) twice, ch 7, sc in next lp, ch 2, shell in next sc, ch 2, sc in next lp, ch 7, sc in middle tr of next shell, repeat from * around, end ch 7, sl st in first sc.

Row 15: Sl st to middle tr of next shell, sc in same tr, * ch 2, shell in next sc, ch 2, sc in middle tr of next shell, ch 2, shell in next sc, ch 2, sc in next lp, ch 7, sc in middle tr of next shell, ch 2, shell in next sc, ch 2, sc in middle tr of next shell, ch 7, sc in next lp, (ch 2, shell in next sc, ch 2, sc in middle tr of next shell) twice, ch 7, sc in next lp, ch 7, sc in middle tr of next shell, ch 7, sc in next lp, ch 7, sc in middle tr of next shell, repeat from * around, end ch 7, sl st in first sc.

Row 16: Sl st to middle tr of next shell, sc in same tr, * ch 2, shell in next sc, ch 2, sc in middle tr of next shell, ch 2, shell in next sc, ch 2, sc in next lp, ch 7, sc in middle tr of next shell, ch 7, sc in next lp, (ch 2, shell in next sc, ch 2, sc in middle tr of next shell) twice, (ch 7, sc in next lp) twice, ch 2, shell in next sc, ch 2, sc in next lp, ch 7, sc in next lp, ch 7, sc in middle tr of next shell, repeat from * around, end ch 7, sl st in first sc.

Row 17: sl st to middle tr of next shell, sc in same tr, * ch 2, shell in next sc, ch 2, sc in middle tr of next shell, ch 2, shell in next sc, ch 2, sc in next lp, ch 7, sc in next lp, (ch 2, shell in next sc, ch 2, sc in middle tr of next shell) twice, (ch 7, sc in next lp) twice, ch 7, sc in middle tr of next shell, (ch 7, sc in next lp) twice, ch 7, sc in middle tr of next shell, repeat from * around, end ch 7, sl st in first sc.

Row 18: Sl st to middle tr of next shell, sc in same tr, * ch 2, shell in next sc, ch 2, sc in middle tr of next shell, ch 2, shell in next sc, ch 2, sc in next lp, (ch 2, shell in next sc, ch 2, sc in middle tr of next shell) twice, (ch 7, sc in next lp) 3 times, ch 2, shell in next sc, ch 2, sc in next lp, (ch 7, sc in next lp) twice, ch 7, sc in middle tr of next shell, repeat from * around, end ch 7, sl st in first sc.

Row 19: Sl st to middle tr of next shell, sc in same tr, * (ch 2, shell in next sc, ch 2, sc in middle tr of next shell) 3 times, (ch 7, sc in next lp) 3 times, ch 7, sc in middle tr of next shell, (ch 7, sc in next lp) 3 times, ch 7, sc in middle tr of next shell, repeat from * around, end ch 7, sl st in first sc.

Row 20: Sl st to middle tr of next shell, sc in same tr, * (ch 2, shell in next sc, ch 2, sc in middle tr of next shell) twice, (ch 7, sc in next lp) 4 times, ch 2, shell in next sc, ch 2, (sc in next lp, ch 7) 4 times, sc in middle tr of next shell, repeat from * around, end ch 7, sl st in first sc.

Row 21: Sl st to middle tr of next shell, sc in same tr, * ch 2, shell in next sc, ch 2, sc in middle tr of next shell, (ch 7, sc in next lp) 4 times, ch 7, sc in middle tr of next shell, (ch 7, sc in next lp) 4 times, ch 7, sc in middle tr of next shell, repeat from * around, end ch 7, sl st in first sc.

Row 22: Sl st to middle tr of next shell, sc in same tr, (ch 7, sc in next lp) 5 times, ch 2, shell in next sc, ch 2, sc in next lp, (ch 7, sc in next lp) 4 times, ch 7, sc in middle tr of next shell, repeat from * around, end ch 7, sl st in first sc.

Row 23: Sl st to center of first lp, sc in lp, (ch 7, sc in next lp) 4 times, * ch 7, sc in middle tr of next shell, (ch 7, sc in next lp) 10 times, repeat from * around, end (ch 7, sc in next lp) 5 times, ch 7, sl st in first sc.

Row 24: Sl st to center of first lp, sc in lp, (ch 7, sc in next lp) 4 times, * ch 2, shell in next sc, ch 2, sc in next lp, (ch 7, sc in next lp) 10 times, repeat from * around, end (ch 7, sc in next lp) 5 times, ch 7, sl st in first sc. End off.

FINISHING: Pin edging to top. Sew or crochet edging to top. Edging can be crocheted to top with sc or ch-7 lps. Make a tassel for each point and notch between points. To make tassel, wind thread (use several balls tog if available) around 6″ cardboard to desired thickness of tassel. Tie strands tog at one end. Cut strands at other end. Wind thread tightly around tassel 1″ below top of tassel for 1″ depth. Fasten off. Trim tassel.

DUST RUFFLE, SHAMS, COVERLET AND CURTAINS
Shown on page 185

EQUIPMENT: Pencil. Yardstick. Paper for patterns. Scissors. Tape measure. Straight pins. Large safety pins. Sewing needle. Sewing machine. Iron.

MATERIALS: Martex "Gazebo" flat sheets: 1 king-size for dust ruffle; 1 twin-size for pillow shams; 2 twin, double, queen or king-size for coverlet; sheets for curtains*. White sewing and buttonhole twist thread. Muslin for dust ruffle; see individual directions for amount. Fairfield Ultra-Loft® batting, two 90″ × 108″ packages for coverlet (all sizes).

*Note: Number and size of sheets needed for curtains will depend upon dimensions and number of windows. See individual directions for measuring fabric for curtains.

GENERAL DIRECTIONS: Remove stitching at hemmed edges of sheets; trim off all selvages; press to remove wrinkles and creases at hems. Measure accurately as directed; use yardstick and tailor's chalk to mark fabric. Cut on straight grain of fabric. When joining strips or making curtains, cut all panels with print in same direction. If stitching pieces together to achieve width, allow for seam allowances and match design carefully. Stitch pieces together with right sides facing and raw edges even, making ½″ seams.

Dust Ruffle: Measure length and width of top of box spring. For underlay, cut muslin 1″ larger than each measurement; piece if necessary. To make hem for head of bed, turn under one short edge of muslin ¼″ twice, enclosing raw edge; press; stitch. To make ruffle strip, determine width of strip by measuring from top of box spring to floor and adding 4″; determine length of strip by measuring around sides and foot of bed (excluding head), multiplying figure by 2½ and adding 8″. Following measurements, cut strips from sheets so that pattern will match when pieces are joined; stitch together at short ends with ½″ seams to make one long strip. Turn raw edges at ends of strip ½″ to wrong side; press. Turn again, 1½″ to wrong side, enclosing raw edges; stitch. Turn bottom of strip ½″ to wrong side; press, and then turn 3″ to wrong side, enclosing raw edges; stitch.

Using buttonhole-twist thread in bobbin, make three rows of machine basting along unfinished edge of strip, starting first row ¼″ from raw edge. Use tailor's chalk to make a point every 12″ along unfinished edge of muslin underlay, and every 30″ along unfinished edge of ruffle strip. Gather strip to fit one side of underlay at a time: Pull bobbin thread, gathering until marks on strip match marks on underlay. Pin strip to underlay, raw edges even and right sides together; baste, then stitch together $\frac{1}{2}''$ from raw edges. Press seam allowance toward underlay; topstitch underlay, securing seam allowances. Place dust ruffle over boxspring. **Note:** If dust ruffle is used on a poster bed, adjust ruffle evenly at corners once dust ruffle is in place on boxspring; cut fabric from hem up to point where post interferes with ruffle. Hem cut edges by turning under $\frac{1}{4}''$ twice and stitching in place.

Pillow Shams: Measure long and short dimensions of your pillow. Adding 1″ to each dimension, use pencil and yardstick to mark paper pattern for front piece. Adding additional 7″ to long dimension, make pattern for back piece. Round corners of patterns. From sheet, cut one top and one back piece for each pillow, using patterns. Fold back piece in half across short dimension and cut into two pieces. Fold each cut edge $\frac{1}{2}''$ to wrong side; press; then fold 2″ for hem and stitch in place. With right sides facing and raw edges even, pin backs to front, overlapping hems at center back; stitch together around all edges, making $\frac{1}{2}''$ seam; clip curves. Turn to right side through opening in back; press. For ruffle, measure perimeter of front piece and triple that dimension for length; width of ruffle is 6″ including hem allowance. Cut strip for ruffle, stitching strips together as necessary for required length. Press seams open. Fold each raw edge of strip $\frac{1}{4}''$ to wrong side twice, enclosing raw edges; machine-stitch in place. Machine-baste 1″ away from one long edge; pull basting, gathering strip to fit around pillow, overlapping ends slightly. Pin strip to pillow front: Position basting line $\frac{1}{4}''$ in from edge so ruffle extends beyond pillow; adjust gathers evenly; stitch in place through all thicknesses.

Coverlet: Prepare two sheets, following General Directions. Press all raw edges of sheets $\frac{1}{2}''$ to wrong side. Place first sheet on large flat surface, wrong side up. Center both layers of batting on top of sheet; smooth out any bumps or wrinkles. Baste batting to sheet by stitching diagonally across in two directions. Place second sheet on top of batting, right side up. Pin all layers together, using large safety pins to hold temporarily. Baste generously through all thicknesses, using white thread and large needle. To prevent shifting, first baste on the lengthwise and crosswise grain of fabric, then baste diagonally across in two directions. Find center of quilt. Safety-pin three layers together at trellis intersection closest to center; quilting pattern radiates from this point. Following

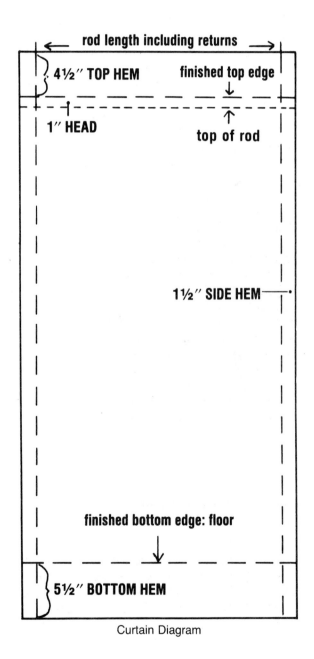

Curtain Diagram

one branch of trellis, safety-pin trellis three intersections away from center. Repeat along same trellis in both directions, then repeat for every third trellis which runs parallel to first trellis until entire quilt is evenly pinned. Tuft quilt starting from center and working around and outward, by tacking three layers securely together at each safety pin as follows: Starting from back and leaving a 2″ end of buttonhole twist thread hanging, bring needle through to top and make two small stitches in the same place. End at back one small stitch from hanging thread. Tie thread ends securely together with two firm knots. Repeat for entire quilt, removing safety pins as you go. When finished, slip-stitch pressed edges of quilt together all around, trimming batting; remove basting.

Curtains: Measure each window individually, with proper fixtures and rods in place, as follows: For finished length, measure from top of rod to floor; for finished width, measure lenth of rod including "returns" (distance the rod extends out from wall on both sides). Following Curtain Diagram, add necessary inches to your finished dimensions for head and hems; calculate fabric needed for each panel. For each window, cut two panels from sheet so pattern begins and ends at same point in the design. Use yardstick and tailor's chalk to mark hems on the fabric, following diagram. Turn all raw edges ½″ to wrong side and press, then turn sides and bottom under again along marked hem lines; press, and stitch in place. For top edge, make doubled hem: Fold and press fabric to wrong side, meeting line for finished top edge; fold again along marked line and press. Stitch 1″ below top edge for head (short dash line on diagram); stitch again close to fold for casing to fit your rod.

TRELLIS CHEST
Shown on page 185

EQUIPMENT: No. 2 pencil. Pencil sharpener. Yardstick. Tape measure. Masking tape: ¼″ and 1″ wide. Putty knife. Drill. Sandpaper: coarse, medium, fine grades; #400 wet or dry. Tack cloth. Paintbrushes: wide, medium #5. Shallow dishes or bowls. Scissors.

MATERIALS: Unfinished wooden chest with three drawers, 30″ × 30″ × 16″ deep, or desired size. Wood filler. Pale blue acrylic paint, one quart. AD Permanent (water-proof) Markers: beige #137, wide-tipped; dark tan #53 and walnut #54, fine-tipped. Three white drawer pulls (optional). Clear acrylic spray.

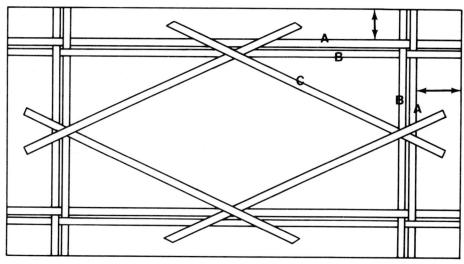

Trellis Chest

DIRECTIONS: Pull out drawers. Remove hardware; seal holes with wood filler if planning new hardware, using putty knife. Sand entire chest first with coarse, then medium, then fine sandpaper. Dust with tack cloth, then paint chest blue; let dry. Spray chest with two coats of acrylic; let dry thoroughly after first coat, then sand lightly with fine sandpaper and dust with tack cloth before applying second coat.

Following Diagram 1, mark 12 branch lines $\frac{1}{2}''$ wide for trellis design on chest top as follows: Draw a branch A parallel to each edge, 2'' from long edges and 3'' from short edges. Draw a branch B $\frac{1}{8}''$ away from and parallel to each branch A. Erase lines at corners for interwoven effect as shown. For diagonal branches C: Find center of each B branch; mark with dots. Connect dots with lightly drawn diagonal lines, then draw branches centered over diagonal lines. Following diagram, erase overlapped lines. Replace drawers. Extending A and B branches from top, mark six pairs of vertical branches down front and sides of chest; keep branches continuous over top and bottom facings, drawer fronts and drawer divider strips; do not draw branches on lower apron. Measuring 3'' below top edge of chest and $5\frac{1}{2}''$ above bottom edge, draw two pairs of horizontal branches around sides and front (top and bottom drawers) of chest. Erase lines at intersections for interwoven effect.

Following illustration on page 185 for details, fill in all branches with wide-tipped beige marker; highlight branches and draw fine lines for twigs at random, using dark tan marker; using walnut marker and short, firm strokes, outline branches and draw grainlines within branches; strengthen trellis effect and mark dots to simulate nails at each intersection.

To complete, spray chest with clear acrylic, letting dry thoroughly and sanding lightly between each coat with wet or dry sandpaper; dust with tack cloth before applying new coats.

Note: Test acrylic spray on small hidden section of chest to ensure that finish will not cause decoration to run or discolor; if this happens, consult your paint supply store. When dry, reattach old hardware or attach new hardware as desired.

DELECTABLE MOUNTAINS QUILT
Shown on page 187

SIZE: About $68\frac{3}{4}'' \times 90\frac{3}{4}''$.

EQUIPMENT: Scissors. Ruler. Thin, stiff cardboard. Tailor's chalk. Light and dark pencils. Sewing and quilting needles. Quilting frame (optional).

MATERIALS: Closely woven cotton fabric 44''-45'' wide: white, $11\frac{1}{4}$ yds. (includes lining); navy, $4\frac{3}{4}$ yds. Cotton or polyester batting. White sewing thread.

DIRECTIONS: Read General Directions for Quilting on page 300. Quilt is made up of twelve $19\frac{1}{2}''$-square blocks set with pieced borders. See Piecing Diagram for one quilt block; smaller blocks within are indicated by heavy lines; dotted lines indicate quilting patterns. Cut cardboard patterns for patch pieces as follows, labeling each pattern: Pattern A—cut a $1\frac{1}{2}''$ square. Pattern B—draw a $1\frac{1}{2}''$ square; draw two corner-to-corner lines, crossing in the center, to divide square into four equal triangles; cut a triangle for pattern. Pattern C—draw a $3\frac{3}{16}''$ square cut in half diagonally for a triangle pattern. Pattern D—draw a $1\frac{1}{2}''$ square; cut in half diagonally for a triangle pattern. Pattern E—cut a $1\frac{1}{16}''$ square. Pattern F—draw a 6'' square; cut in half diagonally for a triangle pattern. Pattern G—draw a $5\frac{5}{16}''$ square; cut in half diagonally for triangle pattern. Cut patch pieces for all quilt blocks as follows; marking patterns on wrong side of fabric and adding $\frac{1}{4}''$ seam allowance all around: from blue fabric, cut 12 A, 1056 B, and 144 C; from white fabric, cut 48 A, 768 B, 96 D, 144 E, 96 F, and 48 G.

To join pieces for one complete quilt block, begin with the star block in center. Right sides together, sew a blue B triangle to a white B triangle on short sides to form a larger triangle; repeat and sew two larger triangles together on long sides to form a square. Make three more pieced squares in same manner. To assemble star block, join four white A squares, one blue A square, and four blue-and-white pieced squares into a block of three rows of three squares each (see Piecing Diagram). Star block should measure $4\frac{1}{2}''$ square, plus outside seam allowance.

For center block (surrounding star block), join

a C triangle to each side of star block. Join a blue B triangle and a white B triangle on long sides to make a square. Make 55 more blue-and-white squares in same manner. Lay 16 blue-and-white squares, four E squares, four D triangles, and eight separate blue B triangles around C triangles of center block as shown in Piecing Diagram, making sure pieced squares are placed as shown; sew pieces into four strips. Sew strips to C triangles to complete center block; piece should measure 8½″, plus outside seam allowance.

For side blocks, sew two C triangles to an F triangle, with C triangles meeting at right angle of F triangle. Lay 10 blue-and-white squares, four blue B triangles, two E squares, and one D triangle around C-F pieced section, following Piecing Diagram and making sure pieced squares are placed as shown. Sew pieces into three strips; sew strips to C-F section to complete side block. Block should measure about 5 5/16″ × 8½″, plus outside seam allowance. Make three more side blocks in same manner.

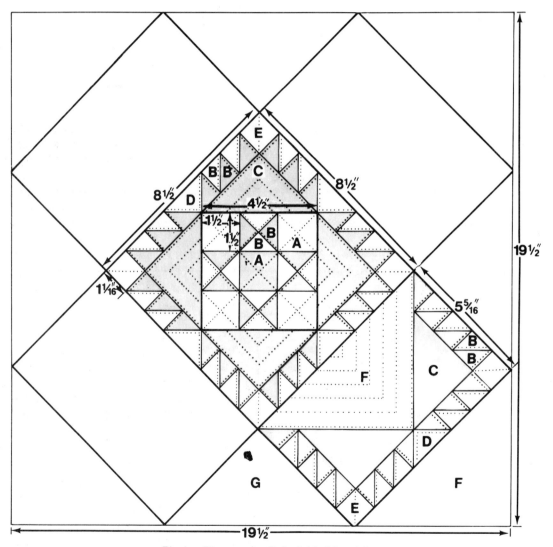

Piecing Diagram for Delectable Mountains

Sew a side block to each side of center block. To complete quilt block, sew four G triangles to sides and four F triangles to corners of piece, making a block about $19\frac{1}{2}''$ square, plus outside seam allowance. Make 11 more quilt blocks in same manner. (**Note:** If blocks do not measure exactly $19\frac{1}{2}''$ square, adjust dimensions in following paragraph so pieced strips will fit blocks.)

For borders and joining strips, cut cardbord pattern $1\frac{7}{32}''$ square (between $1\frac{3}{16}''$ and $1\frac{1}{4}''$ on your ruler); cut square in half diagonally to make triangle pattern. Marking pattern on wrong side of fabric and adding $\frac{1}{4}''$ seam allowance all around, cut 1072 triangles from blue fabric. Cut another cardboard pattern $1\frac{11}{16}''$ square, cut square in half diagonally to make triangle pattern. Cut 536 triangles from white fabric. Join two blue triangles to one white triangle to make a rectangular piece by sewing long side of each blue triangle to each short side of white triangle. Make 535 more rectangular pieces in same manner. Join pieces into strips by sewing long sides together, with white triangles all pointing in the same direction: make nine strips of 16 pieces each, two strips of 52 pieces each, two strips of 70 pieces each, and two strips of 74 pieces each.

To assemble quilt top, join quilt blocks into three horizontal rows of four blocks each, with a 16-piece joining strip between each block; white triangles in joining strips should all point in the same direction. Join the three horiziontal rows by sewing a 70-piece strip between rows, with white triangles pointing in same direction. Sew 52-piece strips to the sides, with triangles on left side pointing up and triangles on right side pointing down. Sew a 74-piece strip across top, white triangles pointing to the right, and a 74-piece strip across the bottom, white triangles pointing to the left. Quilt top should measure about $68\frac{3}{4}'' \times 90\frac{3}{4}''$, including outside seam allowance.

For lining, cut two pieces from white fabric $35\frac{3}{8}'' \times 91\frac{3}{4}''$. Join on long sides, right sides together and with $\frac{1}{2}''$ seams; press seam open. Lining will be $\frac{1}{2}''$ larger all around than quilt top. Cut batting same size as quilt top.

Quilting: With ruler and tailor's chalk, mark straight lines on quilt top, following dotted lines on Piecing Diagram. Make parallel lines on F and C triangles about $\frac{1}{2}''$ apart; repeat same quilting pattern on all the C, F, and G triangles of block. Pin and baste quilt top, batting, and lining together, centering top two layers so that lining extends $\frac{1}{2}''$ all around. Starting in center and working around and outward, quilt on all marked lines. On borders and joining strips, quilt on each long side, close to seam line; quilt also on each white triangle, close to all three seam lines.

To bind edges of quilt, turn excess lining to front, turn under raw edge of lining $\frac{1}{4}''$, and slipstitch to quilt top.

FEATHERED STAR QUILT
Shown on page 186

SIZE: About $74\frac{1}{2}''$ square.

EQUIPMENT: Ruler. Scissors. Thin, stiff cardboard. Tracing paper. Dressmaker's (carbon) tracing paper. Tracing wheel. Tailor's chalk. Sewing and quilting needles. Pencil. Quilting frame (optional).

MATERIALS: Closely woven cotton fabric, 44"-45" wide: $2\frac{1}{2}$ yds. red, $8\frac{1}{4}$ yds. white (including lining). Polyester or cotton batting. White sewing thread.

DIRECTIONS: Read General Directions for Quilting on page 300. Large star is constructed with eight pieced star points joined to a nine-patch center block. Center block has five pieced small-star blocks joined to four plain blocks. To make the small-star blocks, cut a cardboard pattern $2\frac{3}{4}''$ square. Marking pattern on wrong side of fabric and adding $\frac{1}{4}''$ seam allowance all around, cut 20 square patches from white fabric and five square patches from red. Draw two corner-to-corner lines on cardboard pattern, crossing in center, to divide square into four equal triangles. Cut out a triangle for pattern and cut 260 triangles from red fabric and 272 from white, in same manner as for squares. Only 40 of each are used for small-star blocks; remainder are for rest of quilt. Right sides together, sew a red triangle to a white triangle on short sides to form a larger triangle; sew two larger triangles together on long sides to form a square (see star points of small-star blocks in illustration

Continued on page 232

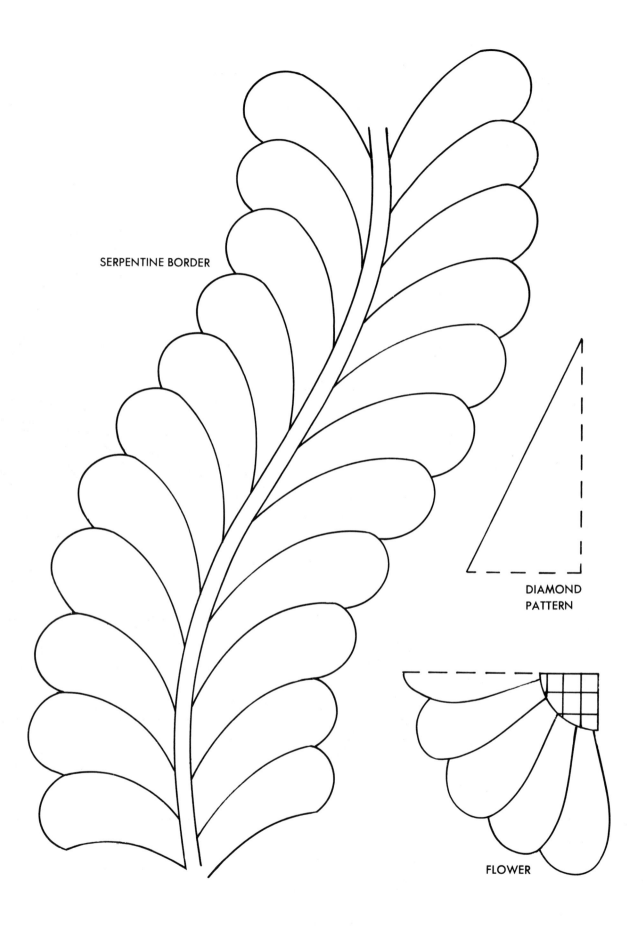

SERPENTINE BORDER

DIAMOND
PATTERN

FLOWER

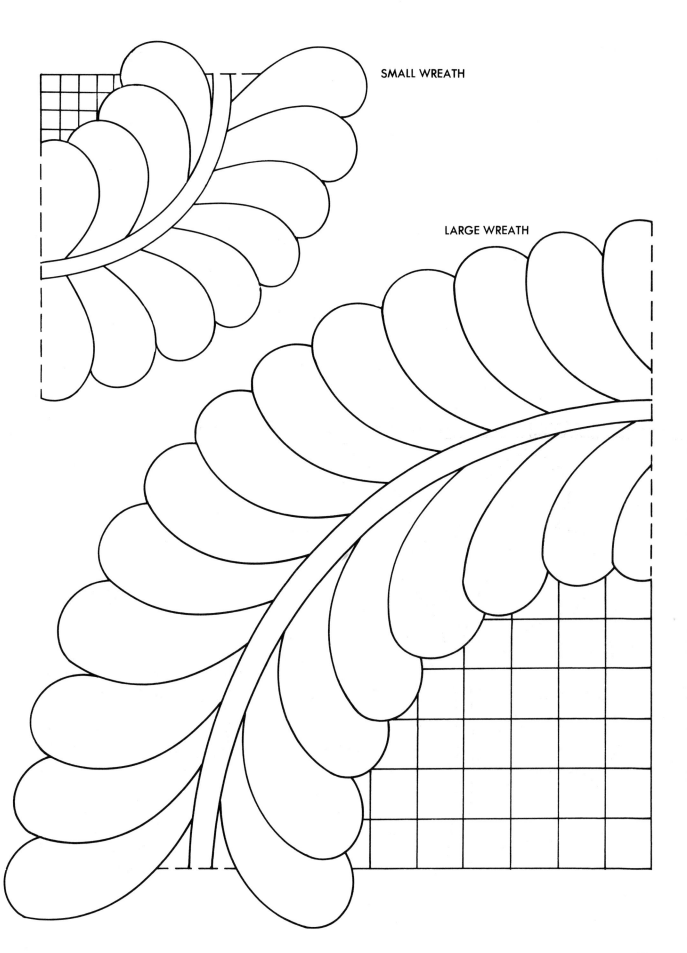

SMALL WREATH

LARGE WREATH

Continued from page 229

for design of squares). Make 19 more pieced squares in same manner. To assemble small-star block, join four white squares, one red square, and four red-and-white pieced squares into one block of three rows of three squares each (see illustration). Make four more small-star blocks in same manner. Blocks should measure $8\frac{1}{4}''$ square, plus outside seam allowance. Make a cardboard pattern $8\frac{1}{4}''$ square and cut four red blocks, adding $\frac{1}{4}''$ seam allowance. Join the small-star blocks and the red blocks into three rows of three blocks each to form center block of large star (see illustration for arrangement). Center block should measure $24\frac{3}{4}''$ square, plus outside seam allowance.

To make star-point blocks for large star, cut cardboard rectangle $9'' \times 10''$; cut in half diagonally to make pattern for large triangle. Cut eight large triangles from red fabric, adding seam allowance. Trace actual-size diamond pattern; complete quarter-pattern indicated by dash lines. Cut eight diamonds from red fabric. Putting aside 16 small white triangles and four small red triangles, join remaining small triangles into $2''$ squares by sewing the long side of a white triangle to the long side of a red triangle. Join squares into strips, placing squares so that all red triangles are on one side of strip: make eight five-square strips, eight seven-square strips, and four 30-square strips.

To assemble a star point, place a large red triangle with $10''$ side vertical at left and long side diagonally at right. Join a five-square strip to $10''$ side of triangle and a seven-square strip to long side. Complete tip of star where the two strips meet by adding two white triangles and a red diamond; see illustration for placement of pieces. Make another star point in same manner, but with the $10''$ side of large triangle at right and long side at left. Join the two star points into a double-pointed block by sewing a red triangle between. Sew the double-pointed block to one side of center block. Make three more double-pointed blocks in same manner and sew to remaining three sides of center block to complete large star.

For white background of star, cut cardboard pattern $14\frac{3}{4}''$ square. Marking on wrong side of fabric and adding $\frac{1}{4}''$ seam allowance, cut four squares from white fabric. Cut pattern in half di-

agonally to make a triangle pattern and cut four triangles from white fabric in same manner. Sew the squares and triangles alternately between the points of large star, to make piece $54\frac{1}{4}''$ square, plus outside seam allowance. Sew a 30-square strip to each side of piece, with red triangles inside and starting first strip flush with edge of pieced center. For white borders, cut four $8\frac{1}{4}''$-wide strips, two $58\frac{3}{4}''$ long and two $74\frac{1}{4}''$ long (measurements include $\frac{1}{4}''$ seam allowance). Sew a shorter strip to each side of quilt top; then sew longer strips to top and bottom of quilt top. Quilt top should measure $74\frac{1}{4}''$ square.

For lining, cut two pieces $37\frac{5}{8}'' \times 75\frac{1}{4}''$. Sew together on long sides, to make lining $\frac{1}{2}''$ larger all around than quilt top. Cut batting same size as quilt top.

Quilting: Trace actual-size quilting patterns; complete quarter-patterns indicated by dash lines. Using dressmaker's carbon and tracing wheel, transfer patterns to quilt top as follows: Place a small wreath in each large red square of large star, in center of each triangle of white background (with a flower in each outer corner), and in each corner of white border, $1''$ from outer edge. Place a large wreath in each corner square of white background. Repeat sepentine border design along center of each white border. With ruler and tailor's chalk, mark straight quilting lines as follows: On small-star blocks, mark diagonal lines $\frac{3}{4}''$ apart in both directions, going through corners; mark same pattern on all blocks with a small or large wreath design, skipping over wreath itself. On points of large star, mark large triangles with diagonal lines $\frac{1}{2}''$ apart in one direction parallel to long side of triangle; mark same pattern on small triangles and diamonds, changing direction of lines so they are parallel to long sides of small triangles; mark same pattern on borders, making lines parallel to triangles of pieced border strips and extending lines across white border; skip over serpentine design.

Pin and baste quilt top, lining, and batting together, centering two top layers so that lining extends $\frac{1}{2}''$ all around. Quilt on all marked lines. To finish quilt turn lining to front, turn in raw edges $\frac{1}{4}''$, and slip-stitch to quilt top. Press edges of quilt.

Three patchwork pillows are simple to sew in country blues and tans. We've used traditional patterns (clockwise from top): Bear Paw, Thousand Pyramids, Dresden Plate. Directions begin on page 268.

233

Capture the charm of another century with these elegant bandboxes that you can create using paper and thread! First used to carry gentlemen's collars, they can hold a myriad of surprises! Directions for bandboxes are on page 270.

*Scrolls and flowers—
the trademarks of
Norse flower art—
transform everyday
wooden objects
into one-of-a-kind
treasures.*

*Rosemaling flourished in Norway
from 1750 to 1850, and each region
had its own distinctive style. Ever-
curving lines and subtle blending of
colors (done with oil paints) create designs steeped in a rich heritage. Directions
and patterns for Rogaland Clock, Hallingdal Chest,
Telemark Bowl, Sognefjord Spoon Holder, begin on page 273.*

Cover a chest in crewel embroidery, and create a treasure to enjoy for years to come. The brightly plumed birds and curving vines, symbols of love and happiness, are stitched in the tradition of 18th century crewelwork. In fact, the graceful motifs were created by an expert in Early American crewel, Doris Thacher. Directions include construction of the 8″ × 16″ chest; see page 281.

Nature provided the materials for our selection of holiday wreaths and a door plaque. Each is pretty enough to use all year 'round! Pine Bough Plaque (25" high) is a clever idea—giant "thistles" are actually toothpicks! Delicate wreath (center) is "frosted" with dainty baby's breath, trimmed with pine cones and a crisp ribbon bow (wreath, 25" across). Nosegay Wreath, 11" across, (top right) looks like spring, even in December. It's made with bright yellow straw flowers, antique lace and a velvet bow. Or, decorate your door with our Apple Wreath (15" across). The bright red of artificial apples is set against a ring of thistles and bleached pine. Directions for all begin on page 285.

*Alphabets in simple stitchery give two plump pillows the
"sampler look." Red brick mansion with a mansard roof is fabric.
The quaint clapboard house with twin chimneys is worked completely in
embroidery. House pillow is about 12½" × 15"; mansion pillow is
about 12¾" × 15½". Directions for Alphabet Pillows are on page 287.*

PINEAPPLE QUILT

Shown on page 186

SIZE: About 70½″ square.

EQUIPMENT: Scissors. Ruler. Pencil. Thin, stiff cardboard. Paper for patterns. Glue. Straight pins. Sewing and quilting needles. Quilting frame (optional).

MATERIALS: Closely woven cotton fabric 44″-45″ wide: red, 5 yds.; white, 2⅔ yds.; fabric for lining, 4⅔ yds. Polyester or cotton batting. Matching sewing thread.

DIRECTIONS: Read General Directions for Quilting on page 300. Quilt is constructed of 49 identical square blocks. To make patterns for patch pieces, first draw an actual-size pattern for a complete 10″-square block, following design and dimensions of Piecing Diagram. Draw all horizontal

and vertical lines of block first, 1″ apart, extending lines to edges of square; intersections will then act as guide points for drawing the triangles. Glue pattern to thin cardboard. Cut along lines of pattern to make an individual pattern for patch pieces A, B, C, D, E, F. Marking patterns on wrong side of fabric and adding ¼″ seam allowance all around, cut patches for entire quilt: from white fabric, cut 49 of patch A, 784 of B; from red fabric, cut 196 each of C, D, E, F.

To join patches for one block, start in the center and work outward, sewing four C triangles to an A square, then four B triangles to the C triangles, then four D strips, then four B triangles, etc., until completing block; piece should measure 10″ square, plus outside seam allowance. Make 48 more blocks in same manner. Join blocks in seven rows of seven blocks each; then sew rows to-

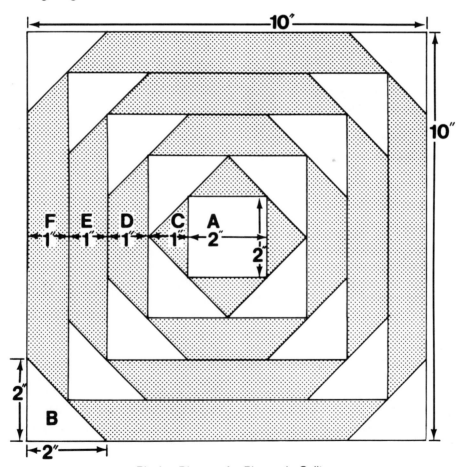

Piecing Diagram for Pineapple Quilt

gether for quilt top. Piece should measure $70\frac{1}{2}''$ square.

For lining, cut two pieces $35\frac{3}{4}'' \times 70\frac{1}{2}''$. Sew together on long sides with $\frac{1}{2}''$ seams. Press seam open. Cut batting same size as lining and quilt top.

Quilting: Quilt near all seam lines, starting in center of quilt and working around and outward.

To bind edges, cut four 1"-wide strips from red fabric, $70\frac{3}{4}''$ long (piece to get these lengths). Stitch to top of quilt, right sides together and with $\frac{1}{4}''$ seams. Turn strips to back of quilt and slip-stitch to lining, turning in raw edges of strips $\frac{1}{4}''$.

ORANGE PEEL QUILT
Shown on page 188

SIZE: About $76'' \times 82\frac{1}{2}''$.

EQUIPMENT: Tracing paper. Thin, stiff cardboard. Pencil. Ruler. Scissors. Straight pins. Sewing and quilting needles. Dressmaker's (carbon) tracing paper in a light color. Tracing wheel. Quilting frame (optional).

MATERIALS: Quilt top: Closely woven cotton fabric 44"-45" wide: $4\frac{2}{3}$ yds. each white and blue. Lining: White fabric 44"-45" wide, $4\frac{1}{4}$ yds. Matching sewing thread. Polyester or cotton batting. White bias tape, 11 yds.

DIRECTIONS: Read General Directions for Quilting on page 300. Trace actual-size patterns; complete half and quarter-patterns indicated by long dash lines. Dotted lines indicate quilting. Make a cardboard pattern for the four-pointed center piece, the petal, and for each of the three border pieces. To cut patches, place patterns on wrong side of fabric with sides of points on the grain; mark and cut, adding $\frac{1}{4}''$ seam allowance all around. From blue fabric, cut 55 four-pointed center pieces, 220 petals, and 88 of border piece B (place left straight side on grain of fabric). From white fabric, cut 55 center pieces, 220 petals, 84 of border piece A (place right straight side on grain of fabric), and 4 of border piece C.

To make a square block, stitch four blue petals in place around a white center piece, right sides together. Block should measure $6\frac{1}{2}''$ square, plus outside seam allowance. Make 54 more blocks in same manner. Make 55 blocks of four white petals stitched in place around a blue center piece. Clip into seams at curves; press to one side.

Beginning and ending with blue-centered blocks, make a vertical strip, alternating six blue-centered blocks with five white-centered blocks. Make four more vertical strips in this manner. Beginning and ending with white-centered blocks, make a vertical strip, alternating six white-centered blocks with five blue-centered blocks. Make four more vertical strips in same manner. Alternating color combinations, sew vertical strips together to form center of quilt top. Piece should measure $65'' \times 71\frac{1}{2}''$, plus outside seam allowance.

Beginning and ending with border piece B, make a border strip, alternating 21 border pieces B with 20 border pieces A. Make another border strip in same manner. Beginning and ending with border piece B, make a border strip, alternating 23 border pieces B with 22 border pieces A. Make another strip in same manner. Place border strips with scallops of border piece B toward you and sew a border piece C to the left end of each strip.

Matching longer strips to longer edges of quilt top and shorter strips to shorter edges, sew border strips to quilt edges. Sew remaining straight edge of border piece C to edge of adjacent strip at each corner. Quilt top should measure about $76'' \times 82\frac{1}{2}''$.

For lining, cut two pieces from white fabric $41\frac{3}{4}'' \times 76''$. Sew together along long edges, right sides together and with $\frac{1}{2}''$ seam allowance. Press seam open.

Quilting: Using dressmakers' carbon and tracing wheel, transfer dotted lines of patterns to appropriate fabric pieces. Following General Directions, pin and baste lining, batting, and quilt top together. Using matching thread, quilt on marked lines, beginning at center and working around and outward. Trim edges of lining and batting even with top layer. Insert quilt edges into fold of bias tape and stitch in place.

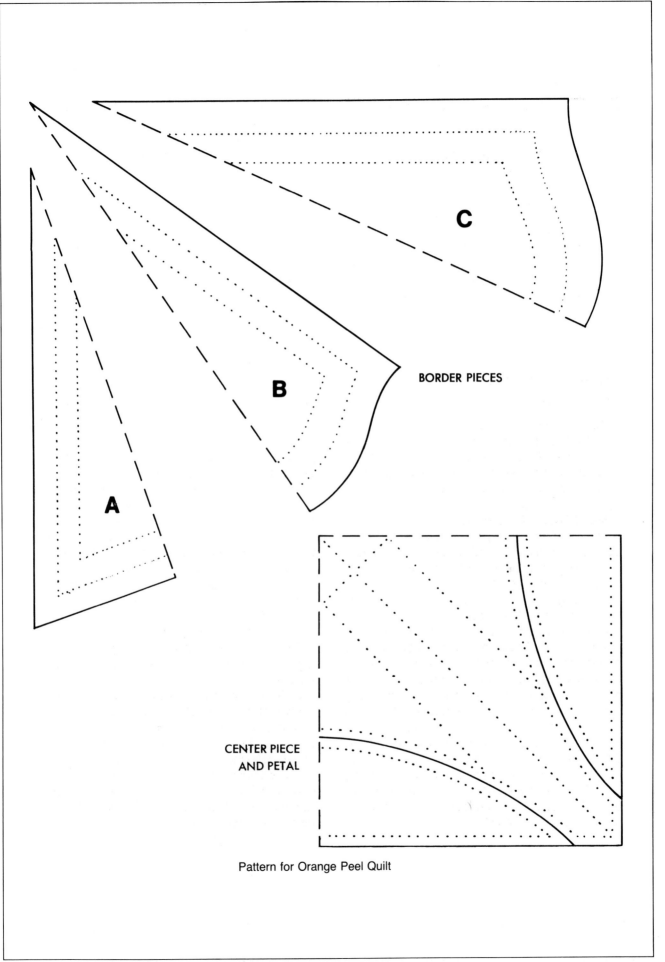

C

B

A

BORDER PIECES

CENTER PIECE
AND PETAL

Pattern for Orange Peel Quilt

COLOR KEY

- ⊠ KELLY GREEN
- ◨ CHERRY RED
- ⊞ TURQUOISE
- ◖ SALMON PINK
- ◪ GOLD

SILHOUETTES

Shown on page 189

EQUIPMENT: Pantograph with manufacturer's instructions. Sharp pencil. Drawing pen. Pointed watercolor brush. Masking tape. Ruler.

MATERIALS: Large sheet of white paper. Smooth white drawing paper. India ink.

DIRECTIONS: Tape large sheet of white paper on wall. Have subject sit in front of paper with light from a strong bulb directed at subject. Adjust light and subject distance from wall so that a strong, clear shadow is cast on the paper at an angle from subject. In this way, you can copy the shadow without an interfering shadow of your own.

Turn off all lights but the strong light and very carefully copy the shadow outline on the large sheet of white paper.

To reduce the silhouette to size desired, use a pantograph. Tape the smooth drawing paper on a large, flat surface, with shadow outline also taped in place; follow manufacturer's instructions to reduce to correct size. Carefully copy shadow outline with stylus of pantograph and it will automatically reproduce silhouette in smaller size. With drawing pen and India ink, trace over reduced outline. Then fill in silhouette with brush and ink. Frame as desired.

"SWEET DREAMS"

Shown on page 189

SIZE: 13″ × 26½″ (unframed).

EQUIPMENT: Masking tape. Tapestry needle. Scissors. Thumbtacks. Ruler. Square. Straight pins.

MATERIALS: White mono canvas 10-mesh-to-the-inch, 18″ × 32″. DMC Laine Tapisserie (tapestry yarn), 8-yard skeins: 6 skeins Cherry Red #7107; 1 skein Turquoise #7807; 6 skeins Salmon Pink #7852; 1 skein Kelly Green #7344; 1 skein Gold #7484. White-faced heavy mounting board, 13″ × 26½″. Short straight pins. Masking tape. Frame, 13″ × 26½″ (rabbet size).

DIRECTIONS: Bind raw edges of canvas with masking tape to keep from raveling. Work needlepoint in continental stitch (see page 306). Cut working strands about 18″ long and use one strand of tapestry yarn in needle. Keep yarn from twisting when working to avoid thin places. Fasten yarn by working over end on back to begin and by going through stitches on back of work to end off strands; clip ends close to canvas. Be careful not to pull yarn too tightly; hold thumb on yarn until you have pulled it through the canvas, then lift thumb, pull yarn into place.

Starting at upper right corner of canvas, measure 3¾″ in, 3¾″ down to start border. Follow chart (which is given sideways) and Color Key. Each square of chart represents one mesh of canvas. Background (blank squares of chart) is left unworked. Work design to end of banner, then repeat angel, border, and spots in reverse to complete picture.

BLOCKING: Cover wooden surface (old table or drawing board) with brown paper; mark on paper the size of canvas (18″ × 32″) being sure corners are square. Place needlepoint, right side down, over this guide and fasten with thumbtacks placed about ½″ apart, near edges of canvas, stretching canvas to marked outline. Wet thoroughly with cold water; let dry.

MOUNTING: With wrong side of canvas facing white side of cardboard, stretch canvas over cardboard, keeping threads straight. Fasten temporarily with pins pushed part way into edge of cardboard. Begin at center of each side and at corners. Continue stretching and pinning along each side. When needlepoint piece is stretched straight, hammer pins all the way into cardboard edges. Tape canvas to back.

PILLOW SHAMS

Shown on page 189

EQUIPMENT: Sewing machine. Tape measure.

MATERIALS: Unbleached muslin. Dark red cotton fabric (or dark red print fabric used for spread). Sewing thread to match.

DIRECTIONS: Cut two pieces of unbleached muslin the size of your pillow, plus 2″ all around for hems and ease. Place two pieces together, right sides facing. Making $\frac{1}{2}$" seams, sew around three sides (leave one end open for pillow insertion); turn right side out. Turn raw edges of open end under; sew.

For ruffles, cut crosswise strips of unbleached muslin $4\frac{1}{2}$" deep; cut crosswise strips of dark red fabric $3\frac{1}{2}$" deep (or strip of dark red print fabric used for center blocks of spread). To determine length, double the measurement around the sham. Seam all lengths of muslin ruffle strips together to make a circle. Do the same for second ruffle. Make $\frac{1}{4}$" hems at top and bottom edges of ruffles. Gather tops of ruffles $\frac{1}{2}$" from edge. Adjust gathers so that ruffle will fit around edges of sham. Place red ruffle over muslin ruffle and baste. Lay ruffles on right side of sham; baste on gathering line $\frac{1}{4}$" in from edge of sham. Sew to double thickness of sham. Press. Insert pillow.

TULIP QUILT

Shown on page 189

SIZE: 80" × 92".

EQUIPMENT: Ruler. Pencil. Tracing paper. Stiff thin cardboard. Scissors. Straight pins. Quilting needle. Quilting frame (optional). Light and dark colored pencils for tracing patterns.

MATERIALS: Cotton fabric, 36" wide, small green print, 3 yards; small dark red print, 3 yards. Unbleached muslin, 72" or 90" wide, 4 yards. Matching sewing thread. Cotton batting, single or double roll.

DIRECTIONS: Trace patterns for each appliqué piece; complete quarter-pattern indicated by dash lines. Make a separate cardboard pattern for each part of appliqué. Trace pattern for quilting motif.

Press fabrics smooth. Place each pattern piece on wrong side of fabric. Trace around pattern using light colored pencil on dark fabric; dark colored pencil on light fabric. When tracing a number of pieces on one fabric, leave space between patterns for seam allowance. Cut out each fabric piece $\frac{1}{4}$" outside marked outline.

From bleached muslin, cut two borders, 6" × 92", and 25 squares, 16" × 16". Cut 25 pointed blocks of dark red print fabric; cut 106 tulip tips and 106 tulip centers (indicated by eliptical shape on tulip pattern) of dark red print fabric; cut 106 tulip cups and stems of green print fabric; cut 106 leaves of green print fabric; reverse pattern and cut 106 more. Read How to Appliqué on page 304, then baste and stitch appliqués in place.

Appliqué the dark red print blocks to centers of each 16" square with points facing each corner. Following pattern and illustration, appliqué one flower motif (tulip, stem and two leaves) to each corner of pointed block. Appliqué three flower motifs across top border (6" × 92" piece), placing one 6" in from left and right edges; one at center. Do the same across bottom border. Join blocks together (five across and five down); join top and bottom borders, being certain that flower motifs run in same direction. Press seams open.

Place quilt top on large flat surface. Using dressmaker's carbon, dressmaker's wheel and quilting motif pattern, mark each square, placing a quilting motif between each flower motif (four quilting motifs to a square).

Cut unbleached muslin lining the same size as quilt top. Place lining, wrong side up, on large flat surface. Place one layer of cotton batting on top of lining. Place quilt top on top of batting, right side up. Pin all together to hold temporarily. Baste through all thicknesses horizontally and vertically across quilt; then baste diagonally across in two directions and around top and bottom.

Read General Directions for Quilting, page 300. Using a quilting needle and strong white thread, quilt by taking tiny, even running stitches through all thicknesses of quilt. Quilting may be done by stretching quilt on a frame, or it may be done over small areas at a time, holding it in your lap. Work quilting motifs first. On remaining areas, including top and bottom borders, work diagonal lines of quilting $\frac{5}{8}$" apart to within $\frac{1}{2}$" of edges.

When quilting is completed, trim away edges of cotton batting $\frac{1}{4}$" all around edge. Turn edges of quilt top over edge of batting. Turn in edges of quilt lining; fold edges of lining over top and stitch all around for finished edge.

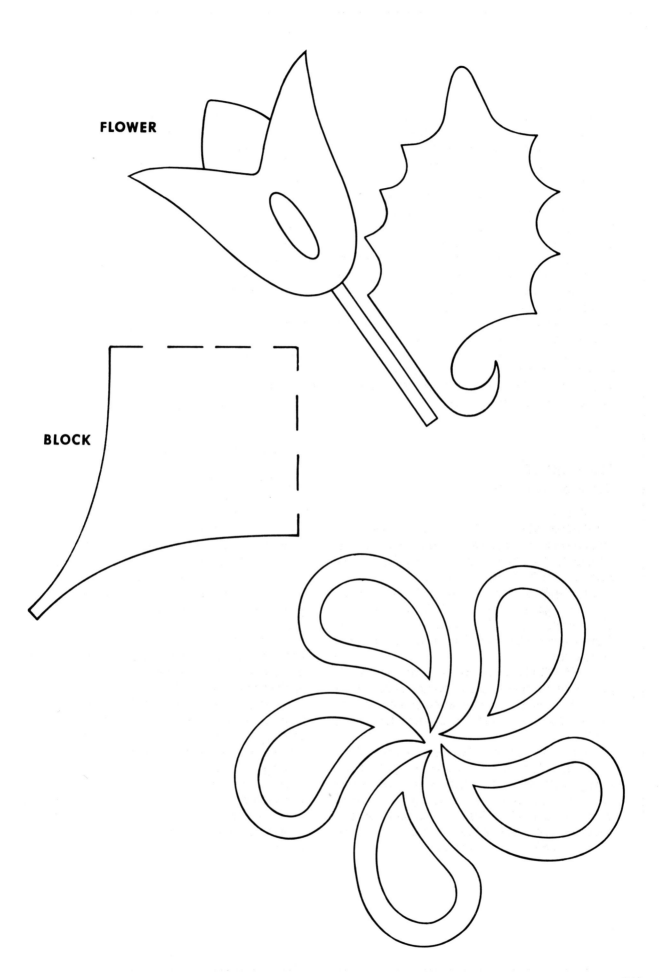

FLOWER

BLOCK

OAK LEAF FRAME

Shown on page 189

EQUIPMENT: Tracing paper. Pencil. Ruler. Hammer. Coping saw. Gouge. Chisel. Sandpaper. Soft rags.

MATERIALS: Bevelled screen stock $\frac{1}{4}''$ thick, $\frac{3}{4}''$ wide: 2 strips, $31\frac{1}{2}''$ long, 2 strips $17\frac{3}{4}''$ long. Lumber $\frac{1}{2}''$ thick, 4" square for each corner trim. Wooden strips $\frac{1}{2}'' \times \frac{1}{2}''$ for rabbet: 2 strips 28" long, 2 strips $13\frac{1}{2}''$ long. Small brads. All-purpose glue. Wood stain.

DIRECTIONS: Trace corner trim half-pattern; to complete, flop pattern over on dash line. Using carbon paper, transfer pattern to $\frac{1}{2}''$ lumber four times. Cut out and shape each corner with coping saw. Following dotted lines on pattern, carve design about $\frac{1}{8}''$ deep using gouge; sand smooth. Put aside until needed.

For frame, form a rectangle of screen stock $14\frac{1}{2}'' \times 28''$ (outside measurements) with ends extending equally. Join with halved cross joint at each corner. To make halved cross joint, place short vertical strips over long strips. With pencil, mark accurately the width $(\frac{3}{4}'')$ and depth $(\frac{1}{8}'')$ of each cut (on top of short strip and bottom of long

strip). Following pencil markings, cut a notch in each strip: clean and smooth inside of notch with chisel. Fit strips into notches to form frame. Glue.

For rabbet strip, glue end of short $\frac{1}{2}'' \times \frac{1}{2}''$ stripping to one long strip with butt joint, long strip overlapping end of short strip. Do the same with the remaining two strips, making sure long piece overlaps the short one. Join the two halves in same manner. Cover one surface of rabbet strip with glue; place on back of frame with outside edges carefully matched; nail together with small brads. With gouge, make irregular grooves along front of frame to give an antique look; sand. Stain frame and decorative trims as desired. Let dry. Glue trim to each corner as shown in illustration.

HARVEST SUN QUILT

Shown on page 190

SIZE: Approximately 89" square.

EQUIPMENT: Ruler. Tracing paper. Thin, stiff cardboard. Light and dark pencils, hard and sharp. Scissors. Needles. Quilting frame (optional).

MATERIALS: Closely woven cotton fabric, 36" wide. Dark color fabric for background, $2\frac{3}{4}$ yards; light or dark fabric (as desired) for lining, $6\frac{3}{4}$ yards; different patterned light and dark-colored fabrics (for diamonds, border squares, and triangles), about 3 yards each of light and dark colors. Cotton batting. Mercerized sewing thread in a color or colors to blend with fabrics.

DIRECTIONS: Read General Directions for Quilting on page 300. Trace diamond pattern, completing the quarter-pattern indicated by dash lines. Cut several diamond patterns from cardboard; replace patterns as they become worn from repeated use.

Center section of quilt contains nine stars. Each star consists of eight diamond-shaped sections radiating from center, and each section is a parallelogram consisting of three rows of three diamonds each. Following General Directions, cut 72 diamonds from fabric for each star. Since this design is most effective when light and dark colors

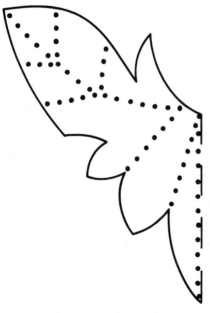

Half-Pattern for Frame Corners

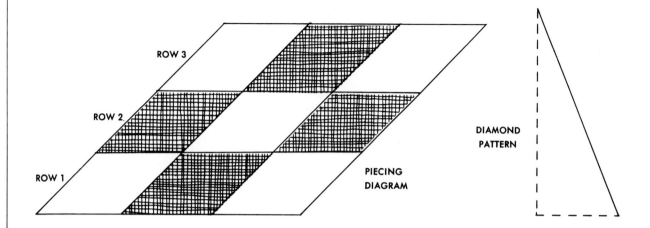

ROW 3

ROW 2

ROW 1

PIECING
DIAGRAM

DIAMOND
PATTERN

alternate in concentric circles, it is suggested that 40 of the 72 diamonds be light, and 32 be dark. Following Piecing Diagram (which represents one assembled diamond-shaped section) for placement, join diamonds in rows of three, with light and dark alternating, as follows: Hold patches together, right sides facing; seam together with small running stitches on pencil lines. Start first row with light, second with dark, third with light. Matching corners carefully, join the three rows to form a parallelogram. Make seven more parallelograms for each star. Having light points together in center, join sections for each half of star; then join star halves. Make eight more stars in same manner.

Cut a cardboard pattern $14\frac{1}{4}''$ square. Use this pattern to cut four squares of background fabric, adding $\frac{1}{4}''$ all around for seam allowance. (**Note:** Before cutting cardboard pattern, place stars point-to-point, as shown in illustration. Measure the large square spaces between stars and deduct $\frac{1}{2}''$ (combined seam allowance). This space should measure $14\frac{1}{4}''$ square; if not, alter cardboard square to fit.) Cut cardboard square in half, forming two rectangles. Use one rectangle as a pattern to cut eight rectangles from the background fabric, adding $\frac{1}{4}''$ all around to these and all other background pieces. Cut second cardboard rectangle in half to form two squares; use one as a pattern to cut twelve squares from background fabric. Cut the small cardboard square in half diagonally to form triangles; use one triangle as a pattern to cut twelve triangles from background fabric. Referring to illustration, stitch background pieces in place. Press seams to one side.

Cut $2\frac{1}{2}''$-wide strips from border fabric (this includes $\frac{1}{4}''$ seam allowance); piece together to fit around quilt edges. Stitch in place around quilt. Cut 96 dark and 120 light diamonds; stitch together to make 24 diamond-shaped parallelograms, as before. Make a cardboard pattern to fit the triangular spaces created between the parallelograms when they are placed point-to-point. Adding $\frac{1}{4}''$ all around, cut 40 triangles from a dark fabric. Cut cardboard triangle in half, forming two right-angled triangles. Use one as a pattern to cut 16 small triangles from the same fabric. Stitch parallelograms and triangles together to form strips as shown, with the small triangles at each end. Stitch strips to edges of quilt. Cut a cardboard square to fit corners. Divide and cut in quarters, to form smaller squares. Cut 16 small squares: 8 dark and 8 light. Alternating light and dark, stitch four small squares together to form a larger square. Sew a large square into each corner.

Cut $2\frac{3}{4}''$-wide strips from border fabric; piece strips together to fit around quilt edges. Stitch in place, making $\frac{1}{4}''$ seams.

Quilting: Pin and baste quilt top, batting, and lining together as directed in General Directions. Quilt diagonally in both directions across each square and border triangles, making the lines about $\frac{3}{4}''$ apart. Quilting lines may first be marked with a ruler and white chalk pencil, if desired.

Trim batting and lining $\frac{1}{2}''$ smaller than quilt top all around. Turn edges of quilt top under $\frac{1}{4}''$; press. Turn under $\frac{1}{4}''$ again, and press. Slip-stitch top to lining all around, trimming away excess fabric at corners.

BOY AND GIRL QUILT SET

Shown on page 191

QUILT SIZE: $41\frac{1}{2}'' \times 57''$.
PILLOW SIZE: $18'' \times 22\frac{1}{2}''$.
EQUIPMENT: Paper for pattern. Pencil. Ruler. Tracing paper. Scissors. Light-colored dressmaker's carbon. Straight pins. Sewing machine with zigzag attachment. Large-eyed needle.
MATERIALS: Red cotton fabric with small print, 44" wide, 4 yards (includes amounts for hats, shoes, and pillow). Ten large pieces (dress takes piece approx. $10'' \times 12''$) or similar patterned fabrics (for dresses, aprons, smocks, and pants on quilt and pillow): five yellow; two purple; one each of medium blue, dark blue, dark green (or colors desired). White cotton fabric, 44" wide, $1\frac{3}{8}$ yards (includes amounts for pillow). Muslin, 44" wide, $1\frac{5}{8}$ yards. Red and white sewing thread. Polyester

fiberfill batting. One skein red pearl cotton embroidery floss.

DIRECTIONS: Read General Directions for Quilting on page 300 and How to Appliqué on page 304. Enlarge patterns by copying onto paper ruled in 2" squares. Trace each hat, shoe piece, dress, smock, apron, and pants separately. The short dash lines on pattern indicate where pieces will be overlapped. The dotted lines on aprons indicate stitching to be done later; they do not indicate separate pieces. Large dots on patterns and Placement Diagram indicate where tying is to be done at the very end.

For quilt lining, cut muslin and red print fabric the full width of fabric and 59" long. Set aside until quilt top is finished.

Referring to Placement Diagram for measurements and adding $\frac{5}{8}''$ to all edges for seam allowances, cut the seven unshaded areas from red

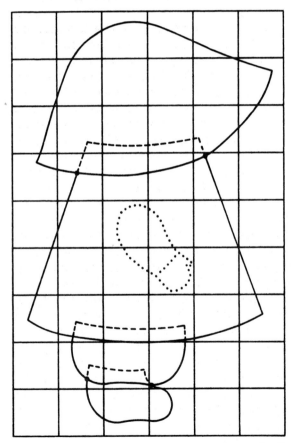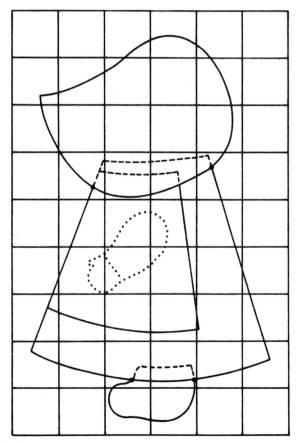

Applique Patterns

print fabric. From white fabric, cut four panels, each $15\frac{1}{4}'' \times 21''$ (shaded areas on diagram); measurement allows for $\frac{5}{8}''$ seam allowances on all edges.

Using patterns, cut two (reversing patterns for each second set) of each appliqué piece; add $\frac{1}{4}''$ along the solid lines only of each piece for turning under. Cut hats and shoes from remaining red print fabric; cut dresses, aprons, smocks, and pants from additional print fabrics. Prepare appliqués as directed in How to Appliqué. Place tracing of apron on fabric apron with carbon paper between. To transfer to fabric, use pencil to go over dotted lines for hand and sleeve outline. Repeat with all apron pieces.

Pin all figure pieces in place in center of each white panel. With machine set for medium-width zigzag stitch, stitch around outline of each piece and along lines for hands and sleeves on aprons.

Following Placement Diagram, pin red strips and white panels together with right sides facing. Stitch, making $\frac{5}{8}''$ seams.

Quilting: Place quilt top, wrong side up, on large, flat surface. Place a layer of batting smoothly on quilt top; pin securely. Turn to right side. Using plain stitch and white thread, machine-stitch around the outline only of each figure and the white panel.

Place muslin piece on large, flat surface. Using pencil, draw diagonal lines $\frac{3}{4}''$ apart across the muslin in the same direction. Repeat lines in opposite directions. Then place quilt lining, wrong side up, on flat surface; place one (or two, depending on thickness desired) layer of batting smoothly on top; place marked muslin on top of batting; pin all thicknesses together. Baste through all thicknesses along lines.

Machine stitching is worked over basting. Using red thread, begin quilting at center of quilt and work toward edges, first all in one direction, then in the opposite direction. Remove basting threads.

To assemble, place quilt top and lining together with right sides facing. If necessary, trim edges so they are even. Trim batting to $\frac{5}{8}''$ in from fabric edges. Leaving a 14" opening in center of one side for turning, sew edges together with $\frac{5}{8}''$ seams. Turn quilt to right side. Turn edges of opening in $\frac{5}{8}''$; slip-stitch closed. Machine-stitch all around quilt 1" in from seam.

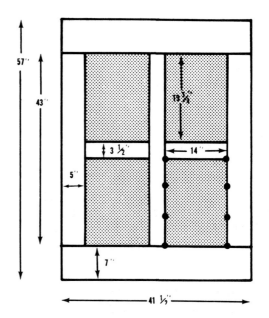

Placement Diagram

For additional stability, quilt is tied at points indicated by large dots on appliqué patterns and Placement Diagram. Insert pins from front to back at these points, mark points on back of quilt with pins. Thread needle with red floss and take a small stitch at each point through all thicknesses except quilt top. Knot floss and tie into bow; trim.

Pillow: Cut white fabric panel, $15\frac{1}{4}'' \times 19\frac{3}{4}''$. Using patterns for one figure, cut pieces from print fabrics and zigzag-stitch onto white panel as for quilt. Cut four strips of red print fabric: two, $3\frac{1}{4}'' \times 23\frac{3}{4}''$; two, $3\frac{1}{4}'' \times 19\frac{1}{4}''$. With right sides facing, pin the two shorter strips at bottom and top of white panel and the longer strips at sides, marking $\frac{5}{8}''$ seams. Pin the strips together where they meet near corners, marking $\frac{5}{8}''$ seams. Sew strips and panel together with $\frac{5}{8}''$ seams. Place pillow top, wrong side up, on flat surface. Put this layer of batting on top. Pin to secure, and turn pillow top to right side. Using plain stitch and white threads, machine-stitch around only the outline of figure. Trim batting to $1\frac{1}{8}''$ in from fabric edge. For pillow back, cut piece of red print fabric the same size as pillow top. Place pillow top and back together with right sides facing. Leaving 6" opening in center of one side, sew top and back together with $\frac{5}{8}''$ seam, leaving an opening for turning. Turn to right side. Stuff pillow neatly with batting. Turn edges of opening in $\frac{5}{8}''$; slip-stitch closed. Sew all around edge of pillow $\frac{1}{2}''$ in from seam.

Patterns for Heirloom Coverlet

HEIRLOOM COVERLET

Shown on page 192

SIZE: Approximately 81″ × 73″.

EQUIPMENT: Paper for patterns. Tracing paper. Ruler. Pencil. Cardboard, piece 8½″ square. Scissors. Dressmaker's tracing (carbon) paper. Dry ball-point pen. Sewing and embroidery needles. Embroidery hoop, 8″ diameter. Piece of soft cloth. Straight pins. Iron.

MATERIALS: Unbleached muslin 45″ wide, 7 yards. Ecru lace edging 3″-4″ wide, 8 yards. Ecru sewing thread. DMC six-strand embroidery floss, red #304, 85 skeins.

DIRECTIONS: Note: We've selected 16 of the original 56 motifs for you to arrange as desired on your coverlet. The coverlet is made up of 56 squares, 7 rows across and 8 down. A square near the middle (4th row across, 5th row down) may feature a personal touch with a name, date, or both.

To Prepare Muslin: From muslin, cut fifty-six 8½″ squares using cardboard square as a pattern. Cut four panels, two 56½″ × 5″ for top and bottom of the coverlet, two 73½″ × 5″ for the sides. Cut two 73½″ × 33″ panels for backing.

Enlarge motifs by copying on paper ruled in 1″ squares. Trace each motif in the center of a piece of 8½″ square tracing paper. After planning the arrangement of squares on your coverlet and determining the number of each motif needed, transfer motifs to muslin squares using carbon and dry ball-point pen. For personalized square, write or print name on tracing paper and transfer to muslin square.

To Work Embroidery: Place muslin square in hoop. Using three strands of floss in needle, work motif lines in chain stitch; see Stitch Details on page 308. When complete, press, placing embroidered side down on a soft cloth.

Assembling Squares: On a large, flat surface, lay out 56 squares as planned. Pin, then stitch top row together, right sides facing and making ¼″ seams. Stitch remaining seven horizontal rows together in same manner. Press seam allowances open. Using three strands of floss in needle, work ¼″-wide herringbone stitch centered over each seam; see page 308.

With right sides facing, pin and then stitch the top two strips of seven squares together, matching seams and stitching ¼″ from edges of fabric. Press the seam allowances open and then work the herringbone stitch over the seam as before. Continue attaching succeeding strips and embroidering the seams in this manner until all eight rows of seven squares each are assembled.

To Complete Coverlet: Right sides facing and edges even, stitch 56½″-long panels of fabric to top and bottom edges of assembled center section. Press seams open and work herringbone stitch over seams. Stitch 73½″-long panels of fabric to side edges of center section and top and bottom panels. Press seams open and work herringbone stitch over side seams between top and bottom seams, so herringbone embroidery meets at corners and forms a square.

Stitch panels for backing together, with ¼″ seam. Press seam open. Right sides facing and all edges even, stitch backing and coverlet together ¼″ from edges, leaving an 18″-long opening along bottom edge for turning. Turn coverlet right side out and press so seams are exactly along edges. Press edges of opening to inside and slip-stitch closed.

To attach lace edging, start at one lower corner and pin wrong side of edging to right side of coverlet, with straight edge of lace overlapping edge of coverlet ⅛″. Ease fullness in around corners so lace lies flat. Join ends of edging where they meet with ¼″ seam. Topstitch along straight edge of lace through all thicknesses around coverlet.

GOOD MORNING PILLOW SHAM

Shown on page 192

SIZE: 20″ × 30″.

EQUIPMENT: Colored pencil. Pencil. Ruler. Paper for pattern. Tape measure. Dressmaker's tracing (carbon) paper. Dry ball-point pen. Scissors. Sewing and embroidery needles. Embroidery hoop, 8″ diameter. Straight pins. Sewing machine. Iron.

MATERIALS: Unbleached muslin 45″ wide, 1 yard. Ecru sewing thread. DMC six-strand embroidery floss, red #304, four skeins.

Pattern for Pillow Shams

DIRECTIONS: Using sharp colored pencil, draw lines across pattern, connecting grid lines. Enlarge pattern by copying on paper ruled in 1″ squares.

Cut muslin into two 21″ × 33″ pieces; press pieces carefully; zigzag - or whip-stitch raw edges to prevent raveling. Set one piece aside for backing. Position enlarged pattern on right side of remaining piece, $3\frac{1}{2}$″ in from both long edges and from left short edge. Carefully pin pattern in place. Place dressmaker's carbon between pattern and fabric, then go over lines of design with dry ballpoint pen to transfer.

To embroider, insert area to be worked first in hoop to keep fabric taut. Begin stitching by leaving end of floss on back and working over it to secure. To end strand or begin a new one, weave end of floss under stitches on back; do not make knots.

Using three strands of floss in needle, embroider pillow as follows (see page 308 for Stitch De-

tails): For letters, use outline stitch, working interior details with straight stitch and dark areas with satin stitch. For girl, work outlines of hair, arm, face, nose, bottom lip and nightgown collar with outline stitch; work eyelashes, fine hair lines and nightgown collar with straight stitch; work curls and remaining facial features with fly stitch. Outline-stitch knobs on bedpost and butterflies on blanket. Straight-stitch shadows on bedpost and bird, and fine lines on pillow. Work all other lines using chain stitch. When embroidery is complete, steam-press on padded surface.

To make sham, pin embroidered front to backing with right sides facing, leaving right edge of design (bedpost edge) open. Stitch pieces together $\frac{1}{2}$″ from raw edges on three sides. On remaining side, fold and press raw edges $\frac{1}{2}$″ to wrong side; fold and press again 2″ to wrong side for hem. Stitch in place, close to edge. Turn sham to right side.

POPCORN SQUARE BEDSPREAD

Shown on page 207

SIZES: Afghan, 57″ × 78″; twin bedspread, 67″ × 100″; double bedspread, 78″ × 100″. Directions are for afghan. Changes for twin and double bedspreads are given in parentheses.

MATERIALS: Columbia-Minerva Nantuk 4-Ply, 4-oz. balls, 20 (31-37) balls. Crochet hook size G (4$\frac{1}{4}$ mm). Yarn needle.

GAUGE: 9 sts = 2″; 9 rows = 2″. Each square is about 11″ square.

AFGHAN: SQUARE (Make 35 (54-63) squares): Ch 12, join with sl st to form ring. Mark beg of rnds.

Rnd 1: Ch 1, sc in next ch, ch 5, (sk 2 ch, sc in next ch) 3 times, ch 5. Join with sl st to first sc, ch 1 on this and all rnds.

Rnd 2: Sc in same st as joining, (sc in next ch-5 lp, ch 5, sc at other end of same ch-5 lp, sc in next sc) 4 times.

Rnd 3: Sc in same st with joining, sc in next sc, sc in next ch-5 lp, (ch 5, sc at other end of same ch-5 lp, sc in next 3 sc, sc in next ch-5 lp) 3 times, ch 5, sc at other end of last ch-5 lp, sc in last sc (5 sc between ch-5 lps).

Rnd 4: Sc in same st as joining, sc in next 2 sc, sc in next lp, (ch 5, sc at other end of same lp, sc in next 5 sc, sc in next lp) 3 times, ch 5, sc at other end of lp, sc in last 2 sc (7 sc between lps).

Rnd 5: Yo hook, draw up a long lp in center sc 3 rows below (row 2), (yo, draw up a lp in same st) twice more (be sure lps are long enough to reach to top of row being worked), yo and through all 7 lps on hook, ch 1 to fasten popcorn, sk sc behind popcorn, sc in next 3 sc, sc in next lp, (ch 5, sc at other end of same ch-5 lp, sc in next 3 sc, popcorn over next st as before, sc in next 3 sc, sc in next lp) 3 times, ch 5, sc in same lp, sc in last 3 sc, join with sl st to ch-1 of popcorn, ch 1.

Rnd 6: Sc in same st as joining, sc in next 4 sc, sc in lp, (ch 5, sc in same lp, sc in next 4 sc, sc in ch 1 of popcorn (do not work in top of popcorn itself), sc in next 4 sc, sc in next lp) 3 times, ch 5, sc in lp, sc in last 4 sc, join, ch 1.

Rnd 7: Sc in same st as joining, popcorn in next sc 3 rows below (row 4), sk sc behind popcorn, sc in next 4 sc, sc in ch-5 lp, (ch 5, sc in same lp, sc in next 4 sc, popcorn in next sc 3 rows below, sk sc behind popcorn, sc in next sc, popcorn in next sc 3 rows below, sk sc behind popcorn, sc in next 4 sc, sc in next lp) 3 times, ch 5, sc in same lp, sc in next 4 sc, popcorn in next sc 3 rows below, join. **Note:** Always work popcorns in sc 3 rows below and sk the sc behind the popcorn.

Rnd 8: Sc in same st as joining, sc in each sc to lp, sc in lp, (ch 5, sc in same lp, sc in each sc and ch 1 of popcorn to next lp, sc in next lp) 3 times, ch 5, sc in lp, sc in next 5 sc, sc in ch 1 of popcorn. Join, ch 1.

Rnd 9: Sc in same st as joining, sc in next sc, popcorn, sc in next 5 sc, sc in lp, (ch 5, sc in same lp, sc in next 5 sc, popcorn, sc in next 3 sc, popcorn, sc in next 5 sc, sc in lp) 3 times, ch 5, sc in lp, sc in next 5 sc, popcorn, sc in last sc. Join, ch 1.

Rnd 10: Work as rnd 8, having 2 more sc in each of the 4 sections (19 sc in each section).

Rnd 11: Sc in same st as joining, sc in next 2 sc, popcorn, sc in next 6 sc, sc in lp, (ch 5, sc in same lp, sc in next 6 sc, popcorn, sc in next 5 sc, popcorn, sc in next 6 sc, sc in lp) 3 times, ch 5, sc in lp, sc in next 6 sc, popcorn, sc in last 2 sc. Join, ch 1.

Rnd 12: Repeat rnd 10 (23 sc in each section).

Rnd 13: Sc in each sc working sc, ch 5, sc in each corner lp (25 sc in each section). Mark the center sc of each side.

Rnd 14: Work in pat with popcorn over marked st and 13 sc at each side of popcorns.

Rnd 15 and All Odd Rnds: Repeat rnd 10.

Rnd 16: Work pat with popcorn at each side of center st, having 14 sc at each side of popcorns.

Rnd 18: Work pat with popcorn at each side of 3 center sts, having 15 sc at each side of popcorns.

Rnd 20: Work pat with popcorn at each side of 5 center sts, having 16 sc at each side of popcorns.

Rnd 21: Repeat rnd 10 (41 sc on each side). End off.

FINISHING: Lightly steam-press squares to shape. Arrange squares in 5 (6-7) strips of 7 (9-

9) squares each. With yarn needle, sew squares tog through back lps only.

Edging: Attach yarn in ch-5 lp and work popcorn, ch 3, popcorn, * sk 2 sc, popcorn in next sc 2 rows below; repeat from * around, working popcorn in each ch-5 lp at square joinings, and popcorn, ch 3, popcorn in each ch-5 corner lp. Join to top of first popcorn, ch 1. Sc in each space between and in top of each popcorn, having 4 sc in each corner. Join, end off. Run in yarn ends.

NOSEGAY ARAN AFGHAN
Shown on page 205

SIZE: 52″ × 70″, plus fringe.

MATERIALS: Brunswick Windrush or Germantown Knitting Worsted, 12 100-gram pull skeins. Knitting needles No. 10½ (6½ mm). Cable or double-pointed needle. Markers.

GAUGE: 4 sts = 1″ (seed stitch); 14 sts = 3″ (bramble stitch); 16 sts = 3¼″ (nosegay pattern).

ABBREVIATIONS: FRONT CROSS (FC). Sl 1 st to double-pointed needle (dpn) and hold in front, p 1, then k 1 from dpn.

FRONT KNIT CROSS (FKC): Same as FC, except knit both sts.

BACK CROSS (BC): Sl 1 st to dpn and hold in back, k 1, then p 1 from dpn.

BACK KNIT CROSS (BKC): Same as BC, except knit both sts.

BRAMBLE STITCH-CABLE PANEL (make 3): Entire panel should measure 9½″ across. Cast on 44 sts.

Row 1 (right side): K 1, p 2, k 2, yo, k 2 tog, p 2, k 1, place marker, p 24, place marker k 1, p 2, k 2, yo, k 2 tog, p 2, k 1.

Row 2: P 1, k 2, p 2, yo, p 2 tog, k 2, p 1, sl marker, * (k 1, p 1, k 1) all in the same st; p 3 tog; repeat from * to marker, sl marker, p 1, k 2, p 2, yo, p 2 tog, k 2, p 1.

Row 3: Repeat row 1.

Row 4: P 1, k 2, p 2, yo, p 2 tog, k 2, p 1, sl marker, * p 3 tog, (k 1, p 1, k 1) all in the same

st; repeat from * to marker, sl marker, p 1, k 2, p 2, yo, p 2 tog, k 2, p 1.

Row 5: Repeat row 1.

Row 6: Repeat row 2.

Row 7: * K 1, p 2, sl 2 to dpn and hold in front, k 2, then k 2 from dpn, p 2, k 1, * purl between markers, repeat between *'s.

Row 8: Repeat row 4.

Row 9: Repeat row 1.

Row 10: Repeat row 2.

Row 11: Repeat row 1.

Row 12: Repeat row 4.

Row 13: Repeat row 1.

Row 14: Repeat row 2.

Row 15: Repeat row 1.

Row 16: Repeat row 4.

Repeat rows 1–16 for pattern until 22 repeats have been knit in all (352 rows).

NOSEGAY-SEED STITCH PANEL (make 4): Entire panel should measure 6¼″ across. Cast on 28 sts.

Foundation Row (right side): K 1, (p 1, k 1) twice, k 1, p 7, k 2, p 7, k 1, (p 1, k 1) twice, k 1.

Row 1: P 1, (k 1, p 1) twice, p 1, k 7, p 2, k 7, p 1, (k 1, p 1) twice, p 1.

Row 2: K 1, (p 1, k 1) twice, k 1, p 6, BKC, FKC, p 6, k 1, (p 1, k 1) twice, k 1.

Row 3: P 1, (k 1, p 1) twice, p 1, k 5, FC, p 2, BC, k 5, p 1, (k 1, p 1) twice, p 1.

Row 4: K 1, (p 1, k 1) twice, k 1, p 4, BC, BKC, FKC, FC, p 4, k 1, (p 1, k 1) twice, k 1.

Row 5: P 1, (k 1, p 1) twice, p 1, k 3, FC, k 1, p 4, k 1, BC, k 3, p 1, (k 1, p 1) twice, p 1.

Row 6: K 1, (p 1, k 1) twice, k 1, p 2, BC, p 1, BC, k 2, FC, p 1, FC, p 2, k 1, (p 1, k 1) twice, k 1.

Row 7: P 1, (k 1, p 1) twice, p 1, (k 2, p 1) twice, k 1, p 2, k 1, (p 1, k 2) twice, p 1, (k 1, p 1) twice, p 1.

Row 8: K 1, (p 1, k 1) twice, k 1, p 2, make bobble (MB) as follows (k 1, p 1) twice into next st, turn and p 4, turn and k 4, turn and (p 2 tog) twice, turn and k 2 tog to complete bobble; p 1, BC, p 1, k 2, p 1, FC, p 1, MB, p 2, k 1, (p 1, k 1) twice, k 1.

Row 9: P 1, (k 1, p 1) twice, p 1, k 4, p 1, k 2, p 2, k 2, p 1, k 4, p 1, (k 1, p 1) twice, p 1.

Row 10: K 1, (p 1, k 1) twice, k 1, p 4, MB, p 2, k 2, p 2, MB, p 4, k 1, (p 1, k 1) twice, k 1.

Repeat rows 1–10 for pattern until 35 nosegay patterns have been knit, then work row 1 once more; do not repeat foundation row—352 rows.

FINISHING: Weave panels together alternating nosegay panels with bramble stitch-cable panels. Knot 4 12″ strands of yarn into every 4th st across each end of afghan.

PINEAPPLES AND DIAMONDS
Shown on page 206

SIZE: 54″ × 74″, plus fringe.
MATERIALS: Worsted weight yarn, 17 100-gram skeins. Crochet hooks sizes H (5 mm) and J (6 mm).
GAUGE: Pineapple panel is 8½″ wide.
AFGHAN: PINEAPPLE PANEL (make 3): With size H hook, ch 28 loosely.

Row 1: Sc in 2nd ch from hook and in each ch across—27 sc. Ch 3, turn.

Row 2: Sk first sc (ch 3 counts as first dc), dc in each sc across. Ch 3, turn.

Rows 3 and 4: Sk first dc, dc in 25 dc, dc in top of turning ch. Ch 3, turn each row.

Row 5: Sk first dc, dc in 6 dc, ch 1, sk 2 dc, shell of (2 dc, ch 2, 2 dc) in next dc, sk 3 dc, shell of (2 dc, ch 4, 2 dc) in next dc, sk 3 dc, shell of (2 dc, ch 2, 2 dc) in next dc, ch 1, sk 2 dc, dc in 6 dc, dc in top of turning ch. Ch 3, turn.

Row 6: Sk first dc, dc in 4 dc, (yo, pull up a lp in next dc, yo and through 2 lps on hook) twice, yo and through 3 lps on hook—1 dc dec; ch 1, shell of (2 dc, ch 2, 2 dc) in ch-2 sp of next shell, 8 dc in ch-4 sp (base of pineapple), shell in next shell, ch 1, 1 dc dec in first 2 dc of border, dc in 4 dc, dc in top of turning ch. Ch 3, turn.

Row 7: Sk first dc, dc in 3 dc, 1 dc dec, ch 1, shell in shell; working across base of pineapple, (dc in dc, ch 1) 7 times, dc; shell in shell, ch 1, 1 dc dec, dc in 3 dc, dc in top of turning ch. Ch 3, turn.

Row 8: Sk first dc, dc in 2 dc, 1 dc dec, ch 1, shell in shell, ch 1, sc in first dc of pineapple, (ch 3, sc in next dc) 7 times, ch 1, shell in shell, ch 1, 1 dc dec, dc in 2 dc, dc in top of turning ch. Ch 3, turn.

Row 9: Sk first dc, dc in next dc, 1 dc dec, ch 1, shell in shell, ch 2, sc in first ch-3 loop, (ch 3, sc in next loop) 6 times, ch 2, shell in shell, ch 1, 1 dc dec, dc in next dc, dc in top of turning ch. Ch 3, turn.

Row 10: Sk first dc, dc in next dc, 2 dc in next dc (an inc), ch 1, shell in shell, ch 2, sc in next ch-3 loop, (ch 3, sc in next loop) 5 times, ch 2, shell in shell, ch 1, 2 dc in first st of border, dc in next dc, dc in top of turning ch. Ch 3, turn.

Row 11: Sk first dc, dc in 2 dc, 2 dc in next dc, ch 1, shell in shell, ch 3, sc in next ch-3 loop, (ch 3, sc in next loop) 4 times, ch 3, shell in shell, ch 1, 2 dc in first st of border, dc in 2 dc, dc in top of turning ch. Ch 3, turn.

Row 12: Sk first dc, dc in 3 dc, 2 dc in next dc, ch 1, shell in shell, ch 3, sc in first ch-3 loop of pineapple, (ch 3, sc in next loop) 3 times, ch 3, shell in shell, ch 1, 2 dc in first st of border, dc in 3 dc, dc in top of turning ch. Ch 3, turn.

Row 13: Sk first dc, dc in 4 dc, 2 dc in next dc, ch 1, shell in shell, ch 3, sc in first ch-3 loop of pineapple, (ch 3, sc in next loop) twice, ch 3, shell in shell, ch 1, 2 dc in first st of border, dc in 4 dc, dc in top of turning ch. Ch 3, turn.

Row 14: Sk first dc, dc in 5 dc, 2 dc in next dc, ch 1, shell in shell, ch 3, sc in first ch-3 loop of pineapple, ch 3, sc in next loop, ch 3, shell in shell, ch 1, 2 dc in first st of border, dc in 5 dc, dc in top of turning ch. Ch 3, turn.

Row 15: Sk first dc, dc in 6 dc, 2 dc in next dc, ch 1, shell in shell, ch 4, sc in ch-3 loop of pineapple, ch 4, shell in shell, ch 1, 2 dc in first st of border, dc in 6 dc, dc in top of turning ch. Ch 3, turn.

Row 16: Sk first dc, dc in 7 dc, 2 dc in next dc, ch 1, shell in shell, dc in ch-4 sp, dc in next ch-4 sp, shell in shell, ch 1, 2 dc in first st of border, dc in 7 dc, dc in top of turning ch. Ch 3, turn.

Row 17: Sk first dc, dc in 9 dc, ch 1, (shell in next shell) twice, ch 1, dc in each of 9 dc of border, dc in top of turning ch. Ch 3, turn.

Row 18: Sk first dc, dc in 9 dc, ch 1, shell in

shell, ch 1, shell in shell, ch 1, dc in 9 dc of border, dc in top of turning ch. Ch 3, turn.

Row 19: Sk first dc, dc in 7 dc, 1 dc dec, ch 1, shell in shell, ch 2, shell in shell, ch 1, 1 dc dec on border, dc in 7 dc, dc in top of turning ch. Ch 3, turn.

Row 20: Sk first dc, dc in 6 dc, 1 dc dec, ch 1, shell in shell, shell in ch-2 sp between shells, shell in shell, ch 1, 1 dc dec on border, dc in 6 dc, dc in top of turning ch. Ch 3, turn.

Row 21: Sk first dc, dc in 5 dc, 1 dc dec, ch 1, shell in shell, shell of 2 dc, ch 4, 2 dc in next shell, shell in shell, ch 1, 1 dc dec on border, dc in 5 dc, dc in top of turning ch. Ch 3, turn.

Row 22: Sk first dc, dc in 4 dc, 1 dc dec, ch 1, shell in shell, 8 dc in ch-4 sp, shell in shell, ch 1, 1 dc dec on border, dc in 4 dc, dc in top of turning ch. Ch 3, turn.

Repeat rows 7–22 until 6 pineapple patterns are complete, then work rows 7–17 for 7th pattern.

Row 18: Sk first dc, dc in 9 dc, 2 dc in center of first shell, ch 3, 2 dc in center of 2nd shell, dc in each dc of border, dc in top of turning ch. Ch 3, turn.

Row 19: Sk first dc, dc in 11 dc, 3 dc in ch-3 sp, dc in 11 dc, dc in top of turning ch. Ch 3, turn.

Row 20: Dc evenly across—27 dc. Ch 1, turn.

Row 21: Sc in each dc across. Cut yarn, leaving a 5″ end.

DIAMOND PANEL: Row 1: Leaving a 5″ end, make lp on hook; from right side, using J hook, sc in side of row 1 of a pineapple panel, 2 sc loosely in end dc of each row of panel to top, making 1 extra sc in last dc row, 1 sc in last sc row—235 sc. End off, leaving a 5″ end.

Row 2: From right side, leaving a 5″ end, beg in first sc of last row, sc in first sc, sc in back lp of each sc across to last sc, sc in both lps of last sc—235 sc. End off, leaving a 5″ end.

Rows 3 and 4: Repeat row 2.

Note: All rows of diamond panel are worked from right side. Begin and end all rows by leaving 5″ ends. Work first and last sc's in both lps, all other sc's in back lp of sts.

Row 5: Sc in 7 sc, * dc in front lp of sc 2 rows below (row 3), sk sc behind dc, sc in 19 sc, repeat from * across, end dc in front lp of sc 2 rows below, sc in 7 sc.

Row 6: Sc in 8 sts, dc in front lp of st 2 rows below, sk sc behind dc, * sc in 17 sts, dc in front lp of st 2 rows below, sk sc behind dc, sc in next st, dc in front lp of st 2 rows below, sk sc behind dc, repeat from * across, end dc in front lp of st 2 rows below, sc in 8 sts.

Row 7: Sc in 9 sts, dc in front lp of st 2 rows below (always sk sc behind dc), * sc in 15 sts, dc in front lp of st 2 rows below, sc in next 3 sts, dc in front lp of st 2 rows below, repeat from * across, end dc in front lp of st 2 rows below, sc in 9 sts.

Row 8: Sc in 10 sts, dc in front lp of st 2 rows below, * sc in 13 sts, dc in front lp of st 2 rows below, sc in 5 sts, dc in front lp of st 2 rows below, repeat from * across, end dc in front lp of st 2 rows below, sc in 10 sts.

Row 9: Sc in 7 sts, dc 2 rows below, sc in 3 sts, dc 2 rows below, * sc in 11 sts, dc 2 rows below, (sc in 3 sts, dc 2 rows below) twice, repeat from * across, end dc 2 rows below, sc in 3 sts, dc 2 rows below, sc in 7 sts.

Row 10: Sc in 8 sts, dc 2 rows below, sc in 3 sts, dc 2 rows below, * sc in 9 sts, dc 2 rows below, sc in 3 sts, dc 2 rows below, sc in next st, dc 2 rows below, sc in 3 sts, dc 2 rows below, repeat from * across, end dc, 3 sc, dc, sc in 8 sts.

Row 11: Sc in 9 sts, dc 2 rows below, sc in 3 sts, dc 2 rows below, * sc in 7 sts, (dc 2 rows below, sc in 3 sts) 3 times, dc 2 rows below, repeat from * across, end dc, 3 sc, dc, sc in 9 sts.

Row 12: Sc in 7 sts; holding back last lp of each dc work 3 dc in front lp of st 2 rows below, yo and through all lps on hook (3-dc cluster made); sc in 2 sts, dc 2 rows below, sc in 3 sts, dc 2 rows below, * sc in 5 sts, dc 2 rows below, sc in 3 sts, dc 2 rows below, sc in 2 sts, 3-dc cluster, sc in 2 sts, dc 2 rows below, sc in 3 sts, dc 2 rows below, repeat from * across, end 3-dc cluster, sc in 7 sts.

Row 13: Repeat row 11.
Row 14: Repeat row 10.
Row 15: Repeat row 9.
Row 16: Repeat row 8.
Row 17: Repeat row 7.
Row 18: Repeat row 6.
Row 19: Repeat row 5.
Row 20: Repeat row 2.

Work same diamond panel on other edge of same pineapple panel. Work same diamond panels on another pineapple panel. The third pineapple panel is center panel of afghan.

TO JOIN PANELS: Work row 1 of diamond panel along one side of center panel. Making sure pineapples face in same direction, sc center panel to side panel: sc in first st of center panel, drop lp off hook, insert hook from front to back through first st of side panel, pull dropped lp through; * sc in next st of center panel, pull loop through next st of side panel, repeat from * across.

Join other side of center panel to second side panel in same way.

FINISHING: Leaving 5″ ends as before, work 2 rows sc in both lps of sts along side edge of afghan.

Cut 10″ strands of yarn. Draw one strand through st on end to make three 5″ ends. Knot 3 ends tog, tightening knot close to edge of afghan. On pineapple panels, knot 2 strands to make fringe in each st across ends.

IRISH FISHERMAN
Shown on page 207

SIZE: About 50″ × 70″.
MATERIALS: Columbia-Minerva Nantuk 4-Ply, 15 4-oz. balls. 29″ circular knitting needle No. 11 (8 mm). Dp or cable needle. Crochet hook size J (6 mm). Markers.
GAUGE: 3 sts = 1″; 4 rows = 1″ (double strand).
Note: Yarn is used double throughout.
PATTERN STITCHES: PATTERN 1 (worked on 17 sts): **Row 1** (wrong side): K 1, p 2, k 1, p 9, k 1, p 2, k 1.

Row 2: P 1, sk next st, k next st without dropping st from left-hand needle, k the skipped st, drop both sts from left-hand needle (Rope St-RS), p 1, k 9, p 1, RS, p 1.

Row 3 and All Odd Rows: Repeat row 1.

Row 4: P 1, RS, p 1, k 3, sl next 3 sts to dp needle and hold at front of work, k next 3 sts, k 3 from dp needle, p 1, RS, p 1.

Row 6: P 1, RS, p 1, sl next 3 sts to dp needle and hold at back of work, k next 3 sts, k 3 from dp needle, k next 3 sts, p 1, RS, p 1.

Rows 7–12: Repeat rows 1 and 2 three times.
Row 13: Repeat row 1. Repeat rows 4–13 for Pattern 1.

PATTERN 2 (worked on 13 sts): **Row 1** (wrong side): K 1, p 2, k 7, p 2, k 1.

Row 2: P 1, RS, p 7, RS, p 1.

Row 3 and All Odd Rows: K the k sts and p the p sts as they face you.

Row 4: P 1, RS, p 3, (insert needle in next st, k 1 but do not drop st from left needle, place lp just made from right needle on left needle, k 1, drop loop from left needle) 5 times (5 new sts on right needle), pass the 2nd, 3rd, 4th, then 5th sts over the first st (popcorn made), p 3, RS, p 1.

Rows 5–10: Repeat rows 1 and 2 three times.
Row 11: Repeat row 1. Repeat rows 4–11 for Pattern 2.

PATTERN 3 (worked on 10 sts): **Row 1** (wrong side): P 2, (k 2, p 2) twice.

Row 2: K 2, (p 2, k 2) twice.

Row 3: Purl.

Row 4: Knit. Repeat rows 1–4 for Pattern 3.

PATTERN 4 (worked on 19 sts): **Row 1** (wrong side): K 1, p 2, k 6, p 1, k 6, p 2, k 1.

Row 2: P 1, RS, p 6, k 1, p 6, RS, p 1.

Row 3: K 1, p 2, k 5, p 1, k 1, p 1, k 5, p 2, k 1.

Row 4: P 1, RS, p 5, k 1, p 1, k 1, p 5, RS, p 1.

Row 5: K 1, p 2, k 4, p 1, (k 1, p 1) twice, k 4, p 2, k 1.

Row 6: P 1, RS, p 4, k 1, (p 1, k 1) twice, p 4, RS, p 1.

Row 7: K 1, p 2, k 3, p 1, (k 1, p 1) 3 times, k 3, p 2, k 1.

Row 8: P 1, RS, p 3, k 1, (p 1, k 1) 3 times, p 3, RS, p 1.

Row 9: K 1, p 2, k 2, p 1, (k 1, p 1) 4 times, k 2, p 2, k 1.

Row 10: P 1, RS, p 2, k 1, (p 1, k 1) 4 times, p 2, RS, p 1.

Row 11: K 1, p 2, k 1, (k 1, p 1) 6 times, p 2, k 1.

Row 12: P 1, RS, p 1, (k 1, p 1) 6 times, RS, p 1.

Row 13: Repeat row 9.
Row 14: Repeat row 10.
Row 15: Repeat row 7.

Row 16: Repeat row 8.

Row 17: Repeat row 5.

Row 18: Repeat row 6.

Row 19: Repeat row 3.

Row 20: Repeat row 4. Repeat rows 1–20 for Pattern 4.

PATTERN 5 (worked on 34 sts): **Row 1** (wrong side): K 1, p 32, k 1.

Row 2: P 1, (sl next 2 sts to dp needle and hold at back of work, k next 2 sts, k 2 from dp needle, sl next 2 sts to dp needle and hold in front of work, k 2, k 2 from dp needle) 4 times, p 1.

Row 3: Repeat row 1.

Row 4: P 1, k 32, p 1.

Row 5: Repeat row 1.

Row 6: P 1, (sl next 2 sts to dp needle and hold at front of work, k next 2 sts, k 2 from dp needle, sl next 2 sts to dp needle and hold at back of work, k next 2 sts, k 2 from dp needle) 4 times, p 1.

Row 7: Repeat row 1.

Row 8: Repeat row 4. Repeat rows 1–8 for Pattern 5.

AFGHAN: With double strand of yarn, cast on 152 sts. Work row 1 of each of the patterns as follows: Pattern 1 over 17 sts, place marker on needle; Pattern 2 over 13 sts, place marker; Pattern 3 over 10 sts, place marker; Pattern 4 over 19 sts, place marker; Pattern 5 over 34 sts, place marker; Pattern 4 over 19 sts, place marker; Pattern 3 over 10 sts, place marker; Pattern 2 over 13 sts, place marker; Pattern 1 over 17 sts. Keeping continuity of all pats, work until there are 14 complete diamond pats, ending with row 20 of Pattern 4. Bind off in patterns.

FINISHING: From right side, work sc in each st along short ends of afghan.

FRINGE: Cut 8 strands 20″ long for each fringe by wrapping yarn around 10″ cardboard 8 times and cutting one end. Knot across afghan, spacing fringe evenly. Divide each fringe in half and knot a second time (see photograph).

STAR BEDSPREAD

Shown on pages 208–209

SIZE: 82″ × 102″, plus fringe.

MATERIALS: Kentucky All-Purpose Yarn (100% rayon), 85 2-oz. skeins. (Yarn can be ordered by mail from Edgemont Yarn Service, R.R. 5, Box 132, Maysville, KY 41056). Knitting needles No. 5 (3¾ mm). Double-pointed needles No. 5, 1 set. Steel crochet hook, No. 00.

GAUGE: Each motif = 11″ square.

BEDSPREAD: MOTIF (make 63): With dp needles, cast on 8 sts. Divide on needles: 3 sts on each of 2 needles, 2 sts on 3rd needle. Join and k 1 rnd.

Rnd 1: (Yo, k 1) 8 times—16 sts.

Rnd 2 and All Even Rnds: K around.

Rnd 3: (Yo, k 2) 8 times—24 sts.

Rnd 5: (Yo, k 3) 8 times—32 sts.

Rnd 7: (Yo, k 4) 8 times—40 sts.

Rnd 9: (Yo, k 5) 8 times—48 sts.

Rnd 11: (Yo, k 1, yo, k 2 tog, k 3) 8 times—56 sts.

Rnd 13: (Yo, k 3, yo, k 2 tog, k 2) 8 times—64 sts.

Rnd 15: (Yo, k 5, yo, k 2 tog, k 1) 8 times—72 sts.

Rnd 17: (Yo, k 7, yo, k 2 tog) 8 times—80 sts.

Rnd 19: (Yo, k 1, yo, k 2 tog, k 5, k 2 tog) 8 times—80 sts.

Rnd 21: (Yo, k 1, yo, k 2 tog, yo, k 2 tog, k 5) 8 times—88 sts.

Rnd 23: * Yo, k 1, (yo, k 2 tog) 3 times, k 4, repeat from * around—96 sts.

Rnd 25: * Yo, k 1, (yo, k 2 tog) 4 times, k 3, repeat from * around—104 sts.

Rnd 27: * Yo, k 1, (yo, k 2 tog) 5 times, k 2, repeat from * around—112 sts.

Rnd 29: * Yo, k 1, (yo, k 2 tog) 6 times, k 1, repeat from * around—120 sts.

Rnd 31: * Yo, k 1, (yo, k 2 tog) 7 times, repeat from * around—128 sts.

Rnds 32–34: K 3 rnds even.

Corners: First Corner: Place first 32 sts on one needle.

Row 1 (right side): P 30 sts, p 2 tog; turn.

Row 2: K 29 sts, k 2 tog; turn.

Row 3: P 28 sts, p 2 tog; turn.

Row 4: P to last 2 sts, p 2 tog; turn.

Row 5: K to last 2 sts, k 2 tog; turn.

Row 6: P to last 2 sts, p 2 tog; turn. Repeat rows 4–6 until 2 sts remain. Work last 2 sts tog. End off; leave long end for sewing.

Place next 32 sts on needle for 2nd corner. Work as for first corner. Repeat for 3rd and 4th corners.

FINISHING: Pin out each motif, face down, to 11″ square. Wet lightweight terry cloth and place over squares. Place a very hot iron over terry cloth. Do not use much pressure. Steam squares thoroughly. Let dry thoroughly before unpinning squares.

Weave squares tog, 7 squares × 9 squares, being sure to have as much stretch in seams as in the knitting.

BORDER: First Side Border: Cast on 15 sts.

Row 1: K 1, * yo, k 2 tog, repeat from * across.

Rows 2 and 3: Knit.

Row 4: Purl.

Rows 5 and 6: Knit. Repeat rows 1–6 for desired length of side edge of bedspread, end row 2.

Shape Corner: Row 3: K to last 2 sts, k 2 tog.

Row 4: P 2 tog, p across.

Row 5: K to last 2 sts, k 2 tog.

Row 6: K 2 tog, k across.

Row 7: K 1, * yo, k 2 tog, repeat from * across.

Row 8: K 2 tog, k across.

Row 9: K to last 2 sts, k 2 tog.

Row 10: P 2 tog, p across.

Row 11: K to last 2 sts, k 2 tog.

Row 12: K 2 tog, k across.

Row 13: K 1, (yo, k 2 tog) twice, k 1.

Row 14: K 2 tog, k across.

Row 15: K 3, k 2 tog.

Row 16: P 2 tog, p 2.

Row 17: K 1, k 2 tog.

Row 18: K 2 tog. End off.

2nd Side Border: Work as for First Side Border to Shape Corner.

Row 3: K 2 tog, k across.

Row 4: P to last sts, p 2 tog.

Row 5: K 2 tog, k across.

Row 6: K to last 2 sts, k 2 tog.

Row 7: K 1, * yo, k 2 tog, repeat from * across.

Row 8: K to last 2 sts, k 2 tog.

Row 9: K 2 tog, k across.

Row 10: P to last 2 sts, p 2 tog.

Row 11: K 2 tog, k across.

Row 12: K to last 2 sts, k 2 tog.

Row 13: K 1, (yo, k 2 tog) twice, k 1.

Row 14: K 4, k 2 tog.

Row 15: K 2 tog, k 3.

Row 16: P 2, p 2 tog.

Row 17: K 2 tog, k 1.

Row 18: K 2 tog. End off.

Bottom Border: Cast on 1 st.

Row 1: K st.

Row 2: K in front and back of st.

Row 3: Cast on 1 st, p 3 sts.

Row 4: K 2, k in front and back of last st.

Row 5: Cast on 1 st, k 5 sts.

Row 6: K 1, yo, k 2 tog, yo, k 2.

Row 7: Cast on 1 st, k 7 sts.

Row 8: K 6, inc in last st.

Row 9: Cast on 1 st, p 9 sts.

Row 10: K 8, inc in last st.

Row 11: Cast on 1 st, k 11 sts.

Row 12: K 1, (yo, k 2 tog) 5 times.

Row 13: Cast on 1 st, k 12 sts.

Row 14: K 11, inc in last st.

Row 15: Cast on 1 st, p 14 sts.

Row 16: K 13, inc in last st—15 sts.

Row 17: K 15 sts. Beg with row 1 of border pat, work even for desired length of bottom edge of bedspread, end row 2. Shape corner as for corner of side border.

Weave borders in place. Work 2 rows of sc across top of bedspread. For fringe, cut yarn in 6″ lengths. Using 3 strands tog, knot a fringe in every row 1 and row 4 of border.

WATER LILY BEDSPREAD

Shown on page 210

SIZE: 86″ × 102″ (double bed size).

MATERIALS: Bucilla Wondersheen, 68 400-yd. skeins. Steel crochet hook No. 7 (1.5 mm).

GAUGE: Each hexagon motif should measure about 13½″ from point to point.

BEDSPREAD: Bedspread is composed of 53

hexagons and 6 half hexagons, arranged as shown on chart and sewed together.

HEXAGON: Ch 9, join with slip st to form ring.

Rnd 1: 18 sc in ring, join with slip st in first sc.

Rnd 2: Ch 3, 4 dc in same st as joining st, drop loop from hook, insert hook in top st of ch 3 and draw dropped loop through, * ch 2, skip 1 sc, 5 dc in next sc, drop loop from hook, insert hook in top of the first of 5 dc just made and draw dropped loop through (popcorn st); repeat from * around (9 popcorns in round), end with ch 2, 1 slip st in top of ch 3 at beginning of round.

Rnd 3: Ch 5, 1 dc in space after first popcorn, * ch 2, 1 dc in top st of next popcorn, ch 2, 1 dc in next space, repeat from * around, end with ch 2, 1 slip st in 3rd st of ch 5 at beginning of round.

Rnd 4: 3 sc in first space, * 1 sc in top of next dc, 3 sc in next space, repeat from * around, ending with 1 sc in joining st at beginning of round.

Rnd 5: 2 sc in first sc, taking up top thread only of st, * 1 sc in each of the next 3 sts (take up top thread only of all sts, until directed otherwise), 3 sc in next st; repeat from * around, ending with 1 sc in each of the last 3 sts before the 2 sc in first st of round.

Rnd 6: 3 sc in first st, * 1 sc in each of the next 5 sts, 3 sc in next st (center st, or point, of the 3 sc below); repeat from * around, ending with 1 sc in each of the last 5 sts before center st of point at beginning of round. Continue in this way to increase (3 sc in 1 st) at center of each of the 18 points, until there are 12 rounds of sc; there will be 2 sts more between points in each successive round; in 12th sc round there will be 25 sts between center sts in points.

Next Round (16th round from beginning): Slip stitch over the first 8 sts, then fold and join pleats as follows: place next point to last point (right side of work inside fold), work 1 sc in next st on both edges, inserting hook under top thread of both sts, join the next 4 edge sts in same way, * ch 4, fold the next 2 points together, skip 8 sts from point and join the next 5 sts of both edges; repeat from * until all "petals" are joined; end with ch 4 and join with a slip st in the first of the 5 joining sts of first petal.

Rnd 17: 1 slip st in next st, 2 sc in next st (the 3rd of the 5 joining sts), * 1 sc in each of the next 26 sts, 3 sc in next st; repeat from * to end of round; there will be 6 increasing points in round (including the first point, which has only 2 sts) and 26 sts between all increases; the round ends just before the first increase.

Rnd 18: 3 sc in next st, * 1 sc in each of the next 28 sts, 3 sc in next st (center st of next point), repeat from * around. Work 4 more rounds of sc, increasing in center st of all points in every round, and ending last round just before the point st.

Rnd 23: 1 slip st in next (top) st, ch 4, 1 dc in same st as slip st, * ch 1, skip 1 st, 1 dc in next st; repeat from * 7 times; ch 1, skip 2 sts, 1 dc in next st, * ch 1, skip 1 st, 1 dc in next st; repeat from last * 8 times, ending with a dc in point st; ch 1, 1 more dc in point st; work in same way on remaining 5 sides of hexagon (19 spaces between each point-space); end with ch 1, 1 slip st in 3rd st of ch 4 at beginning of round.

Rnd 24: 1 sc in first space (point), ch 4, 1 dc in same space, * ch 1, 1 dc in next space, repeat from * to next point, ending with 1 dc in point space, ch 1, 1 dc in same space; continue in same way to end of round, ch 1, 1 slip st in 3rd st of ch 4 at beginning of round.

Rnd 25: 2 sc in next ch st, * 1 sc in each dc (taking up top thread only) and 1 sc in each chain st to next corner space, 3 sc in ch 1 of corner space; repeat from * on remaining 5 sides of hexagon (43 sc between point sts on each side).

Rnd 26: 3 sc in first st (point), 1 sc in each of the next 3 sts (taking up top thread only, as before), * 1 popcorn in next st, 1 sc in each of the next 5 sts, repeat from * until there are 7 popcorns, 1 sc in each of the next 3 sts to point, 3 sc in point st; continue in same way to end of round.

Rnd 27: * 3 sc in point st, 1 sc in each st to next point; repeat from * around.

Rnd 28: 3 sc in point st, 1 sc in each of the next 2 sts, 1 popcorn in next st, * 1 sc in each of 5 sts, 1 popcorn in next st (center st between popcorns in last popcorn row); repeat from * until there are 8 popcorns, 1 sc in each of the remaining 2 sc to next corner st, 3 sc in corner st; continue in this way on remaining 5 sides of hexagon.

Rnd 29: Same as round 27.

Rnd 30: 1 slip st in corner st, ch 4, 1 dc in same corner st, * ch 1, skip 1 st, 1 dc in next st; repeat from * to next corner, ending with 1 dc in corner st, ch 1, 1 more dc in same corner st; repeat from * on remaining 5 sides, ending with ch 1, 1 slip st in 3rd st of ch 4 at beginning of round.

Rnd 31: Same as round 24.

Rnd 32: Same as round 25 (57 sc between points).

Rnd 33: 3 sc in corner st, 1 sc in each of the next 4 sts, * 1 popcorn in next st, 1 sc in each of the next 5 sts; repeat from * until there are 9 popcorns; 1 sc in each of 4 sts to next corner, 3 sc in corner st; continue in this way on remaining 5 sides of hexagon.

Rnd 34: Same as round 27.

Rnd 35: 3 sc in corner st, 1 sc in each of the next 3 sts, * 1 popcorn in next st, 1 sc in each of the next 5 sts; repeat from * until there are 10 popcorns; 1 sc in each of the 3 sts to next corner, 3 sc in corner st; continue in this way on remaining 5 sides.

Rnd 36: same as round 27.

Rnd 37: 3 sc in corner st, 1 sc in each of the next 2 sts, * 1 popcorn in next st, 1 sc in each of the next 5 sts; repeat from * until there are 11 popcorns; 1 sc in each of remaining 2 sts to corner st, 3 sc in corner st; continue in this way to end of round.

Rnd 38: Same as round 27 (69 sc between points).

Rnd 39: Same as round 30.

Rnd 40: Same as round 31. This completes one hexagon.

Half Hexagons: Ch 7, join with a slip st, 12 sc in ring.

Row 2: Turn, ch 5, 1 popcorn in 3rd sc below, * ch 2, skip 1 sc, 1 popcorn in next sc, repeat from * until there are 5 popcorns, ch 5, 3 more sc in ring, ch 3, join with a slip st to 3rd st of turning chain at end of row.

Row 3: Ch 4, 1 dc in same st as slip st just made, ch 1, 1 dc in space before first popcorn, ch 1, 1 dc in top st of popcorn, ch 1, 1 dc in next space, * ch 1, 1 dc in top of next popcorn, ch 1, 1 dc in same place, ch 1, 1 dc in next space, ch 1, 1 dc in top of next popcorn, ch 1, 1 dc in next space; repeat from * once, then ch 1, 1 dc in 3rd st of ch 5 at end of row below, ch 1, 1 dc in same st.

Row 4: Ch 4, turn, 1 dc in first space, 5 even spaces (an even space = ch 1, 1 dc in next space); ch 1, 1 dc in same space as last dc; 5 even spaces, ch 1, 1 dc in same space as last dc; 5 even spaces, ending with a dc in space under turning chain in row below; ch 1, 1 dc in 3rd st of same turning chain.

Row 5: Ch 1, turn, 1 sc in each of the first 13 sts (take up top thread only of sts below), 3 sc in next st, 1 sc in each of the next 11 sts, 3 sc in next st, 1 sc in each of the next 11 sts, 2 sc on turning ch at end of row below; break off.

Row 6: Beginning at same side as 5th row, make 2 sc in first st (taking up top thread only as in preceding row), 1 sc in each of the 2 sts, * 1 popcorn in next st, 1 sc in each of the next 3 sts, repeat from * once; 1 popcorn in next st, 1 sc in each of 2 sts, 3 sc in next st (the center st of the increase in row below); 1 sc in each of the next 2 sts; 3 popcorns, with 3 sc between each; 1 sc in each of 2 sts after the 3rd popcorn, 3 sc in next st (center st of increase below); 1 sc in each of the next 2 sts; 3 popcorns with 3 sc between each; 1 sc in each of 2 sts after the last popcorn, 2 sc in next st (end st of row).

Row 7: Ch 1, turn, 2 sc in first st, 15 sc on the next 15 sts (taking up the top threads only, so that the lower thread shows on right side), 3 sc in next st (corner st); 15 sc on the next 15 sts, 3 sc in next st (corner st); 15 sc on the next 15 sts, 2 sc in last st.

Row 8: Ch 1, turn, 2 sc in first st, 1 sc in each of the next 2 sts (take up top thread as before); 4 popcorns with 3 sc between each; 1 sc in each of the next 2 sts, 3 sc in next st (corner st); 1 sc in each of the next 2 sts, 4 popcorns, with 3 sc between each, 2 sc after the last popcorn; 3 sc in next corner st, 2 sc in each of the next 2 sts, 4 popcorns, with 3 sc between each; 1 sc in each of 2 sts, 2 sc in last st of row below.

Row 9: Ch 1, turn, 2 sc in first st, 1 sc in each st (upper threads of top sts) to first corner, 3 sc in corner st, 1 sc in each st to next corner, 3 sc in corner st, 1 sc in each st to within 1 st of end of row, 2 sc in end st (there will be 21 sts in each section, besides the increased sts).

Row 10: Ch 4, turn, 1 dc in first st, * ch 1, skip 1 st, 1 dc in next st, taking up *back* thread of st; repeat from * to st just before corner st (12 spaces, including space made by turning chain), ch 1, 1 dc in same corner st, 11 spaces to next corner st, ch 1, 1 more dc in corner st; * ch 1, skip 1 st, 1 dc in next st; repeat from * to last st, ch 1, 1 more dc in last st (11 spaces between each corner space).

Row 11: Ch 4, 1 dc in first space, 12 even spaces to corner space, ch 1, 1 dc in same corner space, 12 even spaces to next corner space, ch 1, 1 dc in same corner space, 12 even spaces, ch 1, 1 more dc in last space (under turning chain).

Row 12: Ch 1, turn, 1 sc in first st, taking up top thread, 1 sc in each st (26) to corner, 3 sc in corner st, 1 sc in each st (25) to next corner, 3 sc in corner st, 1 sc in each of the 25 sts to turning

chain at end of row, 1 sc in first st of chain, 1 sc in next st of chain; break off.

Row 13: Beginning at other end, make 2 sc in first st (taking up top thread), 1 sc in each st to corner, 3 sc in corner st, 1 sc in each st to next corner, 3 sc in corner st, 1 sc in each st to end of row, 1 more sc in last st; break off. Work 4 more rows same as last row; these 6 plain rows form the same pattern as the 6 plain rows after the rosette in the full hexagon.

Row 18: Same as row 10 (with 19 spaces between each corner space).

Row 19: Same as row 11 (20 spaces between corner spaces).

Row 20: Same as row 12; break off. From now on follow the design as given for the last 15 rows of the full hexagon, working back and forth as directed for the same patterns in the first part of half hexagon. Work the last 2 rows also on the 4th side of half hexagon.

Make 6 half hexagons.

Arrange the pieces as indicated on chart, and sew them together from wrong side, using the crochet cotton to sew with and taking up top thread only of edge sts.

FRINGE: Wind thread around a 6-inch cardboard, cut at one end, knot 6 strands in each space on edge, on 3 sides of spread.

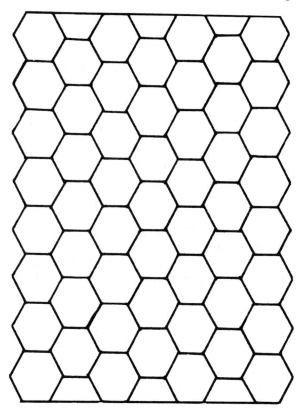

Water Lily Bedspread

BRIDAL ROSE AFGHAN

Shown on page 211

SIZE: 45″ × 60″.

MATERIALS: Dawn Wintuk Sport Yarn, 24 2-oz. skeins White. Aluminum crochet hook size E. Tapestry needle.

GAUGE: One square = $7\frac{1}{2}$″.

SQUARE (make 63): Ch 6, join with a sl st in first ch to form ring. **Rnd 1:** Ch 3 (counts as first dc), 11 dc in ring, join with sl st to top of ch 3.

Rnd 2: Ch 2, hdc in same place as sl st, 2 hdc in each dc around—24 hdc, counting ch 2 as 1 hdc. Join.

Rnd 3: Ch 1, sc in same place as sl st, * ch 5,

sk next 2 hdc, sc in next hdc, repeat from * 6 times, end ch 5, join in first sc—8 lps.

Rnd 4: * In next lp make (sc, hdc, 5 dc, hdc, sc), repeat from * 7 times—8 petals. Join in first sc.

Rnd 5: * Ch 5; holding next petal forward and working behind it, sc around bar of next sc of rnd 3, inserting hook from back to front to back, repeat from * 6 times, ch 5, do not join.

Rnd 6: * In next lp work (sc, hdc, 7 dc, hdc, sc) repeat from * 7 times—8 petals. Sl st in first sc.

Rnd 7: * Ch 7; holding next petal forward and working behind it, sc around bar of next sc of rnd 5, repeat from * 6 times, ch 7, do not join.

Rnd 8: * In next lp work (sc, hdc, 9 dc, hdc, sc), repeat from * 7 times. Sl st in first sc.

Rnd 9: Ch 7, * (dc, ch 4, dc) in 5th dc of next petal for corner, ch 4, dc between petals, ch 4, sc in 5th dc of next petal, ch 4, dc between petals, ch 4, repeat from * 3 times, end last repeat ch 4, sl st in 3rd ch of ch 7.

Rnd 10: Sl st in next ch-4 sp, ch 3, 3 dc in same sp, ch 1; * (2 dc, ch 3, 2 dc) in corner sp, ch 1, 4 dc in next sp, (ch 1, 3 dc in next sp) twice, ch 1, 4 dc in next sp, ch 1, repeat from * 3 times, end last repeat, ch 1, sl st in top of ch 3.

Rnd 11: Sl st in each st across to next corner sp, (ch 3, dc, ch 3, 2 dc) in same sp, * ch 1, sk next 2 dc of corner, dc in each of next 4 dc, ch 1, (dc in each of next 3 dc, ch 1) twice, dc in each of next 4 dc, ch 1, (2 dc, ch 3, 2 dc) in corner sp, repeat from * twice, ch 1, sk next 2 dc of corner, dc in each of next 4 dc, ch 1, (dc in each of next 3 dc, ch 1) twice, dc in top of ch 3, dc over sl sts into each of next 3 dc, ch 1, sl st in top of ch 3.

Rnd 12: Sl st across to corner sp, (ch 3, 2 dc, ch 3, 3 dc) in same sp, * ch 1, sk 2 dc of corner, dc in each of next 4 dc, ch 1, (dc in each of next 3 dc, ch 1) twice, dc in each of next 4 dc, ch 1, (3 dc, ch 3, 3 dc) in corner sp, repeat from * 3 times, end last repeat dc in each of 4 dc, ch 1, sl st in top of ch 3.

Rnd 13: Sl st across to corner sp, (ch 3, 2 dc, ch 3, 3 dc) in same sp, * ch 2, sk 3 dc of corner, dc in each of next 4 dc, ch 1, (dc in each of next 3 dc, ch 1) twice, dc in each of next 4 dc, ch 2, (3 dc, ch 3, 3 dc) in corner sp, repeat from * 3

times, end last repeat dc in each of 4 dc, ch 2, sl st in top of ch 3. End off. Weave in all loose ends.

FINISHING: Thread tapestry needle with yarn. Hold 2 squares with right sides tog; join yarn in upper right-hand corner of one square, sew across, picking up center two strands only (front lps of sts). Carefully match each st and corners. Join rest of squares in same way to make 7 strips of 9 squares each; then join strips across long sides. Lightly steam joinings.

Edging: Rnd 1: From right side, sc in any corner sp, ch 5, sc in same sp, * ch 5, sc in next sp, repeat from * around, being sure to count square corner on each side of every joining as a sp, and working sc, ch 5, sc in each corner of afghan. Sl st in first sc.

Rnd 2: Work petal of (sc, hdc, 5 dc, hdc, sc) in corner sp and in each ch-5 sp around. Sl st in first sc. End off.

COLONIAL BEDSPREAD
Shown on pages 212–213

SIZES: Double bed size, 85″ × 102″. Single bed size, 70″ × 102″. Directions are for double bed size; changes for single bed are in parentheses.

MATERIALS: Bucilla Wondersheen, 47 400-yd. skeins for double bed, 35 skeins for single bed. Steel crochet hook No. 7 (1.5 mm).

GAUGE: Each square should measure $7\frac{1}{2}''$.

SQUARE MOTIF: Ch 8, join with a slip st into a ring.

Rnd 1: Work 16 sc in ring; join with a slip st in first sc of round.

Rnd 2: Ch 3, work 4 dc in joining st of round below, drop loop from hook, insert it in top st of ch 3, insert it also in the dropped loop and draw through (a popcorn at beginning of round), * ch 2, skip next st, 5 dc in next st; drop loop from hook, insert it in top of first dc of the group of 5 dc just made, insert it also in the dropped loop and draw through (popcorn); repeat from * around, end with ch 2, join with a slip st in top of popcorn at beginning of round.

Rnd 3: Ch 5, 1 dc in space after first popcorn,

* ch 2, 1 dc in top of next popcorn, ch 2 and 1 dc in next space; repeat from * around, end with ch 2, join with a slip st in 3rd st of chain 5 at beginning of round.

Rnd 4: Ch 1, work 1 sc in joining st below, * 3 sc in next space, 1 sc in top of next dc; repeat from * around, end with 3 sc in last space, join with a slip st in first sc of round.

Rnd 5: Ch 1, work 2 sc on back thread of joining st in round below, * 1 sc on back thread of each of the next 3 sts, 3 sc on back thread of next st; repeat from * around, end with 1 sc in same place as the first 2 sc of round, join with a slip st in first sc of round. Always work on back thread of all sts unless otherwise mentioned.

Rnd 6: Ch 1, work 2 sc in joining st, * 1 sc in each of the next 5 sts, 3 sc in next st; repeat from * around, end with 1 sc in same place as the first 2 sc of round, join with a slip st in first sc. Continue to work in this way, increasing (3 sc in 1 st) at center of each of the 16 points, until there are 10 rounds completed from beginning, when there will be 15 sts between center sts at points.

Rnd 11: Slip st in each of the next 5 sts, then fold and join pleats as follows: place next point on top of first point (folding right side of work inside), work 1 sc in next st, inserting hook under top thread of both sts, join the next 2 edge sts in same way, * ch 3, fold the next 2 points together as before, skip 5 sts from point and join the next 3 sts of both edges in same way; repeat from * around until all "petals" are joined; end with ch 3 and join with a slip st in the first of the 3 joining sc of first petal.

Rnd 12: Ch 1, work 1 sc on back thread of joining st below, 1 sc on back thread of each st to end of round, join with a slip st in first sc of round.

Rnd 13: Ch 8, work a long treble (3 times over hook) in joining st, taking up both threads of st, ch 1, 1 more long treble in same st, take up both threads of sts in this round, * ch 1, skip 1 st, 1 treble (twice over hook), in next st, ch 1, skip 1 st, 1 dc in next st, ch 1, skip 1 st, work 1 hdc (hdc—half dc—thread over hook, draw up a loop in st, over and through all 3 loops on hook) in next st, ch 1, skip 1 st, 1 sc in each of the next

9 sts, ch 1, skip 1 st, 1 hdc in next st, ch 1, skip 1 st, 1 dc in next st, ch 1, skip 1 st, 1 treble in next st, ch 1, skip 1 st, work a long treble in next st, ch 1, a second long treble in same st, ch 1 and a 3rd long treble in same st, ch 1 and a 4th long treble in same st, ch 1 and a 5th long treble in same st (corner); repeat from * around, end with ch 1 and a long treble in same place as the first group of long trebles at beginning of round, ch 1 and a 2nd long treble in same place, ch 1, join with a slip st in 7th st of chain 8 at beginning of round.

Rnd 14: Ch 1, turn; working on front thread of all stitches in this round, work 2 sc in joining st below, 1 sc in each st to next corner, 3 sc in corner st, 1 sc in each st to next corner, work this corner like last, then continue around, working all corners alike, end with 1 sc in same place the group of 2 sc at beginning of round was worked in, join with a slip st in first sc.

Rnd 15: Ch 6, turn, work 1 treble in joining st below (take up both threads of all stitches in this round), ch 1 and 1 more treble in same st, † * ch 1, skip 1 st, 1 treble in next st; repeat from * 15 times, ch 1, skip next st, work 1 treble in next st (corner), ch 1 and a 2nd treble in same st, ch 1 and a 3rd treble in same st, ch 1 and a 4th treble in same st, ch 1 and a 5th treble in same st; repeat from † around, end with ch 1, a treble in same place as the first group of trebles in round, ch 1 and 1 more treble in same place, ch 1, join with a slip st in 5th st of chain 6 at beginning of round.

Rnd 16: Ch 1, turn, work on front thread of all sts in this round, work 3 sc in joining st, 1 sc in each st to next corner, 4 sc in corner st, 1 sc in each st to next corner, work this corner same as last, then continue in this way around, working all corners alike, end with 1 sc in same place as the first 3 sc of round, join with a slip st in first sc.

Rnd 17: Ch 3, turn, work a popcorn in joining st of round below (as described for popcorn at beginning of round), take up both threads of every st in this round, ch 2, work a regular popcorn in same st, † * ch 2, skip 2 sts, work a popcorn in next st; repeat from * 13 times, ch 2, skip 2 sts, a popcorn in next (corner) st, ch 2 and a 2nd popcorn in same st, ch 2 and a 3rd popcorn in same st; repeat from † around, end with ch 2 and a popcorn in same place as the first 2 popcorns of round; ch 2, join with a slip st in top of first popcorn.

Rnd 18: Ch 1, turn, work 2 sc in top of corner popcorn, 3 sc in each space to next corner, work 3 sc in top of corner popcorn, then 3 sc in each space to next corner, work this corner like last, continue in same way around, working all corners alike, end with 1 sc in same place as the 2 sc at beginning of round, join with a slip st in first sc.

Rnd 19: Ch 6, turn; working on both threads of all sts in this round, work 1 treble in joining st below, ch 1 and another treble in same st, † * ch 1, skip 1 st, 1 treble in next st; repeat from * to next corner, work ch 1 and 1 treble in corner st, ch 1 and a 2nd treble in same st, ch 1 and a 3rd treble in same st, ch 1 and a 4th treble in same st, ch 1 and a 5th treble in same st; then repeat from † around, end with ch 1, work 1 treble in same place as the trebles at beginning of round, ch 1 and 1 more treble in same place, ch 1, join with a slip st in 5th st of chain 6 at beginning of round.

Rnd 20: Ch 1, turn; work all sts of this round on front thread of stitches, work 3 sc in joining st below, * 1 sc in each st to next corner, work 5 sc in corner st; repeat from * around, working all corners alike, end with 2 sc in same place as the 3 sc at beginning of round, join with a slip st in first sc of round.

Rnd 21: Ch 3, turn; taking up both threads of sts in this round, work a popcorn (as at beginning of round) in joining st below, ch 2, a regular popcorn in same place, † * ch 2, skip 2 sts, a popcorn in next st; repeat from * to next corner, work a group of ch 2, 1 popcorn, ch 2, a popcorn, ch 2 and another popcorn,—all in corner st; repeat from † around, end with ch 2, a popcorn in same place as the 2 popcorns at beginning of round, ch 2, join with a slip st in top of first popcorn.

Rnd 22: Ch 1, turn, work 3 sc in joining st below, * 3 sc in each space to next corner, 4 sc in top of corner popcorn; repeat from * around, end with 1 sc in same place as the first 3 sc of round and join with a slip st in first sc.

Rnd 23: Ch 6, turn; working on both threads of all sts in this round, work 1 treble in joining st below, ch 1 and a 2nd treble in same st, † * ch 1, skip 1 st, work a treble in next st; repeat from * 37 times, ch 1 and a 2nd treble in same st, ch 1 and 3rd treble in same st, ch 1 and a 4th treble in same st, ch 1 and a 5th treble in same st then repeat from † around, end with ch 1, 1 treble in same place as the corner group at beginning of round, ch 1 and another treble in same place, ch 1, join with a slip st in 5th st of chain 6 at beginning of round and fasten off thread. This completes one square; make 130 (104) of these squares.

Arrange squares 10 (8) squares in width and 13 squares in length; sew from wrong side with an overhand stitch, taking up top thread of each edge st and being careful to keep seams as elastic as the crocheted fabric.

FRINGE: Wind thread around a 6-inch cardboard and cut at one end; knot a 4-strand fringe in every other space of round on 3 sides of spread (2 long sides and lower edge). Divide fringes in half and tie another knot about 1 inch below first knot, taking 4 strands from first fringe and 4 strands from third fringe. Trim fringe evenly to 5 inches. Darn in all ends neatly.

NAUTICAL STARS AND BARS
Shown on page 214

SIZE: 50" × 56".

MATERIALS: Reynolds Reynelle, 7 4-oz. skeins white, 4 skeins blue, 3 skeins red. Knitting needles No. 7. Steel crochet hook No. 0. Set of bobbins.

GAUGE: 5 sts = 1"; 6 rows = 1".

STRIPS (make 4); With blue, cast on 61 sts. P 1 row. Following chart, beg with row 1 (bottom row has already been worked), work in stockinette st (k 1 row, p 1 row) to top of chart. Use a bobbin for each separate color section. In center section, white can be carried across back of stars.

Repeat from row 1 to top of chart until 6 blocks have been completed.

FINISHING: Weave in ends on wrong side. Sew strips tog.

☐ WHITE
▣ RED
☒ BLUE

ROW 1

Chart for Nautical Star and Bars

Edging: Rnd 1: Join blue in edge of afghan. Sc in 2 sts, * sk 1 st, sc in next 2 sts, repeat from * around, working sc, ch 1, sc in each corner. Join with sl st in first sc.

Rnd 2: Ch 3, dc in st before ch 3, * sk next st, dc in next st, dc in skipped st (cross st made), repeat from * around, working ch 3 between cross sts at corners. Join with sl st in top of ch 3.

Rnd 3: Ch 1, sk first st, sc in next dc, sc in skipped st, * sk next dc, sc in next dc, sc in skipped dc, repeat from * around, working 2 sc, ch 1, 2 sc in each corner sp. Join. End off.

Block afghan using damp cloth and lukewarm iron.

PATCHWORK PILLOWS
Shown on page 233

SIZE: Each, 17″ square.

EQUIPMENT: Pencil. Ruler. Graph paper. Tracing paper. Scissors. Acetate film (or thin, stiff cardboard). Straight pins. Sewing machine. Masking tape.

MATERIALS: For Each Pillow: Off-white, sturdy cotton fabric 45″ wide, $\frac{1}{2}$ yard, for pillow back and cording. Navy cotton fabric 36″ wide, $\frac{1}{8}$ yard for one border. Matching sewing threads. Cording $\frac{1}{4}$″ wide, 2 yards. Fiberfill. Also, closely woven cotton fabrics for patchwork and other border: **Bear Paw:**

Navy with white dots, 36″ wide, $\frac{1}{4}$ yard. Off-white with navy print, 36″ wide, $\frac{1}{8}$ yard. **1000 Pyramids:** Scraps of medium and dark blue prints and off-white prints. Off-white print, 36″ wide, $\frac{1}{8}$ yard. **Dresden Plate:** Scraps of light, medium, and dark blue prints. Off-white print, piece $14\frac{1}{2}$″ square. Light blue print, 36″ wide, $\frac{1}{8}$ yard.

GENERAL DIRECTIONS: For pillow, first assemble a patchwork block, choosing one of the three designs below. **Bear Paw and 1000 Pyramids:** Following individual directions and using ruler and sharp pencil, mark patterns on graph paper; patterns include $\frac{1}{4}$″ seam allowance all around. Make templates from patterns, using acetate film (or thin, stiff cardboard). For patch piece, place each template on designated fabric. Place right angles on straight of goods. For triangles without right angles, place one edge on straight of goods, changing to an alternate edge for alternate colors, so straight edges will be sewn to bias edges. Mark around template with sharp pencil held at an outward angle, so point rests against it. Cut on marked lines.

To piece design by machine, place strip of masking tape on machine plate $\frac{1}{4}$″ from needle line, for seam allowance. To stitch two pieces together, place them with right sides facing, matching edges as directed; place matched edges against tape and stitch. Match a straight edge with a bias edge where possible; if stitching two bias edges together, be careful not to stretch fabric. Press seams under darker piece or as desired and trim off points at corners. When all pieces have been joined, finished block should measure $14\frac{1}{2}$″ square. **Dresden Plate:** Design is appliquéd rather than pieced. See directions below for pattern and sewing.

For all three designs, add borders to complete pillow front, following individual directions for colors: Cut four 1″-wide strips for inner border, two $14\frac{1}{2}$″ long and two $15\frac{1}{2}$″ long. Place a $14\frac{1}{2}$″ strip along one (side) edge of block, right sides facing and raw edges even. Stitch in place with $\frac{1}{4}$″ seam. Sew other $14\frac{1}{2}$″ strip to opposite side, then longer strips to top and bottom, making piece $15\frac{1}{2}$″ square. Cut four $1\frac{3}{4}$″-wide strips for outer border, two $15\frac{1}{2}$″ long and two 18″ long. Sew shorter strips to sides and

longer strips to top and bottom, as before. Pillow front should measure 18″ square.

For pillow back, cut piece 18″ square from solid off-white fabric. From remaining fabric, cut bias strips $1\frac{1}{2}$″ wide, piecing to make strip about 2 yards long. Center cording on wrong side of bias strip; fold strip over cording, aligning edges. Using zipper foot attachment, machine-stitch along strip, close to cording. To attach covered cord to pillow front, begin in middle of one side; pin cord to right side of front, matching raw edges of cord covering and front all around; round corners slightly and overlap ends 1″, cutting off excess. Starting 2″ from beginning of cord, baste all around to 2″ from end of cord, sewing next to seam. Snip out 1″ of cord from overlapping end. Turn under $\frac{1}{2}$″ of extra fabric and, butting ends of cord, fit it over other end. Finish basting seam.

With right sides facing, place front and back together, enclosing cord. Stitch, following line of basting; leave opening in center of one side. Clip corners and turn pillow right side out. Stuff with fiberfill until firm; slip-stitch opening closed.

Bear Paw: Read General Directions. Referring to diagram, mark patterns: A—$2\frac{1}{2}$″ × $2\frac{1}{2}$″. B—right triangle, $2\frac{7}{8}$″ on right-angle sides. C—$4\frac{1}{2}$″ × $4\frac{1}{2}$″. D—$2\frac{1}{2}$″ × $6\frac{1}{2}$″. Make templates and cut patches. From white dotted navy fabric, cut one of A, 16 of B, four of C. From off-white print fabric, cut four of A, 16 of B, four of D. Begin piecing with B triangles: Place a white B with a navy B, matching all edges, and stitch long edges together. Press

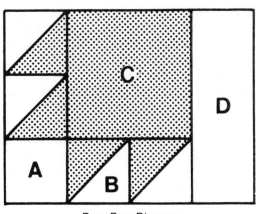

Bear Paw Diagram

and trim, for $2\frac{1}{2}''$ square. Make 15 more B squares. Join four B squares into two strips as shown in diagram, adding a white A square to end of one strip. Join strips to navy C square, then add white D strip, completing one section of block. Make three more sections in same manner. Referring to color illustration on page 233, join sections around the navy A square, for patchwork block. Finish pillow as directed above, cutting inner border from solid navy and outer border from white dotted navy fabrics.

1000 Pyramids: Read General Directions. Mark two triangle patterns: For large triangle, mark $4\frac{5}{16}''$ square; mark midpoint on one side of square; draw a line from midpoint to each of two opposite corners. For small triangle, mark right triangle, $2\frac{7}{16}''$ and $4\frac{13}{16}''$ on right-angle sides. Make templates. From blue print and off-white print fabrics, cut 14 large triangles and four small triangles each. Referring to color illustration, arrange all pieces in four horizontal rows as shown. Begin stitching in top row, at left; place first small and large triangles with right sides facing, matching top angles as shown; stitch, then trim off point of small triangle at bottom. Finish row, then stitch other rows and join. Finish pillow as directed above, cutting inner border from off-white print fabric and outer border from solid navy.

Dresden Plate: Read General Directions. Trace pattern for wedge shape; complete half pattern indicated by dash line. Make template from pattern, using acetate film (or thin, stiff cardboard). For patch pieces, place template on wrong side of fabric with one long edge on straight of goods; mark around with sharp pencil held at an outward angle, so point rests against template. Cut out piece $\frac{1}{4}''$ beyond marked line all around for seam allowance. Cut 18 patches from blue print fabrics. Stitch pieces to off-white square piece; to prepare

background, mark two corner-to-corner diagonal center lines with tailor's chalk; mark two concentric circles—one $3\frac{1}{4}''$ and one $11\frac{1}{2}''$ in diameter. To prepare each patch, press curved edges $\frac{1}{4}''$ to wrong side, clipping if necessary to make piece lie flat. To appliqué first piece, fold one in half lengthwise, matching edges; finger-press fold. Pin piece right side up on muslin, aligning fold line with a diagonal center line of quilting, and inner (small) curve with inner circle. Pin a second piece over first piece, right sides facing and matching all edges. Stitch along right edge, on marked line. Turn top piece over so it lies adjacent to first piece, and press seam, checking to see that inner curve aligns with inner marked circle and "shoulders" of two pieces align with outer circle. Add third piece to second piece in same manner. Continue around in same direction until all pieces are in place and wreath is complete; on final piece, turn under right edge $\frac{1}{4}''$ and slip-stitch in place, covering left edge of first piece. Slip-stitch inner and outer curved edges of wreath. Finish pillow as directed above, cutting inner border from light blue print fabric and outer border from solid navy.

BANDBOXES
Shown on page 234

EQUIPMENT: Paper for patterns. Pencil. Ruler. Tape measure. Compass. Scissors. X-acto knife. Quilting needle. Thimble. Awl (or hammer and nail). Masking tape. Bowl for mixing paste. Bristle or sponge brush, 1″ wide.

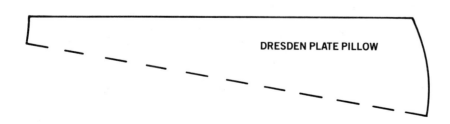

DRESDEN PLATE PILLOW

MATERIALS: Six-ply railroad board, one sheet, 22″ × 28″ (generally used for posters, show cards, tickets and tags), for small boxes. Single-thickness illustration board, two sheets, 30″ × 40″, for larger boxes. (**Note:** Both kinds of board are available at art supply stores.) Wallpaper (samples of leftover pieces for smaller boxes). Newspaper. Wheat paste. Water. Strong thread (linen or buttonhole twist).

GENERAL DIRECTIONS: Each box consists of one bottom, one top, one or two side pieces and one or two rim strips. (The inner measurements of all boxes are given in individual directions.) The patterns given are for the bottoms of some of the boxes. Enlarge them by copying on paper ruled in 1″ squares; complete half- and quarter-patterns indicated by long dash lines. Make patterns for tops $\frac{1}{8}$″ larger all around. See individual directions for sizes of additional pieces.

Cut pieces out of board; cut box sides and rims in direction the board will bend most easily, to avoid cracking.

To Construct and Sew Boxes: To assemble each box, sew the side piece to the bottom and the rim to the top. While sewing, use masking tape to hold pieces in place. Knot thread to start sewing; to end, weave through other stitches. Sew the side piece to the bottom with a whip-stitch, $\frac{1}{8}$″ in from edges, following Diag. 1. End by overlapping ends of side piece, for all but the heart-shaped boxes. Then sew the side seam, following Diag. 2A. Make stitches vertically and horizontally. Then work stitches up diagonally, following Diag. 2B. Sew the rim strip to the top in the same manner. For heart-shaped boxes, do not overlap side seams; to sew, follow Diag. 3 and specific directions. **Note:** For larger boxes, you will have two side pieces and two rim strips. To sew pieces

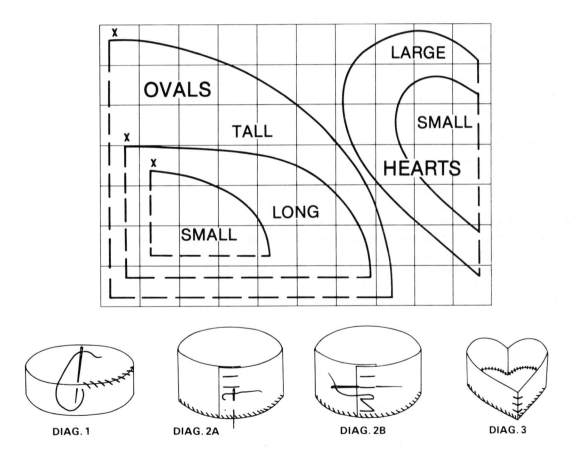

DIAG. 1   DIAG. 2A   DIAG. 2B   DIAG. 3

together, overlap ends $\frac{3}{4}''$; stitch, following Diags. 2A and 2B. For easier sewing, punch holes with awl or hammer and nail into tops and bottoms, $\frac{1}{8}''$ from edges all around.

To Cover with Paper: Use outside measurements for following: For smaller boxes (small heart, small round, and small oval), cut wallpaper for top and bottom pieces $\frac{1}{4}''$ larger all around than box; for side and rim pieces, cut $\frac{1}{4}''$ wider and $\frac{1}{2}''$ longer than box. For larger boxes, cut wallpaper for top and bottom pieces $\frac{1}{2}''$ larger all around than box; for side and rim pieces, cut $\frac{1}{2}''$ wider and 1" longer than box.

Use inside measurements for following: For all boxes, cut top and bottom pieces of wallpaper or newspaper $\frac{1}{4}''$ larger all around than box; cut sides $\frac{1}{4}''$ narrower and $\frac{1}{2}''$ longer than box. For small round and small heart-shaped boxes, cut paper for rims $\frac{3}{16}''$ narrower and $\frac{1}{2}''$ longer than box. For all other boxes, cut rims $\frac{1}{4}''$ narrower and $\frac{1}{2}''$ longer than box.

Add wheat paste to about $\frac{1}{4}$ cup of water to get the consistency of pablum. Apply paste to each area only as you come to it, brushing a thin layer of paste on area of box and to back of wallpaper piece. Smoothly press paper to box. Start by placing box with bottom up; center paper onto box bottom; clip around edges of excess paper every $\frac{1}{2}''$. Apply paste to sides near edge; fold and press excess paper to sides. Turn box right side up. Paste side strip around box, overlapping seam. Clip excess at top; fold down to inside of box and paste.

Clip inside bottom piece $\frac{1}{4}''$ all around edge; paste into box bottom; cover sides. Repeat same procedure for box top and rim. Weight top and bottom separately, while drying. Allow to dry for two or three days.

(**Note:** The following measurements are for inside of box.)

SMALL ROUND BOX (2$\frac{1}{2}''$ diameter, 2" deep): Cut the following pieces from railroad board: One 2$\frac{3}{4}''$-diameter circle for bottom; one 2$\frac{7}{8}''$ circle for top; one 2" × 9" strip for sides and one $\frac{1}{2}''$ × 9$\frac{3}{4}''$ strip for rim. Sew and cover with paper, following General Directions.

SMALL OVAL BOX (4" × 6" × 3" deep): Cut the following pieces from railroad board: One bottom and one top, using patterns; one 3" × 17$\frac{1}{4}''$ strip for sides and one $\frac{3}{4}''$ × 18" strip for rim. Sew bottom of box to side, starting at point X indicated on pattern, so that the seam will be at a long side of the finished box. Sew and cover with paper, following General Directions.

SMALL HEART (4$\frac{1}{4}''$ × 3$\frac{3}{4}''$ × 2$\frac{5}{8}''$ deep): Cut the following pieces from railroad board: One bottom and one top, using patterns; one 2$\frac{5}{8}''$ × 13$\frac{1}{2}''$ strip for sides and one $\frac{1}{2}''$ × 14$\frac{1}{4}''$ strip for rim. Sew bottom to sides, starting at point of heart; crease side strip at indentation and continue sewing around back to point. Trim if necessary for a flush joint. Sew seam as shown in Diag. 3. Sew top to rim in same manner. Cover with paper, following General Directions.

LARGE HEART (5$\frac{7}{8}''$ × 6$\frac{3}{4}''$ × 4" deep): Cut the following pieces from railroad board: One bottom and one top, using patterns; one 4" × 21$\frac{1}{2}''$ strip for sides and one 1" × 22$\frac{1}{2}''$ strip for rim. Sew as for Small Heart. Cover with paper, following General Directions.

LONG OVAL (6$\frac{1}{4}''$ × 12" × 3" deep): Cut the following pieces from illustration board: One bottom and one top, using patterns; two 3" × 16$\frac{3}{4}''$ strips for sides; two 1" × 17$\frac{1}{4}''$ strips for rim. Join side strips for one piece, as directed. Sew bottom to side piece, matching stitched seam to point X indicated on pattern; sew in one direction around to same point on opposite side; from starting point, sew around in other direction to opposite side again. Close open side, using zigzag stitch. Sew rim to top in same manner. Cover with paper, following General Directions.

TALL OVAL HAT BOX (12$\frac{1}{2}''$ × 14$\frac{1}{4}''$ × 12$\frac{1}{2}''$ deep): Cut the following pieces from illustration board: One bottom and one top, using patterns; two 12$\frac{1}{2}''$ × 22$\frac{1}{4}''$ strips for sides; two 1$\frac{1}{2}''$ × 22$\frac{3}{4}''$ strips for rim. Construct as for Long Oval. Cover with paper, following General Directions.

ROUND HAT BOX (13" diameter, 6" deep): Cut the following pieces from illustration board: One 13"-diameter circle for bottom; one 13$\frac{1}{4}''$ circle for top; two 6" × 21$\frac{1}{4}''$ strips for sides, two 1$\frac{1}{2}''$ × 22$\frac{1}{4}''$ strips for rim. Sew as for other large boxes. Cover with paper, following General Directions.

CLOCK, CHEST, BOWL AND SPOON HOLDER WITH ROSEMALING

Shown on page 235

NOTE: Rosemaling is the Norwegian decorative folk art of painting on wood. The designs of flowers, leaves, and scrolls are created by combinations of brushstrokes. Each region of the country developed its individual style with its particular flower and scroll forms and color schemes. These designs—the Telemark bowl, Sognefjord spoon holder, Hallingdal chest, and Rogaland clock—represent four styles of rosemaling.

EQUIPMENT: Newspapers. Scraps of wood for practice. Several sheets of fine sandpaper. Tack cloth (soft, lint-free cloth). Brush 1″ wide for applying enamel backgrounds. Turpentine. Tracing paper. Ruler. Graphite and white Saral paper for transferring designs. Masking tape (optional). Sharp-pointed #2 pencil. Palette (use paper palette or large flat pan or dish) and palette cup. Palette knife. Fine quality red sable brushes: flat, round tapered and pointed, and round long and pointed (see individual directions). Small glass jar. Paper towels. Vaseline. Toothpick and small amount of absorbent cotton. Plastic wrap (optional).

MATERIALS: Enamel undercoat. Semi-gloss enamel and small tubes of oil colors (see individual directions). Boiled linseed oil. Additional materials in individual directions. **NOTE:** Wooden items and materials may be ordered from Sadeen's Scandinavian Gift and Card Shop, 1315 White Bear Avenue, St. Paul, Minn. 55106.

GENERAL DIRECTIONS: To Prepare Wood for Rosemaling: On new, unfinished wood pieces, sand wooden surface smooth; wipe dust off with tack cloth. With 1″ brush, apply enamel primer as smoothly as possible. Let dry for 24 hours. Sand again and wipe with cloth. Apply a coat of enamel with even brushstrokes, working with the grain of wood; let dry for 24 hours. Sand and wipe again. Apply a second coat of enamel and let dry for 24 hours. Do not sand after this coat.

To Transfer Design for Rosemaling: Use sharp-pointed #2 pencil. Patterns provided for chest are full-size; patterns for other projects are reduced as follows: bowl, 70% of original; spoon holder and clock, 65% of original. To enlarge patterns, trace and use a ruler to draw horizontal and vertical lines at $\frac{1}{4}$″ intervals to form a grid. Reproduce by copying onto paper ruled in 1″ squares. Center tracing over enamel-painted wooden surface. Place graphite (on light surfaces) or Saral (for dark surfaces) paper between tracing and wood. Tape to wood if necessary. Trace over design lines to transfer design to wood; use pencil and medium-to-light pressure, being careful to avoid making impressions in the wood. Your surface is now ready for rosemaling.

We recommend that you read the following General Directions through first and practice painting the brushstrokes with the different brushes on scraps of wood before attempting these projects. After rosemaling, let work dry for at least three weeks. To remove any residue from graphite or Saral tracings not covered by paint, place bit of absorbent cotton on toothpick, dip in turpentine and squeeze to remove excess. Dab away the residue being careful not to remove any paint.

To Prepare Paint: Always have a small jar about 2″ full of turpentine handy for rinsing brushes and paper towels for blotting. Also keep palette cup about two tablespoons full of boiled linseed oil, which is used as extender for the oil colors.

Squeeze $\frac{1}{4}$″ to $\frac{1}{2}$″ of oil paint from tubes onto palette. Use palette knife to mix colors. Dip palette knife into linseed oil and mix several drops of linseed oil into the oil color. Press the knife back and forth across the paint to force oil into the paint until you get a thick, creamy consistency (like honey). Add some linseed oil each time you mix in another color. Try to mix enough of one color to complete the project, since matching may be difficult. If you intend to leave mixed paint on palette for a day or two, cover with plastic wrap to keep it from drying. If skin forms over the paint, peel it back with palette knife so you can use the fresh paint underneath.

Care and Use of Brushes: Always use good quality red sable brushes; brushes must be flexible and have spring, therefore camel's hair or bristle brushes will not do for rosemaling.

For best results, make absolutely sure your brushes are thoroughly clean. Rinse brushes in the jar of turpentine immediately after painting, before changing colors, and when work is finished, so that a residue will not form under the ferrule. Do not press or pound the brush down on the bottom of the jar; instead, shake brush from side to side in jar, then blot brush with paper towel. When blotting, hold handle horizontally and draw brushes along the towel with handle end first. If brush stains towel, repeat cleansing process. After brushes have been thoroughly cleaned, lubricate them by applying vaseline to hairs with fingertips and bring them back to natural point or tip. Stand brushes in a jar until ready to use again, then remove vaseline by dipping brush in turpentine and wiping until vaseline is off.

Painting Technique: Sit in a relaxed position with wooden object on table or on knees propped up against the table.

Grasp brush like a pencil, but do not push it like a pencil. Always turn work so that you can pull the brush toward you when painting. For shorter strokes hold brush with the fingers close to the hairs. For longer strokes, hold brush with fingers farther from hairs. Practice holding the brush as far back as possible for long smooth strokes. Use your other arm and hand to support the painting hand or arm. Keep the brush handle pointing back toward your shoulder or up toward the ceiling; do not slant to either side or you will lose control.

Apply paint to brush by pulling brush through the prepared oil color (do not poke at it) several times until paint works its way to the ferrule. Paint must extend up the ferrule, especially on pointed brushes. Shape brush point by pressing gently on palette surface.

Move brush at a moderate even pace. If you move brush too slowly, you will get a stiff or shaky line. If you move brush too fast, you may get a sloppy line. You can control the width of the brushstroke by varying the pressure and the angle of the brush. With round brushes, press and lift; with flat brushes, turn to the flat or side edge of hairs.

STROKES: Paint all strokes continuously from beginning to end or as far as possible. If you run out of paint before finishing the stroke, just stop, refill brush and begin again over the previous painting of incomplete stroke.

"Tear Drop" Stroke: Use the round tapered and pointed brush; liquify paint and fill brush as directed above. This stroke is made by pressing the brush down to its full width, and then gradually lifting it as you pull it towards you so that by the time you have moved $\frac{1}{2}''$, you have reached the very tip of the brush hairs (Fig 1A). Try the same stroke in several sizes, varying it with more or less pressure on the brush at the start, and by moving a longer or shorter distance as you lift. Then try the same stroke with a slight sideways lift so that it becomes a comma shape (Fig. 1B). Now try all of these in reverse, beginning the stroke at the very tip of the hairs of the brush, and then pressing gradually to the full width of the stroke before lifting. The width of the stroke is determined by pressing and lifting.

Scroll Strokes: Use the flat brush for large scrolls; round brush may be used for smaller scrolls. For these strokes, prepare the paint and load the flat brush as follows: Do not mix the linseed oil into the paint, but pick up a tiny bit with the tips of the hairs, then draw it lightly through the oil color, filling only about $\frac{2}{3}$ the length of the hairs of the brush. Practice a scroll by painting the widest part of the scroll with brush held flat, utilizing the fullest width of brush, then gradually turn brush handle so that you will be painting with the edge when you reach the narrow part of the scroll. Practice large comma-shaped scrolls, C-shaped, and S-shaped scrolls (Fig. 2). The width of the stroke is determined by turning to the flat side or the edge of the brush. For curled ends on scrolls, twirl the handle of the brush before lifting it off (Fig. 3). When painting scrolls, begin with the larger ones and flat brush, then paint the smaller ones with round tapered brush. Paint the scrolls that cross the main scroll as close to the main scroll as possible; stop when they intersect, then continue on the other side (Fig. 4). Figures 4A and 4B show direction of strokes when filling out scrolls.

Full Circle Stroke: Using the whole width of the flat brush, press brush straight down on wood. Roll the brush around between thumb and first

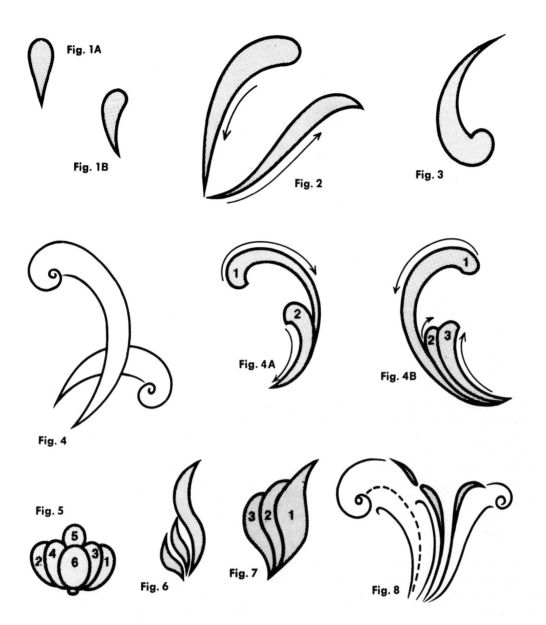

Fig. 1A

Fig. 1B

Fig. 2

Fig. 3

Fig. 4

Fig. 4A

Fig. 4B

Fig. 5

Fig. 6

Fig. 7

Fig. 8

two fingers, keeping full pressure on for entire stroke. To complete, bring brush toward center of circle and pick brush up. For half-circle, paint in same manner with less pressure at the beginning and end of stroke.

For flowers, always start on the outside and work toward the inside with flat or round brushes, using as few strokes as possible (Fig. 5). Numbers indicate order of strokes to avoid smudging. For a complete circle found in the middle or at the base of flowers, use flat brush and twist the brush until the circle is complete; lift up brush.

For leaves, use round brush and mostly a single stroke (Fig. 6). Paint larger leaves with three or more strokes as shown in Fig. 7, or with a stroke on either side, then fill in center. Leaves are done solely with brush pressure; do not twist brush. Try to let the brushstrokes follow the natural growth of the leaves, petals, etc.

Outlining: Use round long pointed brush and

use very much the same method of liquifying the paint and filling the brush as indicated above, but be sure that the paint is fluid enough so that it will run down the length of the hairs to the tip, as you can use it up in the painting of the long lines. Start with the tip and slowly increase pressure on the hairs; lighten pressure for a fine end (see Fig. 8), or keep pressure even for a line of one thickness. When holding the outline brush, try resting your painting hand on your other wrist as it rests on the table. This will brace the hand and keep it from pressing too hard, which results in too thick lines. Practice long lines, straight lines, curved lines with this brush, always keeping lines neat and fine and as long as possible. Paint slowly enough so that the paint can flow down through the hairs.

BOWL: Sandeen's unfinished wooden bowl, C-D beaded shape, 8″ diameter. Enamel paint: rust red and medium soft blue. Oil colors: cadmium red light, yellow ochre, burnt sienna, ultramarine blue, ivory, black, titanium white, raw umber. Red sable brushes: one flat, size 4; one round tapered, size 1; one round long for outlining, size 1.

Prepare wooden surface of bowl following General Directions. Paint entire bowl with enamel un-

BOWL

BOWL RIM

dercoat. Then paint two coats of blue enamel on the inside and top half of outside of bowl; paint two coats of red enamel on bottom and lower part of outside. When dry, transfer pattern to inside of bowl and repeat border design all around outside top of bowl.

Mix necessary oil colors as indicated by letters in each part of pattern; follow key for colors.

Use the flat brush for scrolls and flowers as indicated above. Paint large scroll first, then add the interlacing scrolls. Outline scrolls with white while still wet. Paint full circles for flower centers, half circles for inner petals. Paint leaves and details with round brush using very fluid paint mixture. Make stems and remaining lines with almost dripping brush. Work border continuously all around outside top of bowl.

SPOON HOLDER: Sandeen's unfinished wooden hanging container SCSP c/p 8, 13″ × 4″ × 1½″. Enamel: cream color. Oil colors: yellow ochre, titanium white, cadmium red medium, alizarin crimson, Prussian blue. Red sable brushes: one pointed quill, size 4 and one round pointed outline, size 1.

Prepare wooden surface of container according

Color Key

A. cadmium red light with a little yellow ochre and burnt sienna mixed in to soften and dull.
B. ultramarine blue with small amounts of black and raw umber
C. ultramarine blue with small amount of black, raw umber and white
D. yellow ochre with a little raw sienna
E. white with a bit of raw umber
F. raw umber and black
G. yellow ochre and white
H. cadmium red light with a little yellow ochre
I. prussian blue with a little yellow ochre and white
J. yellow ochre with a little prussian blue
K. chrome green with yellow ochre and raw umber
L. burnt umber and raw umber
M. prussian blue with burnt umber
N. white with yellow ochre and a touch of burnt umber
O. burnt umber
P. lighter shades of blue, add M with a little of N.
Q. alizarin crimson
R. outline or dot with white

SIDE

SPOON HOLDER

to General Directions. Paint with enamel undercoat. Then paint two coats of cream color over entire piece.

Transfer patterns to front, sides and top.

Mix necessary oil colors as indicated by letters on the patterns; follow the key for colors. Use the flat size 4 brush for the wide flower petals; fill brush with very fluid paint mixture. To form blue and white petals, fill the brush with white first. Then dip the brush tip into the blue mixture. Start at stem end of the petal and press to full width of petal; when you reach the end of petal, lift brush carefully, so white forms flip on end of petal. Repeat in same manner for red and white petals.

Very lightly outline fine stems and leaves with outline brush dipped in fluid mixture.

CHEST: Sandeen's unfinished hinged lid, round-topped wooden chest Hus-SS-C8, 8″ × 4¾″ × 4½″. Enamel: rust red and charcoal gray. Oil colors: yellow ochre, titanium white, chrome green, burnt umber, raw umber. Brushes: one round pointed tapered, size 3 and one round pointed outlining, size 1.

Unscrew hinges and set hardware aside. Paint entire chest with enamel undercoat. Paint chest with two coats of rust red. Paint two coats of charcoal gray on chest bottom and around bottom lip. With pencil, draw a straight line ¼″ from each corner on all sides; use illustration as a guide. Paint corners charcoal gray to pencil lines. Paint trim on chest lid in same fashion.

Transfer patterns centered on chest top, front, back and sides.

Mix necessary oil colors as indicated by letters on patterns; follow the key for colors. Use the size 3 brush for the large flower on chest front. Paint blue first. While blue is still wet, fill brush with white and a touch of raw umber. Make the white stroke from top of petal and brush toward the center of the flower over the wet blue paint, lifting gradually to a point.

For flower on lid top, paint the flower center with blue mixture. Then, with white, begin strokes with the pointed brush tip at the inner edge of the petal and pull and press it gradually to the wider outer edge of the petals. Blot the blue paint off the brush after each stroke and add more white.

To make leaves, draw brush with green paint from the stem end to the tip, then make two side strokes of leaves. Paint white details on top of leaves with outline brush while green is still wet.

Use the tip of the size 3 brush to make the petals of the small white flowers.

With the round pointed outline brush, make stems and white border accent.

When chest is thoroughly dry, replace hinges.

Color Key

A. cadmium red light with a little yellow ochre and burnt sienna mixed in to soften and dull.
B. ultramarine blue with small amounts of black and raw umber
C. ultramarine blue with small amount of black, raw umber and white
D. yellow ochre with a little raw sienna
E. white with a bit of raw umber
F. raw umber and black
G. yellow ochre and white
H. cadmium red light with a little yellow ochre
I. prussian blue with a little yellow ochre and white
J. yellow ochre with a little prussian blue
K. chrome green with yellow ochre and raw umber
L. burnt umber and raw umber
M. prussian blue with burnt umber
N. white with yellow ochre and a touch of burnt umber
O. burnt umber
P. lighter shades of blue, add M with a little of N.
Q. alizarin crimson
R. outline or dot with white

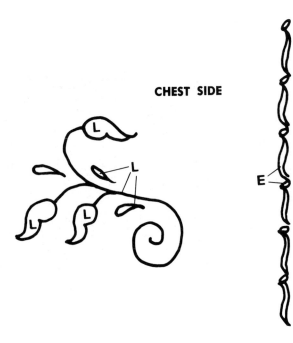

CHEST SIDE

CHEST TOP

CHEST
FRONT

CLOCK

Color Key

A. cadmium red light with a little yellow ochre and burnt sienna mixed in to soften and dull.
B. ultramarine blue with small amounts of black and raw umber
C. ultramarine blue with small amount of black, raw umber and white
D. yellow ochre with a little raw sienna
E. white with a bit of raw umber
F. raw umber and black
G. yellow ochre and white
H. cadmium red light with a little yellow ochre

I. prussian blue with a little yellow ochre and white
J. yellow ochre with a little prussian blue
K. chrome green with yellow ochre and raw umber
L. burnt umber and raw umber
M. prussian blue with burnt umber
N. white with yellow ochre and a touch of burnt umber
O. burnt umber
P. lighter shades of blue, add M with a little of N.
Q. alizarin crimson
R. outline or dot with white

280

CLOCK: Sandeen's Octagonal Clock Board DG-420, $11\frac{1}{2}''$ × $11\frac{1}{2}''$. Battery clockworks including hands. Enamel: rust red and gray blue. Oil colors: titanium white, yellow ochre, burnt umber, Prussian blue, cadmium red light, burn sienna. Brushes: one flat, size 4, one round pointed, size 1, and one round pointed outlining, size 1.

Prepare wooden surface of clock according to General Directions. Paint with enamel undercoat. Paint two coats of rust red on the sides and blue on face and back.

Transfer patterns onto face of clock.

Mix necessary oil colors as indicated by letters on patterns; follow the key for colors. To paint the shading on the scroll motifs, begin with white mixture on flat brush and make a stroke on the inside of the scroll. Then, keeping the light color on brush, add a touch of the blue mixture and paint a stroke slightly overlapping the first. If desired, dip edge of brush in blue and make another stroke.

Use a flat brush dipped in red for tulips. Start at flower center and gently curve the stroke from hub to the end of the petal. With size 1 round brush dipped in very fluid white, make strokes along tips of petals toward center of flower; lift brush about half way when white begins to blend with red. With size 1 round brush dipped in burnt umber, paint shadows. The blue tulips are done in same manner.

With outlining brush dipped in very fluid burnt umber, make fine dark outlines. Assemble clock after paint is dry, according to instructions accompanying clockworks.

EMBROIDERED CHEST
Shown on pages 236 and 237

SIZE: Covered, 8″ deep × 16″ long × $6\frac{1}{2}''$ high.
EQUIPMENT: For Chest Construction: Saber saw. Carpenter's compass. T- or carpenter's square. Pencil. Hammer. Medium to fine sandpaper. Bar or pipe clamps.

For Embroidery: Dressmaker's tracing (carbon) paper. Dry ball-point pen. Scissors. Masking tape. Embroidery hoop. Crewel embroidery needles. Sewing machine. Staple gun and staples.

For Blocking: Softwood surface. Brown wrapping paper. Rustproof tacks.

MATERIALS: For Chest: Clear pine, $6\frac{1}{2}'$ of $\frac{1}{2}''$ × 6″. One piece 18″-square, $\frac{1}{8}''$-thick untempered hardboard. Wire nails, $\frac{3}{4}''$. Finishing nails, $1\frac{1}{2}''$. White glue. One pair $\frac{1}{2}''$ × 1″ brass-plated butt hinges or leather scraps for hinge strips. Antique lock for front closing (optional).

For Embroidered Cover: Natural white medium-weight wool fabric 54″ or 60″ wide, $1\frac{1}{2}$ yards. Appleton Crewel Wool, 30-yard skeins (2-ply, single strand), see Color Key for colors and number of skeins (see Note below). Lightweight cardboard. Small amount of Polyester batting (optional). Olive green velveteen 44″-45″ wide, $\frac{2}{3}$ yards for lining. Matching velvet ribbon $\frac{1}{2}''$ wide, 4 yards. Olive green felt 7″ × 15″.

Note: Appleton Crewel Wool can be mail ordered from American Crewel and Canvas Studio, P.O. Box 298, Boonton, New Jersey 07005.

Continued on page 284

STITCH KEY

A Long and Short Stitch
B Outline Stitch
C Herringbone Stitch
D Buttonhole Stitch
E Seed Stitch
F Bullion Stitch
G Satin Stitch
H Stem with Couching
J Straight Stitch

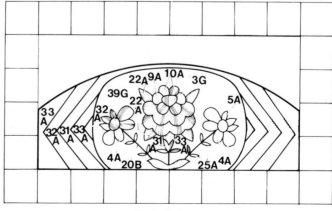

End of chest

Chest Top and Assembly

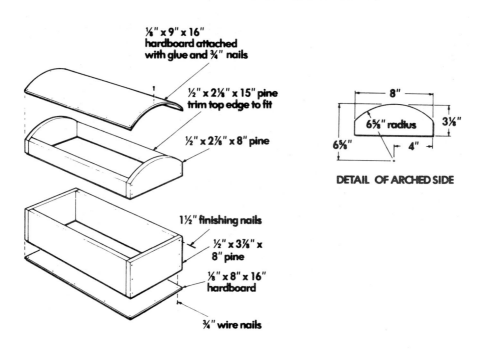

⅛" x 9" x 16"
hardboard attached
with glue and ¾" nails

½" x 2⅛" x 15" pine
trim top edge to fit

½" x 2⅞" x 8" pine

1½" finishing nails

½" x 3⅞" x
8" pine

⅛" x 8" x 16"
hardboard

¾" wire nails

DETAIL OF ARCHED SIDE

8"

6⅝" radius

3⅛"

6⅝"

4"

COLOR KEY

1	HERALDIC GOLD	#840-4	(1)
2	HERALDIC GOLD	#840-1	(1)
3	BRIGHT YELLOW	#550-7	(1)
4	BRIGHT YELLOW	#550-5	(1)
5	BRIGHT YELLOW	#550-4	(1)
6	ORANGE RED	#440-8	(2)
7	ORANGE RED	#440-7	(2)
8	ORANGE RED	#440-6	(2)
9	ORANGE RED	#440-5	(2)
10	ORANGE RED	#440-4	(1)
11	ORANGE RED	#440-3	(1)
12	ORANGE RED	#440-1	(1)
13	SCARLET	#500-4	(1)
14	SCARLET	#500-3	(1)
15	SCARLET	#500-2	(1)
16	SCARLET	#500-1	(1)
17	SCARLET	#500-1a	(1)
18	WINE RED	#710-6	(1)
19	WINE RED	#710-4	(1)
20	EARLY ENGLISH GREEN	#540-8	(3)
21	EARLY ENGLISH GREEN	#540-7	(3)
22	EARLY ENGLISH GREEN	#540-6	(3)
23	EARLY ENGLISH GREEN	#540-5	(3)
24	EARLY ENGLISH GREEN	#540-4	(3)
25	EARLY ENGLISH GREEN	#540-3	(3)
26	EARLY ENGLISH GREEN	#540-1	(3)
27	OLIVE GREEN	#240-5	(2)
28	OLIVE GREEN	#240-2	(2)
29	OLIVE GREEN	#240-1	(2)
30	GREY GREEN	#350-3	(2)
31	DULL CHINA BLUE	#920-9	(2)
32	DULL CHINA BLUE	#920-6	(2)
33	DULL CHINA BLUE	#920-5	(2)
34	CHOCOLATE	#180-7	(1)
35	CHOCOLATE	#180-6	(1)
36	CHOCOLATE	#180-4	(1)
37	CHOCOLATE	#180-3	(1)
38	CHOCOLATE	#180-2	(1)
39	WHITE	#991	(1)
40	TURQUOISE	#520-8	(1)
41	TURQUOISE	#520-7	(1)
42	TURQUOISE	#520-6	(1)
43	TURQUOISE	#520-5	(1)
44	TURQUOISE	#520-3	(1)
45	MID BLUE	#150-3	(1)

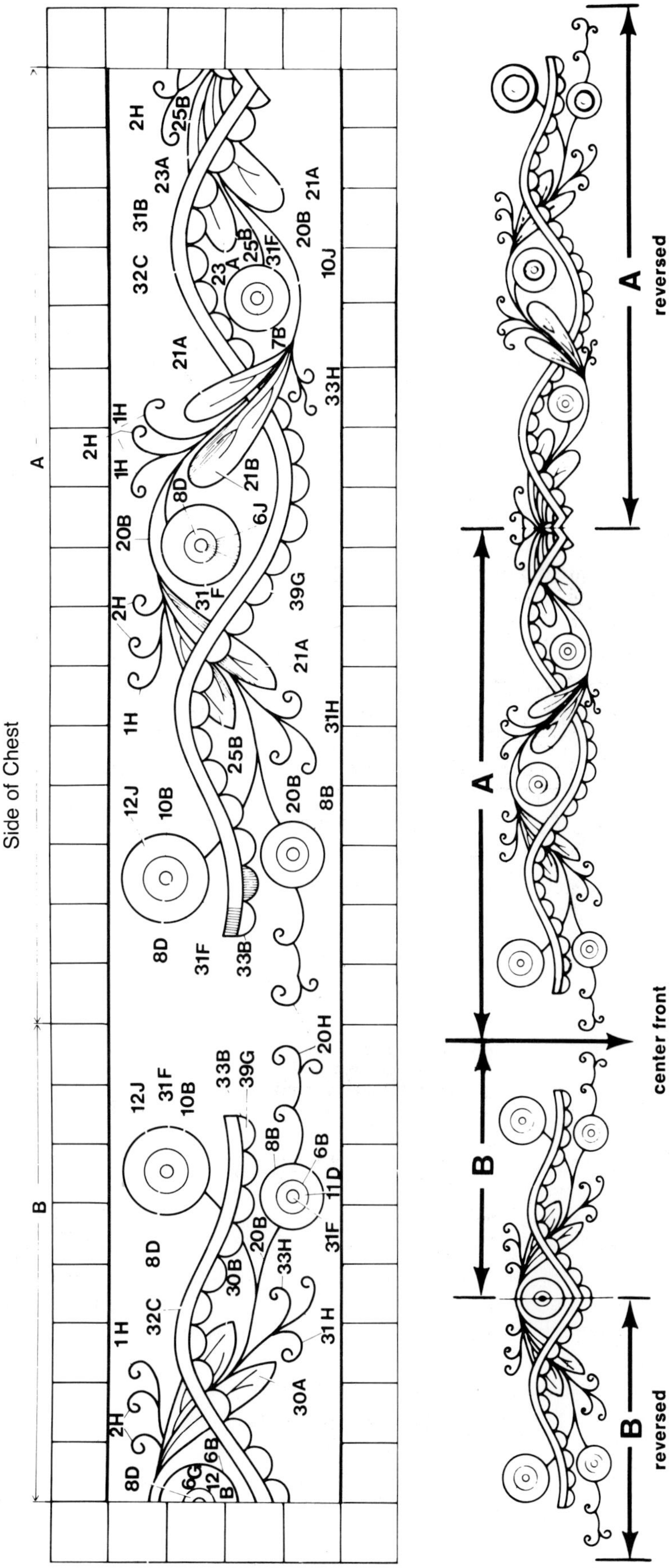

Side of Chest

center front

283

Continued from page 281

DIRECTIONS: To Construct Chest: Following assembly diagram, mark and cut $\frac{1}{2}'' \times 6''$ pine into two $2\frac{1}{8}'' \times 15''$ pieces for long-lid sides and two each $3\frac{7}{8}'' \times 8''$ and $3\frac{7}{8}'' \times 15''$ for chest sides. From remaining pine, refer to detail for lid side to draw arched top edge. Cut out arched lid sides. From $\frac{1}{8}''$ hardboard, cut one $9'' \times 16''$ piece for arched lid and one $8'' \times 16''$ piece for bottom. Assemble pine sides of lid with glue and $1\frac{1}{2}''$ nails. To facilitate bending lid, soak clean cloths in very hot water and wring out. In tub, wrap lid in hot cloths and allow to "steam" for few minutes. Remove cloths and, beginning on one end, bend lid to fit arched sides. Glue and nail as shown. Clamp lid. Trim excess lid edges flush. Sand chest smooth, inside and out; dust.

To Embroider Cover: Using a sharp colored pencil, draw connecting grid lines across each pattern. Enlarge patterns by copying each motif on paper ruled in 1" squares. For side strip, complete pattern as shown in Fig. 1, reversing section A on the right and reversing section B on the left.

From wool fabric, cut the following pieces: One $16'' \times 20''$ for top, two $8'' \times 12''$ for arched lid sides and one $8'' \times 52''$ for continuous strip for box sides. Fold over and whipstitch raw edges or use masking tape to prevent raveling. Transfer embroidery patterns to corresponding fabric piece by positioning pattern on right side of fabric with dressmaker's carbon between. Using dry ball-point pen, transfer all pattern lines. Lift pattern, remove carbon, and go over any design lines that are too faint.

Referring to Stitch Details on page 308, practice stitches on fabric scraps before beginning embroidery. Do not secure yarn on back with knots. Begin by leaving a yarn end on back and working over it to secure it; to end yarn length, weave yarn end under stitches on back. Following Color Key, Stitch Key and patterns, work all embroidery as indicated, repositioning hoop as necessary. Cut yarn into 18" lengths and work with single 2-ply strand in needle throughout.

When embroidery is complete, block following Blocking directions on page 308.

To Upholster Chest: If desired for further padding, cut a piece of batting to same size as curved box lid. Hold batting in place with a few dabs of glue. Center and drape top piece over lid. Carefully pin on lid side piece with excess fabric for seam allowance to outside. Repeat to pin second side piece in place. Remove cover for top, reverse and repin seams on inside, right sides facing. Test-fit cover, checking that design lines match; adjust, if necessary. Stitch side seams and cut away excess fabric, leaving $\frac{1}{4}''$ seam allowance and clipping into curves to ease fit. Reposition cover on lid and turn lid upside down. Wrap and staple raw edge of cover to inside of lid, neatly folding in excess fabric at corners.

To cover chest sides, pin long embroidered piece around box sides, making seam at left back corner edge. Reverse seam to inside; stitch and trim away excess fabric leaving $\frac{1}{4}''$ seam. Slip cover over side and begin wrapping raw edges around inside edge and around bottom. Notch corners to facilitate folding at bottom edge. Staple raw edges to chest.

To line chest, carefully measure each inside wall in chest and lid. Mark and cut a piece of cardboard for each wall $\frac{1}{4}''$ smaller all around than determined dimensions. Test-fit each wall, adjusting if necessary. With walls in place, measure inside of curved lid and floor of chest. Cut cardboard pieces for these dimensions, less $\frac{1}{4}''$ all around. Cut velveteen to wrap each cardboard, allowing $\frac{1}{2}''$ all around to wrap edges. To cover cardboard, center corresponding cardboard piece on wrong side of velveteen. Wrap excess fabric around edges; glue. Repeat to cover all cardboard pieces. Brush glue on one inside wall of chest and press corresponding velveteen-covered cardboard piece in place. Continue around walls in chest and lid. Finally glue curved lid and floor in place. Finish top edges around inside with matching velvet ribbon, glued in place. Finish chest bottom with felt. Cut felt $\frac{1}{2}''$ smaller all around than bottom; glue bottom piece in place.

Following manufacturer's directions, install hinges along back edge. If desired, cut two $\frac{1}{2}'' \times 3''$ leather strips for hinges and nail at back edges with enough slack to allow chest to open. Install lock on front, if desired.

PINE BOUGH PLAQUE

Shown on page 238

SIZE: About 12″ × 25″.

EQUIPMENT: Colored pencil. Ruler. Paper for patterns. Carbon paper. Dry ball-point pen. Sharpened pencil. Jig or coping saw. Drill with $\frac{1}{2}$″ bit. Sandpaper. Tack cloth. Paintbrush for varnish. Wire cutters. Staple gun and staples. Hammer. Scissors.

MATERIALS: Clear pine $\frac{3}{4}$″ thick, 12″ × 25″. One large and two medium-size plastic foam eggs. Round toothpicks. Three large T-pins. Three nails. Floral wire, #18 gauge. Fresh live pine boughs. Red velvet ribbon 1$\frac{1}{2}$″ wide, 1$\frac{1}{4}$ yards. Clear varnish.

DIRECTIONS: Using sharp colored pencil, draw lines across pattern, connecting grid lines. Enlarge pattern by copying on paper ruled in 1″ squares; complete half-pattern, indicated by long dash lines. Center pattern over clear pine with carbon paper in between. Go over lines of design with dry ball-point pen to transfer. Remove pattern and carbon; strengthen lines of design with pencil if necessary.

Cut out plaque, using jig or coping saw; drill $\frac{1}{2}$″-diameter hole through plaque at center top where indicated by circle on pattern. Sand all rough edges; dust with tack cloth. Paint plaque with several coats of clear varnish, sanding lightly between each coat.

To make thistles, insert toothpicks into plastic foam eggs, to cover each egg about $\frac{3}{4}$ of the way around (front and sides) and end to end; leave "back" bare. Placing egg with pointed end at top, insert row of toothpicks $\frac{1}{2}$″ from top, so they point straight up. Insert a second row $\frac{1}{2}$″ below first, pointing up. Continue adding rows of toothpicks, working towards bottom of egg and gradually angling toothpicks outward until they extend out about 90° at bottom.

Wire head of a T-pin with 4″ length of floral wire; wrap other end of wire around a nail, leaving about $\frac{1}{2}$″ space between pin and nail. Insert T-pin into egg bottom so it is firmly embedded in the foam. Repeat for other two eggs, making three thistles.

Arrange pine boughs on plaque and staple stems in place as follows: Staple first row at bottom (opposite drilled hole) so that tips of branches point downward. Staple second row of boughs so tips of branches overlap stems of first row. Continue in this way, covering plaque up to top; angle stems at top to form a point as shown in photograph. Tie ribbon in a bow and staple to plaque, covering stems of top row. Arrange thistles on plaque as shown and nail in place. Cover top of each thistle with some of the pine boughs. Hang as desired.

HOLIDAY WREATHS

Shown on pages 238 and 239.

SIZE: (approximate diameters): Baby's Breath Wreath, 25″; Nosegay Wreath, 11″; Apple Wreath, 15″.

EQUIPMENT: Scissors. Wire cutters. Sequin pins (small straight pins). Measuring tape. Iron.

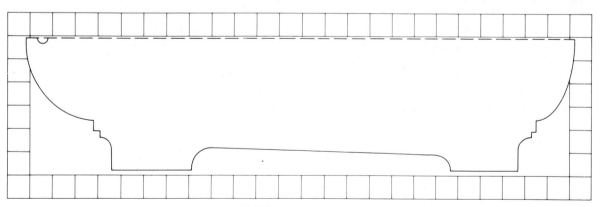

Half Pattern for Plaque

MATERIALS: For Each: Plastic foam ring $1\frac{1}{4}''$ thick, diameters listed below. White floral tape. Floral wire, #18 gauge. Florist's picks. White glue. Clear acrylic spray. **For Baby's Breath Wreath:** Ring, 16″ diameter. Large pine cones. Sprigs of baby's breath flowers. Striped grosgrain ribbon $2\frac{1}{4}''$ wide, 6 yards. Fusible woven interfacing 18″ wide, $\frac{1}{4}$ yard. **For Nosegay Wreath:** Ring, 9″ diameter. Yellow strawflowers. Ruffled lace trim or antique crocheted lace 3″ wide, 1 yard. Yellow velvet ribbon 3″ wide, 1 yard. **For Apple Wreath:** Ring, 9″ diameter. Small artificial apples with attaching wires, 12. Dried thistles, 18. Sprays of bleached pine or other dried branches. Green

grosgrain ribbon $1\frac{1}{2}''$ wide, $3\frac{1}{4}$ yards. Cardboard, $7\frac{1}{2}'' \times 2$·.

GENERAL DIRECTIONS: Prepare plastic foam ring base by wrapping it with white floral tape as shown in Diagram 1. The tape strengthens the ring and prevents disintegration of the foam as flowers and decorations are added.

Before attaching dried flowers to plastic foam base, trim stems to 3″–4″ length (6″ for baby's breath) and bind groups of 7–10 flower heads together around a short florist's pick, using floral tape; see Diagram 2. Insert pick into foam, arranging flowers as directed below.

To wire pine cones, cut a length of floral wire and wrap around base of cone between the scales, following Diagram 3. Twist wire ends together securely. Use as is or attach a florist's pick to wire ends. Wire thistles in same manner; attach to florist's pick.

After wreath is completed, spray entire wreath with clear acrylic, using several light coats rather than one heavy one. Always spray in a well ventilated room; allow to dry before hanging.

BABY'S BREATH WREATH: Wrap ring, following General Directions. To make bow, cut three 36″ lengths of ribbon. Cut six strips of fusible interfacing, each $1\frac{1}{2}'' \times 18''$. Cut three 36″ lengths of wire. Center wire on wrong side of each length of ribbon; center two strips of fusible interfacing over wire and ribbon, matching short edges at center. Fuse interfacing (over wire) to ribbon, using iron and following manufacturer's directions. Fold ends of one ribbon to center, forming two large loops; pin to front of prepared ring. Repeat for other two wired ribbons, placing over first ribbon but angling loops above and below as shown in photograph. Cut 10″ length of ribbon and wrap around ring, covering pinned ends of loops; secure with pins on back side of ring. Cut two 46″ lengths of ribbon for streamers; fold in half and pin to back side of ring, behind bow (see photo). Glue to secure if necessary.

Bind stems of baby's breath to florist's picks, following General Directions; cover most of each pick with tape so it will not be visible when inserted into wreath. Insert bunches of baby's breath all around ring, covering densely. Wire pine cones

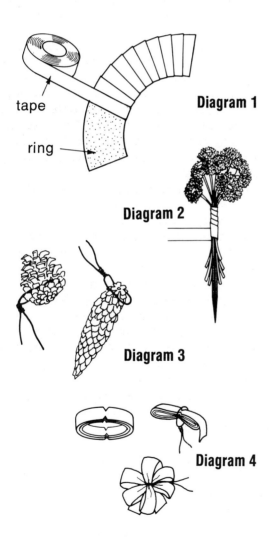

tape

ring →

Diagram 1

Diagram 2

Diagram 3

Diagram 4

as directed and insert into wreath, clustering them near bow as shown in photograph, or interspersed throughout wreath as desired.

NOSEGAY WREATH: Wrap ring, following General Directions. Using sequin pins, attach ruffled lace trim or crocheted lace all around front side of ring, placing trim so ruffled edge extends beyond ring and straight edge is about $\frac{1}{2}''$ in from outer edge of ring; gather lace evenly to fit and pin securely. Glue if necessary.

Attach bunches of strawflowers to florist's picks, following General Directions. Insert into ring, covering entire ring densely. Tie velvet ribbon into a large bow and wire the wrong side of bow to a florist's pick. Insert into ring at an angle as shown in photograph.

APPLE WREATH: Wrap ring, following General Directions. Arrange pine sprays all around ring, overlapping and angling them so branches fan out beyond outer edge of ring as shown in photograph; bind ends of sprays to ring with floral tape. Wire thistles to florist's picks and arrange evenly around ring. Attach apples to ring, evenly interspersed between thistles.

Follow Diagram 4 to make bow. Wrap ribbon around long edge of cardboard six times; carefully remove from cardboard and notch each side as shown. Twist and tighten a piece of wire around notched ribbon. Fan out loops to form the bow as shown. For streamers, cut two 30" lengths of ribbon. Place ribbons together, then twist a wire around centers as for bow. Notch ends of streamers. Attach bow and streamers to florist's picks; insert streamers first, then bow into ring on one side as shown.

ALPHABET PILLOWS
Shown on page 240

SIZES: Mansion Pillow, $15\frac{1}{2}'' \times 12\frac{3}{4}''$; House Pillow, $15'' \times 12\frac{1}{2}''$.

EQUIPMENT: Paper for patterns. Tracing paper. Pencil. Ruler. Dressmaker's tracing (carbon) paper. Scissors. Hard-lead pencil. Straight pins.

Sewing and embroidery needles. Sewing machine with zipper foot attachment. Iron.

MATERIALS: For Mansion Pillow: Heavy unbleached muslin, 10" × 13". Floral prints: 13" × 12" for inner border; $\frac{1}{2}$ yd., 45" wide, for pillow and piping. Assorted fabric scraps for appliqués. Six-strand embroidery floss: 1 skein each yellow-green, emerald green, royal blue, red, cocoa brown.

For House Pillow: Heavy unbleached muslin, $12\frac{1}{2}'' \times 9\frac{1}{2}''$. Floral prints: 13" × 12" for inner border; $\frac{1}{2}$ yd., 45" wide, for pillow and piping. Six-strand embroidery floss: 1 skein each bright yellow, bright pink, black; two skeins each rust and emerald green.

For Both: Matching sewing threads. Muslin for inner pillow. Fiberfill. Cable cord, $\frac{1}{4}''$ diam., enough to go around each pillow.

DIRECTIONS: Enlarge patterns by copying on paper ruled in 1" squares. Dash lines on Mansion's fence indicate where fabric is overlapped.

For Mansion: Read How To Appliqué, page 304. Trace pattern for each appliqué piece. Place separate patterns on wrong side of selected fabrics. Using carbon paper and hard-lead pencil, transfer design to fabrics. Cut out pieces, adding $\frac{1}{4}''$ all around each piece.

Following pattern, pin appliqués in place on background. Using matching sewing threads, appliqué pieces to background.

Using dressmaker's carbon, transfer alphabet and corner motifs to muslin above appliquéd scene.

Use full six strands of floss in embroidery needle. Using satin stitch, embroider royal blue stars, red apples, and yellow-green leaves. Using outline stitch, embroider royal blue alphabet, dark green outlines of leaves and stars, cocoa brown windowpanes and roof slate. Make doorknob in straight stitch. See Stitch Details, page 308.

For House: Using dressmaker's carbon, trace entire pattern and transfer design to unbleached muslin background. Using six strands of floss in needle, embroider as follows: Work lines of house and roof in rust outline stitch. Work alphabet with black in outline stitch and satin stitch on wider parts. Work green leaves, bright yellow flower petals and windows, bright pink flower centers, and rust chimney bricks in satin stitch.

Continued on page 290

Mansion

House

Continued from page 287

Inner Floral Borders: For both pillows, cut $2\frac{1}{2}''$-wide fabric strips as follows: two same length as sides of muslin piece; two 2″ longer than top and bottom of muslin piece. Fold each strip in half lengthwise and turn in $\frac{1}{4}''$ on each long edge; press. Insert $\frac{1}{4}''$ along each side of design piece between turned-in edges of shorter border strips. Slip-stitch border to muslin. Repeat at top and bottom, slipping fabric strips over muslin and side borders; slip-stitch in place.

To Make Pillows: Cut floral fabric for pillowcase: two pieces each 15″ × $13\frac{1}{4}''$ for Mansion; two pieces each $15\frac{1}{2}''$ × 13″ for House. Slip-stitch embroidered piece to center of one pillowcase piece. From remaining floral fabric, cut enough 1″-wide bias strips to fit around outer edge of pillow, seaming strips as necessary for desired length.

Place cable cord along wrong side of bias strip. Bring raw edges together, and stitch along fabric close to cable cord with zipper foot attachment.

With raw edges out and flush with edges of pillow fabric, baste piping around pillow front. To join ends of piping, cut off excess with ends overlapping $\frac{1}{2}''$. Cut $\frac{1}{2}''$ of cable cord off inside one end and turn fabric in $\frac{1}{4}''$. Insert other end and slip-stitch together. Stitch piping in place. Place pillow front and back together right sides facing, with piping between. Stitch together, making $\frac{1}{4}''$ seams. Leave 6″ opening for turning and stuffing. Turn to right side.

For inner pillow, cut two muslin pieces $\frac{1}{2}''$ larger all around than the finished pillowcase. Sew both together, making $\frac{1}{4}''$ seams. Leave a 3″ opening for stuffing. Turn to right side and stuff plumply with fiberfill. Slip-stitch opening closed. Insert inner pillow into pillowcase; sew opening closed.

Knitting Needles and Accessories

Single-pointed needles of aluminum, plastic or wood are used in pairs to knit back and forth in rows. For ease in working, choose a color to contrast with the yarn. Colored aluminum and plastic needles come in 7", 10", and 14" lengths in sizes varying from 1 to 5 in the shorter lengths, and 1 to 10½, 11, 13 and 15 in the longer lengths. Colored aluminum needles also come in size 0. Wood needles, 14" long, come in sizes 11 to 15. Even larger sizes for jiffy knitting-17, 18, 19, 35 and 50 are available in hollow plastic. Flexible "jumper" needles of nylon or nylon and aluminum are available in 18" lengths in sizes 1 to 15.

Double-pointed (dp) needles are used in sets of four for tubular knitting for such items as socks, mittens, gloves and sleeves worked without seams. Of plastic or aluminum, they come in 5", 7" and 10" lengths. Plastic double-pointed needles come in sizes 1 to 15, aluminum in 0 to 8.

Circular knitting needles of nylon come in 16" to 29" lengths in sizes 0 to 10½; the 29" length is also made in sizes 11, 13 and 15; a 36" length is made in sizes 5 to 15. Circular needles are used for knitting skirts without seams, circular yokes

ABBREVIATIONS USED IN KNITTING DIRECTIONS

k—knit	psso—pass slip stitch over
p—purl	inc—increase
st—stitch	dec—decrease
sts—stitches	beg—beginning
yo—yarn over	pat—pattern
sl—slip	lp—loop
sk—skip	MC—main color
tog—together	CC—contrasting color
rnd—round	dp—double-pointed

and other tubular pieces, but may be used for knitting back and forth in flat knitting, too. They are especially useful for afghans and other large pieces that require a great many stitches.

Many accessories are available to the knitter: stitch holders to keep one section of knitting from ravelling while another section is being worked; counters to keep track of increases, decreases, stitches and rows; needle point guards to keep knitting on needles when not in use; bobbins or snap yarn holders to use when knitting in small areas of color; little ring markers; needle gauges to determine correct sizes of needles.

KNITTING NEEDLES	U. S.	0	1	2	3	4	5	6	7	8	9	10	10½	11	13	15
	English	13	12	11	10	9	8	7	6	5	4	3	2	1	00	000
	Continental — mm.	2¼	2½	3	3¼	3½	4	4½	5	5½	6	6½	7	7½	8½	9

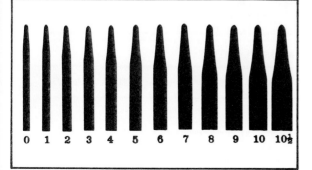

STANDARD U.S. SIZES

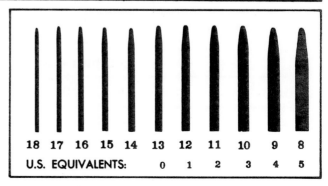

ENGLISH SIZES

Crochet Abbreviations and Stitches

Treble Stitches

Treble or Triple Crochet (tr): With 1 loop on hook put yarn over hook twice, insert in 5th chain from hook, pull loop through. Yarn over and draw through 2 loops at a time 3 times. At end of a row, chain 4 and turn. Chain 4 counts as first treble of next row.

Double Treble (dtr): Put yarn over hook 3 times and work off 2 loops at a time as for treble.

Treble Treble (tr tr): Put yarn over hook 4 times and work off 2 loops at a time as for treble.

How to Turn Your Work

In crochet a certain number of ch sts are needed at the end of each row to bring work into position for the next row. Then work is turned so reverse side is facing the crocheter. Follow the stitch table below for the number of ch sts required to make a turn.

Single crochet (sc)	Ch 1 to turn
Half double crochet (half dc or hdc)	Ch 2 to turn
Double crochet (dc)	Ch 3 to turn
Treble crochet (tr)	Ch 4 to turn
Double treble crochet (dtr)	Ch 5 to turn
Treble treble crochet (tr tr)	Ch 6 to turn

CROCHET ABBREVIATIONS

ch–chain stitch	sc–single crochet
st–stitch	sl st–slip stitch
sts–stitches	dc–double crochet
lp–loop	hdc–half double crochet
inc–increase	tr–treble or triple crochet
dec–decrease	dtr–double treble crochet
rnd–round	tr tr–treble treble crochet
beg–beginning	bl–block
sk–skip	sp–space
p–picot	cl–cluster
tog–together	pat–pattern
lp–loop	yo–yarn over hook

How to Follow Directions

An asterisk (*) is often used in crochet directions to indicate repetition. For example, when directions read "*2 dc in next st, 1 dc in next st, repeat from * 4 times" this means to work directions after first * until second * is reached, then go back to first * 4 times more. Work 5 times in all.

When () (parentheses) are used to show repetition, work directions within parentheses as many times as specified. For example, "(dc, ch 1) 3 times" means to do what is within () 3 times altogether.

"Work even" in directions means to work in same stitch without increasing or decreasing.

CROCHET HOOKS (STEEL)

U.S.	1	2	3	4	5	6	7	8	9	10	11	12	13	14
English	3/0	2/0	1/0	1	1½	2	2½	3	4	5	5½	6	6½	7
Continental—mm.	3	2.5		2		1.75	1.5	1.25	1	0.75		0.6		

CROCHET HOOKS (ALUMINUM OR PLASTIC)

U.S.	1/B	2/C	3/D	4/E	5/F	6/G	8/H	9/I	10/J	10½/K
English	12	11	10	9	8	7	6	5	4	2
Continental—mm.	2½	3		3½	4	4½	5	5½	6	7

Making Hand-Hooked Rugs

For warmth and beauty underfoot, nothing beats a hand-made rug! The techniques described in this section, hand-hooking and braiding, produce rugs which suit perfectly the casual charm of a country-style decor.

The American tradition of hand-hooking seems to derive from early Scandinavians, who hooked clothing and coverlets. They introduced hooking to the Britons, and the Pilgrims brought it to America. The settlers first made hand-hooked coverings for the bed, and later for the floor.

Settlers also covered their floors with braided cornhusk mats. This was a craft that had been practiced as early as 6000 B.C. by Egyptians who plaited rushes into rugs. When the practical and inventive Colonists learned to braid rags into durable and colorful rugs, they instituted a native American craft.

If you're adventurous, use our general directions as a guide for making a hand-hooked or braided rug of your own design.

MATERIALS AND EQUIPMENT: The hand hook for rugmaking resembles a large steel crochet needle embedded in a wooden handle. Firmly woven burlap about 40″ wide is the usual foundation fabric; old burlap bags are often used. There are also cotton and linen foundation fabrics called warp cloth that are woven with a somewhat open mesh, allowing the needle to slip in easily. If foundation fabric is not large enough, it can be pieced by lapping one piece of fabric over the other about two inches and running a line of catch-stitching down both edges. Designs must be shown on the top (right) side of the fabric, since work is done from the top. Although you may be able to hook with the fabric in your lap, most hookers find it easier to stretch it on a rug hoop or frame.

Hand-hooked rugs are usually made from fabric strips cut from old clothing or blankets, although new fabric may be used to supplement it, or even to make an entire rug. Try to use fabric of the same weight, thickness, and fiber content for the whole rug so that it will wear evenly. Wool wears very well and does not show soil as much as silk, rayon or cotton. Stocking or necktie strips may be used as highlights in wool rugs or to hook small ornamental mats.

If you wish to make your rug washable, it is important that the material be absolutely colorfast. New or old, all material should be washed in hot water and borax to loosen and remove any excess dye. Wash each color separately, then rinse until no more dye comes out. (If the material is soiled, use naphtha soap.) Do not wring; hang in the sun to dry. The colors will not seem faded when hooked, because color is relative and depends upon placement of adjacent colors for the overall effect.

To obtain the desired colors, you can dye your fabrics yourself (see section on Dyeing Fabrics). Lovely color effects can be obtained by shading areas. A group of shaded colors for making a motif is known as a "swatch" and is made of five or six 3″ × 12″ pieces of fabric that shade from light to dark in the same hue. Swatches may be purchased at art needlework departments, from rug designers, or may be prepared at home. Interesting effects are also achieved by mixing materials to include tweeds, herringbone weaves, flannels, and twills. The shadings add variety of tone and make the rug more practical—a slightly variegated background shows less soil. Mingling of color is called "wiggling in."

Estimating Amount of Material: Use the general rule that $\frac{1}{2}$ pound of fabric will cover 1 square foot of backing; or, $1\frac{1}{2}$ to 2 square yards of wool or 2 square yards of cotton will hook about 1 square foot.

PREPARING STRIPS AND BACKGROUND FABRIC: The width of strips varies according to the thickness of the material. Strips of the same fabric should be cut in uniform widths, although strips to be used for fine detail in a small section may be cut narrower. A machine that cuts strips evenly is sold in needlework departments and by mail. Most strips are cut on the straight of the goods, but some prefer them cut slightly on the bias for more give. Fabric should be cut as finely as the weave allows. Closely woven fabric such as flannel is cut in strips as narrow as $\frac{1}{16}$" to $\frac{1}{8}$" wide; more loosely woven fabric is cut from $\frac{3}{16}$" to $\frac{5}{16}$". Cotton strips should be $\frac{1}{4}$" to $\frac{1}{2}$".

Before hooking is begun, mark design on fabric and plan the finished edge.

HOOKING: Hand hooking is a simple method of putting loops of narrow strips of fabric through meshes (between threads) of background fabric. If you have never hooked before, practice on a small area outside the rug design. Hold the hook above the foundation fabric in the right hand; hold the fabric strip underneath with the left. Push the hook through the foundation, catch strip, and draw a loop up through to the desired height; then reinsert the hook in the fabric close by and pull up another loop. Give hook a little clockwise twist as you pull the loops through. This makes a firmer and longer wearing pile. Care must be taken to have all loops the same height; height is determined by the fabric used and the width of strip. If loops are to be cut, they should be no longer than usual. For fine hooking, loops are pulled through the mesh about $\frac{3}{16}$"; for coarser hooking, pull the loops approximately about $\frac{1}{4}$" high. You will gauge how far apart your stitches should be by the width or thickness of the strands and the height of the loops; they should be close enough together to stay in place, yet far enough apart so that the rug

will not buckle. Continue inserting hook through burlap and pulling up loops. Do as much of one color as possible at one time. Pull ends through to top when starting and ending a strand; clip ends even with loops.

Usually, the design part of the rug is worked before the background, and the portion of design that appears in "front" or "on top" is worked first in order to keep the shapes from being lost. To obtain an interesting background texture, do not work in straight lines. Fill in background around the motifs, then continue to keep direction of lines irregular. If you are working the rug in a small frame, work all motifs and background around before rolling to new section.

DYEING FABRICS: To obtain the desired colors, you can dye your fabrics yourself. Follow the directions given on the dye package, but do not worry about getting an even tone if fabric is to be used for hooking, as variations in shading give depth and character to the design of a hooked rug.

Fabrics in white or light colors can easily be dyed a darker shade. If you wish to dye a dark material a lighter shade, however, first remove the color.

Lovely color effects can be obtained by shading areas.

To dye several shades of one color, start by making enough dye for all the shades. (Prepare more dye than you think you need; it is better to have too much than not enough, because it will be almost impossible later to match colors exactly.) Dye material about two shades darker when wet than the desired color. Make the color you want for the darkest shade; dye this shade first, remove fabric, then put into the same dye mixture the fabric for the next lighter shade, etc. As each piece absorbs some of the color, the next piece will be a bit lighter.

To shade fabric that is already cut into strips, hold five strips at one end and dip the other end in the dye for five minutes. Reverse the ends and hold in dye for three minutes; hold both ends and dip center in the dye for one minute.

For a mottled effect rather than even shading, wet the material to be dyed, wring it out, and spread out flat on a newspaper. With a teaspoon,

Hooking Detail

drop blotches of dye on the material. Roll up tightly; unroll when dry.

For mottling strips, tie a few together in several knots and drop into the dye. Untie when dry.

After fabric is dyed, each color should be washed in warm water with borax or naphtha soap, rinsed without wringing, and hung in sunlight to dry. This helps to make the rug more washable and colorfast.

RUG FRAMES: Although the use of a rug frame is not absolutely required for hand-hooked rugs, many rugmakers find that the work is easier and their stitches are smoother with a frame. Canvas rugs worked in complicated stitches often require the use of a free hand under the canvas.

There are several types of frames suitable for working hand-hooked rugs.

The standing, easel-type frame is probably the most convenient to use. The easel frame tilts at any desired angle and can be revolved to reveal the underside for inspection; it stands at the usual table height of 30″. Usually these frames have adjustable roller bars at top and bottom that make it easy to turn the foundation material in order to work on one part of the design at a time, rolling up the finished work as it is completed. The roller bars are attached to the side pieces in various ways: the simplest ones use pegs; others use clamps or screws for tightening and have ratchets to avoid slippage.

The foundation is attached to the roller bars, usually by basting through a strip of firm fabric (called listing or webbing) that has been thumb-tacked or stapled to each roller bar. Or—strips of sheeting may be tacked to each bar and wound around to make a firm padding; sew on foundation with close but loose stitches. First, machine-stitch raw edges if foundation is a fabric that tends to ravel. Find the center of both foundation and bar and sew from the centers out, following the same thread across. It is important that the foundation be straight in the frame before work is begun.

The foundation is also attached to the side bars of the frame. You can buy lacing sets, or you can devise your own by lacing heavy twine back and forth, sewing through the foundation and winding around the side bars or through holes drilled in the side bars or around $\frac{1}{2}″$ tacks. To keep the foundation from stretching out in peaks at the sides,

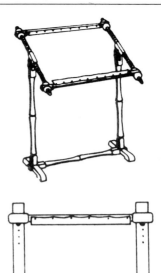

Rug Frames

run a knitting needle in and out along the edge and wind the string around the needle, or use straight pins set closely together along the edge. The strings will be untied and reset when the foundation is rolled to a new area. If the foundation is wider than the frame, attach foundation directly to the frame with $\frac{1}{2}″$ thumbtacks; make a $\frac{1}{2}″$ tuck in foundation on each side and tack to sides through tucks to reduce the strain.

Some may prefer table-model folding frames or lap frames. Lap frames are braced against the side of a chair, against a table, or attached to a table with a C clamp. These frames have the advantage of being more portable than the standing models and are therefore useful for working on away from home.

To make a simple rug frame, glue and nail four strips of pine or softwood together and brace the inside corners with metal angles. To improvise a frame, try using one of the following: a picture frame, window screen, card table with the inside top removed, bassinet stand, stretcher bars for a painter's canvas, or weaver's loom with harnesses removed.

To make an adjustable frame, cut two 4-ft. crosspieces and two $1\frac{1}{2}$-ft sidepieces using 1″ × 2″ lumber. Bore $\frac{1}{2}″$ diameter holes at 3″ intervals on the side- and crosspieces; use wooden pegs in holes to adjust the size of the frame. The remaining side holes can be used for lacing on foundation.

Making Braided Rugs

MATERIALS: Materials can come from many sources. You may collect worn-out clothing from rummage, or buy material from remnant counters and mill-end shops. A variety of fabrics may be used for rug braiding. However, if you combine different types of fabric in a single rug, they will wear unevenly. Generally, wool makes the best rugs; it works up easily, wears well, and shows less soil. Cotton does not wear as well as wool and soils quickly, but it is inexpensive and easily washed. Silks and synthetics, such as old neckties and stockings, might be used for small bedroom rugs or for chair mats not subject to a great deal of wear.

Estimating Amount of Material: Plan the color scheme and the approximate amount and placement of each color before starting to braid. Determine the size of rug in square feet by multiplying length by the width. A woolen rug of average thickness requires about $\frac{3}{4}$ lb. of material for each square foot. If you are buying wool by the yard, one yard, 60″ wide, equals about one pound.

To dye fabric, when desired colors are not available, see below. All fabric should be washed, each color separately, in warm water with borax or naphtha soap, rinsed without wringing, and hung in sunlight to dry. This helps to insure colorfastness and washability.

Dyeing Fabrics: Follow directions given on the dye package. Fabrics in white or light colors can easily be dyed a darker shade. If you wish to dye a dark material a lighter shade, however, first remove the color.

To dye several shades of one color, or to shade fabric that is already cut into strips, refer to Dyeing Fabrics section in Hand-Hooked Rugs.

PLANNING SIZE AND SHAPE: The size must be decided before you start any shape other than round; the starting braid will determine the finished rug shape. To find the proper length for the starting braid of an oval rug, subtract the width of the desired size of the finished rug from the length. To make a rug 52″ × 46″, start with a 6″ long braid in the center.

HOW TO BRAID

Fig. 1: Three Steps in Splicing

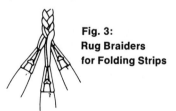

Fig. 2: Starting a Three-Strand Braid

Fig. 3:
Rug Braiders
for Folding Strips

PLANNING COLORS: Lighter shades are usually placed in the center at the start of the rug for the first few rounds. One round of braid is completed when it passes the point it began. Darker shades are added in degrees with each succeeding round. Thereafter the rounds alternate between light and dark. For uniformity make all changes at the end of a complete round.

PREPARING STRIPS: Cut or tear strips on the lengthwise grain of fabric, the width determined by the weight of the fabric in relation to the thickness of the braid. For a large wool rug make the finished braid $\frac{3}{4}$″ or 1″ wide. The cut strip, therefore, should be $1\frac{1}{2}$″ to 2″ wide for medium-weight wool. To make strips desired length, pieces may be joined by sewing together on the bias by hand or machine. Start with strips of different lengths in order to avoid joinings all in the same place.

Strips may also be spliced together. Splicing eliminates having to sew strips together, but it does not make as smooth a braid as sewn strips. Cut a 1″ slit lengthwise in the end of each strip. Pass slit end of strip being braided through slit of new strip. Pass other end of new strip through slit of strip being braided. Pull together (Fig. 1).

To gauge the length of strands needed for each round measure around already completed round and multiply by $1\frac{1}{2}$. Prepare the strips for braiding by folding in the raw edges so that they almost meet at center, then fold the strip in half lengthwise. This may be done by hand as you braid or by using braiding aids (Fig. 3) that fold the strips automatically.

THREE-STRAND BRAID: The simplest type of braid is made with three strands. Pin or sew ends of three folded strands together. Anchor ends firmly, (Fig. 2). Begin braiding by folding right-hand strand over middle strand, then fold left-hand strand over middle strand, keeping open folded-in edges to center. Continue braiding, always folding alternate outside strand over middle strand (Fig. 2). The side facing you is the right side.

BASIC DESIGNS WITH THREE-STRAND BRAID: Three-strand braid may have three of the same color, two dark and one light, or two light and one dark. An Arrowhead design (Fig. A) is a repeated pattern of two rounds, two light and one

Fig. A: Arrowhead

Fig. B: Rail Fence

dark laced to a braid of two dark and one light. A Rail Fence (Fig. B) is a repeated pattern of three rounds, one braid of two dark and one light between two braids of two light and one dark.

ENCLOSED ENDS: Cut wool strip. Fold in half lengthwise, right sides together. Stitch across end and about 2″ along long edge, $\frac{1}{4}$″ from raw edges. Clip corner and turn to right side. Repeat for other strips.

SPIRAL ROUNDS: Braid may be made in a continuous rope and wound spirally in a round or oval shape. To start a continuous rope braid, the braid should have a finished end. Select your three strips and sew the ends of two of these together with a bias seam; trim off corners of strips and press seam flat. Fold joined strip in half lengthwise with edges tucked in to center. Lay joined strip out horizontally with opening of fold at top. Fold in the end of third strip, fold strip in half lengthwise with edges tucked in, and sew end to first strips at point of joining, with opening of fold to the right

**Fig. 4:
Starting a Rope Braid**

(Fig. 4). Anchor end by pinning or nailing to a surface at joining to hold firmly. Braid as directed above.

For a continuous braid, the changes in color combinations are usually made one strip at a time, at staggered intervals, to achieve a gradual blending of color. Sew or lace the continuous rounds of braid together until desired size is reached. The

ending may come at any convenient point; if the rug is oval it will usually be more satisfactory to end around a curve. Taper-trim each strip to a bias cut about 6″ long; braid right to the end, making the tail end very small. Sew tapered end in place along edge, tuck in tail end of braid through a loop of adjoining braid and sew securely.

BUTTED ROUNDS: Many rug makers prefer to butt each round. Butting is used to form a perfect circle, oval, or square, or to make sharp color changes. It eliminates the jogging out of the pattern. Leave both ends of the braid unfinished. Sew braid to rug within 6″ of the point of butting. Cut strips of both unfinished ends diagonally, tapering to a point. Braid strips almost to end. Fold points of strips to back of braid and tuck neatly underneath the loops; spread braid to normal width, keeping square at end for neat joining. Sew fin-

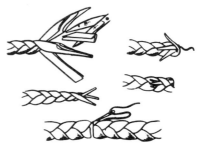

Fig. 5: Four Steps in Butting

ished ends together (Fig. 5). If braids are butted at different points the joinings will be unnoticeable.

JOINING BRAIDS: Braids can be sewn together through adjacent edges with doubled heavy carpet thread, or laced through the braid loops. Work on a flat surface to keep rug flat and even. When sewing, take stitches at center sides of braids, using a curved upholstery needle (Fig. 6).

Fig. 6: Joining by Sewing

To lace, fasten doubled carpet thread to a loop in braid on right, using blunt needle or lacer; push needle through loop of adjacent braid, then into next loop of first braid. Pull thread tightly to lock loops into each other, keeping thread invisible so that rug will be reversible.

DOUBLE LACING: For a rectangular rug of straight strips, we recommend double lacing as the strongest joining. To double lace, fasten carpet thread to loop #1 of first braid with a darning needle, then replace needle with a lacer. Fasten a second piece of carpet thread to loop #3 of first braid, replace needle with second lacer. With first lacer, go through loop #2 on second braid from center out, and down through loop #5. Lay first lacer on table above braids, at left. With second lacer, go through loop #4 on second braid from center out, and down through loop #7, thus crossing threads between braids. Lay second lacer above braids at left. Pull threads tight. Continue

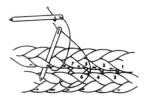

Fig. 7: Joining by Double Lacing

in this manner to end of braids (Fig. 7). Lace another braid to other side of first braid in same manner. Keep center braid straight and continue to lace braids at both sides of center. To keep braids perfectly straight and evenly laced, attach center braid to wooden surface, such as plywood, with thin nails, stretching braid enough to keep work taut; fasten at ends and at equal intervals along braid. Continue lacing braids to each side and fasten a braid to board again after about six rows. When all braids are laced together, steam-press before removing nails.

General Directions for Quilting

Making the Quilt Top

PATTERNS: In making a pieced (patchwork) or appliquéd quilt top, you will need a stiff pattern, also called a template, for each separate part of design. Use thin but firm cardboard for your pattern, such as shirt lining. Some prefer heavy sandpaper, which does not slip on fabric. If the pattern is to be used many times, make duplicates and discard each as its edges become frayed from continued use. Or, cut your pattern from sheet plastic, preferably transparent. Whatever the material, make your stiff pattern with one of the following methods, as directed for each project: 1) Trace actual-size pattern given; glue tracing to cardboard; let dry; then cut. 2) For very simple geometric shapes, such as squares, you simply make the pattern yourself, following dimensions given.

It is essential that patch patterns be accurate. If the patterns are not perfect, neither will be the patches, and they may be impossible to piece together properly. After you have made your patterns, test their accuracy before cutting any patches. If there is a Piecing Diagram, fit patterns together as shown or draw around them on paper. If making a design entirely from hexagons, make sure that six hexagons will fit neatly around the six sides of a center hexagon.

Window Templates: Our patterns are made the size of the finished patch piece, that is, what shows when the quilt top is assembled. The seam

WINDOW TEMPLATES

allowance is not included in the pattern, but is added when patches are cut. If you wish to cut your seam allowance with perfectly even edges, you may want to make a window template. Draw pattern shape as before, then draw another line around it exactly $\frac{1}{4}''$ away. Cut on both lines, leaving a frame. The window template is more difficult and time consuming to make, but it will make patches easier to cut. It is also advisable for using with certain prints, when placement of motifs is important.

PATCH PIECES: Use fabrics that are closely woven, so seams will hold and edges will not fray. The fabric should be fairly soft, but should not be so thin that seam allowances will show through. Before cutting patches, wash new fabrics to preshrink and remove sizing. Wash scraps in a net bag. Press all fabrics smooth. Lay fabric out flat, wrong side up for patch pieces. (See How to Appliqué on page 304.) Lay pattern on fabric, placing it so as many straight sides of pattern as possible are with the crosswise and lengthwise grain of fabric. If necessary, pull threads in both directions to determine grain. Using a sharp, hard pencil (light-colored for dark fabrics, dark-colored for light fabrics), draw around pattern; hold pencil at an outward angle, so that point is firmly against edge of pattern. Reposition pattern $\frac{1}{2}''$ away and draw around as before. Continue marking patterns $\frac{1}{2}''$ apart; do not cut fabric until all the patterns of one color are marked. (**Note:** If large border pieces are to be cut later from the same fabric, be sure to consider their dimensions when marking smaller pieces; you may wish to mark your patches in vertical rows. Do not, however, cut out the border pieces before cutting patches.)

When all patches of one color have been marked,

cut out each patch, $\frac{1}{4}''$ away from marked line, which will be the stitching line. Cut the $\frac{1}{4}''$ seam allowance as accurately as you can, to make piecing easier. To keep patches of same shape and color together, put them in a pile and run a thread through center with a knot in one end; lift off each patch as needed.

PIECING: Several patch pieces will be joined to create a new unit, such as a larger patch or a block. Before sewing, lay out all pieces needed for the block. Begin by joining smallest pieces first, then joining the larger pieces made into rows, then joining rows for completed block.

By Hand: If duplicating one of the antique quilts in this book, you will find it easier to join the small patch pieces by hand. Hand piecing is also advised for patches with curves and sharp angles.

To join two patch pieces, place them together, right sides facing. If pieces are very small, hold firmly to sew. Larger pieces can be pin-basted, matching angles first, then marked lines between. Pin curved pieces together from center out to each corner. For piecing, use #7 to #10 sharp needle, threaded with an 18″ length of mercerized cotton or cotton-wrapped polyester thread. Begin with a small knot, then stitch along marked seam line with tiny running stitches, ending with a few backstitches; if seam is long, take a tiny backstitch every few stitches. Try to make 8 to 10 running stitches per inch, evenly spaced. If thread tends to knot or fray as you sew, run it over a cake of beeswax. If sewing two bias edges together, keep thread just taut enough to prevent fabric from stretching. As you join pieces, press seams to one side, unless otherwise indicated; open seams tend to weaken construction. Try to press seams all in the same direction, although darker fabrics should not fall under lighter ones, lest they show through. As you piece and press, clip into seams of curves and other pieces where necessary, so they will lie flat. Clip away excess fabric, to avoid bunching. Be sure a seam is pressed flat before you cross it with another; take a small backstitch over the crossing.

Joining Hexagons: To keep angles sharp and seams precise, you may find it easier to join hexagons by using a paper liner. You can prepare a

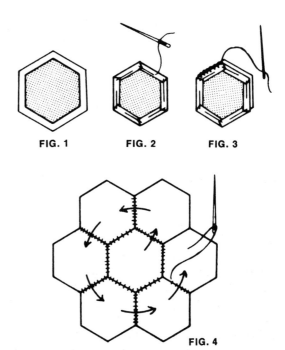

FIG. 1　　FIG. 2　　FIG. 3

FIG. 4

PIECING HEXAGONS BY HAND

paper liner for each hexagon as follows: Cut a firm paper pattern from wrapping or shelf paper the exact size of cardboard pattern. Fit paper liner within pencil outline on wrong side of patch. Hold patch with liner uppermost. Fold seam allowance over each side, and tack to the paper with one stitch on each side, allowing the thread to cross corners; finish by taking an extra stitch on the first side. Cut thread, leaving about $\frac{1}{4}''$. To make removal of tacking easier, do not knot thread or make any backstitches. Press lightly. Hold prepared patches right sides together, matching the edges to be seamed exactly. Whip together with fine, even stitches (about 16 to the inch), avoiding the paper as much as possible. Join hexagons in circular fashion, starting with six hexagons around a center patch. Backstitch where corners meet. The liners may remain in place until the quilt top is completed. To remove liners, snip tacking thread once on each patch and withdraw thread.

By Machine: Quilts of newer design are more apt to be made with larger patches and you might wish to piece them by machine. Set machine for 10 stitches to the inch, unless working with very heavy fabrics, and use needle #14. Use mercerized cotton thread #50 or cotton-wrapped polyester. Follow the same procedures as for hand piecing: Pin-baste, stitch, clip seams, and press. In piecing squares, you need not begin and end your thread with each patch; let thread run on for a continuous chain of patches. Patches will be snipped apart and their seams anchored by cross-seams.

ASSEMBLING QUILT TOP: As you construct your quilt top, building from patches to blocks to rows of blocks to borders, etc., it is important to measure each unit as you make it. Blocks to be joined should be of equal size. It is also important to compare your measurements with those given in the directions and make any necessary adjustments in the size of following pieces. Our measurements are strictly mathematical and do not allow for the variance that may easily result from multiple piecing. For example: We may have calculated that the pieced center of a quilt top should measure $79\frac{1}{2}''$ on the sides and we instruct you to cut side border pieces $79\frac{1}{2}''$ long. If your piece measures 80″, naturally you will want to cut border pieces 80″ long. You may need to adjust size of lining and edging strips as well. That is why we do not recommend cutting the larger pieces of a quilt before the smaller units are assembled.

A MITERED CORNER

To Miter Border Corners: Sew border pieces to quilt top, with an equal amount extending at each end, for the corners of quilt. Lay quilt top flat, right side down. Hold adjacent ends of border pieces together at corners with right sides facing. Keeping border flat, lift up inner corners and pin strips together diagonally from inner corners to outer corners; baste, then stitch on basting line. Cut excess fabric to make $\frac{1}{4}''$ seam; press seam open.

Preparing to Quilt

LINING AND BATTING: Cut or piece lining and batting as directed. If they are to be same size as the quilt top, you may want to make them a little larger to start with, such as 1″ all around, and trim after basting or quilting. For comfortable hand quilting, the lining fabric should be soft; sheets, for example, are too densely woven for the needle to pass through easily.

In planning the batting, consider the style of the quilt and its intended use. Antique quilts with their close, ornate quilting designs usually were made with only a very thin filler. If you wish to duplicate the effect, use a split layer of polyester batting. The thinner the layer of batting, the easier and finer the quilting will be. For simpler quilting designs, or where more loft or warmth is desirable, use one or two full layers of batting. Polyester is generally preferable to cotton batting, as it holds together, does not lump, and will dry quickly if the quilt is washed. If using cotton batting, be sure your lines of quilting are no more than 2″ apart.

BASTING: After quilting design has been marked on the quilt top, assemble top, batting, and lining. Place lining, wrong side up, on large, flat surface. Place batting on top of lining and smooth out any bumps or wrinkles. Before adding quilt top, baste batting to lining by taking two long stitches in a cross. Place quilt top on batting, right side up. Pin

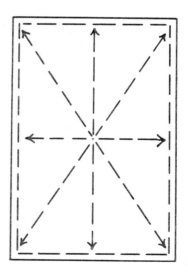

all layers together to hold temporarily, using large safety pins. Baste generously through all thicknesses, using a sturdy thread and a large needle. To prevent shifting, first baste on the lengthwise and crosswise grain of fabric. Then baste diagonally across in two directions and around sides, top, and bottom. If quilting is to be done with a quilting hoop or on the machine, extra care must be taken to keep basting stitches close, so they will hold in place as you work.

Quilting

BY HAND: When quilting by hand, the quilt may be stretched on a frame or in a quilting hoop. If the quilting design is especially ornate, it is best to use the frame; the hoop, on the other hand, is portable and more easily managed. If using neither hoop nor frame, you can quilt in your lap, working over a small area at a time.

Quilting Frame: Sew top and bottom edges of lining to the fabric strips attached to the long parallel bars of frame. Using strong thread so that quilt will not pull away from frame when stretched taut, sew securely with several rows of stitches. After quilt is secured in frame, start quilting midway between the long parallel bars of frame and sew toward you.

Quilting Hoop: Pull quilt taut in hoop and move any extra fullness toward the edges. Start quilting in the center and work toward edges. If necessary, cut basting thread as work progresses. As your quilting comes close to the edge, substitute smaller embroidery hoops for the larger quilting hoop, so that fabric will always remain taut.

Needle and Thread: Use a short, strong needle, between #7 and #10; experienced quilters may prefer a longer needle. If you can find it, use quilting thread which has a silicone coating. If you can't, choose a strong (#50 to #30) cotton mercerized or a cotton-covered polyester thread. If thread knots, frays, or breaks as you quilt try running each strand across a cake of beeswax.

Quilting Stitch: Cut 18″ strand of thread. Knot one end. Bring needle up from lining through quilt top; give a little tug to thread so that knot passes through lining only and lies buried in batting. Sew on marked line with running stitch, in two separate

QUILTING STITCH

motions: Push needle straight down through the three layers with one hand, take needle with other hand, pull thread through and push up close to the first stitch. An experienced quilter may be able to take two or three stitches before pulling needle through, holding quilt down at quilting line with thumb of other hand; do not try this method unless using a frame. Depending on thickness of fabric and batting, make stitches as small and close as you can (5 to 10 per inch); the longer the stitch, the less durable the quilting. Space stitches evenly so they are the same length on both sides of quilt. From time to time, look underneath to check your stitches. To end off, backstitch and take a long stitch through the top and batting only; take another backstitch and clip thread at surface; the thread end will sink into batting. If you are a beginner, practice first on a small piece in an embroidery hoop to find the easiest and best working method for you.

Start in the middle of the quilt and stitch toward you; shift your position as you work, so that the quilting progresses fairly even on all sides toward the outside of the quilt.

BY MACHINE: Quilting can be done on the machine, with or without a quilting foot. When working on a machine the best quilting patterns to use are those sewn on the diagonal or on the bias. Fabric gives a little when on the bias, making it easier to keep work flat.

As a rule, machine quilting is done with a straight stitch. Set stitch length from 6 to 12 per inch. Adjust pressure so that it is slightly heavier than for medium-weight fabrics with the bobbin thread a little loose. If you are using a scroll or floral design, it is best to use the short open toe of the quilting foot. This allows you to follow the curved lines with ease and accuracy.

To begin, roll up half of quilt and place to right of needle. Begin stitching in center of quilt and work to the right, unrolling quilt as you go. Repeat for remaining half.

How to Appliqué

Choose a fabric that is closely woven and firm enough so a clean edge results when the pieces are cut. Cut a pattern piece for each shape out of thin, stiff cardboard, and mark the right side of each pattern. Press fabric smooth.

Place cardboard pattern on right side of fabric. Using sharp, hard pencils (light-colored pencil on dark fabric and dark pencil on light fabric), mark the outline on the fabric. When marking several pieces on the same fabric, leave at least $\frac{1}{2}''$ between pieces. Mark a second outline $\frac{1}{4}''$ outside the design outline. Proceed as directed below, appliquéing by hand or by machine.

BY HAND: Using matching thread and small stitches, machine-stitch all around design outline, as shown in Fig. 1. This makes edge easier to turn and neater in appearance. Cut out the appliqué on the outside line, as in Fig. 2. For a smooth edge, clip into seam allowance at curved edges and corners. Then turn seam allowance to back, just inside stitching as shown in Fig. 3, and press. Pin and baste the appliqué on the background, and slip-stitch in place with tiny stitches, as shown in Fig. 4.

BY MACHINE: Pin and baste appliqués in place; do not turn under excess fabric. Straight-stitch around appliqués on marked lines. Trim away excess fabric to $\frac{1}{8}''$ from straight stitching. Set sewing machine for close zigzag stitch as directed ($\frac{1}{4}''$ wide or less). Zigzag around appliqués, covering straight stitching and excess fabric.

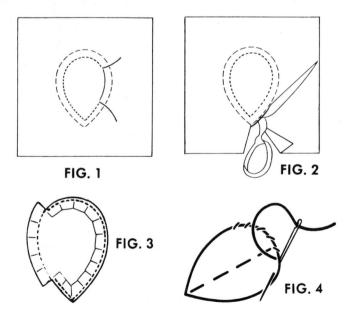

FIG. 1

FIG. 2

FIG. 3

FIG. 4

Stenciling on Fabric

EQUIPMENT: Paper for patterns. Pencil. Ruler. Scissors. Tracing paper. Stencil paper. Rubber cement. Masking tape. Glass or other hard surface for cutting stencil. X-acto knife with #11 blade. Cardboard or stencil paper scraps for palette. Palette knife for mixing paints. Stencil brushes (see below). Soft rag. Newspapers. Transparent tape. Soap.

MATERIALS: Fabric. Acrylic paints.

To Cut Stencil: Cement tracing at edges and corners onto stencil paper. Place stencil paper on glass surface. With knife, cut out design areas indicated. Hold knife at a slight angle, pointing toward cut-out area to make a slightly beveled edge. Cut all the way through in one stroke so edges will be clean. Turn stencil paper so that you always cut toward you. When completely cut out, remove tracing. If you should accidently tear or cut part of a stencil, place a small piece of transparent tape on wrong side of stencil; cut away excess tape with knife.

To Prepare To Stencil: Cover a flat working surface with newspapers. Tape fabric in place; make sure fabric is taut.

To Stencil Design: If you have fewer than the number of stencil brushes required, one per color, wash and dry brushes thoroughly between color changes. Since paints are concentrated, use only a small amount on brush at a time. Dip brush into paint and rub off onto paper until almost dry.

Hold brush upright and work paint into fabric with an up and down dabbing or a stippling motion. Go over area with additional coats of paint if area is not dark enough. When working on one area of stencil, protect areas of fabric you are not stenciling at the moment by covering with pieces of scrap paper. Acrylic paint dries very quickly and makes stenciling fairly easy.

When finished stenciling, wash brush in soap and water and wipe stencils clean with wet rag.

To clean finished stenciled items, wash gently with mild soap and water.

When using acrylic paints on fabric, be sure fabric is washable; most dry-cleaning fluids will remove acrylic paint.

General Directions for Needlepoint

To start a needlepoint piece, mark outline of design in center of canvas, leaving at least a 2″ margin around all sides. Bind all raw edges of canvas with masking tape. Find center of canvas by basting a line from center of one edge to the center of opposite edge, being careful to follow a row of spaces. Then baste another line from center of third edge to center of fourth edge. Basting threads will cross at center.

Designs are represented in chart form. Each square on chart represents one mesh on canvas. Each symbol on chart represents a different yarn color.

Cut yarn strands in 18″ lengths. When starting first strand, leave 1″ of yarn on back of canvas and cover it as the work proceeds; your first few stitches will anchor it in place. To end strand or begin a new one, run yarn under a few stitches on back of work; do not make knots. Keep yarn tension firm and even. Stitching tends to twist the working yarn; untwist from time to time, letting needle hang straight down to unwind. If a mistake is made, run needle under stitch and snip yarn with sharp scissors; do not reuse yarn.

Continental Stitch: Start at upper right corner and work across to left; turn work upside down for return row. Always work horizontal rows from right to left; see Details 1 and 2. Work vertical

DETAIL 1

DETAIL 2

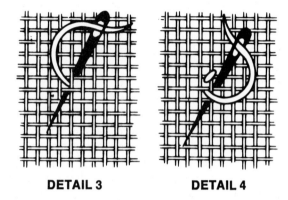

DETAIL 3   **DETAIL 4**

continental stitch from top to bottom; see Details 3 and 4.

Brick Stitch: A series of straight stitches taken over 2 or 4 canvas threads and laid in staggered rows like bricks. Work rows left to right, then right

MOSAIC STITCH

BRICK STITCH

to left. The first row skips a space between each stitch, then this space is used by the second row of stitches. In this way the rows interlock.

Mosaic Stitch: A series of long and short stitches, worked on the diagonal. For short stitch, follow directions for Continental Stitch. Long stitch skips a space, making a stitch twice the length of short stitch. Interlock rows by placing short stitches under long stitches and long stitches under short stitches. In covering a specific area such as square shown here, spaces around the edge are filled in with Continental Stitch.

Blocking: Cover a softwood surface with brown paper. Mark canvas outline and center lines on paper for guide, using T- or carpenter's square. Place needlepoint right side down over guide; if piece has raised stitches, block right side up. Match center markings on canvas with those on paper. Fasten canvas to wood with rustproof tacks spaced about $\frac{1}{2}''$ to $\frac{3}{4}''$ apart along edge of canvas; stretch canvas to match guide. Wet thoroughly with cold water; let dry. If piece is badly warped, block again. (**Note:** If yarn is not colorfast, dissolve salt in cold water. Block with salt water.)

To mount a needlepoint picture: After canvas has been blocked, stretch it over heavy cardboard or plywood cut the same size as worked portion of canvas. Use heavy cardboard for small pictures (12" or less); for larger pictures and panels, use $\frac{1}{4}''$ plywood. If cardboard is used, hold canvas in place with pins pushed through canvas into edge of cardboard. If canvas is mounted on plywood, use carpet tacks. Push pins or tacks only partway into edge; check needlepoint to make sure rows of stitches are straight. Carefully hammer in pins or tacks the rest of the way. Using a large-eyed needle and heavy thread, lace loose edges of canvas over back of cardboard or plywood to hold taut; lace across width, then length of picture.

How to Make a Pillow

To Make Knife-Edge Pillow: After blocking needlepoint, trim canvas margins to $\frac{1}{2}''$. Cut backing fabric same size as trimmed canvas. If cording is desired follow directions below to make fabric cording. With right sides facing, stitch back piece and needlepoint front together, making $\frac{1}{2}''$ seams; leave opening in center of one side. Clip corners of canvas diagonally; seal canvas edges with glue. Whipstitch canvas margins to back of needlepoint; turn pillow right side out. Following directions below, make inner pillow; insert through

opening. Add stuffing to corners if necessary. Turn raw edges $\frac{1}{2}''$ to inside; slip-stitch.

To Make Welting: Welting, a fabric-covered cord used as an edging, is a tailored way to finish a pillow. (It is also called piping or cording.) Welting can be purchased ready-made in some upholstery supply stores or can be easily made. To make welting, measure the perimeter of pillow, then cut $1\frac{1}{2}''$-wide bias strips from fabric to this length, piecing strips and adding 1" for seam allowance. Center welting cord along bias strip on the wrong side; fold strip over cord so that edges are aligned. Using zipper-foot attachment, machine-stitch along strip with needle as close to cord as possible.

To attach welting to pillow cover, begin in the middle of one side; pin welting to right side of cover so that raw edges of welting line up with raw edges of pillow cover; overlap ends 1". Starting 2" from beginning of welting, stitch all around to 2" from end of welting. Snip out 1" of cord from overlapping end. Turn under $\frac{1}{2}''$ of extra fabric and, butting ends of cord, fit it over the start of welting (see diagram 1). Finish stitching welting to pillow cover.

JOINING WELTING ENDS

To Make Inner Pillow: Cut two pieces of muslin the same shape as pillow, but measuring 2" wider and longer than finished pillow size. (For very firmly stuffed pillow, cut muslin 3" wider and longer than pillow size.) Stitch pieces together with right sides facing and making $\frac{1}{2}''$ seams; leave 3" opening in center of one side. Clip seams diagonally at corners; turn to right side. Stuff inner pillow until full. Turn raw edges of opening $\frac{1}{2}''$ to inside; slip-stitch opening closed.

Embroidery Stitches and Directions

To clean: Embroideries made with colorfast threads and washable fabrics can be laundered without fear of harming them. Wash with mild soap or detergent and warm water, swishing the fabric through the water gently–do not rub. Rinse in clear water without wringing or squeezing. When completely rinsed, lift fabric from the water and lay on a clean towel; lay another towel on top and roll up loosely. When the embroidery is sufficiently dry, press lightly on a well padded surface.

After blocking or pressing, an embroidered picture should be mounted right away to prevent creasing.

To block an embroidered picture: With needle and colorfast thread, following the thread of the linen and taking ¼″ stitches, mark guidelines around the entire picture to designate the exact area where the picture will fit into the rabbet of the frame. The border of plain linen extending beyond the embroidery in a framed picture is approximately 1¼″ at sides and top and 1½″ at bottom. In order to have sufficient linen around the embroidered design for blocking and mounting, 3″ or 4″ of linen should be left around the embroidered section. Matching corners, obtain the exact centers of the four sides and mark these centers with a few stitches.

If the picture is soiled, it should be washed, but it should be blocked immediately after washing. In preparation, cover a soft wooden board with a piece of brown paper held in place with rustproof thumbtacks. Draw the exact original size of the linen on the brown paper. Mark center of each side. Be sure linen is not pulled beyond its original size when the measurements are taken. (Embroidery sometimes pulls linen slightly out of shape.) Check drawn rectangle to make sure corners are square.

Wash embroidery; let drip a minute. Place embroidery right side up on the brown paper inside the guidelines and tack down the four corners. Tack centers of four sides matching center marks on paper. Continue to stretch the linen to its original size by tacking all around the sides, dividing and subdividing the spaces between the tacks already placed. This procedure is followed until there is a solid border of thumbtacks around the entire edge. In cross-stitch pictures, if stitches were not stamped exactly even on the thread of the linen, it may be necessary to remove some of the tacks and pull part of embroidery into a straight line. Use a ruler as a guide for straightening the lines of stitches. Hammer in the tacks or they will pop out as the linen dries. Allow embroidery to dry thoroughly.

To mount an embroidered picture: Cut a piece of heavy white cardboard about ⅛″ smaller all around than the rabbet size of the frame to be used. Stretch the embroidery over the cardboard, using the same general procedure as for blocking the piece. Following the thread guidelines, use pins to attach the four corners of the embroidery to the mounting board. Pins are placed at the centers of sides, and embroidery is then gradually stretched into position until there is a border of pins completely around picture about ¼″ apart. When satisfied that the design is even, drive pins into the cardboard edge with a hammer. If a pin does not go in straight, it should be removed and reinserted. The edges of the linen may be pasted or taped down on the wrong side of the cardboard or the edges may be caught with long zigzag stitches. Embroidered pictures can be framed with glass over them, if desired.

How to Cross-Stitch

Care should be taken to make sure that the strands of thread or yarn lie smooth and flat. Begin by leaving an end of floss on back and working over it to secure; run needle under four or five stitches on the back to finish off. Do not make any knots.

It is important when working cross-stitch to have the crosses of the entire piece worked in the same direction. Work all underneath threads in one direction and all the top threads in the opposite direction. Keep the stitches as even as possible. Be sure to make all crosses touch; do this by putting your needle in the same hole as used for the adjacent stitch. Cut strands of embroidery floss 18″ to 20″ long.

To keep the material from raveling as you embroider, bind edges with masking tape; remove when design is finished.

An embroidery hoop will help to keep the fabric taut and stitches even. Lightly press finished picture. Block, if necessary, and mount as directed at left and above.

EMBROIDERY STITCHES

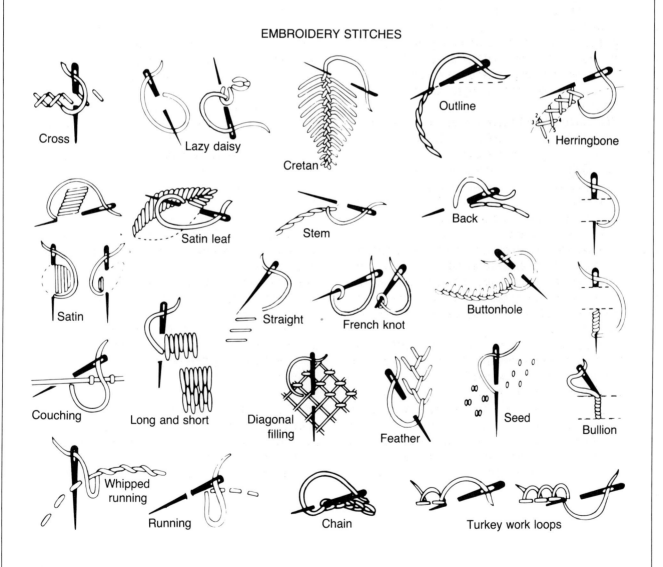

Cross

Lazy daisy

Cretan

Outline

Herringbone

Satin leaf

Stem

Back

Satin

Straight

French knot

Buttonhole

Couching

Long and short

Diagonal filling

Feather

Seed

Bullion

Whipped running

Running

Chain

Turkey work loops

Index

Page numbers in **boldface** are information in illustrations